DICTIONARY
of
SELECTED
COLLOCATIONS

EDITORS

Jimmie Hill
Michael Lewis

Based on the original work of
Christian Douglas Kozłowska
and Halina Dzierżanowska

Language Teaching Publications

114a Church Road, Hove, BN3 2EB, England
ISBN 1 899396 55 1
© LTP 1997

LTP

Language Teaching Publications is an independent publisher of English Language Teaching books. Founded in 1981 by Michael Lewis and Jimmie Hill, it is based in Hove, Sussex and has a worldwide network of distributors. Through the theoretical work of Michael Lewis, LTP has developed teaching materials based on a lexical approach to language and language teaching.

Acknowledgements

We are grateful to Mark Powell for his painstaking editorial work. We are also indebted to George Woolard, Clare West and the many teachers who commented on this dictionary from a pedagogical point of view.

Cover Design by Anna Macleod
Typesetting by Sean Worsfold
Printed in England by Commercial Colour Press Plc, London E7

TRIBUTE

The inspiration for this collocation dictionary came from the work of two academics working in Poland – Christian Douglas Kozłowska and Halina Dzierżanowska.

Halina Dzierżanowska, the late deputy head of the Institute of Applied Linguistics at Warsaw University, was a pioneer of collocation studies. She started a collaboration with Christian Douglas Kozłowska in the late seventies which resulted in 1982 in the noun-based dictionary *Selected English Collocations*. In 1981 they began work on a new dictionary of verb-adverb and adjective-adverb collocations which appeared in 1991 as *English Adverbial Collocations*. Both dictionaries were based on a corpus of post-1960 British English writing.

The aim of the original authors was to produce reference material which learners and translators would find of practical use. It is to their great credit that they published their work many years before anything similar was available to students in the West.

We are grateful to the original Polish publishers – the Polish Scientific Publishers PWN Ltd – for giving us permission to combine the two original books and to edit and up-date them extensively to make them suitable for ELT learners worldwide.

This book is dedicated to Halina Dzierżanowska and Christian Douglas Kozłowska, who understood the importance of collocation long before the rest of us.

Jimmie Hill and Michael Lewis
Hove 1997

CONTENTS

INTRODUCTION

The LTP Dictionary of Selected Collocations

The LTP *Dictionary of Selected Collocations* is not a traditional dictionary. It is a new kind of dictionary to help learners of English to use the words they know more effectively. Most dictionaries help you to find the meaning of words you do not know. This book helps you to **use** the words you know.

Who is the dictionary for?

You will find this dictionary of most use if you are an intermediate or advanced learner. It answers the kind of questions you will have when you need to write, translate or speak English accurately.

How is this dictionary different?

In most dictionaries the entries give the meaning of single words. But words are very rarely used alone. If you want to speak and write naturally, it is the way words combine with other words which is important. This is a dictionary of collocations – word combinations.

Different kinds of collocation

When you speak or write, many different word combinations are **possible**, but some are much more **probable** than others. Some pairs of words occur together very rarely but other pairs occur together so often that when you see one word, you strongly expect that the other word may be there too. These special combinations are called **collocations** and they occur in all languages. The most important kinds listed in this dictionary are:

adjective + noun	*fatal accident, golden opportunity*
verb + noun	*accept responsibility, undermine (my) self-confidence*
noun + verb	*the gap widened, a fight broke out*
adverb + adjective	*highly desirable, potentially embarrassing*
verb + adverb	*discuss calmly, lead eventually to*

This dictionary does not contain all the collocations of English. If it did, it would be very long and difficult to use. The collocations have been selected to make it as useful and easy to use as possible for learners of English.

Very common collocations

The most frequent collocations are almost all made with some of the most common words in English:

a *big* house	*give* a *quick* report
very different	*rather* strong

Many of these are very common in spoken English. When we write or prepare what we are going to say, we use language more precisely and choose our words and combinations more carefully, so we might prefer:

a *magnificent* house	*present* a *preliminary* report
significantly different	*relatively* strong

The lists in this dictionary help you to find combinations like these.

Strong collocations

Some rare collocations are very strong – these usually express fairly unusual ideas, but when you do write about one of these ideas, the particular collocation is almost the only natural way of doing it:

He's been found guilty of *serious professional misconduct*.

One of the most important ways to make your English sound natural is to use these strong collocations. Storing combinations like *declare war, impose rigid discipline* in your memory is one of the best ways to build an effective vocabulary. Collocations of this kind are listed in this dictionary. Browsing through an entry will often remind you of strong collocations you have met, but which may not come to mind when you need them.

Which collocations are included and which are not?

Some very common adjectives such as *good, bad, big, small, old, new* combine with almost any noun. These are not usually included in the lists, but they **are** included if the collocation is very strong, for example, *good/bad luck*. In a similar way, we have omitted very common adverbs such as *really, very, rather, quite*. The most common words are not included and neither are the most common collocations made with common words – *a fast car, have dinner, a bit tired*. If you are using this dictionary, we are confident you will already know these. Nor have we included technical collocations from specialist areas such as medicine or economics. We have also excluded highly colloquial collocations which may sound unnatural if used by learners.

This is a dictionary of **selected** collocations. We have included only those about which we think you may be uncertain or which you will need when you want to use English carefully and precisely.

Grammatical information

If you want to check grammatical information, you will need to consult your ordinary dictionary, grammar book, or teacher. You need to be particularly careful with articles *(a, an, the)*. If in doubt, check. There are several reasons why we have not given detailed grammatical information in the lists:

- you already know a lot about common grammatical patterns
- slightly different meanings of a word sometimes mean different grammar patterns
- giving full grammatical information would make the entries so complicated that the collocational information would be less accessible

Our aim is to make the entries in this dictionary as easy as possible to scan or browse.

How to look something up

The dictionary has two parts. In the first part all the headwords are nouns. You use this section to find the verbs and adjectives which combine with the noun. In the second part the headwords are verbs and adjectives. You use this section to find the adverbs and adverbial expressions which combine with the verbs and adjectives.

Headwords

The noun is often the most important word in a sentence because it is 'what you are talking about'. The other words are built round the noun. Complicated ideas are built in a logical order:

1. What am I talking about? a noun
2. What kind?   adjective + noun
3. What happened to it?   verb + adjective + noun
4. How did it happen?   verb + adjective + noun + adverb/adverbial

NOUN	> ADJECTIVE	> VERB	> (ADVERB)
order	> *urgent*	> *dispatch*	> *by air*
proposal	> *original*	> *modify*	> *drastically*

Then, when you have all the words, you need to put them into the correct grammatical form to say exactly what you want:

We dispatched your urgent order by air yesterday.
The original proposal had been drastically modified before it was accepted.

How to find the collocations you need

Start from the noun and scan all the verbs under the headword quickly. Scanning the words in the entry will help you think more clearly about what exactly you want to say. Ignore any words you do not recognise, and all those where you know the meaning is not what you want. You should find either exactly the verb you are looking for or, perhaps, several verbs with similar meanings so you can choose the one that best expresses what you want to say.

Browsing

Apart from looking for the collocation which says exactly what you mean, you can use an entry, particularly one of the longer ones, to help you to re-activate lots of half-remembered combinations. Use the entry in this way when you are preparing an essay or a talk.

Translating

Scanning the whole entry is particularly helpful if you are trying to translate from your own language. Scanning the entry should refresh your memory and remind you of possibilities. This is particularly the case for those words which are difficult to translate because they have rather little meaning – but they have very long lists of collocations, for example, *idea, information, evidence, manner, plan, scheme.*

Words with more than one meaning

Sometimes there is more than one entry for the same headword. This happens when the word has two or more **clearly distinct** meanings:

SPACE   **SPACE** (cosmic)

SENSE   **SENSE** (smell, sight)   **SENSE** (meaning)

A small number of headwords are given in the plural when this is the **most common** use of the word, for example, *congratulations, circumstances.* Sometimes the plural has a different meaning from the singular:

TALK   **TALK** (lecture)   **TALKS** (negotiations)

9

Sometimes, where the headword is singular, some expressions which are always plural are listed at the end of the entry:

> **RIGHT**
> P: the ~ of free speech, to have/reserve the ~ to, to know/stand up for your *rights*,
>   within (your) *rights*, animal, human, women's *rights*

Many nouns have only one meaning; a few have two or more clearly different meanings (*state = condition; state = nation*). Many words have a range of similar or overlapping uses. The differences in meaning can be very small – *a spelling test, a driving test* and *medical tests* – are all slightly different uses of the word *test*. A word like *story* is much more complicated. Here are some examples:

> *Shall I tell you a funny story?*
> *Despite intensive cross-examination, both witnesses stuck to their stories.*
> *The Government made a statement as soon as the story broke.*

Although they all have the same basic meaning, the word *story* refers to three quite different areas – jokes, testimony in court and a news story. Obviously some of the collocations of *story* are common in one use but unusual or even impossible in the others, but some other collocations can be used with all three slightly different meanings. Separating these overlapping areas is both impossible and unhelpful. Scanning one of the longer entries like *story, idea, system, view* will help you to see the similar but slightly different ways in which these important words are used. As we have already seen, this also helps you to re-activate for immediate use words you only half-remember.

Literal and metaphorical uses

Many of the words which cover overlapping areas like this are used both literally and metaphorically:

> *run the race of a lifetime*   *win a gold medal*
> *run for office*   *win the race for the White House*

Metaphorical uses are common in all forms of writing including newspapers, research, essays and reports.

Remember, when looking at adjective + noun collocations, that many adjectives are ungradable when they are used literally, but gradable when used metaphorically. So although you are unlikely to say *My grandmother is very dead,* you can say *The town is very dead at the weekend.*

Part 1 – The Noun Section

Most entries contain:

- V: a list of verbs which come before the noun
- V: a list of verbs (in the most common tense) which come after the noun
- A: a list of adjectives
- P: phrases which contain the noun

They look like this:

CAREER

V: abandon, be absorbed in, be destined for ~ in, boost, carve out, change, choose, concentrate on, cripple, cut short, damage, determine, develop, devote oneself to, embark on, end, enter upon, further, give up, hamper, have a ~ in (banking), help, hinder, interrupt, launch out on, launch sb on, map out, plan, predict, promote, pursue, put an end to, ruin, sacrifice, salvage, set sb off on, spoil, start, take up, wreck ~

V: ~ blossomed, had its ups and downs

A: amazing, brilliant, chequered, colourful, demanding, difficult, disappointing, distinguished, entire, fine, flourishing, glittering, golden, good, great, honourable, ill-fated, meteoric, modest, promising, splendid, steady, strange, successful, turbulent, unusual, varied ~

P: outset of, peak of, pinnacle of, springboard for, summit of ~, a ~ change

---

The verb lists

The ~ marks the position of the headword in the collocation or phrase. When the ~ comes at the end of a list of verbs, those verbs are used **in front of** the noun. For example: *She interrupted her career to have a family.*

When the ~ comes first, the verbs **follow** the noun. For example: *Her career blossomed after she changed jobs.*

When the ~ comes in the middle, it still shows the position of the headword – *have a career in banking.*

The adjective lists

Most of the adjectives listed can be used before the noun (attributively – *a distinguished career* – and after the noun (predicatively – *his career in the diplomatic service was very distinguished*). Sometimes adjectives can only be used in one position. If you are in doubt, check in your ordinary dictionary or grammar book. Notice in some entries the adjective list contains some words which are normally used as nouns. For example:

Collocations such as *car accident* and *road accident* are common in English and indeed it is impossible to express these ideas any other way. Do not be surprised to find more 'nouns' in the adjective lists than you expect.

Sometimes two grammatically related adjectives collocate with the noun:

realistic / unrealistic assumption

Sometimes the negative word collocates, but there is no positive equivalent, or the positive equivalent does not collocate:

unwarranted assumption

These features appear in the dictionary like this:

> **ASSUMPTION**
> A: arrogant, basic, bold, cautious, charitable, conventional, crucial, fair, false,
>   far-fetched, feeble, foolish, fundamental, (un)likely, logical, obvious, optimistic,
>   pessimistic, plausible, preliminary, (im)probable, (un)realistic, reasonable,
>   reliable, ridiculous, rigid, risky, safe, tacit, (un)tenable, unfounded, unjustified,
>   unwarranted, valid, well-founded, wild ~

Lists of phrases

All the phrases contain the headword in the position shown by the ~. For example – *the peak of his career, a successful career change.*

Only two other symbols are used in the entries:

sb = somebody – *invite sb out for a meal, establish sb's guilt*
sth = something – *entirely, perfectly, totally, wholly consistent with sth*

Sometimes these are combined. If the phrase needs to be completed, this is shown by three dots. For example:

> **CONTEMPTUOUS**
>   faintly, openly, privately *contemptuous* of sb/sth
>
> **REPORT**
> V: ~ calls for sth, came out, draws attention to sth, identifies ...,
>   makes clear that ...

Part 2 – The Adverb Section

The lists in this section tell you which adverb goes with a particular verb or adjective. For the adjectives the adverbs come in front; for the verbs the lists show you where the word or phrase **usually** occurs. In English it is very difficult to give absolute rules for the position of the adverb. Here is some guidance:

1. Adverbial expressions nearly always follow the verb:

     enter *without permission*   disappear *into thin air*

2. Adverbs of manner usually follow the verb:

     manage *efficiently*   nod *approvingly*

3. Time adverbs usually come in front of the verb:

     seldom see   *often* come

but as these are very common we do not usually list them in this dictionary.

4. One important group of words which behave differently consists of certain adverb + verb collocations which function almost like two-word verbs:

     I *strongly disapprove.*

     They were *completely excluded.*

These are shown in the lists, which show you the **most probable** position of the adverb like this:

> **SUGGEST**
> *suggest* diffidently, hesitantly, in good faith, obliquely, politely, repeatedly, wearily
> seriously, strongly, tentatively *suggest* sth/that...

Sometimes there is only one adverb + adjective collocation given:

     greatly encouraged   *highly excitable*

The collocation which is given is very strong although of course you will occasionally find other combinations.

Sentence Adverbs

On pages 286 and 287 we list adverbs which are used at the beginning of a sentence to refer to the whole sentence or paragraph which follows. They explain the status of what follows. Using these sentence adverbs and adverbials makes your writing easier to read because you show the reader the connections between one part of your text and another. For example:

Equally,	Finally,
Essentially,	Firstly,
Even so,	Fortunately,
Eventually,	Fundamentally,
Explicitly,	

Building your vocabulary

One of the best ways to build your vocabulary is to remember collocations rather than single words. If you work or study in a particular area, it helps if you record collocations you find when you are reading. Collocation is one of the best ways to improve your English.

Michael Lewis, Jimmie Hill, Hove 1997

Abbreviations used in this dictionary

~	=	the headword
V	=	verb
A	=	adjective
P	=	phrase
adj	=	adjective
sth	=	something
sb	=	somebody

THE NOUN SECTION

Using the noun section

As you read in the Introduction, the noun is often the most important word in a sentence because it is 'what you are talking about'. The other words are built round the noun.

1. What am I talking about?   a noun
2. What kind?   adjective
3. What happened to it?   verb
4. How did it happen?   adverb/adverbial

noun	> adjective	> verb	> (adverb)
language	> *foreign*	> *learn*	> *naturally*

This example shows you **the order** in which you build an idea:

1. from **noun** to **adjective**
2. from **adjective + noun** to **verb**
3. from **verb + adjective + noun** to any **adverb** or **adverbial expression**
4. add the grammar: *If you want to learn a foreign language naturally . . .*

From noun to verb

Surprisingly, the **last** word in a sentence is often where the idea starts.

I mustn't forget to feed the cat.

As you can see, the sentence is about 'the cat', and although that word comes last, it is the starting point for what you want to say.

A few nouns are typically the grammatical subject and are followed by a large range of verbs. These are often words for kinds of writing. Look, for example, at the entry for *report*.

A

ABILITY
V: appraise, assess, demonstrate, develop, encourage, foster, have, measure, nurse, overrate, recognise, stifle, underrate, use ~
A: average, creative, exceptional, great, inferior, innate, latent, moderate, natural, outstanding, remarkable, striking, superior, uncanny, unique ~

ABOLITION
V: call for, campaign for ~
A: outright, total ~
P: ~ of the death penalty/slavery

ABUSE
V: avoid, check, clamp down on, curb, prevent, put an end to ~
V: ~ is rampant
A: alcohol, blatant, child, drug, horrifying, physical, psychological, sexual, shocking, substance, widespread ~
P: victim of ~

ABUSE (swearing)
V: hurl ~ at, take a lot of ~
P: term of, barrage of, stream of, tirade of, torrent of ~

ACCENT
V: affect, assume, cultivate, detect, disguise, get rid of, have, imitate, lose, put on, speak with ~
A: broad, foreign, funny, heavy, noticeable, pronounced, silly, slight, strong, thick ~
P: no trace of ~

ACCEPTANCE
V: announce, find, gain, meet with, refuse, signify, win ~
A: definite, enthusiastic, general, grateful, immediate, prompt, ready, reluctant, total, universal, unqualified, wholehearted, widespread, unwilling ~

ACCESS
V: acquire, allow, bar, demand, deny, force, gain, get, give, have, obstruct, obtain, permit, provide, refuse ~
A: difficult, (in)direct, easy, free, (un)limited, ready, (un)restricted, unimpeded ~

ACCIDENT
V: avert, avoid, be involved in, cause, have, meet with, precipitate, prevent, suffer, witness ~
A: bad, car, dreadful, fatal, happy, horrible, industrial, nasty, road, serious, slight, terrible, tragic, unfortunate ~
P: cause of, victim of ~, spate of, toll of *accidents*

ACCLAIM
V: be greeted with, receive ~
A: critical, enthusiastic, great ~

ACCOMMODATION
V: book, find, get, have, hunt for, let, look for, offer, provide, rent, reserve, search for, take ~
A: comfortable, high-class, luxury, luxurious, permanent, poor, satisfactory, shabby, sheltered, spacious, standard, suitable, superior, temporary ~
P: scarcity of, shortage of ~

ACCOUNT
V: check, circulate, corroborate, embark on, give, obtain, offer, produce, provide, publish, receive, send in, submit, verify, write ~

V: ~ appeared, is coloured by ..., is consistent with ..., circulated, has come in, tallies with ...

A: (in)accurate, authentic, authoritative, balanced, (un)biased, blow-by-blow, brief, careful, clear, coherent, colourful, compelling, comprehensive, condensed, (un)convincing, definitive, detailed, distorted, dramatic, dreary, elaborate, entertaining, euphemistic, exciting, expert, eye-witness, factual, false, fascinating, fictitious, first-hand, frightening, frank, full, funny, garbled, general, glowing, graphic, gruesome, impartial, incoherent, informative, knowledgeable, leisurely, lively, lucid, misleading, moving, muddled, one-sided, painful, persuasive, powerful, precise, rambling, readable, (un)reliable, riveting, running, scholarly, simple, sober, sparkling, step-by-step, straightforward, succinct, true, truthful, unvarnished, verbatim, vivid ~

ACCOUNT (bill)
V: check, pay, prepare, question, receive, render, send in, settle, square ~

A: itemised, overdue ~

ACCOUNT (bank)
V: add sth to, close, credit, debit, draw on, have, keep, open, overdraw, pay sth into, put sth into, run down ~

V: ~ is in the red/black, is overdrawn/in credit

A: current, deposit, healthy, illicit, interest-bearing, joint, numbered, savings ~

ACCOUNTS (financial)
V: balance, check, do, file, go through, keep, keep a record of, settle, square ~

A: ~ payable, receivable

P: ~ file, manager

ACCURACY
V: improve, maintain, measure, test ~

A: absolute, amazing, commendable, deadly, historical, perfect, reasonable, required, strict, total, uncanny, unerring ~

ACCUSATION
V: be confronted with, bring, counter, defend oneself against, deny, disprove, fabricate, fight, level, make, rebut, refute, withdraw ~

A: absurd, baseless, damaging, dangerous, (grossly) exaggerated, false, furious, grave, groundless, hysterical, malicious, ridiculous, serious, unfair, unfounded, unjust, untrue, unwarranted, wicked ~

ACHIEVEMENT
V: acclaim, acknowledge, admire, appreciate, assess, belittle, disparage, exaggerate, give sb credit for, hail, magnify, make light of, marvel at, note, praise, sneer at, underestimate ~

A: amazing, brilliant, creditable, crowning, dazzling, enduring, enormous, great, imposing, incomparable, joint, lasting, laudable, magnificent, major, memorable, notable, outstanding, phenomenal, remarkable, solid, stupendous, superb, tangible, unique, unparalleled, valuable, wonderful, worthy ~

P: sense of, lack of ~

ACKNOWLEDGEMENT
V: ask for, demand, express, get, make, receive, send ~

A: formal, frank, full, generous, grateful, grudging, modest, polite, prompt, public, reluctant, sincere, slight, unqualified ~

18

ACQUAINTANCE
V: bump into, introduce, make, meet ~
A: casual, distant, new, old, recent ~

ACQUISITION
A: expensive, latest, magnificent, new, pleasant, recent, valuable ~

ACT (see also *action*)
V: commit, perform, perpetrate ~
A: aggressive, altruistic, barbaric, brave, commendable, courageous, cowardly, criminal, deliberate, despicable, disgraceful, foolish, friendly, generous, heroic, hostile, humane, illegal, inexplicable, inhuman, irresponsible, (un)kind, kindly, (un)lawful, mean, noble, provocative, (un)selfish, sensible, solemn, thoughtless, unforgivable ~
P: ~ of aggression, of desperation, of faith, of folly, of kindness, of war

ACT (of Parliament)
V: administer, apply, bring in, enforce, introduce, invoke, look up, refer to, repeal ~
V: ~ applies to sth, bans sth, becomes law, comes into force, empowers sb to do sth, lays down (guidelines), makes sth illegal, provides for sth, requires sth, states sth
P: breach of, contravention of, loophole in ~

ACTION
V: be led into, call for, condemn, condone, contemplate, decide on, defer, hamper, hinder, incite sb to, instigate, judge, justify, perform, postpone, prevent, renew, rouse sb to, take, undertake ~
A: bold, brisk, careless, clumsy, concerted, co-ordinated, corporate, daring, decisive, deliberate, disgraceful, drastic, energetic, evasive, foolish, foolhardy, further, generous, hasty, hostile, hot-blooded, humanitarian, ill-advised, immediate, imminent, impulsive, incomprehensible, instant, joint, legitimate, precipitate, (un)premeditated, prompt, purposeful, quick, retaliatory, ruthless, slow, spontaneous, strenuous, stupid, supportive, sweeping, swift, thoughtless, unprincipled, unwise, urgent, warlike ~
P: day of, freedom of, plan of ~

ACTIVITY
V: ban, be engaged in/involved in/mixed up in, clamp down on, curb, disrupt, go in for, hamper, indulge in, keep an eye on, monitor, prevent, pursue, put an end to, put a stop to, reduce, step up, suppress, sustain, wind up ~
V: ~ extends to sth
A: ceaseless, clandestine, constant, continuous, covert, criminal, detrimental, frantic, frenetic, furious, great, harmful, hectic, heightened, illegal, indoor, intense, leisure, mysterious, outdoor, (un)related, risky, secret, sinister, social, sporting, subversive, suspicious, tremendous, underground, unorthodox, weird ~
P: bout of, flurry of, hive of, surge of, whirl of ~, series of, variety of *activities*

ADAPTATION
V: bring about, hasten, prevent ~
A: gradual, day-by-day, piecemeal ~

ADDRESS (speech)
V: deliver, give ~
A: customary, farewell, final, formal, inaugural, moving, opening ~

ADDICTION
V: cure, develop, feed, get over, overcome, recover from, treat ~
A: chronic, drug, fatal, hopeless, lifelong, long-term, powerful ~
P: ~ to alcohol, to drugs, to gambling

ADJOURNMENT
V: announce, ask for, call for, move, propose, refuse ~
A: brief, temporary ~

ADMINISTRATION
V: be in charge of, be responsible for, streamline, take over, tighten up ~
A: day-to-day, (in)efficient, poor, smooth ~

ADMINISTRATION (governing body)
V: set up, support ~
A: current, incumbent, (in)efficient, outgoing ~

ADMINISTRATOR
V: appoint ~
A: bad, clever, efficient, experienced, hard-headed, level-headed, poor, wise ~

ADMIRATION
V: arouse, attract, be the centre of, be full of ~ for, be worthy of, command, deserve, earn, enjoy, excite, express, feel, give, have, merit, show, win ~
A: breathless, full, great, mutual, sincere, tremendous, undiminished, undying, universal, unstinting, warm, widespread ~
P: gasp of, wave of ~

ADMIRER
A: ardent, devoted, enthusiastic, faithful, fervent, fond, great, old, secret ~

ADMISSION (entry)
V: apply for, ban, demand, deny, forbid, force, grant, refuse ~
A: free, immediate, (un)restricted ~

ADMISSION (confession)
V: come out with, force, make ~ , wring an ~ from sb
A: candid, damning, embarrassing, frank, full, humiliating, misleading, painful, partial, ready, reluctant, revealing, tacit, terse ~

ADVANCE
V: accelerate, achieve, block, check, further, halt, hamper, hold back, hold up, impede, keep back, make, oppose, prevent, repel, slow down, spearhead, speed up ~
V: ~ gathered momentum, lost impetus, slowed down, speeded up
A: breathtaking, dramatic, exhilarating, fitful, great, inevitable, rapid, relentless, remarkable, significant, slow, steady, sudden, swift ~

ADVANTAGE
V: balance, bring, confer, enjoy, exploit, fritter away, gain, give, grasp, have, offer, outweigh, present, press home, represent, squander, take ~ of, use, waste, weigh up, win ~
V: ~ accrued, lies in sth
A: added, apparent, big, built-in, clear, common, decided, distinct, doubtful, great, hypothetical, long/short-term, main, marked, mutual, obvious, prospective, slight, undeniable, undue, unexpected, unfair, vital, well-deserved ~

ADVENTURE
V: go on, have, look for, seek ~
A: amazing, breathtaking, exciting, real, thrilling ~
P: a life of, a love of, a spirit of, a sense of ~

ADVERSARY
V: attack, challenge, confront, conquer, crush, defeat, defy, destroy, deter, encounter, engage, face, fight, kill, meet, overcome, rout ~
A: dangerous, daunting, fierce, implacable, powerful, principal, superior ~

ADVERSITY
V: encounter, endure, meet with, suffer ~
A: great ~
ADVERT(ISEMENT)
V: create, devise, place, produce, run, screen, show ~
A: full-page, job, newspaper ~
P: a good ~ for, a very poor ~ for
ADVERTISING
A: global, subliminal, television ~
P: ~ agency, budget, campaign, executive, expenditure, industry, space
ADVICE
V: accept, act on, adopt, ask, ask for, disregard, follow, get, give, go against, ignore, offer, profit from, receive, refuse, reject, seek, solicit, sweep aside, take, tender ~
A: admirable, bad, badly needed, blunt, cautious, considered, elementary, excellent, expert, fatherly, friendly, good, gratuitous, impartial, invaluable, poor, professional, prudent, reliable, sensible, shrewd, silly, sound, straight, stupid, unbiased, unpalatable, unsolicited, urgent, valuable, welcome, wise ~
P: piece of ~
ADVISER
V: consult ~
A: cautious, clear-headed, economic, experienced, financial, impartial, legal, outside, political, realistic, spiritual, technical, trusted, unbiased ~
AFFAIR
V: arrange, be engaged in, become entangled in, bungle, cover up, deal with, disentangle oneself from, finish with, get involved in, get mixed up in, handle, hush up, resolve, settle, wash one's hands of, withdraw from, wriggle out of ~
V: ~ became public, blew over, came out, came to light, cropped up, dragged on, rankled, was kept dark/kept quiet
A: complicated, compromising, dangerous, delicate, disastrous, embarrassing, foolish, grandiose, illegal, messy, nasty, painful, private, protracted, risky, shady, sinister, sordid, spectacular, tricky, suspicious, ugly, underhand, unfortunate, unhappy, unpleasant, unsavoury, upsetting ~
P: ramifications of ~
AFFAIRS (business of any kind)
V: attend to, be in charge of, deal with, look after, make a mess of, manage, neglect ~
A: everyday, mundane, routine ~
P: state of ~
AFFECTION
V: be hungry for, bestow, crave, demonstrate, display, feel, forfeit, get, give, hanker after, have, hunger for, lack, long for, need, return, show, stifle, win, withhold, yearn for ~
A: deep, enduring, great, growing, lasting, long-standing, warm ~
P: bonds of ~
AGE
V: arrive at, be at, come of, look one's, pass, reach ~
A: advanced, difficult, early, mature, middle, retirement, ripe old, sensible, tender, venerable ~
AGE (era)
V: belong to, date back to, date from, herald ~
A: adventurous, bygone, golden, idyllic, past, remote, turbulent ~

AGENCY (body)

V: act through, apply to, be in charge of, disband, manage, register with, run, set up ~

AGENDA

V: adopt, agree on, appear on, approve, draft, draw up, fix, go through, include on, put sth / an item on, remove sth from, settle, stick to, vote on ~

A: final, full, hidden, provisional ~

AGGRESSION (physical, military)

V: be bent on, be guilty of, commit, condemn, curb, defend sb against, denounce, desist from, engage in, fuel, halt, limit, meet, oppose, plan, step up, stop, resist, unleash, ward off ~

A: armed, blatant, cruel, mounting, naked, open, savage, unprovoked ~

P: act of ~

AGGRESSION (emotional)

V: control, display, express, fuel, get rid of, give vent to, manifest, master, redirect, sublimate, suppress ~

A: hidden, mounting, overt, strong, unconcealed, unprovoked, veiled ~

AGREEMENT

V: abide by, achieve, arrive at, breach, break, by-pass, cancel, carry out, circumvent, come to, conclude, contract out of, endorse, enforce, enter into, express, extend, get out of, go back on, hammer out, honour, ignore, implement, make, negotiate, ratify, reach, reject, remain committed to, renege on, renew, respect, revoke, scrap, secure, seek, sign, sort out, undermine, violate, withhold, work out ~

V: ~ comes into effect/force, expires, holds good, is in force, is null and void, is out-of-date, is valid, provides for sth, runs out, states sth, takes effect, will be superseded by ...

A: advantageous, amicable, awkward, bilateral, binding, broad, complete, complicated, convenient, crucial, equitable, existing, fair, firm, (in)formal, general, gentleman's, lasting, legally-binding, mutual, profitable, provisional, ready, reciprocal, solemn, standing, tacit, tentative, total, verbal, wise, written ~

P: be in full ~ with sb, breach of, stumbling block to, terms of ~

AID

V: allocate, appeal for, be in need of, bring, call for, channel, cut, cut off, depend on, discontinue, distribute, enlist, extend, get, give, offer, lend, need, organise, provide, reduce, refuse, resume, seek, stop, summon, suspend, withdraw, withhold ~

A: covert, (in)direct, economic, effective, emergency, essential, financial, foreign, generous, government, immediate, legal, massive, substantial, Third World, unsolicited ~

AIM

V: accomplish, achieve, be successful in, endorse, fail in, fall short of, fulfil, further, pursue, reach, secure, serve, set oneself, strive towards, succeed in, thwart, work for/towards ~

V: *aims* coincide, collide, conflict, converge, match, overlap

A: apparent, basic, broad, chief, clear, common, conscious, deliberate, (in)direct, distant, far-reaching, final, fundamental, further, general, immediate, implicit, implied, intermediate, joint, laudable, legitimate, lofty, long/short-term, main, noble, overall, overriding, overwhelming, political, primary, principal, real, recognised, secret, single-minded, specific, true, ultimate, underlying, useful ~

AIR (manner)

V: adopt, assume, convey, exude, have ~

A: blunt, cheerful, confident, cool, diffident, friendly, gentle, matter-of-fact, melancholy, military, mysterious, nonchalant, sad, sinister, superior, triumphant ~

AIR
A: clear, filthy, fresh, mountain, polluted, sea, stale, thin ~

ALARM
V: cause, express, feel, give rise to, increase, spread ~
A: considerable, great, growing, mounting, natural, sudden, unnecessary, widespread ~

ALIBI
V: cast doubt on, (double-)check, concoct, confirm, damage, destroy, establish, invent, make up, produce, prove, provide, question, question sb about, reject, supply, support, suspect, test, weaken ~
V: ~ broke down, collapsed, held good
A: cast-iron, convincing, false, good, plausible, poor, strong, watertight, weak ~

ALLEGATION
V: admit, challenge, come out with, contest, defend oneself against, deny, discount, dismiss, disprove, drop, fabricate, make, prove, publish, put forward, react to, refute, spread, substantiate, withdraw ~
A: crude, damaging, dreadful, false, grave, harmful, ill-founded, irresponsible, malicious, serious, sinister, (un)true, unfounded, unsubstantiated, well-founded, wicked, wild ~

ALLIANCE
V: belong to, break, cement, create, dissolve, enter into, forge, form, hold together, join, patch up, resurrect, set up, sever, split, strengthen, support ~
V: ~ broke down, collapsed, foundered, remains in force, still holds
A: ancient, close, flourishing, formidable, hasty, old, shifting, strong, tactical, traditional, uneasy, unhappy, unholy ~
P: breakdown of, collapse of, split in ~

ALLOWANCE
V: ask for, demand, draw, get, give, grant, make, pay, squander, stop ~
A: daily, generous, meagre, miserly, monthly, petty, regular, small, weekly ~

ALLUSION
V: make ~
A: apt, brief, flattering, hidden, passing, polite, tactful, tentative, topical ~

ALLY
V: gain, make, pose as, recruit, support ~
A: close, dependable, doubtful, faithful, false, firm, loyal, reliable, staunch, strong, trustworthy, useful ~

ALTERNATIVE
V: look for, propose, seek, suggest ~
V: ~ presented itself
A: feasible, viable, worthwhile ~
P: choice of, range of *alternatives*

AMBITION (general desire to achieve)
V: be consumed/devoured/driven by, be full of, feed, fire, fuel, satisfy, serve ~
A: inflated, mounting, overwhelming, single-minded ~
P: height of ~

AMBITION (specific aim)
V: achieve, cherish, fail in, foil, frustrate, fulfil, gratify, harbour, have, nurse, realise, thwart, wreck ~
A: burning, chief, great, lifelong, long-standing, main, overriding, secret, strong, vague ~
P: fulfilment of ~, achieve the ~ of a lifetime

AMENDMENT
V: accept, approve, debate, delete, draft, frame, incorporate, introduce, move, oppose, pass, present, propose, put forward, reject, submit, suggest, support, table, vote on ~

AMENITIES
V: offer, preserve, provide, safeguard ~

AMOUNT
V: add up to, calculate, estimate, guarantee, measure, reckon, reduce, spend ~
V: ~ decreased, diminished, fell, grew, increased, remained steady
A: (in)adequate, amazing, available, average, considerable, disproportionate, enormous, exact, full, great, huge, infinitesimal, large, miserly, moderate, modest, negligible, overall, small, specific, (in)sufficient, tremendous, total, vast ~

ANALOGY
V: draw, see ~
A: clear, close, distinct, obvious, slight, vague ~

ANALYSIS
V: carry out, embark on, invalidate, make, produce, undertake, use ~
V: ~ demonstrates, shows, suggests
A: basic, (un)biased, broad, careful, close, detailed, dispassionate, final, forensic, illuminating, in-depth, logical, misleading, painstaking, penetrating, perceptive, precise, preliminary, profound, rigorous, rough, scholarly, systematic, tentative, thorough, wide-ranging ~

ANARCHY
V: encourage, end in, give rise to, incite sb to, lead to, put down, slide into, stir up ~
V: ~ broke out, grew, reigned, spread, was rife
A: complete, general, serious, total, utter, widespread ~

ANGER
V: appease, arouse, avert, be consumed with/filled with/seized with, bottle up, control, contain, curb, explode with, express, feel, fuel, get over, heighten, increase, restrain, seethe with, show, stir up, suppress, turn pale/red with, vent, voice ~
V: ~ abated, broke forth, died down, erupted, exploded, got the better of sb, grew, mounted, subsided, vanished, was dissipated, was (soon) over, was unleashed,
A: bitter, consuming, fierce, mounting, pent-up, uncontrollable ~

ANGLE
V: come at/examine/look at sth from another/a different ~
A: human, interesting, new, unusual ~

ANIMAL
V: behave like, breed, domesticate, hunt, skin, slaughter, stuff, tame, train, trap ~
A: caged, carnivorous, domestic, farm, exotic, herbivorous, predatory, rare, tame, wild ~
P: ~ fat, products, rights

ANIMOSITY
V: fear, feel, get over ~
A: deep, great, instinctive, strong ~

ANNOUNCEMENT
V: broadcast, catch, insert, issue, make, miss, notice, publish, put up, watch for ~
A: final, formal, important, initial, official, preliminary ~

ANOMALY
V: create, do away with, observe, perceive, remove ~
V: ~ arose, exists
A: absurd, distinct, serious ~

ANSWER
V: accept, await, blurt out, call for, come forward with/out with/up with, demand, elicit, evade, expect, get, give, have, insist on, invent, look for, make up, offer, prepare, produce, provide, put forward, receive, record, refuse, reject, require, submit, supply ~

A: abrupt, aggressive, (un)ambiguous, appropriate, awkward, banal, bland, blunt, bold, civil, clear, complete, comprehensive, confused, considered, conciliatory, (in)correct, courteous, cryptic, (in)decisive, (in)definite, detailed, diplomatic, (in)direct, (in)distinct, early, evasive, explicit, favourable, feeble, final, firm, flippant, foolish, frank, fresh, frosty, full, glib, hasty, hesitant, immediate, impertinent, incoherent, ingenious, knowledgeable, mild, negative, non-committal, nonsensical, original, persuasive, plain, polite, poor, positive, precise, prompt, proper, provocative, rash, ready, reasonable, right, roundabout, rude, (un)satisfactory, sensible, silly, simple, straight, straightforward, succinct, thoughtful, unequivocal, vague, wrong ~

ANTAGONISM
V: aggravate, cause, create, feel, get over, give rise to, increase, lead to, overcome, produce, reduce ~

A: fierce ~

ANXIETY
V: add to, allay, alleviate, be filled with, be plagued by, be seized with, cause, compound, conquer, create, dispel, ease, experience, feel, fight, get over, get rid of, give rise to, provoke, relieve, remove, repress, soothe, suffer, suffer from, voice ~

V: ~ comes from ..., disappeared, has to do with ..., is connected/linked with ..., is due to ..., is produced by ..., is tied up with ..., stems from ...

A: acute, deep, great, intense, justifiable, (un)justified, mounting, overwhelming, profound, serious, severe, subconscious, unnecessary ~

P: (no) cause for, fit of, (not much) need for ~

APOLOGY
V: accept, ask for, call for, demand, expect, make, offer, send, tender ~

V: ~ is called for, is due, is in order, is overdue, is required

A: abject, full, humble, public, sincere, unreserved ~

P: send your *apologies*

APPEAL
V: address, answer, be moved by, ignore, issue, listen to, make, refuse, reject, renew, respond to, turn down ~

V: ~ failed, succeeded

A: charity, confident, desperate, (in)direct, dramatic, earnest, emotional, final, fruitless, immediate, moving, nationwide, passionate, pathetic, powerful, public, sincere, successful, television, urgent, vociferous, wide, worldwide ~

APPEAL (attractiveness)
V: diminish, enhance, have ~

V: ~ lies in sth

A: charismatic, enduring, great, instant, irresistible, sex, wide ~

APPEAL (retrial)
V: allow, dismiss, file, grant, hear, lodge, lose, throw out, uphold, withdraw, win ~

APPEARANCE
A: (un)attractive, dowdy, down-at-heel, elegant, imposing, impressive, intimidating, neat, noble, pleasant, pleasing, smart, strange, surprise, (un)tidy, unprepossessing ~

APPEARANCE (act of appearing)
V: make, put in ~
A: final, guest, last, personal, public, regular, sudden, television, unexpected, welcome ~
APPETITE
V: blunt, dull, give, satisfy, sharpen, spoil, stimulate, take away, tempt, whet, work up ~
A: formidable, good, healthy, huge, insatiable, jaded, poor, ravenous, sharp, tremendous ~
APPLAUSE
V: draw, greet sb with, meet with, win ~
V: ~ broke out, died down, went on
A: deafening, dutiful, enthusiastic, generous, polite, prolonged, rapturous, sustained, thunderous, tumultuous, wild ~
P: burst of, ripple of, round of, storm of ~
APPLICATION
V: accept, consider, examine, file, fill in, grant, invite, lodge, make, process, put in, receive, refuse, reject, send in/out, submit, turn down, vet, withdraw, write ~
V: ~ failed, was successful, went ahead
A: detailed, formal, immediate, personal, prompt, written ~
P: ~ forms; deluge of, flood of, wave of *applications*
APPLICATION (use)
V: foresee, have ~
A: (un)limited, narrow, obvious, practical, universal, widespread ~
APPOINTMENT (arrangement to meet)
V: (re)arrange, break, cancel, fail to turn up for, fix, grant, have, keep, make, miss, postpone ~
APPOINTMENT (post)
V: announce, hold, obtain, receive, resign from, take up ~
A: permanent, recent, temporary ~
APPREHENSION
V: be filled with, feel, overcome ~
A: considerable, great, little, needless ~
APPROACH
V: adopt, attempt, change, cling to, choose, decide on, employ, favour, follow, have, make, modify, pursue, recognise, reject, settle for, show, take, try, use, welcome ~
A: aggressive, balanced, basic, belligerent, bold, broad, broad-based, brutal, careful, careless, cautious, clear, concerted, conciliatory, (un)constructive, cool, co-ordinated, crude, determined, (in)direct, dispassionate, doctrinaire, energetic, firm, flexible, fresh, (un)friendly, hard-line, helpful, holistic, hostile, (un)imaginative, lackadaisical, logical, low-key, mature, measured, neutral, novel, partisan, positive, pragmatic, realistic, (un)reasonable, resolute, revolutionary, rigid, rigorous, scholarly, scientific, sensitive, slapdash, soft, tentative, timid, traditional, (un)usual, useful, useless, vigorous ~
APPROVAL (agreement)
V: apply for, ask for, express, gain, get, give, grant, have, meet with, obtain, receive, refuse, request, seek, signify, solicit, voice, win ~
A: definite, enthusiastic, firm, friendly, full, hearty, hesitant, immediate, instant, out-and-out, provisional, reluctant, tentative ~
P: chorus of, nod of, seal of ~
APPROVAL (warm regard)
V: enjoy, look for, lose, want, win ~
A: benign, decided, grudging, hearty, warm, wholehearted ~

APTITUDE
V: demonstrate, develop, display, encourage, foster, have, inherit, lose, possess, show ~
A: decided, definite, distinct, great, marked, natural, outstanding, pronounced, rare, remarkable, special ~
ARBITRATION
V: decide sth by, go to, refer sth to, send sth to, submit sth to ~
AREA (space)
V: cover, denote, designate, develop, earmark, extend, fix, increase, locate, map, mark, measure, reduce, survey ~
V: ~ extends/stretches from ... to ... , increased, is bounded by ... , is situated (some-where), lies (somewhere), measures (30m by 20m)
A: adjacent, adjoining, built-up, catchment, central, cramped, disaster, extensive, huge, large, (un)limited, neighbouring, remote, total, vast, whole ~
AREA (military)
V: annex, conquer, cordon off, occupy, subjugate, take possession of ~
A: adjacent, adjoining, extensive, huge ~
ARGUMENT (disagreement)
V: become involved in, cause, cut short, end, engage in, enter into, get into, give rise to, have, hold, provoke, put an end to, settle, start, take part in ~
V: ~ arose, broke out, developed, ensued, went on
A: acrimonious, bitter, endless, ferocious, fierce, friendly, fruitless, furious, futile, heated, lively, loud, never-ending, noisy, pointless, serious, silly, stupid, unpleasant, violent ~
ARGUMENT (specific piece of reasoning)
V: accept, acknowledge, add weight to, advance, agree with, be backed by, brush aside, check, cite, clinch, confuse, counter, deal with, deny, dismiss, employ, express, grasp, invalidate, invoke, keep to, look into, offer, press, put aside/forward, raise, refute, reinforce, reject, repeat, see the force of, stand by, support, test, undermine, unravel, use, voice ~
V: ~ carries weight, centres round sth, fails, holds good, is sustained by sth, looks thin, makes sense, rests on sth, is wearing a bit thin
A: balanced, basic, biased, classic, cogent, complicated, convenient, (un)convincing, dangerous, detailed, down-to-earth, dubious, effective, evasive, fair, false, (un)familiar, feeble, flimsy, flippant, forceful, impassioned, incomprehensible, inconclusive, indefensible, ingenious, irrefutable, lame, legitimate, logical, lucid, ludicrous, misleading, novel, obscure, patient, persuasive, plausible, powerful, preposterous, rational, realistic, reasonable, reasoned, shaky, shallow, shrewd, silly, solid, sound, spurious, straightforward, strange, strong, telling, usual, weak, weighty, well-founded, woolly ~
P: basis of, cogency of, essence of, flaw in, force of, gist of, merits of, strength of, substance of, thread of ~
ARMAMENTS (large weapons)
V: build up, control, limit, pile up, reduce, stockpile ~
ARMS (smaller weapons)
V: bear, carry, lay down one's, pile up, take up, traffic in ~
P: ~ control, race, talks; cache of, clash of, flow of, trickle of ~

27

ARMY

V: build up, collect, command, create, crush, defeat, deploy, disband, draw up, equip, face, field, join, mobilise, outflank, outmanoeuvre, raise, regroup, train, supply, surprise ~

V: ~ advanced, fought, hung on, marched, rested, retreated, was in disarray, went into action, withdrew

A: disciplined, efficient, great, huge, ill/well-trained, invincible, mighty, ragged, rebel, regular, victorious ~

P: ~ officer

ARRANGEMENT

V: alter, arrive at, cancel, come to, conclude, conform to, hammer out, have, keep to, make, proceed with, reach, seek, work out ~

V: ~ covers sth, fell through, holds good, (no longer) holds, (still) holds, is in force

A: amicable, binding, careful, convenient, definite, detailed, final, firm, fixed, flexible, friendly, general, handy, informal, loose, makeshift, meticulous, mutual, necessary, permanent, poor, previous, regular, routine, satisfactory, sound, standby, standing, steady, suitable, systematic, temporary, tentative, unworkable ~

ARREST

V: avoid, be under, escape, make, place/put sb. under, resist ~

A: citizen's, false, house ~

P: spate of, wave of *arrests*

ARRIVAL

V: await, count on, expect ~

A: early, imminent, impending, late, new, sudden, unexpected ~

ARTS

P: ~ degree, sponsorship; appreciation of, flowering of ~

ARTICLE

V: edit, print, publish, review, skim, submit, summarise, work on, write ~

V: ~ deals with sth, discusses sth

A: brilliant, controversial, dull, inspiring, interesting, libellous, scathing, scholarly, seminal, sensible ~

P: string of *articles*

ASPECT

V: analyse, be aware of, consider, constitute, demonstrate, examine, fasten on, have, ignore, look at, neglect, omit, pass over, reveal, study, survey, take into account, view ~

V: ~ became more pronounced, came to the fore

A: chief, controversial, deeper, disturbing, essential, frightening, gratifying, gruesome, hopeful, human, humorous, (un)important, instructive, key, main, marginal, negative, obvious, ominous, principal, puzzling, questionable, refreshing, serious, striking, superficial, troubling, true, underlying, unexpected, unfortunate, unusual, upsetting, useful, vital, worrying ~

P: the most (worrying) ~ of this is ...

ASPIRATION

V: achieve, cherish, fail in, fulfil, gratify, profess, realise, satisfy ~

ASSAULT

V: be arrested for, carry out, commit, conduct, direct, launch, lead, make, repel, repulse, resist, suffer, ward off ~

A: armed, dangerous, daunting, direct, indecent, massive, military, physical, relentless, ruthless, savage, sexual, sudden, surprise, unjustified, unprovoked, violent ~

ASSENT
V: give, grant, refuse ~
A: ready, reluctant ~

ASSERTION
V: accept, bear out, challenge, contest, contradict, deny, disprove, make, put forward, refute, reject, substantiate, support ~
A: bare, blunt, bold, broad, confident, dangerous, dubious, explicit, false, firm, implied, (un)justified, questionable, (un)reasonable, strong, (un)true, wild ~

ASSESSMENT
V: agree on, arrive at, carry out, give, make, offer, produce, reach ~
A: (in)accurate, balanced, broad, careful, charitable, considered, continuous, (in)correct, critical, (un)fair, false, favourable, fresh, hasty, judicious, limited, overall, poor, realistic, reasonable, rough, shrewd, true, wise, wrong ~

ASSETS
V: accumulate, acquire, build up, draw on, freeze, impound, own, pile up, possess, recover, release, seize, sequester, squander, strip sb of ~
V: ~ are tied up (in ...), declined, disappeared, dwindled, grew, shrank
A: capital, considerable, extensive, frozen, liquid, movable, solid, (in)tangible, valuable ~

ASSIGNMENT
V: allocate, carry out, fulfil, give, undertake ~
A: crucial, dangerous, secret, special ~

ASSISTANCE
V: call for, count on, deny, get, give, invite, lend, offer, provide, receive, refuse, reject, rely on, seek, summon, supply ~
V: ~ arrived, came, was forthcoming
A: economic, financial, generous, great, immediate, mutual, prompt, ready, tangible, technical, useful, vital, welcome ~

ASSOCIATION (relationship)
V: break off, enter into, forge, form, have, sever ~
A: brief, clandestine, close, fruitful, harmful, harmless, intimate, long, loose, permanent, pleasant, useful ~

ASSOCIATION (society)
V: belong to, form, join, resign from, run ~

ASSORTMENT
V: choose from, offer ~
A: mixed, motley, odd, strange, varied, wide ~

ASSUMPTION
V: accept, act on, admit, bear out, challenge, contradict, deny, disprove, prove, put forward, question, rebut, refute, rely on, rest on, revert to, rule out, share, start from, support, test, underline, undermine, weaken ~
V: ~ holds good, is (no longer) true, was proved right/wrong
A: arrogant, basic, bold, cautious, charitable, conventional, crucial, fair, false, far-fetched, feeble, foolish, fundamental, improbable, logical, obvious, optimistic, original, pessimistic, plausible, preliminary, (un)realistic, reasonable, reliable, ridiculous, risky, safe, tacit, unfounded, unjustified, unlikely, unwarranted, valid, well-founded, wild ~

ASSURANCE
V: ask for, deliver, demand, extract, give, have, obtain, offer, receive, seek, want ~
A: categorical, empty, firm, formal, repeated, solemn, welcome ~

ATMOSPHERE
V: be aware of, be sensitive to, calm, create, ease, encourage, enjoy, evoke, express, feel, foster, generate, improve, lead to, preserve, relieve, sense, spoil ~

V: ~ became tense, changed, cooled down, pervaded sth, prevailed, was conducive to sth

A: aggressive, artificial, awkward, business-like, calm, (highly-)charged, conciliatory, congenial, constructive, deadly, eerie, electric, encouraging, (un)favourable, festive, (un)friendly, frightening, frosty, frustrating, gloomy, harmful, heady, hopeful, hostile, hot-house, loving, oppressive, relaxed, stable, stifling, stimulating, strained, stuffy, tense, uneasy, weird ~

ATROCITIES
V: be guilty of, commit, cover up, perpetrate, reveal ~

V: ~ have come to light

A: cruel, terrible ~

ATTACK (physical or verbal)
V: be immune/subject/vulnerable to, beat back, blunt, call off, carry out, come under, condone, deter, direct, drive home, evade, fend off, head off, initiate, instigate, intensify, intercept, launch, lead, make, mount, press home, provoke, renew, repel, repulse, resist, scale down, spearhead, step up, suffer, sustain, thwart, ward off ~

V: ~ escalated, failed, fizzled out, gathered momentum, got into its stride, petered out, reached a new pitch, succeeded

A: abortive, all-out, audacious, barbaric, blistering, bold, brutal, bungled, callous, concentrated, concerted, courageous, cowardly, cruel, dangerous, daring, direct, ferocious, fierce, frenzied, fresh, frontal, full-scale, furious, imminent, impending, impetuous, major, massive, mis-timed, murderous, savage, sudden, surprise, sustained, treacherous, unexpected, unjustified, unprovoked, vicious, vigorous, violent ~

P: brunt of, ferocity of, resumption of, savagery of, suddenness of, victim of, vulnerable to ~; series of, spate of, wave of *attacks*

ATTACK (verbal)
V: deliver ~

A: crude, forthright, impassioned, outspoken, passionate, scathing, scurrilous, unwarranted, vehement, venomous, virulent, withering ~

ATTEMPT
V: abandon, abort, be involved in, bring off, brush aside, bungle, cancel, circumvent, combat, cripple, defy, embark on, fail in, foil, frustrate, give up, jeopardize, make, prevent, succeed in, thwart, undermine, undertake, wreck ~

V: ~ collapsed, failed, foundered, miscarried, succeeded, went badly wrong

A: abortive, all-out, belated, bizarre, bold, brave, calculated, cautious, clumsy, concerted, confident, co-ordinated, courageous, creditable, crude, daring, deliberate, desperate, determined, disastrous, energetic, feeble, final, foolhardy, frantic, frenzied, fresh, fruitless, futile, gallant, genuine, half-hearted, hazardous, heroic, hopeless, ill-fated, ineffectual, ingenious, initial, laudable, misguided, misjudged, overdue, patient, preliminary, protracted, reckless, risky, savage, sincere, sinister, sly, (un)successful, sudden, sustained, systematic, tentative, vain, valiant, veiled, well-meaning ~

ATTENTION
V: absorb, attract, call for, capture, compete for, concentrate, deflect, demand, deserve, devote, distract, divert, earn, engage, escape, focus, get, give, hold sb's, invite, lavish ~ on, occupy, pay ~ to, receive, require, rivet, secure, seize, solicit, summon, switch, transfer ~

V: ~ flagged, wandered, was taken up, wavered

A: close, constant, full, marked, meticulous, rapt, undivided, whole ~
P: bid for, centre of, focus of ~

ATTITUDE
V: adopt, affect, foster, harden, influence, maintain, sense, show, stand by, take, undermine, vindicate ~
V: ~ changed, hardened, is ingrained, persisted, softened, stiffened, worsened
A: absurd, affable, aggressive, amicable, ambiguous, ambivalent, antagonistic, arrogant, attentive, austere, basic, bellicose, belligerent, benevolent, benign, (un)biased, businesslike, casual, cautious, cavalier, common, conciliatory, condescending, (in)consistent, (un)constructive, (un)conventional, (un)co-operative, (un)critical, current, defiant, enigmatic, entrenched, (un)equivocal, (un)fair, (un)favourable, firm, (in)flexible, flippant, frank, (un)friendly, grasping, grim, helpful, hostile, hypocritical, impersonal, intransigent, lackadaisical, lenient, liberal, loving, ludicrous, mean, militant, negative, objective, one-sided, patronizing, positive, predatory, prevailing, prevalent, (un)realistic, rigid, robust, sensible, sentimental, sound, straightforward, strict, stringent, supercilious, (un)sympathetic, threatening, unbending, uncompromising, understanding, unrepentant, venomous, wholesome, workmanlike ~
P: shift in, set of *attitudes*

ATTRACTION
V: feel, have, see ~
A: fatal, immediate, irresistible, mutual, physical, sexual, strong ~

AUDIENCE
V: address, appeal to, attract, bore, build up, captivate, capture, draw, electrify, enchant, enthral, establish, hold, hold ~ captive, move, pander to, please, rivet, rouse, shock, stir, sway ~
V: ~ applauded, booed, heckled, jeered, walked out, whistled
A: appreciative, attentive, critical, discerning, enthusiastic, impressive, noisy, packed, potential, receptive, (un)responsive, sizeable, sparse, spellbound, (un)sympathetic, vast ~

AUTHENTICITY
V: attest, cast doubt on, challenge, check, doubt, feel confident of, establish, prove, question ~

AUTHOR
V: enjoy, like, hate ~
A: anonymous, best-selling, classic, children's, contemporary, established, famous, favourite, prolific, successful, rising, talented, well-known ~

AUTHORITY
V: abuse, accept, acknowledge, add to, assert, assume, defy, delegate, deny, divest sb of, endow sb with, enforce, enhance, establish, erode, evade, exercise, exert, flout, have, impair, impose, invoke, maintain, oppose, overstep one's, overthrow, question, rebel against, recognise, resist, respect, restore, show, support, transfer, undermine, uphold, use, wield ~
V: ~ collapsed, dwindled, is vested in sb, is at stake, stems from sth
A: absolute, dubious, great, inherited, innate, legal, paternalistic, relevant, superior, supreme, unimpaired, wide ~
P: erosion of ~

AUTHORITY (authorisation)
V: claim, give, grant, make use of, recognise, take away ~
A: full ~

AUTHORITY (recognised expert)
V: consult, quote, recognise sb as an ~
A: best, eminent, foremost, great, renowned, worldwide ~

AUTHORITIES (*the authorities* = official body)
V: anger, apply to, defy, fall foul of, inform, (dis)obey, rebel against ~
A: proper ~
AVERSION
A: deep, deep-rooted, emotional, immediate, mild, natural, pet, strong ~
AWARD
V: carry off, establish, give, grant, present, receive, set up, win ~
A: annual, coveted, famous, generous, highest, miserly, prestigious ~
AWARENESS
V: arouse, develop, diminish, dull, have, heighten, raise, sharpen, show ~
A: deep, ecological, full, keen, political, spiritual ~

B

BABY
V: expect, abandon, adopt, breastfeed, calm, cradle, change, comfort, deliver, give away, have, look after, lose, nurse, put ~ up for adoption, rock ~ to sleep, soothe ~
V: ~ is bawling, is teething, is crawling, is crying, is dribbling, kept (us) up all night
A: newborn, premature, still-born, test-tube ~
BACKGROUND
V: be the product of one's, check sb's, come from ~
A: academic, criminal, cultural, cultured, deprived, educational, exalted, humble, modest, narrow, obscure, political, privileged, questionable, respectable, superior ~
BACKGROUND (details, setting)
V: describe, fill in, give, sketch in, supply ~
BACKGROUND (position)
V: keep to, lurk in, relegate sb to, remain in, stay in ~
BALANCE
V: achieve, create, destabilise, destroy, disturb, establish, hold, keep, lose, maintain, overturn, redress, shift, strike, threaten, throw sb off, tip, tilt, upset ~
V: ~ shifts
A: delicate, good, healthy, precarious, sensible, stable, steady, subtle ~
BALL
V: bounce, catch, drop, fumble, hit, kick, miss, pass, play, roll, throw ~
BALLOT
V: be elected by, hold, put it to, re-run ~
A: open, secret ~
BAN
V: announce, apply, beat, break, bring in, call for, declare, defy, disregard, do away with, ease, enforce, evade, ignore, impose, introduce, keep, lift, maintain, (dis)obey, place, proclaim, put ~ on, put ~ into force, rebel against, recognise, relax, remove, rescind, respect ~
V: ~ applies to sth, is confined to sth, comes into force, (still) holds
A: complete, controversial, effective, immediate, limited, partial, rigid, rigorous, strict, total, unpopular, worldwide ~

BANK
A: central, commercial, high street, international, merchant, savings ~
P: ~ account, balance, charges, details, draft, loan, manager, rate, transfer

BARGAIN
V: arrive at, keep to, make, reach, strike ~
A: fair, hard, tough ~

BARRIER
V: be faced with, break down/through, build, burst through, come up against, construct, create, cross, demolish, destroy, erect, form, get through, lower, meet, overcome, penetrate, place, put up, remove, set up, take down ~
V: ~ collapsed, disappeared, fell, held
A: cultural, daunting, firm, formidable, impenetrable, (in)effective, insuperable, insurmountable, racial, rigid, solid ~

BASICS
V: get down to, go back to, know, learn, master ~

BASIS
V: build, change, constitute, create, destroy, form, lay down, maintain, provide, strengthen, undermine, upset ~
A: broad, common, ethical, firm, joint, narrow, permanent, reliable, scientific, shaky, solid, sound, strong, uncertain, whole ~

BATTLE
V: engage in, fight, force, go into, join in, lose, take part in, win ~
V: ~ continues, dragged on, ended in stalemate, is in progress, raged
A: bitter, bloody, crucial, decisive, fierce, final, great, gruelling, hard-fought, historic, hopeless, important, last-ditch, long, long-running, major, mock, pitched, real, relentless, running, successful ~
P: fight a losing ~, outcome of ~

BEACH
V: clean up, contaminate, laze on, lie on, overlook ~
A: beautiful, clean, crowded, deserted, golden, isolated, naturist, nudist, pebble, polluted, private, public, sandy, stony, unspoilt ~

BEAUTY
V: ~ fade, last
A: breathtaking, classical, dazzling, exceptional, fragile, great, haunting, indescribable, inherent, outstanding, radiant, serene, sheer, singular, skin-deep ~

BEHAVIOUR
V: be responsible for, censure sb for, disapprove of sb's, emulate, govern, imitate, indulge in, influence, inhibit, justify, modify, observe, predict, restrain, tone down ~
V: ~ appalled (me), baffled (me), deteriorated, improved, shocked (me), stems from ...
A: absurd, (un)acceptable, annoying, antisocial, aggressive, arbitrary, atrocious, bad, boisterous, bullying, callous, civilised, complex, conventional, correct, cowardly, despicable, disgusting, disruptive, eccentric, errant, erratic, exemplary, frivolous, gentlemanly, good, illogical, impulsive, inconsiderate, inconsistent, inexcusable, infantile, instinctive, irrational, irresponsible, irritating, mysterious, noisy, (ab)normal, obstreperous, odd, off-hand, outrageous, overt, peculiar, polite, provocative, reserved, restrained, riotous, rowdy, rude, (un)satisfactory, scandalous, shocking, stereotyped, strange, undisciplined, unorthodox, unpredictable, unruly, unsportsmanlike ~
P: patterns of, standards of, be on (your) best ~

BELIEF

V: (re)assert, cherish, cling to, corroborate, deny, destroy, endorse, express, give up, heighten, inculcate, induce, instil, lose, maintain, shake, share, shatter, stick to, strengthen, support, sustain, undermine, uphold, weaken ~

V: ~ crumbled, faded, grew, is based on sth/derives from sth, persists, prevails, remains unshaken, survives, wavered

A: basic, common, deep-rooted, false, fanatical, fervent, firm, fond, genuine, honest, instinctive, intuitive, invincible, justifiable, misguided, mistaken, obsessive, obstinate, passionate, popular, preposterous, robust, solemn, steady, strong, tenacious, undying, uneasy, unhesitating, unjustified, unshakeable, unsubstantiated, unswerving, unwarranted, unwavering, widespread ~

BELIEF (credibility)

V: destroy, stretch ~

P: bounds of ~, beyond all ~

BELIEFS (religious)

V: abandon, disseminate, fight for, give up, hold, hold firm to, jettison, profess, refute, reject, renounce, repudiate, stick to, undermine, subscribe to, uphold ~

V: ~ conflict with sth, inspired sb, are founded on sth

A: discredited, false, fanatical, former, heretical, inherited, (un)orthodox, outdated, religious, traditional ~

BENEFIT

V: acknowledge, bring, derive, enjoy, feel, foresee, gain, get, look for, obtain, produce, reap, weigh up ~

V: ~ accrues, ensued, resulted from ..., stemmed from ...

A: considerable, definite, enormous, great, immediate, immense, important, infinitesimal, little, major, mutual, negligible, obvious, positive, substantial, tangible, tremendous, unique, visible, worthwhile ~

BENEFIT (money)

A: child, disability, housing, sickness, unemployment ~

P: ~ concert, match

BIAS

V: avoid, have, manifest, see, show ~

A: clear, covert, deep-rooted, distinct, implicit, implied, marked, obvious, perceptible, strong ~

BIBLIOGRAPHY

V: compile, draw up, look up, prepare, provide ~

A: comprehensive, exhaustive, extensive, full, select, up-to-date ~

BILL (Parliamentary)

V: alter, amend, approve, boycott, bring forward/in/out, contest, debate, delay, discuss, draft, enact, force through, introduce, oppose, pass, prepare, present, propose, push through, put through, reject, rush through, shelve, support, table, throw out, vote against/for/on, withdraw ~

V: ~ became law, was read, went to committee

A: controversial, emergency ~

BILL

V: ask for, foot, get, pay, present, receive, reduce, send, send in, settle, split, submit ~

V: ~ came in, is (over)due/outstanding,

A: crippling, excessive, outrageous, shocking, steep, stiff ~

BIOGRAPHY
V: produce, publish, write ~
A: accurate, (un)authorised, critical, entertaining, exhaustive, fascinating, illuminating, lively, objective, outstanding, readable, revealing, scholarly, stylish, well-researched, witty ~

BIRTH
V: announce, attend, await, be present at, celebrate, expect, mark, record, register ~

BITTERNESS
V: cause, create, engender, feel, get over, lead to, overcome ~
A: great, lasting, marked, unending, unnecessary ~

BLAME
V: absolve sb from, accept, acknowledge, apportion, attach, attribute, bear, carry, deny, distribute, exonerate sb from, fix ~ on sb, lay/place/put ~ on sb, share, shift, shoulder, take ~
A: full, main, real, whole ~

BLAST
V: be caught in, cause, keep away from, set off, shelter from ~
V: ~ blew ... out/up, broke/damaged/destroyed/shattered/shook sth, injured/killed sb
A: terrific, tremendous, violent ~

BLAST (of wind)
V: encounter, feel, shelter from, struggle against ~
V: ~ caught/hit/struck sb/sth
A: fierce, furious, great, icy, strong, sudden, tremendous ~

BLAZE
V: add to, control, extinguish, put out ~
V: ~ was out of control, consumed/destroyed sth, died down, spread to ...
A: fierce, great, terrible ~

BLOCKADE
V: break through, get past/through, impose, lift, maintain, raise, remove, run, set up ~
A: naval, partial, strict, tight, total ~

BLOOD
V: draw, give, let, lose, poison, shed, spill, test ~
V: ~ circulates, clots, coagulates, congeals, flowed, flowed out, is getting thinner, gushed out, oozed out, thickened, spurted out
P: ~ bank, donor, transfusion; mark of, spot of, traces of, trail of ~

BLOW (mental)
V: experience, get over, receive, recover from, soften, suffer, sustain ~
V: ~ fell on sb, stunned sb
A: cruel, devastating, grievous, heavy, severe, unexpected ~

BLOW (physical)
V: administer, aim, avoid, deliver, feel, give, inflict, parry, receive, strike, survive, sustain ~
V: ~ dazed/felled/hit/hurt/killed/missed/stunned sb, knocked sb down/out
A: cowardly, cruel, dangerous, deadly, decisive, destructive, devastating, direct, dull, final, glancing, hard, heavy, knock-out, massive, mortal, nasty, painful, powerful, serious, severe, sharp, slight, swift ~

BLUNDER
V: admit, allege, avoid, come across, commit, correct, cover up, discover, make, minimise, point out, rectify, stumble upon ~
A: colossal, crass, definite, distinct, fatal, grave, hopeless, monumental, obvious, regrettable, serious, stupid, terrible, unfortunate, unnecessary ~

BOARD
V: appear before, appoint sb to, attend, form, head, resign from, serve on, set up, sit on ~
P: ~ decision, meeting
BODY (organised group of people)
V: axe, refer a matter to, set up ~
A: advisory, authorised, elected, governing, government, independent, official, professional, representative, school, student ~
BOMB
V: defuse, detonate, dismantle, drop, explode, hurl, make, manufacture, plant, release, remove, set, set off ~
V: ~ exploded, went off
A: atomic, car, huge, letter, live, nuclear, petrol, powerful, stray, terrorist, time, unexploded ~
P: ~ disposal; spate of, wave of *bombs*
BOND
V: create, destroy, forge, form, make, strengthen, tighten ~
A: close, emotional, firm, fragile, inseparable, spiritual, strong, tenuous, unbreakable, weak ~
P: ~ of friendship
BOOK
V: annotate, ban, bring out, censor, compile, contribute to, dedicate, digest, edit, glance through, illustrate, issue, launch, leaf through, licence, (re)print, produce, promote, proofread, publicise, publish, pulp, remainder, research, review, revise, scan, translate, write ~
V: ~ is due out, is out of print/stock, was reissued, has been remaindered, was serialised, is unavailable, came out, covered ..., dealt with ..., described ..., explored ..., revealed ..., touches on ...
A: absorbing, admirable, ambitious, amusing, authoritative, brilliant, coffee-table, comprehensive, controversial, delightful, dull, encyclopaedic, engrossing, entertaining, enthralling, fascinating, flawless, fine, forthcoming, gripping, hilarious, important, informative, instructive, interesting, libellous, lively, long, moving, powerful, readable, reliable, repetitive, sensible, stimulating, thought-provoking, trite, useful, wise ~
P: scope of, subject of, substance of, thread of ~
BOOKS (accounts)
V: balance, check, cook, do, go over, go through, inspect, keep ~
BOOM
V: cope with, enjoy, forecast, see ~
A: baby, economic, postwar, sales, sudden, travel, unexpected, unprecedented ~
P: ~ in popularity
BORDER
V: close, cross, establish, fix, guard, mark, patrol, seal, seal off, slip across/over, smuggle sth across the ~
V: ~ runs/stretches from ... to ..., shifted
A: common, disputed, natural, open, shared, unguarded ~
BOREDOM
V: do sth out of, relieve, suffer ~
A: excruciating, sheer, utter ~
BOUNDARY
V: alter, change, create, cross, define, demarcate, determine, (re)draw, establish, extend, extend along/beyond, fix, follow, form, impose, keep within, lay down, make, mark, move, push back, reach, reach beyond, recognise, respect, run along, set, set up, settle, shift ~

V: ~ extends/stretches from ... to ..., runs, separates ... from ...
A: arbitrary, clear, definite, distinct, extensive, narrow, natural, rigid, state ~

BRAIN
A: acute, agile, fine, good, excellent, first-class, quick, superb ~
P: tax one's, use one's ~; is the *brains* behind sth, has got *brains*, pick (your) *brains*, rack (your) *brains*

BRAND
A: best-selling, popular ~
P: ~ awareness, image, leader, loyalty, management, manager, war

BREACH (of relations)
V: cause, heal, lead to, make up ~
A: sudden, total ~

BREAKDOWN
V: cause, end in, lead to, patch up, prevent, result in ~
A: complete, inevitable, nervous, partial, rapid, regrettable, sudden, surprising, temporary, unfortunate, total ~

BREAKTHROUGH
V: achieve, bring about, lead to, mark, reach ~
V: ~ was made, came about
A: major, medical, scientific, significant, spectacular ~

BREATH
V: catch/hold/save/waste (your) ~, draw, get (your) ~ back, say sth under (your) ~
A. deep, long, shallow ~
P: with bated ~; a ~ of fresh air, it took (my) ~ away

BREATHING
A: (barely) audible, heavy, irregular, laboured, rapid, regular, shallow, slow, soft, uneven ~
P: ~ difficulties, problems

BRIDGE
V: build, construct, cross, demolish, design, destroy, erect, pull down, put up ~
V: ~ was blown down (by the wind), was blown up (by a bomb), was washed away, carries the (main road), collapsed, crosses ..., joins ... with ..., spans the (Rhine)

BRINK
V: balance on, come to, cross, get near, go over, hover on, teeter on ~

BUDGET
V: announce, balance, draw up, exceed, increase, introduce, keep to/within, operate within, overstep, overstretch, pass, reduce, set oneself, tighten, vote on ~
A: annual, expansionary, fixed, generous, harsh, interim, low, modest, monthly, rigid, tight ~

BUILDING
V: alter, blow up, (re)build, construct, convert, damage, demolish, design, erect, flatten, gut, inspect, knock down, look after, look over, maintain, occupy, pull down, put up, refurbish, renovate, repair, restore, shore up, survey ~
V: ~ collapsed, is deteriorating, fell down, fell into ruin, houses ..., stands, towers over sth
A: ancient, attractive, beautiful, crumbling, decrepit, derelict, deserted, dilapidated, dingy, distinguished, disused, famous, fine, handsome, historic, huge, imaginative, imposing, listed, low, multi-storey, neglected, prominent, rambling, ramshackle, spectacular, sprawling, tall, well-proportioned ~
P: lease of, upkeep of ~

BULLETIN
V: issue, pin up, print, publish, read out ~

A: daily (hourly, weekly, etc), final, latest, official, regular ~

P: news ~

BURDEN
V: assume, bear, carry, cast off, ease, impose, lay ~ on sb, lessen, lighten, pick up, place, relieve, remove, shoulder, take on, throw off ~

V: ~ lies on sb, rests on sb, wore sb down/out, weighed sb down ~

A: great, growing, heavy, increasing ~

BUREAUCRACY
V: cut down/out, do away with, eliminate ~

A: cumbersome, government, overgrown, slow, sluggish ~

BUSINESS (firm, with a/*the*)
V: build up, carry on, close down, establish, finance, give up, have, manage, modernise, open, prop up, restructure, run, set up, start, streamline, take over, wind up ~

V: ~ amalgamated with ..., closed down, declined, is expanding, failed, went bankrupt, prospered

A: defunct, efficient, excellent, family, flourishing, growing, large, long-established, lucrative, profitable, prosperous, run-down, successful, thriving ~

BUSINESS (affairs)
V: attend to, conduct, get down to, handle, interfere in sb else's, to stick your nose in sb else's, transact ~

A: current, official, personal, private, routine, urgent ~

BUSINESS (trade)
V: be in, carry on, do, drum up, encourage, find, give up, go after/into/out of, hunt for, look for, promote, set up in ~

V: ~ is bad/brisk/good/poor/slow/sluggish, declined, expanded, flourished, picked up, is thriving

P: ~ contact, lunch, matters, objectives, opportunities, relationship, trip

C

CABINET (government)
V: form ~

A: shadow ~

P: ~ minister, reshuffle

CALCULATION
V: do, make, make a mistake in ~

V: ~ was wide of the mark, was (all) wrong

A: accurate, approximate, faulty, precise, rapid, rough, wrong ~

CALL (phone)
V: accept, give sb, make, place, put ~ through, return sb's, take, wait for ~

A: alarm, business, collect, early morning, emergency, local, long-distance, personal, private, urgent ~

CALL (visit)
V: make, pay, receive, return ~
A: brief, courtesy, (in)formal, friendly, official, unexpected ~
CALL (appeal)
V: answer, heed, issue, make, respond to, send out, support, take up ~
A: ardent, clarion, despairing, desperate, emotional, moving, passionate, rousing ~
CALM
V: disturb, restore, ruffle, shatter, upset ~
A: dead, perfect, unruffled, usual ~
CAMERA
V: be caught on, focus, (un)load, point, rewind ~
V: ~ is in/out of focus, clicked, flashed, ran out of film
A: automatic, complicated, digital, disposable, easy-to-use, simple, 35 mm. ~
CAMPAIGN
V: back, be involved in, boost, conduct, embark on, engage in, enter upon, fight, give direction
    /impetus to, inaugurate, initiate, intensify, join, launch, lead, manage, mount, open, oppose,
    organise, pursue, run, spearhead, sponsor, start, step up, support, take part in ~
V: ~ fizzled out, got off to a good start
A: active, bitter, boisterous, brief, brilliant, chaotic, confused, covert, determined, energetic,
    fierce, inept, intensive, international, limited, lively, long-drawn-out, losing, noisy, political,
    presidential, strident, (un)successful, uninspiring, vicious, vigorous, widening, winning,
    worldwide ~
P: failure/futility/height/ineptness/success of ~
CAMPAIGN (military)
V: conduct, fight, launch, lead, wage ~
V: ~ ended in stalemate, lost impetus
A: bloody, brilliant, daring, disastrous, fierce, lengthy, lightning, risky, successful, victorious ~
CAMPAIGNER
A: experienced, seasoned, shrewd, skilful ~
CANDIDATE
V: adopt, back, drop, elect, nominate, offer oneself as, put forward/up, reject, select, stand as,
    support, vote for ~
V: ~ got in, is standing, stood down, won, withdrew
A: independent, likely, local, (un)official, (un)popular, prospective, reliable, risky, safe,
    (un)suitable, surprise ~
CANDLE
V: blow out, extinguish, (re)light, snuff out ~
V: ~ burned, burned low, flickered, went out
P: ~ flame
CAPABILITIES
V: assess, be endowed with, cast doubt on, consider, examine, exploit, extol, exceed, have, list,
    make use of, manifest, overrate, possess, praise, question, take advantage of, test, underrate,
    use, waste, weigh up ~
A: great, hidden, immense, obvious, outstanding, reputed, true, undoubted, useful, wide ~
CAPACITY
V: exceed, exhaust, have, measure, use ~
A: abundant, (in)adequate, large, maximum, peak, sufficient ~
P: was filled to ~; a ~ crowd

39

CAPACITY (ability)

V: be endowed with, blunt, develop, have, impair, lack, nurture, use ~

A: amazing, boundless, enormous, great, infinite, innate, latent, matchless, natural, necessary, outstanding, superior, tremendous, unique, unrivalled

CAPACITY (position)

V: act in, have ~

A: administrative, advisory, official, private, professional ~

CAPITAL

V: amass, accumulate, borrow, break into, build up, inherit, invest, lay out, pay back, pile up, provide, put up, raise, require, run out of, save up, squander, tie up, transfer, waste ~

V: ~ is locked up, brings in sth, dwindled, grew, ran out

CAR

V: back (up), break into, crash, drive, hire, park, push, register, rent, repair, reverse, road-test, run, run in, service, smash up, start, steal, stop, tow, wreck, write off ~

V: ~ broke down, came/went off the road, packed up, ran into sth, screeched to a halt, skidded, swerved, was written off

A: economical, estate, family, flashy, luxury, powerful, second-hand, sports, used ~

CARDS (games)

V: cheat at, cut, deal, lose at, play, shuffle, win at ~

A: picture, playing ~

P: deck of, game of, house of, pack of ~

CARE

V: bestow, give, lavish, need, provide, take sb into ~

A: constant, extra, great, meticulous, proper, scrupulous, special, utmost ~

P: tender loving ~ (TLC)

CARE (sorrow, anxiety)

V: be free from, be weighed down by ~

CARE (caution)

V: call for, exercise, take ~

A: extra, good, great, proper, special ~

CAREER

V: abandon, be absorbed in, be destined for ~ in, boost, carve out, change, choose, concentrate on, cripple, cut short, damage, determine, develop, devote oneself to, embark on, end, enter upon, further, give up, hamper, have a ~ in (banking), help, hinder, interrupt, launch out on, launch sb on, map out, plan, predict, promote, pursue, put an end to, ruin, sacrifice, salvage, set sb off on, spoil, start, take up, wreck ~

V: ~ blossomed, had its ups and downs

A: amazing, brilliant, chequered, colourful, demanding, difficult, disappointing, distinguished, entire, fine, flourishing, glittering, golden, good, great, honourable, ill-fated, meteoric, modest, promising, splendid, steady, strange, successful, turbulent, unusual, varied ~

P: outset of, peak of, pinnacle of, springboard for, summit of ~, a ~ change

CASE (matter)

V: alter, argue, clinch, deal with, (re)examine, go into, investigate, press, review, solve, study ~

A: complicated, controversial, unusual ~

CASE (instance)

V: cite, describe, highlight, quote, take ~

A: authentic, authenticated, borderline, classic, clear, clear-cut, difficult, glaring, hypothetical, illuminating, intriguing, isolated, obvious, perfect, special, textbook, unique, unusual ~

CASE (argument)

V: argue, back up, complete, expound, give support to, go over, make ~ for/against, make out, outline, press, put, put forward, review, submit, (over)state, sum up, weaken ~

V: ~ collapsed

A: classic, convincing, good, irrefutable, plausible, persuasive, poor, strong ~

CASE (court)

V: adjourn, answer, appear in, bring, contest, decide, defend, dismiss, drop, hear, judge, lose, postpone, refer to, report, resume, settle, study, sum up, throw out, try, turn down, win, withdraw ~

V: ~ came before the court, comes up, collapsed, forms a precedent, was referred to (a higher) court, went badly/well

A: capital, civil, controversial, criminal, murder, notorious, sensational, test ~

P: outcome of ~

CASH

V: be out of, be short of, carry, pay (in), prefer, raise, run out of, send ~

A: hard, petty ~

P: ~ card, in advance, on delivery

CASUALTIES

V: inflict, report, suffer, sustain ~

A: crippling, heavy, light, serious ~

CATALOGUE

V: compile, look sth up in, publish, receive, revise, send sb, send for, study, update ~

A: autumn/spring, current, free, full, full-colour, latest, mail-order, trade ~

CATASTROPHE

V: avert, avoid, be heading for, bring about, cause, deal with, face, foresee, forestall, head off, lead to, precipitate, prevent, provoke, suffer, trigger off ~

V: ~ faced sb, happened, hit sb, lay ahead, looms, lurks, occurred, overtook sb, struck sb, took place, threatened

A: absolute, certain, devastating, final, grave, huge, impending, inevitable, major, mounting, overwhelming, senseless, serious, terrible, total, unavoidable, unforeseen, unheard-of, unprecedented, utter ~

P: aftermath of, cause of ~

CATEGORY

V: assign sth to, be in/outside, belong to, come into, define, fall into, fit, place sth in, put sth into, slot sth into ~

A: bottom, broad, definite, exclusive, fuzzy, hard and fast, inferior, loose, main, middle, narrow, principal, rigid, special, strict, superior, top, unique, unusual, well-defined, wide ~

CATTLE

V: brand, breed, drive, graze, herd, raise, rear, round up, show, slaughter ~

A: beef, dairy, prize ~

P: head of, herd of ~

CAUSE (reason)

V: analyse, ascertain, be due to, determine, diagnose, discover, eliminate, enquire into, eradicate, establish, examine, ferret out, find out, investigate, look for, seek, stem from, study, trace ~

A: apparent, basic, chief, common, (in)direct, extraneous, fundamental, further, immediate, implicit, inherent, latent, main, major, mysterious, obscure, obvious, original, overriding, primary, prime, principal, remote, root, sole, specific, tangible, true, ultimate, underlying ~

CAUSE (goal)

V: abandon, adopt, advance, advocate, aid, be dedicated to, be loyal to, believe in, betray, champion, damage, deal with, defend, die for, embrace, espouse, fight for, follow, further, have sympathy with, join, neglect, preach, promote, pursue, rally to, sacrifice oneself for, serve, support, take up, work for ~

A: altruistic, common, deserving, good, higher, hopeless, lost, noble, obscure, radical, worthwhile, (un)worthy ~

P: all in a good, devotion to ~

CAUTION

V: abandon, call for, cast ~ aside, exercise, maintain, need, proceed with, require, take, throw ~ to the winds, treat sth with, use ~

A: extreme, great, utmost ~

CEASEFIRE

V: agree on/to, announce, arrange, break, negotiate, observe, sign, violate, work out ~

A: permanent, temporary ~

CELEBRATION

V: arrange, call for, have, hold, organise, spoil ~

A: dazzling, formal, glittering, great, joyous, marvellous, noisy, quiet, solemn, special, splendid, tremendous ~

CELEBRITY

V: acquire, achieve, bring sb, enjoy, seek, shun ~

A: great, unsolicited, unwanted, unwelcome ~

CENSORSHIP

V: abolish, enforce, exercise, impose, introduce, lift ~

A: film, press, rigid, strict ~

CENSUS

V: carry out, conduct, hold, take ~

CENTRE

V: attend, close, establish, open, run, set up ~

A: business, civic, commercial, community, crisis, health, job, leisure, popular, sports ~

CENTURY

P: close of, turn of ~

CEREMONY

V: arrange, attend, cancel, conduct, hold, officiate at, organise, perform, postpone, take part in, televise, view, watch ~

A: age-old, ancient, annual, closing, colourful, dignified, imposing, impressive, impromptu, inauguration, inspiring, majestic, moving, opening, quiet, religious, sad, solemn, stately, time-honoured, traditional, wedding ~

CERTIFICATE

V: apply for, ask for, award, check, demand, examine, forge, get, give, have, issue, make a copy of, obtain, possess, produce, qualify for, require, show, stamp, supply, win, work for ~

V: ~ attests/proves/shows/states that ...

A: false, formal, genuine, official, useful ~

CHALLENGE

V: accept, answer, be confronted with, constitute, cope with, face (up to), invite, issue, meet, offer, overcome, pose, present, put up, reject, represent, respond to, rise to, take up, throw down ~

A: ambitious, big, concerted, dangerous, daunting, definite, fearsome, formidable, great, immediate, imposing, irresistible, real, renewed, serious, strong, urgent ~

CHAMPION
V: be up against, beat, become, defeat, take on ~
A: defending, former, national, reigning, unbeaten, undisputed, world ~
CHANCE
V: affect, assess, boost, calculate, count on, destroy, eliminate, endanger, enhance, estimate, forfeit, get, give sb, grab, have, improve, increase, lose, make the most of, miss, offer, present sb with, reduce, ruin, see, spoil, take, take advantage of, use, wait for, waste, welcome, weigh up, wreck ~
V: ~ arose, cropped up, has gone, improved, offered itself, won't come again
A: best-ever, excellent, exceptional, fair, fighting, fine, fleeting, fortunate, good, infinitesimal, lucky, negligible, only, outside, poor, rare, realistic, reasonable, remote, slight, slim, small, splendid, sporting, unexpected, unique, welcome ~
CHANGE
V: adapt to, advocate, avoid, be conducive/opposed to, block, bring about, call for, cause, cope with, counteract, effect, encounter, experience, face, facilitate, favour, get used to, go through, impede, induce, initiate, instigate, institute, introduce, justify, lead to, make, necessitate, observe, obstruct, perceive, prevent, produce, promote, resist, restrict, see, sense, show, signal, spark off, speed up, stimulate, welcome, witness ~
V: ~ accelerated, affected sb, came about, ensued, led to sth, occurred, reflected sth, resulted in sth, slowed down, was evident
A: abrupt, alarming, appreciable, badly-needed, beneficial, broad, considerable, constant, continuous, crucial, (un)desirable, discernible, disturbing, drastic, extensive, far-reaching, fundamental, gratifying, great, immediate, inevitable, infinitesimal, initial, invigorating, irresistible, irreversible, major, marginal, marked, material, merciful, modest, painful, perceptible, principal, profound, quick, radical, rapid, refreshing, revolutionary, sensational, sharp, slight, slow, speedy, substantial, subtle, sudden, sweeping, tangible, tremendous, unexpected, unfortunate, unsettling, violent, visible, welcome, widespread ~
P: magnitude of, management of, process of, speed of ~; sea ~
CHAOS
V: be in a state of, cause, create, descend into, end in, endure, precipitate, prevent, produce, provoke, sink into ~
V: ~ broke out, prevailed, reigned
A: absolute, indescribable, utter, widespread ~
P: ~ theory; state of ~
CHARACTER (of a person)
V: be endowed with, build, change, develop, form, have, have an effect on, improve, influence, leave a stamp on, mark, mould, reflect sb's, reform, shape, test, transform, warp ~
V: ~ changed, developed, improved, matured
A: dependable, depraved, despicable, determined, difficult, fine, independent, noble, (un)reliable, (un)stable, (un)steady, strong, undisciplined, upright, weak ~
P: blot on, flaw in, insight into ~
CHARACTER (nature of something)
V: affect, alter, analyse, appreciate, assume, be struck by, determine, develop, discover, exhibit, identify, keep, maintain, modify, possess, preserve, restore, retain, reveal, ruin, show, spoil, stamp, study, take into account/consideration, take on, understand ~
V: ~ became apparent/blurred, is clear/evident, showed itself
A: basic, beneficial, complicated, controversial, definite, different, distinct, erratic, fundamental, genuine, harmful, indeterminate, indigenous, individual, intrinsic, obvious,

ordinary, original, outstanding, paradoxical, prominent, provisional, real, strange, traditional, true, typical, underlying, vivid ~

CHARACTER (unusual person)

A: amiable, amusing, colourful, disreputable, eccentric, formidable, lazy, mean, nasty, notorious, peculiar, quaint, questionable, strange, suspicious, terrible, unique, unreliable, well-known ~

CHARACTERISTIC

A: basic, defining, exasperating, intrinsic, main, salient, striking, typical, unusual ~

CHARGE (responsibility)

V: accept, assume, divest oneself of, entrust sb with, take ~

A: complete, full, heavy, immediate, sole ~

CHARGE (accusation)

V: admit, be brought up on, be sensitive to, bring ~ against sb, confess to, counter, deny, dispute, drop, evade, examine, face, lay/level a ~ against sb, make, press, prove, rebut, refute, specify, substantiate, support, withdraw ~

A: damaging, false, flimsy, formal, official, petty, serious, trumped-up ~

CHARGE (financial)

V: collect, demand, impose, levy, make, pay, waive ~

A: heavy, reasonable, regular, ridiculous, small ~

CHARITY (organisation)

V: do sth for, donate money to, give (money) to, make a donation to, raise money for, run, set up, sponsor sb for ~

A: children's, global, local, (inter)national, official, popular, registered ~

P: ~ appeal, ball, concert, event

CHARM

V: exert, ooze, use one's ~

A: considerable, great, indefinable, infinite, irresistible, natural, perennial, tremendous ~

CHARTER

V: be a signatory to, draw up, flout, give, grant, put ~ into effect, sign, tear up ~

CHASE

V: abandon, embark on, enter on, follow, give ~ to, give up, join in, pursue, take part in, take up ~

A: exciting, hopeless, (un)successful, wild-goose ~

CHASM

V: bridge ~

V: ~ appeared, divides ... from ...

A: deep, gaping, unbridgeable, wide, yawning ~

CHAT

V: drop in for, have, have time for, stop for ~

A: friendly, little, long, occasional, pleasant, quiet ~

CHECK (inspection)

V: carry out, make, run, submit to, subject sb to ~

V: ~ revealed sth

A: close, nationwide, regular, rigorous, rough, routine, spot, thorough ~

CHECK (restraint)

V: come up against, encounter, impose, meet with, remove ~

A: important, serious, severe, sudden, unavoidable, unexpected ~

CHEQUE

V: bounce, cash, forge, handle, issue, make out, process, sign, write ~

V: ~ bounced, was returned, went through

A: blank, crossed, generous, large, post-dated, travellers', worthless ~

CHEESE
A: blue, cottage, cream, full-fat, hard, low-fat, grated, mild, soft, smoked, strong, toasted ~
P: lump of, piece of, slice of ~

CHILD
V: abuse, adopt, bring up, educate, foster, give birth to, have, indulge, look after, mistreat, neglect, nurse, raise, spoil, support ~
V: ~ developed, grew up
A: badly/well behaved, foster, gifted, illegitimate, love, naughty, only, precocious, sensitive, sick, spoilt, unwanted ~

CHOCOLATE
A: bitter, dark, hot, melted, milk, plain, rich, sweet, thick, white ~
P: bar of, piece of ~

CHOICE
V: affect, face, force ~ on sb, give sb, have, inflict ~ on sb, influence, limit, make, place ~ before sb, put off, restrict ~
V: ~ lies before sb/with sb, rests with sb
A: awkward, basic, careful, conscious, considered, deliberate, difficult, easy, final, first, fundamental, happy, hard, heart-rending, immediate, indiscriminate, inevitable, inspired, intelligent, judicious, instinctive, invidious, last, limited, narrow, painful, poor, random, second, shrewd, straight, stupid, unambiguous, unavoidable, unenviable, unprecedented, wise ~

CIGARETTE
V: extinguish, light, put out, roll, smoke, stub out ~
A: king-size, low-tar, mild, strong ~
P: ~ butt, case, end, holder, lighter, packet

CIRCLE (set of people)
V: be admitted to, belong to, form, gain admittance to, move in ~
A: close, close-knit, exclusive, inner, innermost, large, narrow ~   ·
P: wide ~ of friends

CIRCLES (social)
V: move in ~
A: avant-garde, elevated, exclusive, fashionable, high, influential, intellectual, official, old-fashioned, powerful, sophisticated, wide ~

CIRCULATION
V: be in, put into, withdraw from ~
A: enormous, general, limited, international, nationwide, small, wide ~
P: a ~ war

CIRCUMSTANCES
V: accustom oneself to, adapt oneself to, adjust oneself to, alter, avoid, be aware of, be brought up in, blame, change, deplore, discover, examine, get used to, have, investigate, improve, know, live in, misjudge, reveal ~, take ~ into consideration, take place in ~
V: ~ altered, are against sb, change, deteriorated, improved
A: adverse, affluent, alarming, (in)auspicious, baffling, bizarre, clear, comfortable, compromising, difficult, distressing, easy, exceptional, extenuating, favourable, fortunate, harsh, humble, incongruous, incriminating, luxurious, mitigating, modest, mysterious, obscure, ordinary, plain, poor, precarious, privileged, prosperous, reduced, straitened, strange, suspicious, true, unaccustomed, unfortunate, unprecedented, vague ~
P: force of, irony of, set of ~

CITIZEN
A: good, law-abiding, naturalised, ordinary, respectable, second-class, senior ~

CITIZENSHIP
V: acquire, adopt, apply for, change, claim, deprive sb of, forfeit, grant, lose, refuse, renounce, strip sb of ~

CITY
V: ~ expanded, grew up

A: ancient, attractive, beautiful, capital, cosmopolitan, densely populated, flourishing, great, historic, industrial, inner, interesting, modern, overcrowded, popular, sophisticated, ugly

CIVILIZATION
V: bring, destroy ~

V: ~ collapsed, declined, disappeared, flourished, reached its peak, was at its peak

A: advanced, alien, ancient, budding, early, foreign, indigenous, mature, primitive, sophisticated, superior ~

P: dawn of, passing of, rise and fall of ~

CLAIM (assertion)
V: acknowledge, admit, advance, attack, bear out, be sceptical of, challenge, concede, defend, deny, discount, dismiss, dispute, doubt, examine, maintain, make, modify, persist in, prove, put forward, question, refute, reject, repudiate, substantiate, support, test, uphold, verify, weaken ~

V: ~ does not stand examination, is open to doubt, rests on ...

A: ambitious, angry, astonishing, bold, controversial, doubtful, exaggerated, excessive, exciting, extravagant, fanciful, feeble, fundamental, impressive, inadmissible, indefensible, initial, just, justifiable, justified, legitimate, ludicrous, novel, original, outrageous, paradoxical, plausible, presumptuous, reckless, ridiculous, strong, tenuous, unique, unsubstantiated, worthless ~

CLAIM (financial)
V: abandon, acknowledge, agree to, admit, amend, bring, check, consider, contest, deal with, disallow, discuss, drop, endorse, enter, establish, file, follow up, forfeit, further, give up, handle, justify, lodge, make, make out, meet, negotiate, pay, press, put in, question, recognise, reduce, refuse, reinforce, resist, satisfy, settle, shelve, submit, succeed in, verify, waive, withdraw, write off ~

V: ~ applied to sth, failed, involved sth

A: exaggerated, excessive, fair, false, heavy, insurance, justifiable, large, modest, outstanding, pay, pressing, strong, substantial, well-founded, worthless ~

P: in pursuit of ~; spate of, string of *claims*

CLAIM (to a right or title)
V: acknowledge, defend, give up, ignore, justify, keep up, lay, maintain, press, prove, pursue, put forward, question, recognise, refute, reinforce, reject, relinquish, renew, renounce, repudiate, set up, stake, succeed in, support, uphold, waive, weaken, withdraw ~

V: ~ is based on sth, came to nothing, failed, rests on sth, succeeded

A: bogus, controversial, doubtful, false, justifiable, legitimate, overriding, potential, presumptuous, prior, spurious, strong, substantial, unique, valid ~

P: in pursuit of ~

CLASH
V: avoid, end in, lead to, precipitate, prevent ~

A: armed, bitter, bloody, dangerous, furious, great, head-on, inevitable, personality, serious, tremendous, unavoidable, unpleasant, vicious, violent ~

CLASS (social)
V: abolish, belong to, come from, move in, rise in ~
A: educated, impoverished, inferior, managerial, lower, middle, (under)privileged, ruling, superior, under-, upper, wealthy, working ~
P: ~ conflict, struggle

CLASS (lesson)
V: attend, cancel, give, go to, hold, miss, sit in on, skip ~
A: advanced, beginners', boring, compulsory, evening, intermediate ~

CLASSES (categories)
V: arrange sth in, divide sth into, sort into ~

CLICHE
V: repeat, use, utter ~
A: meaningless, stale, well-worn ~

CLIMATE
V: enjoy, have, regulate ~
A: changeable, excellent, extreme, harsh, (in)hospitable, humid, invigorating, mild, moderate, poor, relaxing, severe, temperate ~

CLIMAX
V: approach, bring sth to, build up to, come to, get over, mark, move towards, near, overcome, pass, reach, rise to, survive, work up to ~
A: alarming, dangerous, dramatic, exciting, mighty, serious, thrilling, tremendous ~

CLIMB
A: arduous, dangerous, difficult, easy, exhausting, gradual, hard, rough, steep, tortuous ~

CLOCK
V: put ~ back, put ~ forward, regulate, set, wind (up) ~
V: ~ is fast/right/slow
A: alarm, cuckoo, electric, grandfather, wall ~

CLOTHES
V: change, have ~ altered, put on, rip off, slip into, take off, tear off, try on ~
A: second-hand, shabby, summer, tatty, threadbare, trendy, warm, winter, worn-out ~

CLOUDS
V: blow away, disperse ~
V: ~ (dis)appeared, approached, built up, came up, covered sth, drifted, gathered, went away, hide sth, lifted, obscure sth, piled up, raced, sailed, swirled
A: angry-looking, cumulus, dark, heavy, high, huge, low, massive, menacing, rain, scattered, stationary, storm, thick, thunder, wispy ~

CLUB
V: be a member of, belong to, form, join, run, set up, start ~
A: exclusive, private, youth ~
P: ~ member, membership, secretary, treasurer

CLUE
V: come across, decipher, discover, examine, find, follow, look for, miss, overlook, provide, pursue, study, stumble on, uncover ~
A: faint, false, hidden, important, misleading, mysterious, obvious, principal, useful, vital ~

COALITION
V: break up, dissolve, forge, form ~
V: ~ broke up, fell apart
A: multi-party, national, strong ~

CODE
V: break, change, crack, decipher, invent, set up, transcribe sth into, use ~
A: (top) secret, simple, sophisticated ~

COERCION
V: apply, give way to, resist, submit to, use ~

COEXISTENCE
V: aim at, promote, strive towards, work towards ~
A: friendly, peaceful ~

COINCIDENCE
V: come across, encounter, meet with ~
A: convenient, curious, (un)fortunate, happy, interesting, (un)lucky, mere, odd, pure, remarkable, sheer, strange, timely, unusual, weird ~
P: chain of, string of *coincidences*

COLD (with *the*)
V: come in out of, get out of, feel ~
A: biting, bitter, extreme, freezing, intense, severe, unbearable ~

COLLABORATION
V: benefit from, establish, rely on ~
A: close, fruitful ~
P: basis of ~; work in ~ with

COLLAPSE
V: avert, avoid, bring about, cause, end in, entail, lead to, prevent, result in, suffer ~
A: complete, devastating, serious, sudden, swift, total, unexpected, utter ~
P: state of ~

COLLECTION
V: acquire, build (up), donate, exhibit, form, have, make ~
A: comprehensive, distinguished, fine, impressive, national, rare, rich, splendid, stamp/coin etc, superb, unique, unprecedented, unsurpassed, valuable ~

COLLEGE
V: be thrown out of, apply to, be accepted by, be away at, be fresh out of, be rejected by, drop out of, finish, go (back) to, graduate from, leave, put sb through ~
A: business, famous, Oxbridge, prestigious, technical ~
P: ~ drop-out, graduate, of further education, of higher education

COLOUR
A: bright, brilliant, cheerful, garish, gaudy, glaring, glowing, harsh, loud, natural, neutral, pastel, rich, soft, sombre, subdued, vivid, warm ~
P: combination of, range of *colours*

COMBAT
V: abandon, break off, carry on, engage in, enter into, join ~
A: armed, bitter, close, deadly, fierce, half-hearted, hand-to-hand, mortal, unarmed ~

COMEDY
A: alternative, black, dark, hilarious, light, musical, riotous, serious ~

COMFORT
V: bring, derive, draw, find, give, live in, offer, provide, seek, take ~
A: cold, complete, great, physical, spiritual ~
P: be a ~ to sb; feeling of, words of ~

COMMAND (order)

V: carry out, disregard, execute, fulfil, give, ignore, issue, (dis)obey ~

A: direct, explicit, express, sharp ~

COMMAND (authority)

V: assume, be under sb's, exercise, give up, hand over, have, hold, lose, question sb's, relegate, relinquish, resign, take over, transfer ~

A: direct, full, highest, overall, supreme, temporary, total ~

COMMENT

V: express, ignore, invite, make, offer, refrain from ~

A: adverse, angry, appropriate, apt, biting, blunt, brief, derogatory, fair, favourable, forthright, frank, ironic, nasty, outspoken, pithy, rude, sarcastic, scathing, sharp, shrewd, silly, sincere, stupid, succinct, sympathetic, tart, terse, vicious, withering ~

COMMENTARY

V: add, broadcast, give, produce, write ~

A: balanced, brief, brilliant, colourful, eye-witness, fair, full, lively, lucid, running, vivid ~

COMMERCIAL

V: ban, broadcast, create, devise, produce, run, screen, show, sponsor ~

A: award-winning, hard-hitting, popular, powerful ~

P: ~ break

COMMISSION

V: carry out, entrust sb with, execute ~

COMMITMENT

V: abandon, acknowledge, assume, avoid, deny, enter into, express, feel, fulfil, get out of, go back on, have, honour, keep to, make, meet, recognise, take on ~

A: casual, close, deep, firm, heavy, important, passionate, previous, prior, solemn, strong, total ~

COMMITTEE

V: appear before, appoint, be a member of, chair, elect, form, head, serve on, set up, sit on ~

V: ~ considered ..., dealt with ..., decided ..., discussed ..., drew up a report, met, recommended ..., reported back, studied ..., suggested ..., are taking steps to ..., urged ...

A: ad hoc, advisory, consultative, executive, influential, inter-departmental, joint, mixed, organising, parliamentary, special, top-level ~

COMMUNICATION

V: break off, cut, ease, enter into, establish, get into, hamper, have, improve, interrupt, keep in, lack, maintain, restore, sever, stop ~

V: ~ broke down

P: breakdown in, means of, speeding up of ~

COMMUNITY

V: belong to, establish, form, found, join, reform, represent, revitalise, serve, set up, stabilise ~

A: balanced, close, closed, close-knit, exclusive, flourishing, international, local, native, primitive, scattered, self-reliant, tightly-knit, vigorous, worldwide ~

P: access to, membership of, pillar of ~

COMPANION

A: amusing, close, constant, delightful, excellent, faithful, inseparable, stimulating, travelling ~

COMPANY

V: find oneself in, have, invite, keep, keep away from ~

A: amusing, bad, boring, congenial, doubtful, dull, entertaining, exalted, good, intellectual, mixed, noisy, pleasant, polite, rowdy, shady, stimulating, suspicious, undemanding, undesirable, unsuitable ~

COMPANY (firm)

V: buy out, close down, downsize, establish, float, form, found, join, launch, liquidate, manage, nationalise, register, reorganise, rescue, re-structure, run, sell off, set up, start, take over, wind up ~

V: ~ employs ..., expanded, failed, grew, is in trouble, ran into difficulties/trouble, started up, is thriving, trades, went bankrupt/bust/into liquidation, went under

A: ailing, bankrupt, blue-chip, defunct, dynamic, efficient, emerging, enterprising, excellent, expanding, foremost, giant, go-ahead, holding, huge, limited, medium-sized, moribund, multi-national, old-fashioned, parent, private, (un)profitable, rival, shady, sister, sound, subsidiary, well-run, young ~

P: group of *companies*

COMPARISON

V: avoid, draw, make ~

A: close, (un)fair, far-reaching, (un)favourable, instructive, invidious, true, unwelcome ~

P: basis of ~

COMPASSION

V: arouse, feel, show ~

A: deep, profound, strong ~

P: exercise of, show of ~

COMPENSATION

V: award, claim, demand, get, give, grant, make, obtain, offer, pay, receive, refuse ~

A: (in)adequate, ample, due, fair, full, generous, just, miserly ~

P: ~ clause, package

COMPETITION

V: be up against, come up against, encounter, encourage, face, meet, reduce, stimulate ~

A: close, cut-throat, domestic, fierce, formidable, great, healthy, intense, international, keen, local, rigorous, serious, severe, sharp, stiff, strong, Third World, tremendous ~

COMPETITION (sports)

V: announce, be the winner in/of, enter for, go in for, hold, judge, sponsor, stage, take part in, win, withdraw from ~

A: exciting, nationwide, local, national, popular ~

COMPLAINT

V: acknowledge, accept, admit, bring, confront sb with, consider, deal with, dismiss, examine, file, get, handle, hear, ignore, inquire into, investigate, justify, lodge, make, put in, put ~ right, raise, receive, refer to, register, reject, reply to, respond to, study, uphold, voice, withdraw ~

V: ~ involves sth, stands

A: bitter, disturbing, grave, justifiable, legitimate, preposterous, serious, worrying ~

P: chorus of, flood of, string of *complaints*

COMPONENTS

A: basic, essential, key, main, vital ~

P: set of ~

COMPLIMENT

V: accept, pay, return ~

A: back-handed, dubious, genuine, sincere, tremendous ~

50

COMPLIMENTS
V: fish for ~, lavish ~ on, send sth with one's ~, shower ~ on
P: with the ~ of the house, with the ~ of the management; ~ of the season
COMPROMISE
V: agree on/to, aim at, arrive at, come to, effect, negotiate, patch up, reach, reject, seek, work out ~
V: ~ failed, worked
A: acceptable, definite, early, fair, good, potential, reasonable, (un)satisfactory, shaky, tacit, uneasy, working ~
COMPULSION
V: be driven by, feel, give way to, resort to, subject sb to, submit to, use ~
A: inner, irresistible, overpowering, overwhelming, strange, strong, tremendous ~
COMPUTER
V: back up, hack into, operate, program, run sth through, use ~
V: ~ is down, bombed, controls, has crashed, stores
A: home, laptop, mainframe, palmtop, personal ~
P: ~ age, animation, error, graphics, operator, program, programmer, software, studies
CONCENTRATION
V: call for, demand, disturb, improve, need, require, spoil ~
V:~ is focused on, improved, wavered
A: complete, constant, continuous, deep, great, grim, high-powered, immense, intense, marked, persistent, poor, prolonged, steady, superhuman, total ~
P: ~ span; lapse of ~
CONCEPT
V: abandon, accept, adhere to, arrive at, attack, broaden, build, build up, cast doubt on, challenge, create, deny, develop, embrace, formulate, grasp, have, invent, keep to, lead to, produce, put forward, question, reject, search for, subscribe to, support ~
A: abstract, astounding, bold, brand-new, broad, classical, clear, creative, current, dangerous, daring, difficult, established, existing, false, fresh, general, illusory, imaginative, ingenious, narrow, nebulous, novel, original, overall, pioneering, plausible, revolutionary, total, true, unique, unlikely, useful, vague ~
CONCEPTION
V: broaden, create, deny, develop, favour, have, lead to, put forward, support ~
A: broad, clear, erroneous, false, general, inflated, mistaken, obscure, original, overall, true ~
CONCERN
V: be filled with, cause, display, evoke, express, feel, give rise to, harbour, heighten, hide, intensify, share, show, voice ~
V: ~ is mounting
A: acute, considerable, constant, deep, deep-seated, foremost, genuine, grave, great, growing, high-level, humanitarian, intense, international, justified, laudable, legitimate, main, major, marked, national, obvious, overriding, overt, passing, pressing, primary, prime, principal, profound, proper, real, serious, sharp, sincere, slight, widespread ~
P: grounds for, matter of ~
CONCERT
V: cancel, give, go to, hold, put on, stage ~
A: charity, classical, jazz, live, open-air, pop, rock, sell-out ~
CONCESSION
V: deserve, earn, extract, finalise, get, grant, make, obtain, offer, win ~
A: generous, modest, significant, sizeable, slight, substantial, sweeping, welcome ~
P: string of *concessions*

CONCLUSION (belief)
V: arrive at, be driven to/forced to, be unable to escape, bear out, come to, confirm, draw, favour, form, invalidate, jump to, lead to, overturn, question, reach, resist, support ~
V: ~ emerged, holds true, stands
A: astonishing, awkward, biased, bleak, certain, correct, definite, depressing, devastating, disturbing, erroneous, false, final, firm, foregone, happy, hasty, inescapable, inevitable, irresistible, justifiable, logical, mistaken, obvious, one-sided, orthodox, premature, rash, right, sad, self-evident, tentative, unanimous, unavoidable, unpalatable, wrong ~
P: cannot escape the ~ that ...; (the result) was a foregone ~

CONCLUSION (end)
V: anticipate, bring sth to, lead sth to ~
A: abrupt, rapid, satisfactory, speedy, successful, triumphant ~

CONDEMNATION
V: call for, deserve, issue, meet with ~
A: bitter, firm, general, harsh, indignant, resolute, strong, sweeping, universal ~

CONDITION (health)
V: get into, get out of, help, treat ~
V: ~ has become more serious, deteriorated, improved, remains stable, worsened
A: critical, low, poor, satisfactory, stable, weak, weakened ~
P: deterioration in, improvement in ~

CONDITION (state of a thing)
V: be blind to, examine, improve, report on ~
V: ~ has deteriorated
A: disgraceful, dreadful, excellent, filthy, fine, first-class, flourishing, fresh, good, immaculate, perfect, pitiable, pitiful, poor, prime, pristine, shabby, splendid, superb, thriving, top, wretched ~
P: deterioration in, improvement in ~

CONDITIONS (terms)
V: accept, agree on/to, alter, approve, break, change, define, examine, fix, fulfil, get out of, haggle over, ignore, impose, insist on, keep to, lay down, make, meet, obey, obtain, offer, propose, reject, satisfy, set down/out, settle, specify, spell out, state, stipulate, study ~
V: ~ apply, are binding, are in force, (still) hold, tie sb down, vary
A: advantageous, detailed, diverse, exacting, (un)fair, favourable, firm, generous, harsh, indispensable, lenient, prior, provisional, rigid, rigorous, severe, stiff, stringent, unacceptable ~
P: set of ~

CONDITIONS (circumstances)
V: adapt oneself to, adjust to, alter, be kept in, bear, cope with, create, encounter, experience, find oneself in, improve, live in, provide, restore, stand up to, suffer, survive, tolerate ~
V: ~ affect sth, are conducive to sth, deteriorated, improved, worsened
A: adverse, appalling, austere, changing, comfortable, confined, difficult, dreadful, easy, existing, filthy, fluctuating, frightful, grim, hard, harsh, hygienic, inhospitable, inhuman, intolerable, (ab)normal, poor, prevailing, rigorous, shocking, squalid, stable, (un)suitable, surrounding, terrible, trying, varying, wretched ~

CONDUCT
V: affect, approve of, commend sb for, criticise sb for, deplore, excuse, get an award for, influence, justify, modify, punish, reward sb for ~
V: ~ is an example to sb, deteriorated, improved, inspired sb, served as an example

A: appalling, bad, brave, courageous, cowardly, deplorable, disgraceful, dishonourable, disorderly, exemplary, frivolous, generous, good, idle, ignorant, impeccable, improper, inconsistent, inexcusable, inexplicable, irresponsible, loyal, selfish, shameful, shocking, strange, stupid, subsequent, treacherous, unethical ~

P: code of, motives behind sb's ~

CONFERENCE

V: attend, be away at, call, convene, go to, hold, organise, preside over, speak at, wind up ~

V: ~ carried a resolution, dealt with sth, debated sth, disbanded, discussed sth, met, opened, reached agreement on sth, recommended sth, took place

A: annual (monthly, etc), international, one-day (etc), stormy ~

P: ~ circuit, goer, participant, press ~

CONFESSION

V: beat a ~ out of sb, demand, elicit, extract, force a ~ from sb, make, obtain, retract ~

A: deathbed, detailed, frank, full, terrible ~

CONFIDENCE

V: affirm, bolster, boost, (re)build, build up, declare, dent, deserve, destroy, display/show ~ in sb, erode, express ~ in sb, exude, feel, gain, give sb, have, inspire sb with, keep up, lack, lose, maintain, ooze, preserve, reinforce, restore, shake/shatter sb's, take away sb's, undermine ~

V: ~ collapsed, diminished, dwindled, ebbed, evaporated, faltered, flagged, grew, mounted, plummeted, vanished, waned, wavered

A: absolute, awe-inspiring, blind, complete, full, gratifying, great, overweening, overwhelming, perfect, quiet, reduced, total, touching, unbounded, unshaken ~

P: erosion of, lack of, loss of ~

CONFINES

V: keep within, mark, set, stick to ~

A: broad, close, exact, narrow, strict, wide ~

CONFIRMATION

V: ask for, await, expect, receive, require, wait for ~

A: final, firm, fresh, immediate, (un)official, reliable, urgent ~

CONFLICT

V: aggravate, avert, avoid, be at the centre of/at the root of, be engaged in, carry on, confine, create, eliminate, end in, escalate, exploit, extend, fuel, give rise to, inflame, isolate, lead to, limit, localise, plunge sth into, resolve, settle, solve, sow the seed of, stir up ~

V: ~ arose, broke out, came to a head, died down, erupted, escalated, festered, flared up, got out of hand, grew, raged, simmered, smouldered, spread, took place, threatened

A: acute, all-out, armed, bitter, brief, constant, dangerous, desperate, direct, disturbing, fierce, fresh, genocidal, imminent, inevitable, long-drawn-out, mounting, open, prolonged, protracted, savage, serious, severe, sharp, unfortunate, useless, widening, widespread ~

P: dimensions of, nub of, roots of, seeds of ~

CONFRONTATION

V: avoid, bring about, come a step nearer to, end in, head for, lead to, prevent, provoke ~

A: dangerous, direct, head-on, inevitable, serious, unavoidable ~

CONFUSION

V: add to, aggravate, avoid, cause, clear up, create, generate, increase, lead to, prevent, produce, sort out, throw sth into ~

V: ~ arose

A: complete, general, great, growing, hopeless, indescribable, total, utter, widespread ~

P: scene of, state of ~

CONGRATULATIONS
V: offer ~
A: best, hearty, sincere, warmest ~

CONJECTURE
A: bold, mere, pure, wild ~
P: be a matter of, be reduced to ~

CONNECTION
V: break, break off, discover, establish, forge, form, foster, have, interrupt, keep, keep up, look for, lose, maintain, make, observe, perceive, point out/to, provide, see, sever, strengthen, suspect, trace ~
A: advantageous, causal, clandestine, clear, close, complicated, definite, direct, existing, firm, flimsy, fortuitous, friendly, genuine, important, initial, logical, loose, natural, (no) necessary, obvious, obscure, only, profitable, spurious, strong, tangible, tenuous, unavoidable, useful, vague, visible ~

CONQUEST
V: attempt, complete, consolidate, embark on, make, set off on, undertake ~
A: decisive, easy, final, important, legendary, military, rapid, sexual, swift, total, valuable ~

CONSCIENCE
V: appeal to, ask, ease, go by, have a/no, have sth on, jolt, listen to, obey, salve, soothe, trouble, weigh on ~
V: ~ gnawed at sb, troubled/worried sb
A: bad, clear, guilty, tortured, troubled, uneasy ~
P: pangs of, voice of ~

CONSCIOUSNESS
V: drift in and out of, lose, recover, regain ~
A: heightened ~
P: sth creeps into one's ~; stream of ~

CONSENSUS
V: arrive at, destroy, endorse, (try to) reach ~
A: broad, general ~

CONSENT
V: apply for, ask for, call for, express, get, give, grant, have sb's, obtain, refuse, request, withhold ~
A: enthusiastic, full, general, grudging, immediate, joyful, mutual, parental, reluctant, tacit, wholehearted ~
P: age of, by common ~

CONSEQUENCES
V: abide by, accept, alleviate, avoid, bear, brave, calculate, contemplate, cope with, deal with, escape, examine, face, fear, foresee, have, ignore, investigate, lead to, minimise, mitigate, pay for, produce, realise, reckon with, result in, shut one's eyes to, soften, suffer, take, take ~ into account, weigh ~
V: ~ ensue, follow from sth, result from sth, stem from sth
A: adverse, alarming, appalling, beneficial, catastrophic, certain, clear-cut, damaging, (un)desirable, devastating, dire, (in)direct, disastrous, far-reaching, fatal, (un)fortunate, grave, happy, harmful, harsh, hazardous, horrendous, immediate, (un)important, incalculable, inevitable, irreparable, irrevocable, (un)likely, lamentable, long/short-term, momentous, (un)predictable, probable, regrettable, sad, serious, severe, startling, tragic, unforeseeable, unforeseen, unfortunate, unimaginable, unique, violent ~

CONSIDERATION
V: be due for, be under, call for, give ~ to, leave sth out of, need, repay, require, show, take sth into ~
A: brief, careful, close, due, full, great, little, marked, mature, urgent ~
CONSPIRACY
V: crush, expose, foil, hatch, organise, reveal ~
A: criminal, political ~
P: ~ theory; ~ to commit (crime), to murder, to overthrow (government etc), of silence
CONSOLATION
V: afford, bring, deprive sb of, get, give, offer ~
A: great, little, slight ~
CONSTITUTION
V: adopt, alter, amend, approve, contravene, draft, draw up, frame, grant, introduce, make, model ~ on sth, preserve, safeguard, set up, suspend, ratify, (re)write ~
P: amendment to, shortcomings of ~
CONSTRAINTS
V: impose, place, put, remove ~
A: severe ~
CONSULTATIONS
V: arrange/ask for, conduct, grant, hold, seek, take part in ~
A: close, discreet, emergency, friendly, immediate, joint, regular, secret, urgent, useful, wide, wide-ranging ~
CONSUMER
V: appeal to, attract, encourage, protect, put ~ off, warn ~
P: ~ affairs, choice, confidence, demand, goods, products, protection, rights, spending, survey
CONSUMPTION
V: ban, check, curb, encourage, estimate, hold down, increase, keep down, measure, predict, promote, reduce, stimulate ~
V: ~ decreased, fell, increased, went down/up, levelled off, remains steady, rose, is shrinking, slumped, soared
A: annual (etc), diminished, excessive, heavy, high, low, mass, unnecessary ~
P: drop in, rise in ~
CONTACT
V: ban, be in ~ with sb, break off, cut off, enter into, establish, hamper, have, keep in, lose, maintain, make, remain in, retain, stay in ~
A: close, constant, (in)frequent, general, intermittent, intimate, loose, (ir)regular, restricted, steady ~
P: lose all ~ with sb
CONTACTS (personal)
V: build up, develop, foster, have, increase, keep up, open up, strengthen ~
A: broad, friendly, tenuous, useful, wide ~
P: network of, web of ~
CONTEMPT
V: deserve, earn, express, feel, have, hold sb in, show ~
A: complete, profound, utter ~
CONTENT
V: analyse, criticise, describe, digest, explain, follow, study, summarise, sum up ~
A: clear, factual, obscure, political, technical ~

CONTENTS
V: (re)arrange, ascertain, check, empty, examine, inspect, list, look through, recall, turn out ~
V: ~ fell/spilled/tumbled out

CONTEST
V: enter, go in for, hold, judge, take part in ~
A: close, closely fought, fair, final, heated, keen, open, rough ~

CONTEXT
A: cultural, different, historical, original, political, social ~
P: be in the ~ of; be out of, put sth in, see sth in, take sth out of, quote sb out of ~

CONTINGENCY
V: allow for, deal with, foresee, meet, plan for, prepare for, provide for ~
A: sudden, unexpected ~
P: ~ plan

CONTINUITY
V: break, destroy, ensure, lack, maintain, preserve ~
P: sense of ~

CONTRACT
V: break, carry out, (re-)draft, draw up, enter into, finalise, fulfil, get, get out of, give up, go over, go through, grant, have, honour, implement, initial, keep to, lose, make, (re)negotiate, renew, sign, tear up, terminate, win ~
V: ~ binds sb to do sth, comes into effect/to an end, expires, is in force, lapses, runs, runs out
A: binding, exclusive, final, good, huge, important, non-renewable, original, profitable, temporary, unworkable, valid ~
P: breach of, terms of ~

CONTRADICTION
V: acknowledge, be aware of, do away with, eliminate, explain, get round, ignore, lessen, notice, perceive, resolve, see, solve, take account of, take into account ~
V: ~ is embodied in sth, was evident, has become less marked, came about, emerged, existed
A: apparent, basic, clear, definite, direct, distinct, glaring, inherent, intrinsic, lasting, logical, marked, obvious, plain ~
P: ~ in terms; mass of *contradictions*

CONTRAST
V: bring out, emphasise, examine, express, form, heighten, highlight, make, note, notice, perceive, reduce, see, stress, study, underline ~
A: astonishing, bleak, definite, glaring, harsh, important, obvious, refreshing, remarkable, sharp, significant, slight, stark, startling, striking, strong ~
P: in marked ~ to

CONTRIBUTIONS
A: token, unsolicited, voluntary ~
P: flood of ~

CONTROL
V: abandon, acquire, allocate, assume, be in/out of/under, bring under, come under, consolidate, establish, exercise, exert, extend, get, get under, give up, hand over, hang on to, have, impose, increase, keep, lack, loosen, lose, maintain, regain, relax, relinquish, retain, share, submit to, take over, tighten, win, wrest ~
A: absolute, complete, day-to-day, (in)direct, effective, exclusive, firm, full, heavy-handed, inadequate, insufficient, intermittent, limited, overall, partial, proper, regular, rigid, strict, supreme, tenuous, tight, total ~

CONTROLS
V: call for, devise, ease, impose, introduce, lift, relax, remove, tighten ~
A: stiff, strict, tough ~

CONTROVERSY
V: arouse, avoid, cause, create, end, end in/up in, engage in, excite, fuel, generate, give rise to, inflame, intensify, lead to, prevent, provoke, put an end to, renew, re-open, settle, spark off, stifle, stimulate, stir up ~
V:~ arose, centres on sth, erupted, flared up, intensified, mounted, quietened down, raged, subsided
A: acrimonious, acute, bitter, fierce, furious, heated, important, lively, never-ending, prolonged, sharp, vigorous, violent ~
P: height of ~

CONVENTION (international)
V: accede to, adhere to, breach, break, draft, draw up, honour, implement, negotiate, ratify, repudiate, sign, violate ~
V: ~ applies to sth, comes into force, covers sth, governs sth, lays down (rules), regulates sth

CONVENTION (social)
V: be a slave to, defy, flout, follow, obey, observe, outrage, respect, uphold, violate ~
A: accepted, mere, narrow, obsolete, rigid, social, strict ~

CONVERSATION
V: break off, carry on, continue, dominate, enter into, get into, have, hold, interrupt, lead, listen to, monopolise, overhear, steer, strike up, take part in, terminate ~
A: agreeable, amicable, amusing, animated, awkward, brief, casual, cheerful, earnest, embarrassing, endless, entertaining, fascinating, fleeting, forced, frank, general, halting, important, (un)interesting, intimate, (un)pleasant, polite, private, serious, short, stimulating, strange, useful, witty, worrying ~
P: gap in, lull in, pause in, scrap of ~

CONVICTION
V: be swayed by, embrace, express, have, hold, lose, reinforce, shake, share, state, strengthen, undermine, upset ~
A: abiding, absolute, burning, dangerous, deep, deep-rooted, definite, established, firm, growing, instinctive, lifelong, profound, reasonable, steady, strong, unshakeable ~
P: have the courage of your *convictions*

CO-OPERATION
V: build up, count on, develop, encourage, establish, expand, expect, foster, hope for, look forward to, promote, refuse, rely on, strive for, value, withhold ~
V: ~ is lacking, ceased, developed, flourished, grew
A: close, friendly, full, good, greater, growing, helpful, international, regular, renewed, useful, wholehearted ~
P: spirit of ~

CO-ORDINATION
V: achieve, ensure, establish, promote ~
A: close, excellent, perfect, satisfactory ~

COPY
V:~ examine, make, print, run off, take ~
A: accurate, (un)authorised, backup, bad, clean, clear, exact, excellent, fair, good, hard, illicit, legible, master, perfect, poor, rough, (un)satisfactory, true, worn ~

CORRESPONDENCE
V: break off, carry on, conduct, deal with, edit, file, get, handle, keep up, publish, receive, reply to ~
A: acrimonious, brief, business, extensive, intimate, lengthy, long, private, regular, scholarly, secret, vast, voluminous ~

CORRUPTION
V: curb, detect, investigate, root out, stamp out ~
P: ~ is common, is endemic, is rife

COST
V: amortize, bear, bring down, calculate, count, cover, cut, defray, determine, entail, estimate, fix, increase, incur, inflate, involve, meet, minimise, obscure, offset, pay, put up, reckon, recoup, recover, reduce, repay, trim, write off ~
V: ~ climbed, escalated, fell, went down/up, increased, remained steady, rose, rocketed, spiralled
A: appalling, average, basic, crippling, ever-rising, excessive, exorbitant, extra, fearful, fixed, heavy, hidden, high, huge, inordinate, likely, low, maximum, minimum, moderate, mounting, prohibitive, real, rising, soaring, staggering, unnecessary ~

COUNTRY
V: govern, liberate, rule, run, take over ~
A: adjacent, backward, (under)developed, developing, distant, friendly, host, hostile, mother, native, neighbouring, neutral, poor, powerful, primitive, prosperous, rich, Third World ~

COUNTRYSIDE
A: picturesque, surrounding, unspoilt ~
P: fabric of, preservation of ~

COUP
V: avert, be behind, carry out, engineer, execute, foil, forestall, plan, plot, prevent, pull off, stage, support, trigger off, ward off ~
A: abortive, attempted, audacious, bloodless, bloody, bold, clever, daring, (un)successful ~

COURAGE
V: display, give sb, have, inspire sb with, keep ~ up, lack, lose, pluck up, possess, show, summon up, take ~
V: ~ failed, faltered
A: admirable, amazing, commendable, exemplary, great, heroic, indomitable, legendary, outstanding, rare, remarkable, tremendous ~

COURSE (of study)
V: attend, cancel, complete, discontinue, do, drop, drop out of, embark on, enrol for, fail, finish, follow, hold, offer, organise, plan, provide, register for, repeat, run, sign up for, start, tackle, take ~
A: advanced, beginners, boring, compulsory, correspondence, crash, demanding, difficult, easy, elective, evening, exacting, extra-curricular, full, full-/part-time, helpful, in-service, intensive, intermediate, introductory, long, one-to-one, optional, postgraduate, practical, pre-service, refresher, regular, rigorous, short, special, specialist, technical, training, undergraduate, useful, vocational ~

COURSE (direction)
V: alter, be on/off, change, deviate from, follow, keep to, steer, stray from, swerve from, take ~
A: direct, proper, roundabout, straight, wrong, zig-zag ~

COURSE (of action)
V: adopt, advise, advocate, commend, decide on, deviate from, embark on, follow, keep to, recommend, reject, take, threaten ~

A: audacious, best, bold, dangerous, defeatist, desperate, expedient, honest, initial, obvious, proper, prudent, right, risky, sensible, steady, (un)usual, wise, wrong ~

COURT

V: address, appear before, bring sb before, get to, go to, preside over, settle sth out of, take sb to ~

V: ~ adjourned a case, allowed/dismissed/heard an appeal, increased/imposed/pronounced/quashed/reduced a sentence, dealt with sth, decided sth, determined sth, discharged sb, dismissed the case, found sb (not)guilty, has (no) jurisdiction over ..., heard evidence, imposed a fine, made a fresh order, ordered a new trial, released sb (on probation/remand), remanded a prisoner, sentenced sb

A: civil, criminal, crown, higher, municipal, supreme ~

P: ~ case, hearing, of appeal, proceedings

COURTESY

V: demonstrate, extend ~ to sb, show sb every ~

A: common, great, professional, simple, unfailing, the utmost ~

P: act of, matter of ~

CRASH

V: avoid, be damaged/hurt/involved/killed in, be responsible for, cause, end in, have ~

A: car, fatal, head-on, nasty, plane, serious, terrible ~

CREATURE

A: fantastic, ferocious, grotesque, horrible, large, mythical, strange, tiny ~

CREDIT

V: accept, allow sb, be in, buy on, deny sb, give sb, grant sb, extend, offer sb, refuse sb ~

A: further, interest-free, six months' etc ~

P: ~ account, agreement, balance, card, control, limit, period, terms

CRIME

V: combat, commit, crack down on, cut down, detect, encourage, fight, keep down, perpetrate, prevent, reduce, stamp out, take to, wipe out ~

V: ~ escalated, flourished, grew, proliferated, spread

A: appalling, atrocious, brutal, major, outrageous, perfect, petty, serious, vicious, violent, widespread ~

P: ~ figures, ~ of passion; annals of, complicity in, epidemic of, outbreak of, perpetrator of, prevalence of, surge in, upsurge in, victims of, wave of ~

CRIMINAL

A: born, common, dangerous, desperate, hardened, master, petty, violent ~

CRISIS

V: aggravate, avert, be affected by, be in the grip of, be through, break out of, bring things to, cause, come through/to, create, deal with, defuse, divert, encounter, exacerbate, face, find a way out of, get over, go through, head for, meet, overcome, pass, precipitate, prevent, provoke, reach, resolve, ride out, solve, stand up to, stave off, stir up, survive, weather, withstand ~

V: ~ arose, blew over/up, came to a head, deepened, developed, dragged on, erupted, escalated, gripped sth, grew, grew worse, has repercussions, hit sb, passed, is simmering, subsided, widened

A: acute, alarming, approaching, dangerous, deep, explosive, imminent, impending, intense, international, mild, mounting, perpetual, political, profound, recurrent, serious, severe, unavoidable, violent, worrying ~

P: aftermath of, depth of, gravity of, handling of, heart of, resolution of, seeds of, solution to, in the wake of ~

CRITERIA
V: adopt, apply, define, establish, fit, fix, fulfil, keep to, lay down, meet, satisfy, select, set ~
A: basic, clear-cut, demanding, exacting, existing, fundamental, precise, strict, stringent ~

CRITICS
V: annoy, charm, confound, confront, defy, delight, disarm, entrance, face, gag, oppose, placate, please, shock, silence, win over ~
A: articulate, ferocious, harsh, impartial, lenient, outspoken, persistent, severe, strong, unkind ~

CRITICISM
V: accept, agree with, answer, arouse, attract, be discouraged by/exposed to/impervious to/rattled by/subjected to/upset by, blunt, come in for/under/up against, crush, defend oneself against, deflect, deserve, encounter, escape, evoke, express, forestall, give rise to, ignore, invalidate, justify, level ~ against sb, meet with, offer, overcome, provoke, react to, reject, reply to, rise above, run into, shrink from, silence, soften, stifle, subject sb to, suffer, voice, weather, withstand, yield to ~
V: ~ centres on sth, comes from sb, died down, grew, hardened, hit home, is relevant, mounted, revolved around ...
A: adverse, basic, biased, bitter, blunt, common, constant, destructive, devastating, (un)fair, ferocious, fierce, friendly, fundamental, furious, harsh, helpful, hostile, implicit, incisive, lively, merciless, mild, muted, objective, oblique, open, overt, penetrating, perceptive, personal, savage, searing, severe, sharp, sincere, stinging, stringent, strong, subjective, tough, trenchant, unjust, unprecedented, useful, useless, (thinly) veiled, widespread ~
P: chorus of, flood of, spate of, torrent of, wave of, whiff of ~

CROP
V: bring in, cultivate, damage, gather, get, grow, harvest, have, plant, produce, raise, reap, rotate, ruin, save, spoil, spray, yield ~
A: bumper, cash, disappointing, excellent, fine, good, heavy, miserable, poor, record, splendid, successful ~

CROWD
V: address, attract, break up, control, deal with, direct, disperse, draw, face, follow, gather, handle, restrain, sway ~
V: ~ advanced, broke up, collected, dispersed, gathered, got out of control/hand, grew, invaded ..., met, melted away, panicked, retreated, scattered, spilled onto ..., surged forward, swelled, thinned out, turned out, went on the rampage
A: aggressive, angry, dangerous, dense, disorderly, happy, hostile, huge, large, menacing, motley, noisy, restless, riotous, rowdy, seething, ugly, unmanageable, unruly, vast ~
P: ~ control; capacity ~

CRUELTY
A: appalling, barbarous, callous, deliberate, indescribable, mental, physical, psychological, sadistic, savage, terrible, unspeakable, unthinking, utmost, wanton ~
P: act of, victim of (appalling) ~

CRY
V: give, let out, raise, utter ~
A: angry, anguished, loud, piercing, rallying, startled ~
P: ~ for help, of despair, of horror, of outrage, of pain, of protest, of terror

CULTURE (the arts)
V: neglect, promote, revive, spread, subsidise ~
A: folk, high, popular, regional, traditional ~
P: centre of, expansion of, renaissance of, spread of ~

CULTURE (a particular civilization)

V: destroy, study ~

V: ~ declined, disappeared, flourished, influenced sb, penetrated ..., reached its peak, spread, vanished

A: advanced, alien, ancient, foreign, indigenous, inferior, native, primitive, superior ~

P: ~ clash, shock

CURE (recovery)

V: achieve, bring about, effect, guarantee, produce ~

A: absolute, certain, complete, gradual, instant, miraculous, sensational, spontaneous, successful, swift, systematic, total, wonderful ~

CURE (remedy)

V: apply, believe in, discover, find, invent, look for, recommend, seek, try, undertake ~

A: drastic, effective, good, infallible, instant, magic, miracle, miraculous, old-fashioned, painful, radical, rapid, simple, well-known, wonderful ~

CURFEW

V: end, impose, keep to, lift ~

A: midnight, strict ~

CURIOSITY

V: arouse, burn with, excite, feel, fill sb with, give rise to, rouse, satisfy, whet ~

A: great, healthy, idle, insatiable, intellectual, lively, natural, unwelcome ~

CURRENCY

V: accept as, change, issue, withdraw ~

A: (non-)convertible, foreign, hard, local, soft, stable, strong, weak ~

P: ~ crisis, deal

CURRENT

V: be carried along by, chart, go against/with, resist, reverse, stem, swim against/with ~

V: ~ swept sb along

A: political, popular, powerful, prevailing, rapid, strong, swift, treacherous ~

CUSTODY

V: award sb, be in, be held in, be placed in, be remanded in, give sb, grant sb, receive, take, take sb into ~

A: joint, police, protective, safe ~

P: ~ battle, of the children

CUSTOM

V: abolish, adopt, advocate, deviate from, do away with, encounter, eradicate, establish, follow, introduce, keep to, maintain, obey, observe, preserve, respect, stamp out ~

V: ~ dates back to (the 12th Century), died out, disappeared, existed, flourished, grew up, has its origin in sth, persists, survives, vanished

A: age-old, ancient, bizarre, colourful, common, cruel, curious, deep-rooted, exotic, foreign, general, harmful, local, national, old, old-established, outdated, popular, rare, recent, sensible, strange, traditional, tribal, unique, universal, unusual, vulgar, well-established, widespread ~

CUSTOMER

V: attract, entertain, deal with, look after, meet, serve ~

A: best, good, important, irate, prospective, regular, satisfied ~

P: ~ relations, satisfaction, service

D

DAMAGE
V: assess, avoid, cause, (un)do, inflict, make good, mend, prevent, repair, report, restore, save sth from, suffer, sustain ~
V: ~ occurred, took place, was confined/restricted to ...
A: appreciable, enormous, excessive, extensive, great, heavy, huge, irreparable, lasting, massive, negligible, permanent, potential, serious, severe, slight, substantial, tremendous, untold, visible, wartime, widespread ~
P: trail of ~

DAMAGES (compensation)
V: assess, award, claim, demand, get, pay, receive, recover, sue sb for, win ~
A: heavy, punitive, substantial ~

DANGER
V: alert sb to, avert, avoid, be aware of, be exposed to, be in/out of, beware of, cause, confront, detect, disregard, eliminate, encounter, expose sb to, face, flee from, foresee, ignore, keep out of, keep clear of, look out for, magnify, make light of, pinpoint, realise, recognise, risk, run into, scent, sense, smell, spell out, wake up to, warn sb of ~
V: ~ evaporated, faded, loomed, passed, receded, threatened
A: acute, considerable, constant, ever-present, grave, great, hidden, imaginary, immediate, imminent, impending, mortal, obvious, potential, (very)real, remote, serious, slight, worst ~

DARKNESS
V: illuminate, lighten, peer into, pierce, penetrate, relieve, see through ~
V: ~ came down/on, covered sth, enveloped sth, fell, gave way to sth, lifted
A: complete, impenetrable, inky, pitch-black, thick, total, utter ~

DATA
V: access, accumulate, acquire, amass, arrange, assemble, assess, capture, check, classify, collate, collect, compile, enter, evaluate, examine, fabricate, fake, falsify, feed ~ into sth, gather, get, handle, interpret, keep, look up, mix up, obtain, organise, process, produce, record, retrieve, sift, store, study, supply sb with, tag ~
V: ~ applies to ..., concerns ..., pertains to ..., proves ..., refers/relates to ..., shows ...
A: accurate, (in)adequate, available, basic, bogus, comparable, complete, comprehensive, conflicting, consistent, current, exhaustive, final, latest, preliminary, provisional, raw, recent, relevant, reliable, right, significant, (in)sufficient, supporting, up-to-the-minute ~
P: ~ base, bank, processing; access to, flow of, mass of, reliability of, wealth of ~

DATE
V: agree on, arrange, bring forward, change, confirm, decide, fix, mark, name, pencil in, postpone, propose, set, settle ~
V: ~ is approaching, arrived, is drawing near
A: actual, awkward, (in)convenient, definite, distant, early, final, latest, provisional, remote, suitable, tentative ~

DAY
V: celebrate, look forward to, mark, spend, start ~
V: ~ is near/nigh/past, came, dragged on
A: blissful, busy, cheerless, delightful, dreadful, entire, eventful, full, happy, historic, idle, long, memorable, pleasant, red-letter, special, typical, whole, working ~

DAYS (period with *the*)
V: bring to mind, look back on, recall, recollect, remember, yearn for ~
V: ~ are gone/numbered/over/past
A: bad old, carefree, dark, difficult, early, good old, halcyon, last, later, old, olden ~
P: end (your) ~; in ~ gone by

DEADLINE
V: extend, fix, (fail to) meet, miss, pass, set, work to ~
V: ~ is approaching, is (long) past, loomed
A: definite, flexible, strict, tentative, tight ~

DEAL
V: accept, agree on, aim at, approve, arrive at, block, blow, bring off, cancel, clinch, close, complete, conclude, do, enter into, get, get out of, honour, make, negotiate, pull off, reach, reject, screw up, secure, set up, sign, spoil, strike, swing, turn down, veto, wrap up, wreck, wriggle out of ~
V: ~ is off/on, broke down, collapsed, came into effect, emerged, fell through, involved ..., went ahead, went smoothly
A: acceptable, ambitious, astute, advantageous, bad, clever, cut-price, dodgy, dubious, (un)fair, (un)favourable, firm, (dis)honest, huge, lucrative, poor, profitable, risky, shady, shrewd, square, tentative ~

DEALINGS
V: avoid, enter into, have ~
A: clandestine, complicated, difficult, dubious, fraudulent, frequent, illicit, regular, routine, secret, shady, successful, underhand ~

DEATH
V: be near/ready for/reconciled to/responsible for sb's, bring about sb's, cause, cheat, come near to, condemn sb to, escape, fear, meet, mourn, plot/precipitate/prevent sb's, put sb to, sentence sb to, suffer ~
V: ~ is approaching, awaits sb, came, drew nigh, occurred, took place, took sb away, was a (happy) release
A: agonizing, certain, cruel, early, horrible, imminent, inevitable, instant, lingering, natural, painful, peaceful, premature, slow, sudden, tragic, unexpected, untimely, violent ~
P: ~ penalty, sentence; at *death's* door

DEBATE
V: adjourn, close, conclude, end, engage in, have, hold, interrupt, lead, open, resume, spark off, start, suspend, take part in, win, wind up ~
A: acrimonious, animated, bitter, boring, brief, brilliant, crucial, furious, genuine, heated, inconclusive, interminable, leisurely, lengthy, lively, long, momentous, noisy, open, prolonged, protracted, rational, short, spirited, stormy, tense, vigorous ~

DEBT
V: acknowledge, be in, be weighed down by, collect, discharge, fall into, get into/out of, incur, offset, owe, pay, recover, reduce, repay, run into, run up, settle, take on/over, wipe out, write off ~
V: ~ is due, becomes due
A: bad, enormous, huge, National ~
P: ~ of gratitude/honour

DEBTS
V: accumulate, amass, have, honour, pay off, re-schedule, service ~
V: ~ are mounting up
A: gambling, heavy, staggering, substantial, unmanageable ~

DECAY
V: arrest, deal with, fall into, halt, hasten, prevent, stop, speed up ~
V: ~ set in, spread, started
A: incipient, progressive, serious, widespread ~
DECEPTION
V: discover, perpetrate, prevent, uncover ~
V: ~ came to light
A: barefaced, blatant, bold, deliberate, disgraceful, flagrant, gross ~
DECISION
V: abide by, adhere to, affect, alter, announce, appeal against, approve of, arrive at, be faced
   with, cancel, challenge, change, come to, confirm, contest, defer, endorse, enforce, face,
   form, give, go ahead with, go back on, hesitate over, ignore, implement, justify, lie behind,
   make, overrule, overturn, postpone, prompt, put off, question, ratify, reach, reconsider,
   rescind, reverse, revise, revoke, scrap, take, uphold, vindicate ~
V: ~ depends on ..., is binding/final, opens the way for ..., remains in force, rests with sb, stands,
   takes effect
A: agonizing, arbitrary, basic, binding, clear-cut, conscious, correct, critical, crucial, daring,
   definite, delicate, difficult, emotional, (un)fair, (un)favourable, final, foolhardy, forceful,
   frightening, hard, harsh, hasty, immediate, irreversible, irrevocable, joint, key, landmark,
   lightning, major, momentous, (un)popular, previous, prompt, proper, quick, rash, recent,
   ruthless, sensible, snap, split, straightforward, swift, ultimate, unlawful, unpalatable, vital,
   wise, wrong ~
DECLARATION
V: implement, issue, keep to, make, respect, sign, support, uphold ~
A: blunt, courageous, false, final, firm, frank, fresh, important, joint, open, outspoken,
   preliminary, previous, rousing, solemn, unanimous, unilateral, unsolicited, voluntary ~
DECLINE
V: accelerate, arrest, cause, go into, halt, hasten, lead to, prevent, start, suffer ~
A: gradual, headlong, inevitable, inexorable, marked, nationwide, rapid, serious, sharp, slow,
   spectacular, steady, steep ~
DECREASE
V: bring about, cause, lead to, note, observe, result in, show ~
A: considerable, definite, dramatic, gradual, marked, moderate, notable, overall, rapid,
   regrettable, serious, sharp, (in)significant, slight, slow, steady, substantial, tremendous ~
DECREE
V: issue, lift, pass, rescind, revoke ~
DEDUCTION
V: draw, make, reach ~
A: logical, obvious, sweeping ~
DEED
V: do, perform ~
A: brave, daring, dirty, evil, good, heroic, noble, wicked ~
DEFEAT
V: acknowledge, admit, avert, avoid, bring about, cause, concede, end in, ensure, escape,
   experience, face, inflict, lead to, mark, recover from, result in, suffer ~
A: abject, complete, crucial, crushing, decisive, disastrous, final, heavy, humiliating,
   ignominious, inevitable, narrow, resounding, serious, shattering, staggering, stunning, total ~
P: ~ is staring sb in the face; aftermath of, scale of, scene of, spectre of ~

DEFECT
V: correct, cure, eliminate, eradicate, get rid of, have, make good, notice, rectify, remedy, remove, repair, report, suffer from ~
V: ~ became apparent, is inherent in sth
A: congenital, crucial, glaring, hereditary, incurable, serious, slight ~
P: catalogue of *defects*

DEFENCE
V: annihilate, break down/through, crush, destroy, mount, offer, overcome, pierce, put/set up ~
V: ~ collapsed, failed, held, was useless/of no avail
A: brave, courageous, (in)effective, formidable, heroic, hopeless, masterly, spirited, strong, stubborn, successful, ultimate, weak ~

DEFENCES (military)
V: breach, build up, destroy, erect, get through, outflank, overrun, penetrate ~
A: impenetrable, impregnable, intact ~

DEFENDERS
A: beleaguered, brave, stalwart, staunch, stout ~

DEFICIENCY
V: cover, diagnose, discover, identify, make good, rectify, remedy, reveal, spot, suffer from ~
V: ~ came to light, made itself felt
A: dangerous, decided, important, inherent, marked, obvious, serious, slight ~

DEFICIT
V: accumulate, build up, cut, get rid of, incur, make good, make up, reduce, run up, show, wipe out, write off ~
V: ~ doubled (trebled, etc), increased, widened
A: alarming, enormous, huge, large, narrow, serious ~

DEGREE
V: achieve, gain, have, reach, show, win ~
V: ~ varies
A: amazing, certain, considerable, extreme, fair, great, high, immense, inordinate, large, lesser, major, marked, minor, moderate, similar, slight, small, substantial, wide ~

DEGREE (academic)
V: confer ~ on sb, fail to get, get, have, hold, study for, take, try for, work for ~
A: excellent, first, first class, good, masters, obscure, respectable, satisfactory ~

DELAY
V: apologise for, avoid, cause, expect, experience, face, have, suffer ~
A: long, slight, unavoidable, unexpected ~

DELEGATION
V: appoint, be a member of, belong to, head, lead, recall, send, serve on ~
A: foreign, government, large, official, powerful ~

DELIVERY
V: accept, hold up, include, make, promise, take ~
A: emergency, free, immediate, overnight, prompt, special, urgent ~
P: ~ charge, date, note, point, service; cash on ~ (COD)

DELUSION
V: cling to, labour under ~
A: dangerous, serious ~
P: suffer from *delusions* of grandeur

DEMAND (business)

V: boost, cater for, check, control, create, curb, depress, encourage, estimate, keep track of, keep up with, lessen, match, meet, reduce, regulate, restore, revive, satisfy, step up, stimulate ~

V: ~ is on the increase, developed, diminished, exceeded ..., fell (away/off), fluctuated, grew, increased, outstripped ..., recovered, rose, rocketed, shifted, slowed down

A: changing, constant, current, diminishing, domestic, dwindling, ever-growing, excessive, fluctuating, great, healthy, heavy, huge, poor, potential, (ir)regular, rising, seasonal, soaring, steady, tremendous, unprecedented, urgent, varying, visible ~

P: boom in, collapse in, fall in, rise in, upsurge in, upturn in ~, a big ~ for, supply and ~

DEMAND (request)

V: accede to, accept, acknowledge, agree to, announce, back, be confronted with, be indifferent to, carry out, come out with, comply with, concede, disregard, drop, endorse, enforce, express, fulfil, give in to, give way to, ignore, issue, make, meet, modify, oppose, press, put forward/in, refuse, reiterate, reject, repeat, renew, resist, respond to, satisfy, shelve, soften, stand out against, step up, submit, submit to, surrender to, turn down, voice ~

A: absurd, ambitious, crazy, extortionate, final, firm, forceful, formal, fresh, immediate, inexorable, (un)just, last-minute, modest, (un)official, outrageous, peremptory, powerful, preposterous, ridiculous, sensible, solemn, tough, unacceptable, unavoidable, unprecedented, unreasonable, urgent ~

P: lower/reduce (your) *demands*; excessive, exorbitant, extravagant, repeated, sweeping *demands*

DEMOCRACY

V: abandon, encourage, set up, support ~

A: ~ emerging, nascent

P: spread of, travesty of, triumph of ~

DEMONSTRATION

V: ban, break up, call off, control, deal with, lead, mount, organise, stage, take part in ~

V: ~ got out of hand

A: hostile, huge, mass, noisy, orderly, peaceful, public, spontaneous, violent ~

P: ban on, spate of, wave of *demonstrations*

DENIAL

V: accept, believe, come out with, issue, persist in, reject, repeat, retract, stick by/to ~

V: ~ (failed to) convince sb, persuaded sb, sounded convincing

A: emphatic, firm, flat, indignant, repeated, strenuous, strong, uncompromising ~

DEPARTMENT

V: axe, be in charge of, build (up), expand, manage, move, run, set up, sort out, streamline, work in ~

A: different, newly-formed, personnel/accounts/export etc, separate, special ~

DEPARTURE

V: await, bring forward, cancel, delay, fix, hasten, mark, postpone, put off, signal ~

A: abrupt, delayed, hasty, imminent, mysterious, sudden, undignified, unexpected ~

DEPOSIT (money)

V: ask for, claim ~ back, give, hold sb's, leave, make, pay, put down, require ~

A: cash, (non-)refundable, regular, substantial ~

DEPRESSION (economic)

V: be affected by, be in the grip of, cause, come through, cure, face, find a way out of, get out of, go into/through, head for, survive, weather ~

V: ~ hit sb, loomed, passed

A: acute, alarming, deep, imminent, major, minor, recurrent, serious, severe, worrying ~

DEPRESSION (mental)

V: come out of, conquer, fall into, get over, succumb to, suffer from ~

A: chronic, deep, severe, total ~

P: bout of, state of ~

DERISION

V: be greeted with, be met with, provoke, treat sb with ~

A: total, universal ~

P: howls of, note of, object of, shouts of, target of ~

DESCENT

A: direct, gradual, perilous, rapid, sharp, sudden, swift ~

DESCRIPTION

V: answer to, defy, fit in with, give, issue, match, offer, produce, provide, submit, supply ~

V: ~ is wide of the mark, fits, matches, reminds sb of sth, tallies with ...

A: accurate, apt, clear, colourful, comprehensive, convincing, detailed, dramatic, eye-witness, exact, exhaustive, faithful, false, first-hand, full, lively, misleading, poor, reliable, (un)satisfactory, superficial, systematic, thorough, vague, vivid, wrong ~

DESIGN (pattern)

V: copy, create, have, modify, produce, repeat, spoil ~

A: adaptable, attractive, basic, complicated, conventional, elaborate, elegant, exquisite, geometric, overall, pleasing, poor, simple, superb ~

DESIGN (of machine, etc)

V: adopt, create, follow, introduce, modify, pirate, produce, replace, streamline ~

A: advanced, basic, complicated, conventional, excellent, exciting, imaginative, innovative, modern, old-fashioned, original, out-of-date, revolutionary, simple, standardised, successful, traditional ~

DESIRE

V: arouse, be motivated by, curb, dampen, experience, express, feel, frustrate, fulfil, give way to, have, manifest, overcome, reiterate, resist, satisfy, signal, suppress ~

A: atavistic, burning, compelling, consuming, deep, earnest, faint, fervent, foolish, frustrated, genuine, great, growing, heartfelt, insatiable, instinctive, intense, irresistible, keen, laudable, overpowering, overwhelming, persistent, powerful, recurring, secret, strong, unfulfilled, urgent ~

DESPAIR

V: alleviate, be filled with, be in, cause, drive sb to, feel, give way to, overcome, sink into, succumb to, wallow in ~

V: ~ drove sb to do sth, engulfed/overwhelmed/seized sb

A: black, bottomless, deep, infinite, limitless, profound, sheer, total, utter ~

P: depths of ~

DESTRUCTION

V: carry out, cause, connive at, end in, lead to, plan, prevent, repair, result in, spread, suffer ~

A: accidental, barbaric, deliberate, mass, partial, permanent, ruthless, senseless, serious, swift, systematic, total, unprecedented, wanton, widespread ~

P: trail of, wave of, weapons of mass ~

DETAIL

V: describe every, go into, have an eye for, pay attention to ~

P: richness of, wealth of ~

DETAILS

V: analyse, ascertain, divulge, elicit, examine, explain, fill in, formulate, furnish, give, go into/over, itemise, learn, obtain, offer, omit, overlook, produce, provide, publish, release, reveal, sort out, spare sb, study, supply ~

A: exact, full, gory, graphic, gruesome, harrowing, lurid, mere, minor, minute, petty, precise, (ir)relevant, rough, significant, sordid, technical ~

DETENTE

V: achieve, aim at, bring about, build up, destroy, revive, strive for, threaten, work towards ~

DETERIORATION

V: cause, halt, prevent, see, slow down, speed up, suffer, witness ~

A: dramatic, gradual, progressive, rapid, steady, sudden, terrible, tremendous ~

DETERMINATION

V: be filled with, be full of, feel, have, lack, lose, persist in, show, strengthen, take the edge off, undermine, weaken ~

V: ~ faltered, grew, paid off, waned, wavered, weakened

A: absolute, cold, deadly, dogged, fierce, firm, great, grim, inflexible, marked, ruthless, sheer, single-minded, surprising, total, unswerving ~

DEVALUATION

V: announce, bring about, cause, go in for, decide on, prevent, stop ~

A: modest, serious ~

DEVELOPMENT

V: affect, aid, aim at, arrest, assess, ban, call for, check, control, curb, determine, direct, encourage, ensure, follow, foster, further, give an impetus to, go ahead with, guarantee, halt, hamper, hasten, herald, hinder, influence, inhibit, lay the foundations for, lead to, maintain, mastermind, mould, obstruct, outline, plan, promote, retard, shape, speed up, stimulate, support, undergo ~

V: ~ accelerated, ceased, came to a halt, continued, ground to a halt, improved, proceeded, slowed down, speeded up, stopped, went on

A: all-round, balanced, erratic, extensive, favourable, full, full-scale, haphazard, intensive, ominous, overall, poor, progressive, proper, rapid, recent, (un)satisfactory, smooth, spasmodic, startling, uneven, widespread ~

P: pace of, scale of ~

DEVELOPMENTS (events)

V: await, follow, jeopardize, wait for ~

A: further, latest, ominous, recent, startling, unforeseen ~

DEVICE

V: adapt, adopt, design, employ, fit, install, invent, hit upon, resort to, use ~

V: ~ works

A: ancient, artificial, clever, complicated, crafty, cunning, handy, imaginative, ingenious, labour-saving, machiavellian, simple, sophisticated, tricky, unusual, useful ~

DEVOTION

V: demonstrate, prove, show ~

A: absolute, blind, boundless, complete, deep, eternal, fervent, great, selfless, slavish, undying, unstinting, unswerving, utter ~

DIAGNOSIS

V: arrive at, attempt, confirm, give, look for, make, make a mistake in, offer, produce ~

A: accurate, confident, correct, definite, faulty, mistaken, penetrating, preliminary, proper, quick, right, rough, sensible, swift, tentative, wrong ~

DIAGRAM
V: draw, examine, make, produce, refer to, study ~
V: ~ demonstrates, illustrates, makes clear, shows
A: clear, detailed, rough ~
P: the ~ above/below/opposite
DIALOGUE
V: call for, conduct, end, enter into, hold, take part in ~
A: friendly, lengthy, meaningful, meaningless, protracted, useful, useless ~
DIARY
V: keep, publish ~
A: fascinating, genuine, intimate, personal, regular, secret ~
DICTATORSHIP
V: establish, fight against, live under, overthrow, rule by, set up ~
A: absolute, benevolent, brutal, military, ruthless ~
DICTIONARY
V: compile, consult, look up, produce, refer to, revise, update, use ~
A: bi-lingual, children's, collocation, comprehensive, concise, corpus-based, EFL, electronic, English-English, excellent, extensive, handy, picture, pocket, poor, reliable, specialised ~
DIET
V: be on, change, follow, go on, improve, put sb on, recommend, stick to, supplement ~
A: balanced, crash, fat-free, (un)healthy, high-fibre, inadequate, low calorie, natural, nutritious, poor, rich, special, starvation, steady, strict ~
DIFFERENCE
V: accentuate, appreciate, be aware of, blur, bring out, define, distinguish, eliminate, exaggerate, highlight, ignore, intensify, level out, magnify, make, make ~ clear, note, notice, observe, overcome, perceive, pinpoint, point out, recognise, reduce, reinforce, reveal, see, sharpen, tell, transcend, underline, widen ~
V: ~ arises, consists of ..., cropped up, disappears, emerged, exists, grew, increased, lies in sth, stands out (clearly), vanishes
A: all-important, apparent, basic, chief, clear, confusing, considerable, crucial, decided, distinct, enormous, essential, extreme, fundamental, glaring, great, huge, important, infinitesimal, inherent, innate, interesting, intrinsic, irrelevant, main, major, marked, material, minor, noticeable, obvious, palpable, (im)perceptible, profound, pronounced, qualitative, quantitative, radical, real, regrettable, serious, sharp, significant, slight, striking, substantial, superficial, tremendous, true, visible, vital ~
P: a ~ of opinion, a ~ in degree/kind
DIFFERENCES (eg of opinion)
V: exploit, gloss over, have, make up, patch up, put aside, reconcile, resolve, settle, thrash out ~
V: ~ crystallized, hardened, occurred, resolved themselves
A: deep, irreconcilable, profound, regrettable, sharp, violent ~
DIFFICULTY
V: acknowledge, be confronted/faced with, come across, deal with, discover, encounter, exaggerate, face, get over, get rid of, gloss over, handle, have, ignore, make light of, meet, overcome, realise, see, tackle ~
V: ~ arose, cropped up, defeated/deterred/discouraged/intimidated sb, emerged, resolved itself
A: acute, appalling, considerable, extreme, formidable, frightening, great, imaginary, inherent, insoluble, insurmountable, insuperable, overwhelming, serious, slight, tremendous, unforeseen, unfortunate ~

DIFFICULTIES (obstacles)

V: be aware of, brush aside, cope with, create, exaggerate, experience, find oneself in, get into, make, present, raise, run into ~

V: ~ crowded in, are mounting up, multiplied, overwhelmed sb, are piling up, proliferated, stand in the way, terrified sb, vanished

DILEMMA

V: avoid, be confronted with/faced with, create, deal with, encounter, face, find oneself in, get out of, land in, place sb in, pose, resolve ~

V: ~ arose, occurred

A: agonizing, awkward, bewildering, difficult, grave, hopeless, painful, serious ~

DIMENSIONS

V: give, have, measure, state, supply ~

A: approximate, awkward, basic, exact, harmonious, imposing, maximum, minimum, pleasing, rough ~

DIPLOMA

V: be awarded, get, grant, have, issue, obtain, present, receive, study for, work for ~

DIRECTION

V: alter, change, determine, deviate from, fix, follow, go in/off in, indicate, keep to, lose, mark, move in, plot, set, shift, show, take ~

A: customary, definite, general, obvious, opposite, precise, proper, reverse, right, straightforward, wrong ~

DIRECTIONS (instructions)

V: follow, get, give, go against, ignore, issue, lay down, misunderstand, (dis)obey, question ~

A: ambiguous, clear, conflicting, confused, confusing, contradictory, definite, detailed, explicit, firm, misleading, precise, straightforward, unequivocal, vague ~

DIRECTIVE

V: adopt, carry out, draft, fulfil, implement, issue, obey, send out ~

A: (un)ambiguous, clear, draft, detailed, explicit, final, immediate, plain, precise, preliminary ~

DISABILITY

V: aggravate, compensate for, cure, fight, have, incur, overcome, suffer from ~

V: ~ prevents sb from doing sth

A: congenital, dangerous, distressing, grave, permanent, serious, severe, slight, temporary, total, worrying ~

DISADVANTAGE

V: accept, be aware of, compensate for, constitute, disregard, get over/round, have, ignore, involve, labour under, lead to, make up for, offset, outweigh, overcome, put up with, realise, remove, suffer, suffer from ~

A: chief, definite, main, marked, principal, serious, slight, unfortunate ~

DISAGREEMENT

V: cause, express, prevent, result in, sow ~

V: ~ was rife

A: deep, fundamental, growing, increasing, profound, sharp, total, violent ~

P: basis of, grounds for ~

DISAGREEMENT (slight quarrel)

V: get over, have ~ with sb, heal, lead to, make ~ public, resolve, result in, settle, solve ~

V: ~ arose, broke out, occurred, surfaced

A: bitter, fierce, lasting, nasty, painful, serious, slight, unpleasant ~

P: area of, cause of, reason for, source of ~

DISAPPEARANCE
V: bring about, cause, conceal, effect, engineer, explain, lead to ~
A: abrupt, mysterious, sudden, unexplained ~

DISAPPOINTMENT
V: cause, experience, express, feel, get, get over, have, make up for, offset, prevent, put up with, soften, suffer ~
A: big, bitter, deep, great, painful, profound, serious, slight, tremendous, unexpected ~

DISAPPROVAL
V: arouse, cause, evoke, express, feel, give rise to, incur, lead to, meet with, mitigate, sense, show, voice ~
A: deep, definite, evident, general, instant, loud, obvious, open, popular, serious, severe, total, universal, widespread ~

DISARMAMENT
V: achieve, agree on, discuss, strive for, work for/towards ~
A: complete, general, multilateral, nuclear, partial, phased, total, unilateral, universal ~

DISASTER (in general)
V: avoid, cope with, court, end in, head for, lead to, recover from, result in, ward off ~
V: ~ lies ahead, loomed, overcame sb, struck, threatened
A: catastrophic, complete, devastating, imminent, impending, inevitable, major, minor, national, natural, near, sheer, total, tragic, unmitigated, unqualified, utter ~
P: on the verge of ~

DISASTER (a single misfortune)
V: avert, cause, meet with, mitigate, overcome, precipitate, result in, suffer ~
V: ~ ensued, happened, occurred, took place
A: fatal, grave, humiliating, incalculable, irretrievable, overwhelming, potential, serious, terrible, tragic, unforeseen, unprecedented ~
P: aftermath of, scale of ~; catalogue of, crop of, sequence of, series of, succession of *disasters*

DISBELIEF
V: shake one's head in ~
A: complete, total, utter ~
P: cries of, gasps of, groans of ~

DISCIPLINE
V: accept, apply, call for, establish, exercise, expect, get, impose, keep, maintain, obey, observe, rebel against, relax, subject sb to, submit to, tighten, undermine ~
V: ~ broke down, got better/worse, improved
A: effective, excessive, firm, good, hard, harsh, lax, poor, rigid, rigorous, severe, slack, strict ~

DISCLOSURES
A: frank, sensational, startling ~

DISCOMFORT
V: aggravate, alleviate, bear, cause, suffer ~
A: considerable, extreme, mild, minor, slight, unbearable ~

DISCONTENT
V: add to, aggravate, air, anticipate, arouse, cause, counter, divert, express, feel, gauge, generate, give rise to, harbour, increase, lead to, make for, prevent, produce, renew, sow, spread, stir up, vent ~
V: ~ arose, boiled over/up, caused ..., erupted, made itself felt, quietened down, simmered, spread, vanished, was caused by sth
A: considerable, general, grave, great, growing, increasing, public, serious, universal, widespread ~

DISCOUNT
V: agree, ask for, be available at, give, get, negotiate, offer, sell (off) at ~
A: generous, high, modest, (20) percent, special, student, usual ~
DISCOVERY
V: make, publish, report ~
V: ~ came to light
A: amazing, appalling, disconcerting, dramatic, dreadful, earth-shattering, exciting, exhilarating, famous, genuine, great, horrible, horrific, incredible, ingenious, major, obvious, (un)pleasant, revolutionary, sensational, startling, terrible, tremendous, unexpected, unique, wonderful, worrying ~
DISCREPANCY
V: come across, diminish, discover, do away with, find, ignore, indicate, note, notice, perceive, point out, remove, reveal, show, widen ~
A: considerable, distinct, disturbing, fundamental, glaring, growing, important, inherent, marked, obvious, serious, slight, striking, surprising, unfortunate ~
DISCRETION
V: exercise, handle sth with, leave sth to sb's, show, use ~
A: complete, total, utmost ~
DISCUSSION
V: avoid, begin, be under, break off, call for, carry on, come under, complete, (dis)continue, conduct, cut short, embark on, encourage, end, engage in, enliven, enter into, get involved in, give rise to, hold, initiate, instigate, interrupt, join in, lead, lead to, liven up, monopolise, need, open, organise, proceed to, prolong, provoke, put an end/a stop to, resume, start, start off, stop, summarise, sum up, take part in, terminate, wind up ~
V: ~ began, centres on ..., came to a close, continues, developed, ended, livened up, petered out, resumed, switched to ..., went on
A: absorbing, acrimonious, amicable, animated, boring, brief, broad, careful, comprehensive, confidential, detailed, earnest, endless, exploratory, fierce, final, frank, free-ranging, fresh, friendly, frivolous, fruitful, full, full and frank, furious, healthy, heated, helpful, inconclusive, intense, intensive, interminable, lengthy, long, loud, noisy, one-sided, open, orderly, painful, pointless, protracted, quiet, rambling, rational, reasonable, renewed, sensible, serious, stimulating, stormy, superfluous, unbiased, unnecessary, useful, useless, violent, wide-ranging ~
DISEASE
V: aggravate, alleviate, be struck down by/worn out by, be the victim of, carry, cause, combat, come down with, contract, control, cure, diagnose, die of, eradicate, fall ill with, fall prey to/victim to, fight, guard against, have, identify, inoculate sb against, pass on, prevent, spread, succumb to, suffer from, transmit, treat, wipe out ~
V: ~ affects/afflicts/attacks sb, broke out, claimed (victims), disappeared, got out of hand, incapacitated sb, is carried by sb/sth, is prevalent, is rampant, is widespread, kills, manifests itself, paralyses, spread, struck
A: chronic, (un)common, communicable, congenital, contagious, cruel, dangerous, deadly, degenerative, endemic, fatal, grave, hereditary, incurable, infectious, killer, malignant, mysterious, obscure, painful, progressive, rare, recurrent, sexually transmitted, unfamiliar, untreatable, venereal, virulent, wasting ~
P: detection of, immunity from, incidence of, onset of, outbreak of, prone to, spread of, susceptible to, susceptibility to, virulence of ~

DISGRACE
V: bring ~ on sb, fall into, get over, suffer ~
A: absolute, deep, dire, public, terrible, total ~

DISGUISE
V: adopt, assume, be in, don, put on, see through, shed, take off, throw off ~
A: brilliant, clever, cunning, feeble, ridiculous, thin ~

DISGUST
V: air, cause, conceal, disguise, exhibit, express, feel, show, vent ~
A: deep, profound, total ~

DISINTEGRATION
V: bring about, cause, detect, end in, lead to, result in ~
A: complete, incipient, progressive, total ~

DISLIKE
V: conceal, conceive, develop, disguise, express, feel, get over, have ~ for, hide, overcome, show, state ~ , take ~ to
A: active, deep, deep-rooted, great, hearty, instinctive, intense, marked, selfish, strong, unconcealed, violent ~

DISMAY
V: cause, express, feel, fill sb with, voice ~
A: deep, profound, total, utter, widespread ~

DISOBEDIENCE
V: be guilty of, punish, tolerate ~
A: open, rank, wilful ~

DISORDER
V: cause, deal with, encourage, handle, incite, put down, suppress, whip up ~
V: ~ broke out, got out of hand, took place
A: serious, violent, widespread ~

DISPLAY
V: admire, give, make, provide, put on ~
V: ~ impressed sb
A: brave, dazzling, elaborate, extravagant, fine, gallant, gaudy, glittering, imposing, impressive, indecent, lavish, magnificent, marvellous, modest, ostentatious, rare, remarkable, shocking, spectacular, splendid, stupendous, vulgar, wonderful ~

DISPLEASURE
V: arouse, brave, cause, hide, incur, show ~
A: deep, serious ~

DISPOSITION (character)
A: benevolent, cheerful, easy-going, energetic, friendly, irritable, lazy, nervous, pleasant, sunny ~

DISPUTE
V: abandon, aggravate, arbitrate in, be engaged in/locked in, cause, decide, end, get involved in, give rise to, influence, intensify, intervene in, lead to, provoke, put an end to, resolve, settle, spark off, take part in, terminate ~
V: ~ arose, blew up, broke out, cropped up, developed, erupted, escalated, flared up, loomed, was put to arbitration, went on
A: acrimonious, bitter, brief, damaging, fierce, heated, long, long-drawn-out, long-standing, mild, prolonged, petty, senseless, sharp, simmering, slight, ugly, unlawful, violent ~
P: heart of, key to, reason for ~

DISQUIET
V: cause, conquer, express, feel, give rise to, relieve, soothe, voice ~
A: considerable, obvious, profound, serious ~

DISSATISFACTION
V: cause, express, feel, voice ~
A: deep, general, growing, keen, profound, widespread ~

DISSENT
V: express, show, silence, suppress, tolerate ~
A: strong ~

DISTANCE
V: calculate, cover, cut, estimate, increase, mark, measure, note, reckon, record, reduce, shorten, widen ~
V: ~ grew, shrank
A: approximate, considerable, exact, good, great, overall, precise, safe ~
P: within shouting, striking, walking ~

DISTASTE
V: develop, express, feel, look at sb/sth with, show ~
A: faint, growing, strong, violent ~

DISTINCTION
V: be aware of, blur, draw, draw attention to, emphasise, feel, ignore, make, note, obliterate, observe, perceive, point out/to, recognise, see, stress ~
A: arbitrary, artificial, basic, clear, clear-cut, crude, definite, dubious, essential, fine, formal, fundamental, important, key, main, meaningful, obvious, precise, primary, real, slight, subtle, underlying, valid ~

DISTRESS
V: alleviate, cause, ease, feel, get over, occasion, relieve, suffer ~
A: acute, considerable, deep, great, growing, obvious, serious, severe ~

DISTRIBUTION
V: arrange for, control, hamper, increase, organise ~
V: ~ broke down, collapsed, worked
A: chaotic, (in)efficient, equitable, even, erratic, (un)fair, international, limited, proper, (ir)regular, (un)satisfactory, uniform, wide, worldwide ~
P: ~ channels, costs, network, system

DISTRUST
V: arouse, awaken, feel, get over, overcome ~
A: deep, deep-rooted, immediate, instinctive, irrational, mutual, profound ~

DISTURBANCE
V: cause, create, deal with, give rise to, handle, put down, stir up ~
V: ~ broke out, died down, erupted, occurred, took place
A: racial, serious, violent ~

DIVERGENCE
V: lessen, minimise, reduce ~
A: grave, growing, sharp, wide ~

DIVIDEND
V: announce, declare, offer, pay (out), receive ~
A: annual, enormous, healthy, poor, quarterly, regular ~

DIVISION (disagreement)

V: aggravate, create, heal, narrow, widen ~

V: ~ arose, came about, occurred, took place

A: deep, intractable ~

DIVISION (distribution)

V: abolish, do away with, create, draw, form, make, mark, see ~

A: clear, clear-cut, conventional, distinct, equitable, fair, glaring, rough, sharp, superficial, wide, yawning ~

DIVORCE

V: apply for, be involved in, contest, file for, get, grant, obtain, seek ~

V: ~ came through, is pending, was made absolute

A: amicable, damaging, messy, uncontested ~

P: ~ settlement

DOCTRINE

V: abandon, adhere to, adopt, advocate, apply, believe, believe in, counter, deny, discard, disseminate, espouse, establish, expound, fight, hold, hold to, inculcate, instil, invent, keep to, obey, oppose, overthrow, preach, proclaim, put forward, reject, spread, stick to, subscribe to, support, teach, test, undermine, uphold, work out ~

A: basic, dangerous, explosive, fallible, false, harmful, hateful, heretical, narrow, noxious, (un)orthodox, political, religious, revolutionary, rival, sound, startling, strict, traditional, universal, usual, useful, useless ~

DOCUMENT

V: annotate, check, circulate, clarify, complete, conceal, copy, draft, draw up, examine, falsify, file, forge, glance through, go over, inspect, interpret, issue, look up, mislay, obtain, pass over, peruse, piece together, possess, prepare, produce, question, receive, refer to, release, retrieve, scan, scrutinize, sign, stamp, store, submit, suppress, study, vet, withdraw, withhold ~

V: ~ is circulating, details/proves/records/reveals/states/suggests that ...

A: authentic, classified, compromising, confidential, dangerous, detailed, fake, false, forged, fresh, genuine, historic, important, incriminating, key, lengthy, missing, necessary, obscure, official, original, relevant, revealing, sensational, sensitive, subversive, suspicious, top-secret, valid, vital ~

P: armful of, batch of, bundle of, cache of, hoard of, pile of, series of, set of, sheaf of *documents*

DOG

V: breed, keep, keep ~ under control, mistreat, muzzle, train, walk ~

V: ~ is barking, bit sb, growled, howled, savaged sb, snapped, snarled, was put down, whimpered, whined, yelped

A: family, fierce-looking, friendly, mad, pedigree, rabid, savage, stray, vicious ~

DOMINANCE

V: accept, achieve, acknowledge, challenge, enjoy, establish, exert, exploit, (re)gain, maintain, recognise, rebel against, reject, submit to, take advantage of, threaten, undermine ~

V: ~ declined, dwindled, grew

A: clear, definite, great, lasting, marked ~

DOMINATION

V: assert, break, challenge, come under, destroy, establish, exert, extend, fight, gain, get rid of, impose, live under, lose, maintain, oppose, rebel against, resist, struggle against, suffer under ~

A: foreign ~

DOOR
V: answer, break down, close, force, kick ~ in, knock on, (un)lock, open, shut, slam ~
A: glass, heavy, open, revolving, sliding, solid, thick ~

DOSE
V: administer, decrease, give, increase, measure out, prescribe, take ~
A: correct, fatal, lethal, recommended ~

DOUBT (in general)
V: cast ~ on sth, experience, express, feel, have no, imply, raise, remove, spread ~
V: ~ arose, crept in, exists, grew, lurked in sb's mind, persisted, remained, surrounds sth
A: growing, profound, real, serious ~
P: beyond reasonable/a shadow of ~

DOUBTS (personal)
V: air, clear up, conceal, confirm, dismiss, dispel, disperse, entertain, express, feed, get rid of, give way to, overcome, put ~ behind sb, raise, resolve, suppress, voice ~
V: ~ arose, centre on ..., concern ..., cropped up, crystallized, disappeared, grew, haunted sb, prevented sb from doing sth, remain, revolve around ..., tormented sb, troubled sb, vanished
A: grave, growing, lingering, nagging, niggling, passing, persistent, serious, slight ~

DOWNFALL
V: accelerate, be behind, be the cause of, bring about, cause, engineer, hasten, lead to, mark, plot, prevent, result in ~
A: certain, immediate, inevitable, sudden, total, unexpected ~

DRAFT
V: alter, amend, check, correct, draw up, make, prepare, produce, publish ~
A: final, first, preliminary, rough ~

DRAWBACK
V: overcome, pinpoint, suffer from ~
A: biggest, important, main, serious ~

DREAD
V: fill sb with, live in ~
A: constant, great ~

DREAM (in sleep)
V: have, interpret, interrupt, recall ~
V: ~ came to sb, faded, means ...
A: bad, beautiful, colourful, confused, confusing, disturbing, horrible, prophetic, realistic, recurrent, strange, vivid ~

DREAM (of the future)
V: achieve, chase, cherish, dispel, fulfil, indulge in, realise, shatter, sustain, wreck ~
V: ~ collapsed, came to nothing, came true, dissolved, receded, vanished
A: childhood, (un)realistic, rosy, vague, wonderful ~

DRESS
A: battle, casual, elegant, evening, fancy, fashionable, (in)formal, national, smart, traditional ~
P: ~ code, sense

DRIVE
V: be engaged in, conduct, initiate, launch, make, mount, organise ~
A: big, massive, recruitment ~

DROP
A: alarming, big, dramatic, marked, noticeable, perceptible, rapid, sharp, sudden, swift, tremendous ~

DRUG
V: administer, develop, discover, prescribe, research, take, test ~
A: (non-)addictive, effective, (non-)habit-forming, mild, miracle, powerful, prescription, prescribed, restricted, strong, weak, wonder ~
P: ~ abuse, addict, addiction, culture, pusher, problem, smuggler, smuggling, trafficking, trials; the side effects of the ~

DRUGS
V: be on, come off, peddle, push, smuggle, supply, take, traffic in ~
A: dangerous, designer, hard, illegal, illicit, soft ~

DUST
V: be covered in, collect, crumble into, gather, raise ~
V: ~ collected, settled
P: cloud of, layer of, particle of, speck of ~

DUTY (moral)
V: be aware of, be conscious of, do, forget, fulfil, know, neglect, remind sb of ~
P: breach of, dedication to, dereliction of, devotion to, sense of ~

DUTY (task)
V: allocate, allot, apportion, assign, assume, carry out, delegate, discharge, free sb from, fulfil, give up, have, impose, neglect, perform, relieve sb of, remind sb of, shirk, take on/over ~
V: ~ devolves upon sb, weighed sb down
A: boring, civic, grim, heavy, moral, official, onerous, painful, (un)pleasant, professional, regular, sad, solemn, statutory, tiresome, trivial, voluntary ~

E

EARNINGS
V: declare, have, increase, save, spend, squander, supplement ~
A: adequate, annual, average, full-/part-time, gross, high, increased, low, net, overtime, real, reduced, regular, satisfactory, total ~

ECHO
V: produce, send back ~
A: distant, disturbing, faint, muffled, rumbling ~

ECONOMY
V: affect, assist, boost, change, control, depress, develop, drain, expand, hit, influence, kickstart, (mis)manage, mishandle, paralyse, plan, prop up, put the brakes on, reflate, reform, regulate, rejuvenate, reorganise, repair, restore, revive, run, sabotage, salvage, steer, stimulate, straighten out, strain, transform, wreck ~
V: ~ is booming, collapsed, contracted, expanded, flourished, is on the mend, is picking up, plummeted, prospered, recovered, slowed down, stagnated, is thriving
A: advanced, ailing, backward, booming, buoyant, command, crumbling, depressed, deteriorating, entire, fast-growing, flagging, fragile, global, healthy, inefficient, market, mixed, primitive, prosperous, run-down, shaky, shattered, sick, sluggish, sound, stagnant, strong, Third World, vigorous, weak ~
P: boost to, imbalance in, mismanagement of, mobilization of, (poor) performance of, revival of, slump in, state of, upturn in ~

ECONOMY (saving)
V: call for, exercise, practise ~
A: false, rigid, strict ~
P: ~ drive
EDITION
V: bring out, issue, launch, prepare, print, publish, put out ~
V: ~ appeared, came out, was published
A: (un)abridged, cheap, compact, critical, deluxe, earlier, expanded, first, hardback, illustrated, latest, limited, low-priced, luxury, new, omnibus, paperback, pirate, pocket, popular, private, recent, revised, unexpurgated ~
EDUCATION
V: improve, make cuts in, neglect, prioritise, provide, put money into, reform, revolutionise, spread ~
A: adult, compulsory, continuing, free, further, higher, primary, private, professional, religious, secondary, sex, state, universal, university, vocational, widespread ~
EDUCATION (of an individual)
V: broaden, complete, finish, get, give, have the benefit of/the advantage of, interrupt, neglect, provide sb with, receive, waste ~
V: ~ equipped (him) to ... , teaches/trains (you) to ... , widens (your) horizons
A: (in)adequate, all-round, basic, broad, classical, excellent, general, good, liberal, narrow, one-sided, poor, progressive, restricted, rudimentary, thorough ~
EFFECT
V: aggravate, aim at, alleviate, ameliorate, amplify, assess, attribute, avoid, be worried about, bring about, bring sth into, cancel, cancel out, compound, counter, counteract, cover up, cushion, deplore, destroy, draw attention to, emphasise, enhance, ensure, envisage, estimate, examine, exert, give, have, heighten, ignore, jeopardize, lead to, lessen, magnify, make, mar, maximise, minimise, mitigate, observe, offset, prevent, produce, provoke, recover from, reduce, reproduce, show, soften, spoil, stem from, study, suffer from, sum up, underestimate ~
V: ~ (dis)appeared, became evident, developed, faded, is due to sth, lasted, persisted, reverberated, subsided, tailed off, wore off
A: acute, advantageous, adverse, alienating, astounding, bad, beneficial, bewildering, catastrophic, cathartic, chief, combined, confusing, conspicuous, corrosive, crippling, crushing, cumulative, damaging, dazzling, deadly, debilitating, decisive, desired, destructive, deterrent, devastating, diffuse, (in)direct, disarming, disastrous, disruptive, dramatic, dubious, evil, excellent, exhilarating, faint, far-reaching, (un)fortunate, full, general, good, harmful, hilarious, immediate, important, imposing, incalculable, inhibiting, iniquitous, inspiring, instant, instantaneous, knock-on, lasting, lethal, likely, limited, long/medium/short-term, magical, main, minimal, notable, noticeable, obnoxious, obvious, odd, overall, paralysing, permanent, placebo, poor, practical, (un)predictable, profound, pronounced, rare, remarkable, remedial, reverse, ruinous, salutary, sharp, shattering, shocking, side, significant, sinister, speedy, staggering, startling, stimulating, striking, strong, stultifying, stunning, subsequent, surprising, telling, terrible, terrifying, theatrical, traumatic, unexpected, visible, widespread ~
EFFECTIVENESS
V: add to, assess, cast doubt on, check, destroy, diminish, enhance, improve, increase, measure, promote, reduce, restrict, spoil, test ~
V: ~ diminished, increased, varied

EFFICIENCY
V: assess, bring about, encourage, impair, improve, increase, lose, promote, raise, reduce, reward, step up ~
V: ~ is falling, grew, improved
A: all-round, great, peak, outstanding, real, remarkable ~

EFFORT (expenditure of energy)
V: call for, devote, exert, expend, need, put ~ into sth, put in, repay, require, sustain ~
V: ~ paid off, was wasted, was worth it, was worthwhile
A: considerable, great, maximum, minimal, real, tremendous ~

EFFORT (with *a/an*)
V: make ~
V: ~ failed, succeeded
A: abortive, all-out, ambitious, big, brave, ceaseless, concerted, concentrated, conscious, conscientious, covert, desperate, effective, final, frantic, gallant, half-hearted, initial, joint, last, major, massive, mighty, real, special, successful, supreme, sustained, team, ultimate, unceasing, vain ~

EFFORTS
V: back, combine, concentrate, consolidate, continue, co-ordinate, dedicate, defy, devote, direct, double, extol, frustrate, give up, hamper, harness, make, oppose, persist in, rebuff, redouble, spoil, stimulate, thwart, undermine, undo, waste ~
V: ~ are under way, backfired, bore fruit, came to a halt, came to nothing, failed, foundered, lead to ... , received a setback, resulted in ... , succeed, were of no avail, were rewarded
A: abortive, agonizing, arduous, careful, combined, conscientious, consistent, constructive, continual, co-operative, covert, creditable, crude, desperate, determined, disastrous, energetic, faltering, feeble, feverish, frantic, frenzied, futile, gallant, gruelling, half-hearted, heroic, intensive, modest, piecemeal, prolonged, sterling, strenuous, strong, successful, superhuman, sustained, tedious, tireless, tremendous, unavailing, united, untiring, valiant, vigorous, wasted, well-meaning ~

EGO
V: boost, dent, feed, flatter, hurt ~
A: bruised, enormous, fragile, inflated, massive ~
P: ~ trip

ELATION
V: fill with ~
A: sheer ~
P: look of, mood of, surge of ~

ELECTION
V: call, call for, concede, contest, decide, disrupt, enter, fight, fix, have, hold, lose, organise, postpone, rig, swing, vote in, win ~
V: ~ came round, came up, is pending, loomed
A: close, closely fought, hotly contested ~
P: ~ campaign, fever; run-up to ~

ELECTRICITY
V: conduct, cut off, generate, produce, provide, waste ~
V: ~ flowed
A: static ~
P: crackle of, flow of, surge of ~; a build-up of static ~

ELEMENT (factor)

V: find, perceive ~

V: ~ appeared, arose, came to the fore, crept in, cropped up

A: basic, critical, crucial, curious, dangerous, encouraging, extraneous, frightening, fundamental, human, important, key, odd, permanent, puzzling, significant, startling, strange, surprising, unavoidable, uncommon, underlying, unexpected, unique, unusual, vital, volatile, worrying ~

ELEMENTS (parts)

V: assemble, be comprised of, combine, differentiate, discern, discover, distinguish, find, notice, reduce sth to (its) ~

A: basic, complicated, component, conflicting, constituent, contrasting, critical, crucial, disparate, diverse, essential, fundamental, identical, individual, interlocking, main, principal, separate, dissimilar ~

ELITE

V: become one of, join ~

A: small, intellectual, privileged, ruling, social ~

P: member of ~

EMBARGO

V: break through, get round, impose, lift, order, place/put an ~ on, raise, remove, tighten ~

A: immediate, strict, total ~

EMBARRASSMENT

V: apologise for, cause, conceal, die of, disguise, feel, get over, get rid of, give rise to, hide, prevent, relieve, show ~

V: ~ grew, was evident/obvious

A: acute, constant, faint, great, perpetual, profound, serious, unwitting ~

EMBRACE

A: close, lingering, long, loving, passionate, tender, tight, warm ~

EMERGENCY

V: avert, cause, cope with, create, deal with, declare, face, foresee, handle, lead to, meet, prepare for ~

V: ~ arose, cropped up, is over, occurred, passed, took place

A: serious, sudden ~

P: to declare a state of, lift the state of ~

EMINENCE

V: achieve, reach, rise to, win ~

A: great, true ~

EMOTION

V: be blinded/carried away/overcome/ruled by, contain, control, curb, experience, express, feel, generate, give way to, hide, master, show, speak with, stir up, suppress, whip up ~

V: ~ got the better of sb, overcame sb, ran away with sb, was infectious

A: deep, exalted, heady, intense, overpowering, passionate, pent-up, powerful, strong, unguarded ~

P: display of, flicker of, flood of, rush of, show of, upsurge of ~

EMOTIONS

V: appeal to, be guided by/swayed by, disguise, give in to, keep a tight rein on, keep hold of, pander to ~

A: conflicting, mixed, strong, volatile ~

EMPHASIS
V: give ~ to, lay ~ on sth, place ~ on sth, put ~ on sth, shift ~
A: great, growing, heavy, increasing, main, particular, sharp, special, strong, unnecessary ~
P: shift of ~
EMPIRE
V: add to, belong to, break up, build, conquer, destroy, dismantle, establish, expand, found, get
    rid of, give up, govern, rule, rule over, set up ~
V: ~ collapsed, came into being, came into existence, crumbled, disintegrated, embraced ... ,
    expanded, fell, grew, lasted
A: ancient, business, far-flung, great, huge, mighty, powerful ~
P: decline of, downfall of, fall of, heyday of ~
EMPLOYEE
V: discipline, dismiss, engage, fire, hire, lay off, let ~ go, make ~ redundant, recruit, sack, take
    on, train ~
A: full-time, loyal, part-time ~
EMPLOYMENT
V: boost, create, encourage, find, generate, get, give, give up, guarantee, look for, obtain,
    provide, seek, stimulate, take up ~
A: available, casual, full, full-/half-/part-time, regular, seasonal, steady, suitable ~
ENCOUNTER
A: bloody, brief, casual, chance, close, emotional, exciting, famous, fruitful, lucky, moving,
    mysterious, remarkable, risky, sexual, strange, sudden, unexpected, unfortunate, upsetting ~
ENCOURAGEMENT
V: derive, find, give, need, offer, provide, seek ~
A: constant, every, great, guarded, much, unfailing ~
END
V: accomplish, achieve, serve, work towards ~
A: common, desirable, desired, distant, (un)selfish, ultimate ~
ENDEAVOUR
V: appreciate, back, direct, encourage, further, give up, intensify, keep up, persist in, reward,
    step up, stop, support, use ~
A: bold, desperate, earnest, energetic, feeble, frantic, heroic, intensive, intermittent, noble,
    persistent, previous, prolonged, sincere, unwelcome, useless ~
ENDORSEMENT
V: get, give, obtain, receive, seek, win, withdraw ~
A: definite, enthusiastic, firm, full, immediate, prompt, (un)qualified, warm ~
ENDURANCE
V: be beyond, build up, have, show, stretch, test ~
A: colossal, great, patient, remarkable ~
P: limits of, powers of ~
ENEMY
V: ambush, annihilate, attack, beat, beat off, confront, conquer, crush, deceive, defeat, defy,
    destroy, deter, disperse, encircle, encounter, engage, face, fight, get the better of, harass,
    harbour, head off, kill, make, mislead, outflank, outmanoeuvre, outwit, overcome, placate,
    repel, repulse, resist, rout, surround ~
A: aggressive, arch, bitter, chief, crafty, cunning, dangerous, determined, formidable,
    implacable, lifelong, mortal, mutual, natural, powerful, redoubtable, ruthless, superior,
    sworn, traditional, treacherous, worst ~

ENERGY
V: apply, be bursting with, be full of, build up, conserve, consume, derive ~ from sth, (re)direct, generate, get, give, have got, lack, put ~ into doing sth, release, sap, save, spend, use, waste ~
A: boundless, excess, great, latent, limitless, overflowing, sufficient, tremendous, unfailing ~
P: burst of, lack of ~; channel (your) *energies* into (work)

ENGINE
V: cut, kill, lubricate, operate, recondition, repair, replace, rev (up), run, service, stall, start, stop, switch off/on, tune, turn off/on, turn ~ over, warm up, wear out, wreck ~
V: ~ broke down, died, flooded, functioned, overheated, rattled, runs on (fuel), stalled, was idling, works
A: diesel, electric, jet, noisy, powerful, quiet, steam, under-powered ~
P: ~ failure, problems

ENJOYMENT
V: curb, derive, destroy, express, get, give, inhibit, kill, mar, provide, restrict, spoil, stop ~
A: evident, full, genuine, great, immense, personal, real, total, tremendous, true ~

ENQUIRIES
V: assist in, complete, conclude, follow up, handle, instigate, make, pursue, spark off ~
A: anxious, complex, detailed, discreet, door-to-door, energetic, exhaustive, extensive, full-scale, high/top-level, immediate, impartial, inconclusive, internal, lengthy, official, routine, searching, (un)successful, thorough, time-consuming ~
P: flood of ~

ENQUIRY (investigation – with *an*)
V: adjourn, attend, call for, conduct, hold, launch, order, press for, set up, suspend, take part in ~
A: Government, impartial, lengthy, official, police, public, secret, top-level, undercover ~

ENTERPRISE
V: abandon, embark on, undertake ~
A: adventurous, ambitious, audacious, bold, challenging, dangerous, daring, foolhardy, rash ~

ENTERTAINMENT
V: offer, provide, put on ~
A: brilliant, dazzling, intriguing, lavish, live, magnificent, modest, sophisticated ~

ENTHUSIASM
V: arouse, be full of, bubble with, cause, create, curb, dampen, exhibit, express, feel, fill sb with, generate, give rise to, inspire sb with, keep up, lose, meet with, profess ~ for, radiate, show, stir up, temper ~
V: ~ caught on, died down, faded, flagged, is exhausted, lasted, spread, subsided, vanished
A: boundless, catching, eager, fanatical, great, guarded, infectious, lasting, lukewarm, overwhelming, tremendous, violent, wild ~
P: surge of, wave of, without much ~

ENTRANCE
V: await, gain, make an ~
A: dramatic, grand, noisy, spectacular, sudden, triumphant ~

ENVIRONMENT (natural, scientific)
V: adapt to, affect, alter, belong to, change, clean up, control, create, damage, improve, influence, live in, master, modify, pollute, preserve, protect, provide, ravage, save, spoil ~
V: ~ has deteriorated, has an effect/influence on ... , is improving
A: clean, controlled, (un)favourable, flourishing, harmful, harsh, healthy, hostile, ideal, immediate, natural, optimum, perfect, polluted, sterile, suitable ~
P: protection of the ~

ENVIRONMENT (social)

V: adapt oneself to, adjust to, be affected by, be at odds with, belong to, come from, control, create, fit in with, get out of, improve ~

A: adverse, attractive, caring, chosen, competitive, congenial, demoralizing, deprived, difficult, familiar, favourable, (un)happy, harmful, immediate, narrow, perfect, (un)pleasant, poor, restrictive, rich, safe, (un)satisfactory, (un)stable, stifling, stimulating, stultifying, suitable, superior, working ~

ENVY

V: arouse, be consumed with/filled with/tinged with, cause, excite, express, show ~

P: object of, green with ~

EPIDEMIC

V: be in the throes of, cause, contain, control, experience, go through, lead to ~

V: ~ broke out, spread

A: dangerous, virulent, worldwide ~

EPISODE

V: recall, record, recount, witness ~

A: brief, comical, dramatic, exciting, extraordinary, famous, humorous, important, interesting, momentous, outrageous, scandalous, strange, thrilling, touching, tragic, unusual ~

EQUALITY

V: achieve, bring about, claim, enjoy, preach, recognise, strive for, win ~

A: absolute, complete, full, racial, total ~

EQUILIBRIUM

V: achieve, come back to, disturb, keep, lose, maintain, preserve, reach, recover, seek, upset ~

EQUIVALENT

A: approximate, close, exact, precise ~

ERA

V: belong to, come from, enter, hail, herald, inaugurate, mark, symbolize, usher in ~

A: bygone, classical, decadent, early, (long-)forgotten, former, golden, later, legendary, past, post-war, primitive, remote ~

ERROR

V: admit, avoid, be guilty of, commit, compound, correct, cover up, detect, discover, disregard, eliminate, eradicate, examine, expose, find, ignore, make, note, notice, overlook, point out, predict, profit from, rectify, understand ~

V: ~ appears, crept in, cropped up

A: basic, blatant, characteristic, common, costly, crucial, elementary, fundamental, glaring, grave, gross, important, main, major, serious, (in)significant, simple, slight, stupid, unfortunate ~

ESCAPE

V: engineer, foil, make, make good one's, organise, plan, prevent, thwart ~

A: attempted, daring, difficult, fortunate, lucky, miraculous, narrow, near, providential, remarkable, (un)successful ~

ESTEEM

V: bask in, earn, enjoy, fall in sb's, forfeit, go up/down in (my), hold sb in, inspire, lower oneself in sb's, rise in sb's, retain, show ~

A: great, high ~

P: mark of ~

ESTIMATE

V: accept, agree with, arrive at, ask for, come up with, decide on, endorse, exceed, give, increase, lower, make, offer, produce, provide, put in, raise, reduce, reject, revise, study, submit, supply ~

V: ~ covers ... , includes ... , provides for ...

A: accurate, cautious, conservative, crude, exact, exaggerated, fair, final, high, low, misleading, modest, preliminary, provisional, realistic, reasonable, reliable, rough, tentative, written ~

EVENT

V: announce, attend, await, cancel, celebrate, cover, enter for, follow, hail, hold, lead up to, mark, observe, organise, overshadow, postpone, precipitate, prevent, put off, report, take part in, watch, witness ~

V: ~ happened, occurred, started, will take place

A: brilliant, casual, catastrophic, chief, colourful, coming, dignified, disastrous, dramatic, embarrassing, exciting, (in)formal, forthcoming, frequent, happy, historic, historical, important, impressive, key, lively, main, major, momentous, notable, (un)official, outstanding, principal, remote, shattering, shocking, special, social, solemn, spectacular, tragic, trivial, unique, unsatisfactory, unusual ~

EVENTS

V: alter/change the course of, await, be overtaken by, dominate, follow, keep up with, observe, recall, reconstruct, review ~, set ~ in motion

V: ~ overtook sb, ran/took their course, turned out ..., unfolded

A: current, world ~

P: chain of, in the normal course of, sequence of, series of, succession of ~

EVIDENCE

V: accept, accord with, accumulate, admit, assemble, attack, back up, be based on/supported by, believe, bring forward, call, challenge, check, cite sth as, collate, collect, come across, conceal, conclude from, confuse, contain, contradict, corroborate, demand, dig up, discover, discredit, disprove, dispute, disregard, evaluate, (re-)examine, exclude, fabricate, face, falsify, fit, fit in with, furnish, gather, get, give, go over, hear, ignore, interpret, lack, look for, obtain, offer, present, produce, provide, question, quote, record, reject, rely on, reveal, rule out, scrutinize, secure, set out, sift, store, sum up, supply, suppress, survey, take, tamper with, throw doubt on, tone down, trust, turn up, twist, uncover, unearth, use, weigh, weigh up, withhold, yield ~

V: ~ agrees with ... , arose, bears out that ... , came to light, came to the fore, came up, confirms sth, conflicts with sth, corroborates sth, demonstrates sth, emerged, fits, indicates sth, is against sb, is in sb's favour, matches sth, mounted up, piled up, points to ... , proves ... , reveals ... , shows ... , speaks for itself, suggests ... , supports ... , turned up

A: abundant, additional, ambiguous, ample, biased, bogus, circumstantial, clear, cogent, compelling, comprehensive, (in)conclusive, concrete, confidential, conflicting, confusing, contradictory, convincing, corroborative, damaging, damning, (in)direct, disturbing, documentary, embarrassing, existing, experimental, extensive, factual, false, first-hand, flimsy, foolproof, forensic, fresh, further, genuine, hard, impressive, incontestable, incriminating, independent, indisputable, insubstantial, insufficient, internal, intriguing, irrefutable, material, mounting, objective, overwhelming, painful, persuasive, plausible, positive, powerful, reliable, scientific, shadowy, shaky, slender, slight, solid, sound, startling, striking, strong, substantial, supporting, tangible, unequivocal, valid, vital ~

P: body of, bulk of, clash of, matter of, piece of, rules of, not a scrap of, scrutiny of, not a shred of, weight of ~

EVIDENCE (legal, in court only)

V: admit, call, hear, set much store by, withhold ~

V: ~ implicates sb

A: (in)admissable, circumstantial, hearsay, incriminating ~

EXAMINATION (test)

V: administer, do badly/well in, enter for, fail, fail in, get through, go in for, hold, invigilate, pass, revise for, set, (re)sit, sit for, study for, supervise, take, work for ~

A: competitive, difficult, easy, entrance, final, oral, preliminary, professional, psychological, qualifying, stiff, written ~

EXAMINATION (inspection)

V: carry out, make, subject sb/sth to ~

A: careful, close, forensic, medical, meticulous, rigorous, routine, scrupulous, thorough ~

EXAMPLE (instance)

V: cite, encounter, give, quote ~

V: ~ is found, occurs, shows sth

A: blatant, characteristic, classic, (un)common, concrete, eloquent, excellent, extreme, fine, glaring, good, hideous, illuminating, obvious, powerful, spectacular, striking, supreme, telling, typical, impressive, unique, valuable ~

EXAMPLE (model)

V: act as, afford, copy, follow, give, hold sb up as, imitate, provide, refer to, serve as, set ~

V: ~ inspired sb

A: bad, excellent, glaring, good, praiseworthy, shining, useful, worthy ~

EXCITEMENT

V: arouse, cause, conceal, contain, control, create, curb, display, feel, generate, hide, keep up, lead to ~

V: ~ died down, evaporated, grew, mounted, rose

A: considerable, feverish, general, great, intense, mounting, tremendous ~

P: fever of, flurry of, gasp of, shiver of ~

EXCURSION

V: go off on, go on, join, make, organise, set off on ~

EXCUSE

V: accept, believe, concoct, give, invent, look for, make, manufacture, offer, produce, provide, reject, seek, think up ~

A: (un)convincing, credible, easy, familiar, feeble, flimsy, formal, good, lame, legitimate, obvious, official, perfect, plausible, poor, ready, ready-made, ridiculous, silly, superficial, transparent, unlikely ~

EXEMPTION

V: apply for, ask for, claim, demand, get, grant, refuse ~

A: absolute, partial, temporary, total ~

EXERCISE

V: do, engage in, get, take ~

A: aerobic, brisk, deep-breathing, gruelling, hard, healthy, keep-fit, light, regular, strenuous, vigorous, warm-up ~

P: ~ bike, programme; form of ~

EXHAUSTION

V: be overcome by, collapse from, die of, suffer from ~

A: complete, mental, nervous, physical, total ~

P: state of ~

EXHIBITION
V: arrange, hold, house, launch, mount, open, organise, present, put on, see, stage, visit ~
A: absorbing, (bi-)annual, biennial, centenary, contemporary, entrancing, exhilarating, historical, international, large, magnificent, major, memorable, one-man, permanent, retrospective, special, splendid, thematic, touring, unique ~
P: ~ hall, catalogue, stand

EXISTENCE
V: eke out, have, lead, scrape ~
A: aimless, bare, comfortable, drab, dull, happy, happy-go-lucky, hazardous, independent, interesting, isolated, lonely, meagre, miserable, monastic, monotonous, narrow, nomadic, peripatetic, poverty-stricken, precarious, primitive, quiet, settled, solitary ~

EXPANSION
V: block, bring about, check, curb, encourage, foster, further, halt, hamper, look for, prevent, promote, put a stop to, stop ~
A: enormous, gradual, great, marked, rapid, slight, substantial, unchecked, unlimited ~

EXPECTATIONS
V: cherish, come up to, create, disappoint, exceed, fall short of, fulfil, go beyond, have, meet, realise, satisfy, surpass, thwart ~
A: diminished, exaggerated, excessive, false, foolish, great, high, low, modest, (un)realistic ~

EXPEDITION
V: embark on, finance, go (off) on, head, lead, make, mount, organise, set off on, take part in ~
A: Arctic, dangerous, hunting, long, mountaineering, risky ~

EXPENDITURE
V: account for, allow for, approve, budget for, calculate, control, curtail, curb, cut, cut down, cut out, detail, eliminate, estimate, freeze, increase, justify, keep down, limit, monitor, note down, plan, predict, prune, reduce, restrict, sanction, scrutinize ~
V: ~ covers sth, decreased, exceeded ..., fell, got out of hand, grew, mounted, remains at ..., rose, soared, went down/up
A: annual, average, colossal, current, excess, excessive, extra, government, initial, lavish, legitimate, modest, monthly, public, total, unforeseen, unnecessary, wasteful ~

EXPENSE
V: afford, avoid, bear, contribute to, cover, curtail, defray, entail, estimate, have, incur, involve, keep down, limit, pay, reduce, share, take on ~
A: considerable, crippling, extra, great, heavy, incidental, initial, joint, legitimate, negligible, slight, substantial, unnecessary ~

EXPENSES
V: claim, cover, defray, have, pay, pay for, recover, reduce, reimburse sb (for), share ~
A: current, day-to-day, heavy, hotel, incidental, joint, out-of-pocket, running, travelling ~

EXPERIENCE
V: come through, describe, endure, enjoy, get over, go through, have, meet with, pass through, recall, relish, remember, share, undergo ~
A: alarming, appalling, beneficial, bitter, chastening, common, damaging, dangerous, delightful, disconcerting, distressing, disturbing, early, electrifying, enlightening, exciting, exotic, fascinating, formative, fresh, frustrating, grim, gruelling, harmful, harrowing, heartening, horrible, horrifying, hurtful, interesting, learning, memorable, moving, nasty, nerve-racking, novel, painful, (un)pleasant, poignant, refreshing, revealing, sad, salutary, sexual, shattering, sickening, sordid, stimulating, strange, testing, thrilling, traumatic, trivial, trying, uncomfortable, unique, unnerving, unusual, upsetting, useful, vital ~

EXPERIENCE (acquired knowledge)

V: accumulate, acquire, amass, apply, assimilate, digest, gain, gather, get, give, have, learn by, learn from, provide ~

V: ~ came in handy, teaches (us) that ...

A: first-hand, fresh, genuine, good, hands-on, invaluable, long, practical, previous, useful, valuable, wide, worldly ~

P: realm of, wealth of ~

EXPERIMENT

V: carry out, conduct, do, embark on, make, perform, ruin, run, scrap, set up, try, write up ~

A: audacious, bizarre, brave, careful, complicated, control, controlled, dangerous, doubtful, fraudulent, fruitful, laborious, original, pioneering, promising, reckless, risky, simple, straightforward, useful ~

EXPERT

V: ask, call in, consult, leave sth to, refer sth to ~

A: acknowledged, recognised, self-styled, so-called, well-known ~

P: body of, panel of, team of *experts*

EXPERTISE

V: acquire, develop, gain, have, lack, show ~

A: considerable, necessary ~

P: degree of, level of ~

EXPLANATION

V: accept, arrive at, believe, come forward with, demand, fabricate, furnish, give, go into, hit on, look for, manufacture, offer, produce, provide, put forward, reject, seek, suggest, supply ~

A: (un)acceptable, (in)adequate, banal, clear, clumsy, complicated, (un)convincing, credible, devious, false, fantastic, far-fetched, full, (un)helpful, hurried, ingenious, innocent, involved, lame, (un)likely, logical, long, long-winded, lucid, obvious, plausible, poor, probable, prosaic, rambling, rational, (un)reasonable, repeated, (un)satisfactory, scientific, simple, simplistic, straightforward, succinct, tentative, true, unintelligible, valid ~

EXPLOIT

V: embark on, go off on, set off on ~

A: amorous, dangerous, daring, fantastic, heroic, rash, wild ~

EXPORTS

V: ban, boost, curb, diversify, encourage, increase, reduce, restrict, step up, stimulate, suspend ~

V: ~ dwindled, fell, held up, increased, remain strong, tapered off, went down/up

A: invisible ~

EXPRESSION

V: assume, change, disguise, have, put on ~

V: ~ altered, changed, froze

A: alert, angry, anxious, bad-tempered, bewildered, blank, bored, calm, cheerful, contented, cool, dead-pan, ferocious, fierce, flat, friendly, gloomy, glum, grave, grim, happy, haughty, hostile, hypocritical, inscrutable, intense, lively, momentary, morose, obstinate, open, outraged, pained, (un)pleasant, puzzled, sad, self-satisfied, serene, serious, sharp, shy, smiling, sour, spontaneous, stupid, thoughtful, vacuous, wary, worried ~

EXPRESSION (phrase)

V: come across, delete, put in, use ~

V: ~ came into use, fell out of use

A: colloquial, colourful, common, everyday, figurative, fixed, familiar, frequent, handy, idiomatic, literary, offensive, rare, rude, strong, useful, vivid, well-known ~

EXTENT
V: assess, estimate, gauge, measure, reckon ~
A: approximate, certain, full, great, negligible, real, slight, small, startling, true ~
P: to a large ~
EXTINCTION
V: be close to, be doomed to, face, hunt to, push to, save sth from, threaten sth with ~
A: total, virtual ~
P: on the edge/point/verge of ~
EXTRADITION
V: ask for, fight, grant, oppose, request, seek ~
P: ~ agreement, order, proceedings, treaty

F

FACE
V: go red in the, hide, punch, screw up, scrub, slap, wash, wipe ~
A: angelic, attractive, beautiful, bloated, chubby, expressive, familiar, fat, fine, freckled, fresh, funny, gaunt, handsome, happy, hard, hideous, honest, kind, miserable, nondescript, odd, ordinary, oval, (un)pleasant, pock-marked, pretty, red, round, ruddy, rugged, sad, serious, soft, sour, square, strange, sweet, tanned, thin, ugly, weary, young ~
FACILITIES
V: have, improve, offer, provide, use ~
A: (in)adequate, ample, available, decent, excellent, good, incredible, modern, old-fashioned, poor, splendid, state-of-the-art ~
P: growth of, improvement of, lack of, provision of ~
FACT
V: accept, account for, acknowledge, announce, ascertain, assess, be aware of, be oblivious to, bear out, bear witness to, bemoan, check, come up against, conceal, confirm, consider, contemplate, contest, deduce, deny, deplore, disclose, discover, disguise, distinguish, divulge, drive home, elicit, emphasise, establish, face, gloss over, hide, ignore, keep in mind, leave out, make no mention of/secret of, note, obscure, overlook, pick up, point to, proclaim, question, quote, recognise, record, refer to, reject, spring from, state, stress, take account of, take into consideration, testify to, underline, wake up to ~
V: ~ came out, emerged, proves sth, shows sth, suggests that ...
A: accepted, accomplished, alleged, awkward, bald, bare, basic, bewildering, brutal, cold, concrete, distressing, disturbing, essential, established, hard, harsh, horrifying, inescapable, interesting, intriguing, irrefutable, little-known, mere, noticeable, obscure, obvious, pertinent, plain, principal, real, relevant, sad, salient, simple, significant, solid, stark, startling, trivial, true, ugly, undeniable, underlying, undisputed, unpalatable, unpleasant, unquestionable, well-documented, well-known ~
FACTS
V: classify, collect, dig into, distort, embellish, embroider, evaluate, (re-)examine, gather, give, go over, interpret, investigate, misrepresent, pour out, present, produce, review, search out, select, stick to, study, sum up, trace, twist, unravel, weigh up ~
A: bare, cold, detailed, hard ~

FACTIONS
V: be divided into, split into ~
A: breakaway, extremist, opposing, powerful, radical, rebel, rival, warring ~

FACTOR
V: analyse, consider, detect, determine, discover, distinguish, eliminate, examine, pick out, point to, reveal ~, take ~ into account/consideration
A: additional, adverse, all-important, common, complicated, constant, contributory, crucial, deciding, decisive, determining, dominant, harmful, hidden, important, incidental, key, limiting, main, major, mysterious, obvious, only, powerful, primary, principal, probable, puzzling, related, relevant, significant, single, specific, unexpected, unknown ~

FACTORY
V: close, close down, manage, (re)open, relocate, run, set up, shut down ~
V: ~ (re-)opened, shut down

FACULTIES (mental)
V: be in (full) possession of, develop, lose, use ~
V: ~ are failing
A: critical, dormant, imaginative, intellectual, mental ~

FAILURE
V: admit, be resigned to, cause, end in, experience, lead to, meet with, precipitate, prevent, result in ~
V: ~ ensued
A: abject, abysmal, complete, continued, definite, disastrous, dismal, hopeless, inevitable, miserable, partial, pathetic, predictable, sensational, serious, temporary, total, tragic, unfortunate, utter ~

FAITH (religion)
V: adopt, betray, defend, give up, lose, renounce, restore, strengthen ~
A: abiding, Christian/Muslim etc, deep, perfect, profound, pure, true ~

FAITH (confidence)
V: (re)affirm, assert, break, declare, destroy, have, lose, place/put ~ in sb, question, retain, shake, strengthen, undermine ~
A: absolute, blind, boundless, complete, firm, great, indomitable, strong, total, unfaltering ~
P: breach of ~

FALL
V: break sb's, have, soften ~
A: awkward, bad, nasty, painful, serious ~

FALL (financial)
V: bring about, cause, (under)estimate, head for, lead to, prevent, take ~
A: alarming, considerable, disappointing, dramatic, gradual, serious, sharp, significant, slight, steady, sudden, swift, tremendous, unprecedented ~

FAME
V: achieve, court, enjoy, pursue, rise to, seek, win ~
V: ~ dwindled, faded, grew, spread
A: declining, enduring, eternal, everlasting, great, growing, lasting, overnight, undying, unexpected, unwanted, widespread, worldwide ~
P: height of, lure of, peak of, pinnacle of, pursuit of, trappings of ~

FAMILY (human)

V: be related to, belong to, break up, bring up, clothe, come from, educate, establish, feed, have, look after, maintain, raise, rear, split, start, support, uproot ~

V: ~ broke down, broke up, died out, flourished, grew, split up, stuck together

A: adoptive, affluent, ancient, aristocratic, average, close, close-knit, contented, devoted, distinguished, dysfunctional, eminent, extended, famous, (un)happy, illustrious, immediate, impoverished, influential, large, middle/upper/working-class, modest, natural, notorious, nuclear, old, ordinary, poor, powerful, (under-)privileged, problem, prosperous, respectable, respected, rich, single-parent, talented, typical, unusual, well-known, wealthy ~

FAMINE

V: cause, eliminate, relieve, suffer ~

V: ~ is endemic, raged, struck

A: devastating, severe, terrible, widespread ~

P: ~ relief

FANTASY

V: act out, be haunted by, conjure up, fulfil, have, indulge in, weave ~

A: childhood, childish, dangerous, elaborate, escapist, grotesque, mere, persistent, private, pure, recurring, sexual, sheer, strange, unreal, vivid, wild ~

P: live in a ~ world

FASCINATION

V: experience, feel, have ~ for sb, hold ~ for sb, succumb to ~

A: curious, deep, fatal, great, irresistible, morbid, strong, unhealthy ~

FASHION

V: adopt, be in/out of, come into, create, follow, go out of, introduce, set ~

A: attractive, brief, current, extravagant, fleeting, high, latest, popular, present, street, teenage ~

P: height of ~

FATE

V: avoid, be condemned to, be resigned to, decide, deserve, determine, encounter, escape, expect, have, meet, meet with, run away from, seal, settle, share, submit to, suffer, tempt ~

A: blind, common, cruel, dire, dreadful, hopeless, horrible, impending, inevitable, mysterious, strange, terrible, tragic, uncertain, unfortunate, unhappy, universal, unusual ~

P: irony of, twist of ~

FATIGUE

V: battle against, be overcome by, feel, overcome, succumb to, suffer from ~

A: chronic, crippling, emotional, extreme, incredible, mental, physical, severe, total, tremendous ~

P: feeling of, sense of, signs of ~

FAULT

V: cause, correct, detect, diagnose, discover, draw attention to, eliminate, examine, find, get rid of, have, indicate, mend, notice, perceive, point out, put ~ right, rectify, remedy, repair, report, see, trace ~

V: ~ appeared

A: basic, fundamental, human, main, obvious, permanent, radical, serious, slight, tiny, visible ~

FAULTS (personality)

V: cure, excuse, gloss over, have, ignore, make allowances for, overlook, point out, put up with, realise, turn a blind eye to ~

V: ~ became noticeable

A: annoying, glaring, irritating, minor, petty, serious, silly, unfortunate, worst ~

FAULT (responsibility)
V: admit, confess to ~
A: entire, main, principal, whole ~
FAVOUR
V: be anxious for, count on, curry, enjoy, find, (re)gain sb's ~, look with ~ on sb/sth, lose, meet with, solicit, win ~
FAVOUR (with *a/an*)
V: ask, beg, decline, do sb, expect, get, grant, offer, receive, refuse ~
A: big, enormous, extra, great, kind, special, unexpected, unsolicited ~
FEAR
V: arouse, be filled with, be gripped/haunted/obsessed/overcome/plagued by, be the victim of, cause, confess to, control, develop, disguise, ease, experience, express, feel, get rid of, give rise to, have, hide, instil, overcome, show, strike ~ into sb, suffer from, whip up ~
A: acute, chilling, constant, deadly, deep, deep-seated, dreadful, exaggerated, great, hidden, immediate, irrational, justified, lasting, latent, main, nagging, overpowering, overwhelming, real, recurrent, renewed, slight, strong, subconscious, superstitious, unfounded, vague ~
FEARS (anxieties, apprehension)
V: allay, alleviate, arouse, be obsessed by, be the victim of, calm, confirm, dispel, disperse, entertain, exploit, express, feel, increase, intensify, justify, magnify, mitigate, pooh-pooh, quieten, raise, reinforce, remove, revive, ridicule, soothe, suppress, voice ~
V: ~ came true, mounted, multiplied, subsided
A: chronic, foolish, grave, growing, groundless, realistic, recurrent, serious, stupid, unreasonable, vague ~
P: (my) worst ~
FEAT
V: accomplish, achieve, bring off, match, perform, pull off, record ~
A: amazing, astonishing, astounding, bold, brave, brilliant, courageous, daring, heroic, incredible, miraculous, noble, notable, outstanding, prodigious, remarkable, singular, stunning, superhuman ~
P: ~ of endurance, of strength
FEATURE
V: draw attention to, exhibit, have, incorporate, know, manifest, share, show ~
A: added, appealing, attractive, basic, characteristic, colourful, common, conspicuous, constant, current, disappointing, disconcerting, distinct, distinctive, distinguishing, disturbing, dominant, encouraging, endearing, essential, excellent, existing, extraordinary, hopeful, important, indispensable, main, major, man-made, memorable, noble, notable, novel, obvious, outstanding, particular, permanent, pernicious, principal, prominent, recognisable, redeeming, regrettable, remarkable, reprehensible, sad, salient, significant, special, strange, surprising, striking, typical, unfortunate, universal, unique, unmistakable, unusual, vague, vivid ~
FEATURES (facial)
A: chubby, coarse, delicate, exquisite, feminine, fine, gaunt, handsome, hard, heavy, masculine, prominent, regular, soft, striking, strong ~
FEE
V: charge, pay, quote, share, split, waive ~
A: extortionate, exorbitant, fat, huge, nominal, normal, (un)reasonable, ridiculous, usual ~

FEELING
V: cause, create, develop, evince, experience, give sb, have, lead to, make, manifest, produce, remove, spoil, strengthen ~
A: acute, carefree, confused, confusing, curious, dazed, deep, definite, depressed, exhilarating, (un)familiar, genuine, gloomy, guilty, happy, heady, heightened, inexplicable, instinctive, marked, nagging, nasty, profound, real, sensitive, sinking, strange, strong, subtle, sudden, thrilling, transient, uncomfortable, uneasy, vague ~

FEELINGS
V: arouse, conceal, consider, control, disguise, experience, express, get rid of, give way to, have, hurt sb's, ignore, inflame, numb, overcome, question, reciprocate, repress, reveal, share, show, sublimate, suppress, swallow, trust (your) ~
A: aggressive, amicable, bitter, conflicting, confused, delicate, evil, guilty, hard, hostile, innermost, joyful, mixed, nasty, negative, patriotic, pent-up, positive, real, subconscious, submerged, tender, true, unworthy, vague, warm ~

FEELING (physical sensation)
V: have, lose, recover ~
V: ~ came back, disappeared, returned
A: dull, itchy, numb, painful, sharp, tingling ~

FESTIVAL
V: attend, cancel, go to, hold, organise, visit ~
A: annual, Arts, dance, elaborate, extravagant, jazz, local, music, opera, pop, spectacular ~

FEUD
V: cause, create, lead to, mediate in, put an end to, settle, stir up, take part in ~
V: ~ arose
A: bitter, bloody, family, long-drawn-out, long-standing, ongoing, unending, violent ~

FEVER
V: be in bed with, be running, come down with, develop, get over, go down with, have ~
A: mild, slight, terrible ~

FIELD (area of activity or study)
V: be first in (his), be outside (my), break into, develop, dominate, enter, know, promote ~
A: fascinating, interesting, little-known, lucrative, popular, related, specialist ~
P: expert in the ~ of ...

FIGHT
V: ask for, arrange, avoid, carry on, challenge sb to, enter, get embroiled in/involved in/mixed up in, get into, have, hold, interrupt, lead to, lose, pick, provoke, put up, start, stop, take up, win ~
V: ~ broke out, started
A: bitter, bloody, brave, clean, courageous, desperate, dirty, disastrous, (un)fair, fierce, free, gallant, good, heroic, hopeless, nasty, poor, rough, stiff, tough, valiant, vicious ~
P: ~ for survival, to the death/finish

FIGHTING
V: ~ broke out, died down, erupted, escalated, quietened down, raged, resumed, stopped
A: bitter, fierce, hand-to-hand, heavy, renewed ~
P: lull in, outbreak of, renewal of, upsurge of ~

FIGURE (person)
A: alarming, beloved, celebrated, charismatic, comic, conspicuous, contemporary, controversial, courageous, dashing, disreputable, enthralling, established, exotic, familiar, famous, fascinating, forlorn, glamorous, grotesque, imposing, leading, literary, lonely,

ludicrous, major, minor, mysterious, nondescript, popular, picturesque, powerful, prominent, remote, ridiculous, shadowy, solitary, sorry, striking, substantial, towering, tragic, well-known ~

FIGURE (physique)

A: ample, erect, handsome, neat, slender, slim, stocky, wonderful, youthful ~

FIGURE (amount)

V: agree to, calculate, maintain, mention, peak, propose, quote, reach, rise to, top, work out ~

A: approximate, astronomical, ball-park, exact, final, high, large, low, modest, precise, preliminary, real, (un)realistic, ridiculous, tentative, true ~

P: drop/rise in the unemployment *figures*

FIGURES (financial)

V: accept, achieve, add up, amend, announce, arrive at, assess, check, compare, compile, conceal, confirm, confuse, doctor, draw up, establish, estimate, examine, falsify, give, go over, go through, interpret, issue, manipulate, massage, mix up, obtain, produce, publish, query, question, refer to, release, report, reveal, round ~ up/down, scrutinize, study, supply, support, trim, trust, verify ~

V: ~ appear, are available, climbed, conceal ..., demonstrate sth, hide ... , have improved, indicate/mean/prove/show/signify/suggest/support ..., shot up, speak for themselves, went down

A: (in)accurate, alarming, annual, approximate, basic, confidential, corresponding, deceptive, detailed, disappointing, disastrous, disquieting, dubious, encouraging, exact, exaggerated, excellent, false, final, genuine, good, heartening, high, horrendous, impressive, inflated, low, misleading, (un)official, overall, phenomenal, poor, precise, preliminary, real, realistic, ridiculous, rough, round, satisfactory, staggering, true, worrying ~

P: mass of ~

FILES

V: (re)check, consult, close, cross-check, destroy, enter sth in, examine, falsify, go through, have, keep, look up, make, mislay, open, refer to, release, scrutinize, suppress, update ~

V: ~ are in a muddle, contain ... , date back to ... , have disappeared, got lost, piled up, show ...

A: accurate, careful, comprehensive, confidential, damaging, detailed, missing, private, secret, sensitive, thick, up-to-date ~

FILES (computer)

V: activate, disable, compress, copy, close, create, delete, duplicate, get into, go into, lose, merge, modify, name, open (up), save, update ~

FILM

V: ban, censor, cut, direct, edit, finance, make, preview, produce, promote, put on, release, review, see, shoot, show, star in, watch ~

A: adventure, award-winning, black and white, classic, colour, commercial, documentary, exciting, fast-moving, feature, great, gripping, horror, impressive, lousy, low-budget, marvellous, profitable, science fiction, sentimental, silent, unforgettable, violent, 35mm ~

FINANCE

V: apply for, arrange, look for, provide, seek, supply ~

FINANCES

V: examine, go over, repair ~

V: ~ are in a mess, in order, shaky, sound

FINE

V: avoid, impose, let sb off with, levy, pay, receive ~

A: heavy, hefty, immediate, on-the-spot, stiff, token ~

FIRE
V: bring/keep ~ under control, catch, contain, extinguish, put out, set ~ to, start ~
V: ~ broke out, burned, died down, enveloped sth, raged, roared, smouldered, spread, swept through ..., went out
A: accidental, dangerous, deliberate, devastating, forest, mysterious, raging, roaring ~

FIRM
V: belong to, close, found, manage, reorganise, run, run down, set up, take over ~
V: ~ amalgamated with sth, came into being, closed down, collapsed, expanded, flourished, is doing well, is in liquidation, merged with sth, prospered, is thriving, went bankrupt/bust/into liquidation/to the wall/under
A: (in)efficient, family, giant, long-established, prosperous, reliable, reputable, successful, well-known ~

FISH
V: catch, fillet, fry, grill, gut, poach, prepare ~
A: baked, battered, dried, filleted, fresh, freshly-caught, fried, frozen, grilled, meaty, oily, poached, raw, smoked, steamed, white ~
P: fillet of, piece of ~

FLAG
V: display, fly, hoist, lower, run up, salute, unfurl, wave ~
V: ~ was flying (at half-mast)

FLAT
V: decorate, furnish, lease, move into/out of, renovate, rent ~
A: comfortable, cosy, cramped, dingy, enormous, (first-)floor, hideous, luxurious, one-/two-bedroomed, poky, roomy, shabby, smart, spacious, spotless, (un)tidy, tiny, well-kept ~

FLAVOUR
V: add, be full of, give sth, impart, improve ~
A: bitter, crisp, definite, delicate, distinct, exotic, fruity, odd, (un)pleasant, magnificent, mild, natural, salty, smooth, strange, strong, subtle, sugary, superb, tangy, unmistakable, unusual, wonderful ~

FLAW
V: correct, detect, develop, discern, eradicate, expose, get rid of, have, hide, perceive, rectify, remedy, repair, reveal ~
A: basic, considerable, evident, fatal, fundamental, inherent, major, noticeable, obvious, serious, slight ~

FLIGHT
V: board, book, catch, cancel, change, delay, get, miss, take ~
A: bumpy, comfortable, delayed, domestic, dreadful, dull, epic, gruelling, international, ill-fated, long-haul, maiden, memorable, non-stop, pleasant, rough, smooth, tedious, turbulent ~

FLOW
V: accelerate, aid, check, encourage, halt, hasten, impede, interrupt, keep up, limit, maintain, regulate, slow down, stem ~
A: constant, even, free, non-stop, rapid, (ir)regular, smooth, steady ~

FLOWERS
V: arrange, collect, cut, grow, pick, plant, water ~
V: ~ bloomed, are dying/fading, have opened/revived/wilted/withered
A: artificial, bright, colourful, cut, dead, exotic, fragrant, fresh, garden, lovely, rare, spring, wild, woodland ~

FOG
V: ~ came down, cleared, closed in, lifted, rolled down/in, shrouded sth, swirled, thickened
A: billowing, dense, heavy, patchy, severe, thick, thickening ~
P: bank of, patches of, shrouded in ~

FOOD
V: bolt, cook, distribute, grow, gulp, (re)heat, hoard, prepare, process, produce, search for, scavenge for, swallow, waste ~
A: appetizing, delicious, disgusting, exotic, frozen, healthy, Indian/Italian etc, junk, local, luxury, natural, nourishing, packaged, plain, revolting, simple, spicy, tasty, typical, vegetarian, wholesome ~
P: abundance of, scarcity of, shortage of ~

FOOL
A: complete, damn, downright, poor (old), silly (old), utter, young ~
P: act the, behave like, play the ~; make ~ of sb

FORCE
V: act as, apply, exert, exhaust, give into, give way to, have, increase, lose, measure, oppose, reduce, resist, resort to, stop, submit to, use ~
V: ~ diminished
A: active, beneficial, blind, brute, considerable, deadly, definite, disruptive, divisive, dynamic, excessive, extreme, great, harmful, massive, moral, potent, powerful, real, sheer, spent, spiritual, superior, sufficient, tremendous, unnecessary, whole ~
P: come into, show of ~

FORCE (of an argument)
V: accept, admit, carry, lose, recognise ~

FORECAST
V: draw up, issue, make ~
A: (in)accurate, bleak, chilling, discouraging, encouraging, extravagant, gloomy, immediate, long-term, optimistic, pessimistic, rash, realistic, short-term ~

FORM
V: adopt, alter, assume, change, decide on, have, introduce, keep to, retain, take, take on ~
V: ~ developed, disappeared, emerged
A: acute, appropriate, awkward, basic, bizarre, complicated, concrete, dangerous, definite, devastating, distinct, distorted, elementary, embryonic, exact, exceptional, existing, final, grotesque, human, identical, material, modified, novel, original, perfect, popular, precise, primitive, proper, regular, restricted, rigid, rudimentary, stable, strange, suitable, tenuous, traditional, unique, universal, (un)usual, vague, visible ~

FORMULA
V: abandon, adopt, agree on, alter, amend, apply, arrive at, change, come out with, create, decide on, deduce, determine, devise, discover, establish, find, follow, hammer out, invent, keep to, lay down, produce, propose, revise, seek, settle, test, use, work out ~
A: acceptable, appropriate, clever, complicated, convincing, correct, definite, existing, face-saving, final, ingenious, magic, novel, permanent, proper, ready-made, revolutionary, successful, temporary, tentative, workable ~

FORTUNE
V: accumulate, acquire, add to, amass, build up, claim, come into, estimate, have, inherit, lose, make, manage, possess, spend, squander, win ~
V: ~ disappeared, grew
A: considerable, huge, large, small, substantial, vast ~

FOUNDATION
V: build (on), create, destroy, establish, form, lay, make, provide, reinforce, rest on, serve as, shake, undermine ~
V: ~ collapsed, crumbled
A: firm, lasting, permanent, reliable, secure, shaky, solid, sound, steady, strong, weak ~

FRAMEWORK
V: build, construct, create, destroy, erect, fit into, lay down, make, place sth in, provide, put sth in, set up, work within ~
A: balanced, basic, conceptual, convenient, loose, proper, regular, reliable, rigid, solid, strong, suitable, tight ~

FRAUD
V: accuse sb of, be guilty of, commit, convict sb of, deny, detect, discover, engage in, expose, perpetrate, prevent, suspect, uncover ~
A: large-scale, petty ~

FREEDOM
V: abuse, achieve, cherish, curtail sb's, deprive sb of, desire, endanger, enjoy, ensure, fight for, forfeit, gain, get, give, grant, guarantee, guard, jeopardize, limit, lose, preserve, promise, restore, restrict, secure, take away, threaten, value, win ~
V: ~ has been eroded, is at risk/in danger/threatened ~
A: absolute, academic, comparative, complete, hard-won, individual, lasting, (un)limited, new-found, perfect, personal, political, relative, religious, total ~

FRICTION
V: aggravate, avoid, cause, create, generate, give rise to, lead to, produce, reduce, remove ~

FRIEND
V: keep, lose, make, win ~
A: best, close, dangerous, fair-weather, faithful, false, family, firm, good, intimate, lifelong, loyal, mutual, new, old, personal, school, special, sympathetic, true ~

FRIENDSHIP
V: break off, cement, cultivate, destroy, develop, form, promote, spoil, strike up, value ~
A: abiding, close, deep, firm, intimate, lifelong, long, personal, sentimental, unstinted, warm ~
P: act of, bonds of, ties of, token of ~

FRONT (defence)
V: adopt, display, form, make, present, set up, show ~
A: common, solid, united, wide ~

FRONTIER
V: alter, change, close, create, cross, (re)define, determine, draw, establish, fix, guard, mark, move, open, push back, recognise, redraw, violate ~
V: ~ has changed, moved, runs/stretches from ... to ...

FRUIT
V: bear, grow, pick ~
A: bitter, citrus, dried, exotic, firm, fleshy, fresh, juicy, luscious, ripe, rotten, soft, succulent, tinned, tropical, wild ~

FRUSTRATION
V: bottle up, give vent to, suffer, vent ~
A: continual, deep, great, immense, inevitable, pent-up, understandable ~

FULFILMENT
V: achieve, bring, lead to, prevent, reach, seek, strive for ~
A: complete, immediate, instant, partial, personal, sexual, total ~

FUNCTION
V: allocate, assign, assume, be given, carry on/out, define, delegate, discharge, exercise, fulfil, give up, have, hold, perform, take on ~
A: basic, central, chief, crucial, different, everyday, important, key, legitimate, main, normal, official, onerous, only, primary, prime, proper, real, responsible, separate, sole, special, supreme, true, unique, useful, (un)usual, vital ~

FUND
V: add to, administer, build up, close, contribute to, create, draw on, establish, feed, (mis)manage, open, operate, replenish, set aside, set up, subscribe to, support, wind up ~
A: charitable, common, contingency, emergency, existing, growing, healthy, secret, separate, special, voluntary ~

FUNDS
V: add to, administer, allocate, (mis)appropriate, attract, build up, collect, cut off, deplete, dip into, draw on, earmark, embezzle, exhaust, feed, generate, have, make ~ available, need, provide, raise, replenish, run out of, set aside ~
A: ample, available, common, generous, large, (un)limited, limitless, modest, public, separate, special, substantial, (in)sufficient, vast, vital ~
P: allocation of, outflow of, shortage of ~

FURY
V: fill sb with, unleash ~
P: outburst of ~

FUTURE
V: be worried about, build, control, dread, envisage, foresee, foretell, look to, look forward to, look towards, plan, plan for, point to, predict, provide for, see, shape, threaten ~
V: ~ looks bleak/gloomy/bright etc
A: assured, better, bleak, bright, brilliant, depressing, doubtful, dreadful, gloomy, great, horrible, immediate, lonely, long-term, magnificent, marvellous, miserable, promising, prosperous, rosy, secure, splendid, terrible, uncertain, worrying ~
P: make provision for (your) ~

G

GAIN
V: cancel out, consolidate, forfeit, look for, produce, reduce, result in, wipe out ~
A: considerable, definite, enormous, financial, important, lucky, material, maximum, negligible, permanent, real, slight, substantial, tremendous, unexpected, visible ~

GAINS (financial)
V: accumulate, acquire, bring, collect, consolidate, fritter away, look for, make, pile up, share, squander, wipe out ~
A: further, huge, ill-gotten, impressive, large, long/short-term, massive, remarkable, significant, spectacular, total ~

GAMBLE
V: justify, take ~
V: ~ came off, failed, paid off
A: big, huge, legitimate, pure, tempting ~

GAME
V: develop, devise, follow, introduce, invent, play ~

A: ancient, ball, board, dangerous, demanding, exhausting, indoor, intellectual, outdoor, popular, rough, slow, team ~

P: ~ of chance, of skill

GAME (match)
V: abandon, arrange, be beaten in, call off, challenge sb to, fix, go to, have, interrupt, lose, play, postpone, ruin, take part in, watch, win ~

A: close, crucial, difficult, dirty, excellent, exciting, exhausting, friendly, important, leisurely, pleasant, poor, quick, tiring, tough ~

GAP
V: bridge, close, create, cross, fill, fill in, leave, narrow, open, perceive, plug, reduce, shrink, widen ~

V: ~ appeared, arose, has closed, emerged, exists, has narrowed, opened up, has shrunk, has widened

A: awesome, awkward, deep, distinct, enormous, growing, important, irreducible, large, narrow, permanent, real, serious, unbridgeable, unfortunate, wide, yawning ~

GARDEN
V: lay out, landscape, plant, tend to, water, weed ~

A: country, herb, landscaped, overgrown, rock, rose, roof, sunken, terraced, vegetable, walled, well-kept ~

GAZE
A: benevolent, bewildered, quizzical, steady, stern ~

GENERATION
A: baby-boomer, coming, future, last, lost, new, next, older, past, preceding, present, rising, the Sixties, succeeding, younger ~

GENEROSITY
V: count on, enjoy, extend, show, strain, take advantage of ~

A: great, splendid ~

GENIUS
V: demonstrate, show ~

A: absolute, budding, real, true ~

P: stroke of ~

GESTURE (physical)
V: make, repeat ~

A: decisive, forceful, impatient, meaningful, meaningless, menacing, playful, rude, soothing, threatening, violent, warning ~

GESTURE (attitude)
A: appropriate, bold, extravagant, friendly, generous, kind, noble, pointless ~

P: ~ of defiance, of goodwill

GIFT
V: accept, appreciate, bring, decline, get, give, make, offer, present sb with, receive, refuse ~

A: charming, expensive, extravagant, generous, lavish, lovely, modest, precious, small, special, splendid, spontaneous, token, unusual, useful, valuable, welcome ~

GIFT (talent)
V: be endowed with, develop, have, inherit, make use of, waste ~

A: authentic, divine, enormous, genuine, great, marvellous, natural, obvious, outstanding, real, remarkable, tremendous, true, undoubted, unequalled, unique ~

GLANCE

V: cast, catch, dart, direct, give, shoot, steal, take ~

A: admiring, anxious, backward, casual, cold, conspiratorial, contemptuous, cursory, disapproving, disdainful, envious, fleeting, fond, furtive, hostile, indignant, involuntary, last, long, odd, passing, perfunctory, quick, quizzical, rapid, scornful, sideways, surreptitious, unhappy ~

GLIMPSE

V: catch, get, give ~

A: brief, faint, fleeting, momentary, quick, tantalizing, unprecedented ~

GLORY

V: achieve, add to, be covered in/with, bring, enjoy, reflect, win ~

P: bask in reflected, blaze of ~

GOAL

V: accomplish, achieve, adopt, agree on, aim at, choose, drop, give up, have, pursue, reach, seek, set oneself, strive for, succeed in, work for/towards ~

A: altruistic, ambitious, appropriate, broad, chief, common, definite, difficult, direct, distant, final, fresh, general, immediate, intermediate, joint, long/short-term, main, real, (un)realistic, specific, true, ultimate, (un)attainable ~

GOD

V: appeal to, believe in, embrace, fear, praise, pray to, reject, thank, worship ~

A: almighty, all-knowing, all-powerful, Christian/Jewish/Hindu etc, immortal, invisible, living, merciful, omnipotent ~

GOODS

V: buy, carry, check, distribute, export, handle, import, manufacture, package, produce, sell, ship, store, transport, waste ~

A: consumer, damaged, durable, fragile, high-quality, luxury, perishable, (un)saleable, shoddy, sought-after, stolen, valuable ~

GOODWILL

V: enjoy, exude, feel, lose, show, win ~

P: expression of, gesture of, legacy of, sign of ~

GOVERNMENT

V: appoint, bring down, bring in, change, defeat, destabilize, discredit, dismiss, drive out, elect, establish, form, head, oust, overthrow, prop up, put in, set up, support, swear in, throw out, topple, undermine, vote against/for, wreck ~

V: ~ acted, banned sth, came into/to power, collapsed, decided sth, enacted legislation to ... , fell, placed a ban on sth, remained in office, resigned, survived, was in power from ... to ...

A: autocratic, caretaker, central, coalition, (in)competent, corrupt, democratic, enfeebled, fledgling, incoming, independent, inept, interim, local, outgoing, precarious, provisional, puppet, representative, repressive, shaky, stable, strong, vulnerable, weak, wise ~

GRANT

V: apply for, award, cancel, cut, get, give, increase, make, obtain, qualify for, withdraw ~

A:(in)adequate, discretionary, generous, large, miserly, nominal, regular, substantial ~

GRASP (understanding)

V: acquire, have, lose ~

A: excellent, good, instinctive, keen, thorough, total ~

GRATITUDE

V: convey, earn, express, feel, show ~

A: deep, enormous, eternal, heart-felt, profound, sincere, tremendous, warm ~

GREETINGS
V: convey, exchange, extend, send ~
A: cordial, customary, friendly, fraternal, warm, warmest ~
GRIEF
V: alleviate, be overcome by, cause, express, feel, get over, give way to, suffer ~
A: deep, inconsolable, lasting, overwhelming, profound, unbearable ~
GRIEVANCE
V: air, harbour, have, nurse, remove, settle, suffer, voice ~
A: deep-seated, genuine, legitimate, long-standing, serious ~
GRIP
V: adjust, get a ~ on sth, let go, loosen, lose, relax, release, take, tighten ~
A: firm, iron, loose, powerful, strong, tight, vice-like, weak ~
GROUNDS (reasons)
V: discuss, establish, examine, explain, give, go into/over, have, raise, set forth ~
A: (in)adequate, ample, basic, doubtful, excellent, firm, flimsy, fresh, good, moral, obvious, plausible, poor, rational, (un)reasonable, reliable, secure, serious, solid, (in)sufficient, valid, well-established ~
GROUP
V: assign sb to, belong to, break away from, constitute, disband, distinguish, establish, form, gather, join, set up, start up ~
V: ~ comprises sth, consists of sth, embraces sth, includes sth
A: autonomous, breakaway, blood, broad, characteristic, close, close-knit, compact, definite, different, elite, ethnic, heterogeneous, homogeneous, important, independent, influential, large, loose, militant, minority, motley, narrow, peer, pressure, prominent, prosperous, representative, select, self-help, shadowy, similar, sizeable, special, splinter, tightly-knit, typical, uniform, well-defined, wide ~
P: ~ dynamics, pressure
GROUPS
V: arrange sth in, classify sth into, differentiate between, fall into, segregate sth into ~
A: basic, distinct, primary, separate, various ~
GROWTH
V: accelerate, achieve, aim at, anticipate, boost, bring about, check, control, curb, curtail, cut back, encourage, expect, foster, halt, hamper, hinder, hold down, impede, inhibit, limit, measure, prevent, promote, record, restrain, retard, show, slow down, speed up, stifle, stimulate, stop ~
V: ~ accelerated, faltered, increased, mushroomed, outstripped ... , reached (5%), remains steady, slowed down, stopped, took place
A: amazing, average, dramatic, economic, explosive, fast, gradual, healthy, intermittent, marked, maximum, normal, permissible, phenomenal, poor, quick, rapid, relentless, renewed, satisfactory, steady, steep, sustained, unparalleled, unprecedented, weak, zero ~
P: rate of ~
GRUDGE
V: bear, have got, hold, nurse ~
GUARANTEE
V: ask for, demand, get, give, have, offer, produce, promise, provide, receive, rely on, require ~
V: ~ is out of date, has run out
A: absolute, cast-iron, dependable, firm, foolproof, genuine, lifetime, money-back, proper, reliable, satisfactory, solid, unconditional, valid, worthless, written, (3)-year ~

GUESS
V: hazard, make ~
A: accurate, close, correct, good, informed, lucky, rough, shrewd, wild, wrong ~

GUEST
A: entertaining, frequent, perfect, ill-mannered, (un)invited, occasional, overnight, regular, surprise, unexpected, unwanted, (un)welcome ~
P: ~ of honour

GUIDANCE
V: accept, follow, issue, offer, provide, refuse, seek ~
A: careful, clear, detailed, expert, friendly, moral, parental, professional, proper, spiritual, urgent, vocational, wise, wrong ~

GUIDE (book)
V: compile, consult, digest, edit, look sth up in, provide, publish, refer to, use ~
A: authoritative, clear, compact, comprehensive, concise, detailed, essential, excellent, handy, helpful, in-depth, indispensable, (well-)illustrated, infallible, informative, reliable, simple, straightforward, useful, valuable ~

GUIDELINES
V: adhere to, draw up, follow, issue, keep to/within, lay down, observe, provide, rewrite, set, set down, study, violate ~
A: basic, broad, clear, comprehensive, detailed, established, main, satisfactory, strict, useful ~

GUILT
V: admit, be haunted by, be burdened by/with, bear, confess, deny, establish sb's, get rid of, prove, shed, shoulder ~
P: feelings of, sense of ~; racked with ~

GULF
V: bridge, create, eliminate, narrow, reduce, remove, widen ~
V: ~ (dis)appeared, exists, is apparent/visible, opened, has widened
A: alarming, broad, deep, serious, unbridgeable, vast, wide, yawning ~

GUN
V: aim, carry, draw, drop, empty, fire, hold ~ to sb's head, (un)load, point, produce, pull, put down ~, turn ~ on sb
A: concealed, heavy, light, loaded, replica, toy ~

H

HABIT
V: abandon, acquire, adopt, break, develop, drop, fall into, follow, form, get into/out of, get rid of, give up, grow out of, have, keep to, kick, learn, lose, pick up, revert to, take up ~
V: ~ developed, grew, grew up, persists, stuck
A: annoying, bad, compulsive, dangerous, disgusting, filthy, (un)healthy, horrible, ingrained, irritating, nasty, normal, obnoxious, odd, offensive, persistent, (un)pleasant, regular, reprehensible, repulsive, strict, undesirable, unfortunate, useful ~

HAIR

V: bleach, brush, colour, comb, cut, do, dye, grow, lose, part, perm, plait, set, stroke, style, tint ~

V: ~ fell out, grew, is receding, is thinning, went grey/white

A: auburn, blond, bushy, curly, dark, floppy, flowing, frizzy, greasy, grey, greying, immaculate, lank, lifeless, long, luxuriant, mousy, red, shiny, short, shoulder-length, straggly, straight, thick, thin, thinning, unkempt, unmanageable, unruly, wavy, white, wiry ~

P: have (my) ~ cut/done/permed/tinted

HALT

V: bring sth to, call, come to, grind to, screech to, skid to ~

A: abrupt, complete, final, grinding, screeching, sudden ~

HAND

V: clasp sb's, close, hold sb's, grab sb's, grasp sb's, lead sb by, offer sb, open, shake sb's, raise, take sb's, take sb by ~

HANDS

V: clap, cup, hold ~, lay ~ on, shake, wring ~

V: ~ shook, trembled

A: bare, chubby, clammy, cold, delicate, gentle, muscular, rough, soft ~

HANDICAP

V: compensate for, conquer, constitute, cope with, get over, have, impose, overcome, recognise, remove, represent, suffer from ~

A: awkward, considerable, crippling, daunting, great, grave, serious, severe, terrible ~

HAPPINESS

V: achieve, discover, feel, find, look for, search for ~

A: complete, elusive, perfect, real, short-lived, supreme, true ~

P: source of ~

HARDSHIPS

V: bear, endure, face, go through, overcome, put up with, suffer, survive, undergo ~

A: appalling, great, incredible, severe, terrific, tremendous, unbelievable, unimaginable, unspeakable ~

HARM

V: bring, cause, come to no, do, escape, get over, intend, keep sb from, mean no, prevent, protect sb from, repair, shield sb from, suffer ~

A: considerable, great, incalculable, (un)intentional, irreparable, permanent, potential, real, serious, untold ~

HARVEST

V: bring in, gather, reap ~

A: abundant, bountiful, bumper, disastrous, exceptional, grain/rice etc, poor, record, rich, unpredictable ~

HASTE

V: avoid, be in, make ~

A: great, maximum, terrible, undue, unseemly, untoward ~

HATE

V: be filled with, be the object of, channel, deserve, express, feel, overcome, suppress ~

A: incredible, intense, pure, relentless ~

HATRED

V: arouse, cause, create, develop, express, feel, generate, instil, preach, revive, show, stir up ~

A: abiding, absolute, bitter, blind, burning, deep, deep-seated, fanatical, intense, pure, strong ~

HEAD

V: bow, bury one's ~ in one's hands, hang, lift, lower, nod, raise, scratch, shake, toss ~, turn ~ away

P: nod of the, shake of the ~

HEAD (of an organisation)

V: appoint, consult ~

A: acting, departmental, effective, (un)official, permanent, strong, temporary, titular, weak ~

P: ~of State, the family

HEADLINES

V: hit, make ~

A: front-page, huge, main, sensational, tabloid ~

HEALTH

V: affect, be bursting with, enjoy, have, look after, neglect, regain, ruin, suffer, undermine, watch ~

V: ~ broke down, collapsed, declined, deteriorated, is failing, improved, took a turn for the worse

A: bad, declining, excellent, failing, fine, fragile, good, ill, improved, perfect, poor, precarious, robust, sound, uncertain ~

P: a ~ hazard; bad/good for (your), be in good/poor, deterioration in, improvement in ~

HEALTH SERVICE

V: be employed in, bring ~ to a standstill, dismantle. improve, make cuts in, make use of, modernise, organise, privatise, run, set up, use ~

V: ~ broke down, collapsed, deteriorated, worked (well, etc)

A: (in)efficient, excellent, National, unwieldy ~

HEART

V: break, gladden, harden, speak from, steal, win ~

A: broken, cold, cruel, generous, hard, heavy, kind, soft, tender ~

HEAT

V: absorb, emit, feel, generate, give off, give out, produce, radiate, stand ~

A: blistering, dry, extreme, fiery, humid, intense, oppressive, overpowering, stifling, suffocating, sultry, sweltering, terrific, unbearable ~

HEIGHT

V: clear, climb to, estimate, have, lose, measure, reach, rise to ~

A: awesome, commanding, dizzy, enormous, great, imposing, impressive, tremendous ~

HEIR

V: acknowledge sb as, appoint, claim to be, name, recognise sb as ~

A: direct, lawful, legitimate, next, putative, rightful, sole, true, worthy ~

P: ~ apparent, presumptive

HELP

V: appeal for, ask for, beg, bring, call for, canvass, clamour for, come forward with, cry for, enlist, ensure, guarantee, get, give, mobilise, need, offer, organise, proffer, promise, provide, receive, refuse, reject, request, scream for, seek, send, shout for, solicit, spurn, summon, want, withdraw ~

A: additional, all-round, constant, crucial, down-to-earth, effective, efficient, enormous, essential, generous, great, immediate, immense, indispensable, inestimable, instant, intermittent, invaluable, kind, large-scale, massive, necessary, practical, real, substantial, tremendous, urgent, useful, widespread, willing ~

P: appeal for, cry for ~

HERO
V: become, make sb a, play the ~
A: anti-, conquering, childhood, local, mighty, national, real, romantic, sporting, unlikely, unsung, war ~
HIERARCHY
V: belong to, destroy, establish, rise in/through, set up ~
A: age-old, government, inflexible, intellectual, political, religious, rigid, social, traditional
HINT
V: drop, give, take ~
A: broad, friendly, gentle, merest, mild, obscure, plain, subtle, tactful, tantalizing, timely, useful, vague ~
HISTORY
V: distort, follow, go down in, make, relate, (re)write ~
A: accurate, amusing, ancient, authentic, bloody, competent, condensed, entertaining, false, fascinating, glorious, incredible, lengthy, potted, recent, strange, superficial, true, unique ~
P: course of, landmark in, slice of, turning-point in ~
HISTORY (of a person)
A: chequered, complex, complicated, dramatic, fascinating, interesting, romantic, sad, strange, tragic, turbulent, uneasy ~
HOME (family)
V: abandon, belong to, come from, create, desert, enjoy, find, leave, make, set up ~
A: adopted, bad, broken, caring, criminal, deprived, good, (un)happy, loving, poor, proper, quiet, real, rich, rough, rowdy, (un)satisfactory, second, (un)settled, spiritual, strict, suitable ~
HOME (house)
V: build, establish, have, provide, run, set up, work from ~
A: ancestral, comfortable, magnificent, second, starter ~
HONOUR
V: attack, defend, guard, insult, lose, offend, redeem, save, value ~
P: do sth in sb's ~
HONOUR (an award)
V: bestow, deserve, give ~
A: great, high(est) ~
HOPE
V: abandon, bring, cherish, cling to, encourage, entertain, express, extinguish, give, give up, have no, hold out, lose, maintain, offer, preserve, restore, retain, revive, see, take away ~
V: ~ died, disappeared, dwindled, evaporated, faded, flourished, grew, lives on, persists, receded, returned, is running out, survived
A: abiding, ardent, bleak, constant, desperate, eternal, faint, false, fervent, firm, fleeting, flickering, fond, foolish, fragile, frail, fresh, fundamental, futile, great, increasing, last, lingering, negligible, only, paradoxical, profound, real, (un)realistic, remote, renewed, sincere, slight, slim, strong, undying, vague, vain ~
P: flicker of, glimmer of, ray of, last vestige of ~
HOPES
V: betray, blight, dash, destroy, disappoint, entertain, frustrate, fulfil, pin one's ~ on sth, raise, revive, shatter, underpin, wreck ~
A: empty, foolish, future, high, modest ~
P: have high ~ for sb, setback for (our) ~

HORROR

V: be overcome with, be struck dumb with, experience, express, feel, fill sb with, get over, have a ~ of sth, scream in ~

V: ~ gripped sb, haunted sb, struck sb

A: absolute, real, utter ~

P: the full ~ of the situation

HORRORS

V: describe, dwell on, experience, go through, realise, remember, suffer, witness ~

A: incredible, indescribable, unbelievable, unimaginable, unspeakable ~

HORSE

V: back, break in, fall off, harness, mount, ride, saddle, shoe ~

V: ~ cantered, galloped, kicked, neighed, reared up, stampeded, trotted, walked, whinnied

A: bay, chestnut, dappled, fiery, fine, frisky, nervous, piebald, placid, powerful, spirited, unmanageable ~

HOSPITALITY

V: abuse sb's, enjoy, extend, offer, return, show, take advantage of, take advantage of sb's ~

A: characteristic, corporate, generous, lavish, legendary, traditional ~

P: ~ box, package, tent

HOSTILITIES (war)

V: break off, call off, open, renew, start, stop, suspend ~

V: ~ began, broke out, ceased, continue, went on

A: renewed, serious ~

P: cessation of, outbreak of, resumption of ~

HOSTILITY

V: aggravate, cause, conceal, create, disguise, encounter, express, intensify, feed, feel, give rise to, provoke, show ~

A: fierce, great, growing, marked, obvious, open, undiluted, vociferous, widespread ~

HOUSE

V: alter, build, (re)decorate, demolish, extend, let, move, pull down, put up, refurbish, renovate, rent, rent out, tear down ~

A: attractive, comfortable, compact, derelict, (semi-)detached, dilapidated, dream, elegant, empty, exquisite, haunted, hideous, imposing, large, magnificent, newly-built, pleasant, rambling, ramshackle, spacious, sprawling, terraced, unpretentious ~

HUMILIATION

V: endure, subject sb to, suffer ~

A: abject, crushing, deep, painful, utter ~

HUMOUR

A: acid, bitter, black, caustic, dark, deadpan, dry, earthy, gentle, madcap, self-directed, sly, subtle, wicked, wry, zany ~

P: brand of, sense of ~

HUNGER

V: allay, alleviate, die of, satisfy ~

A: insatiable, ravenous ~

P: pangs of ~

HURDLE

V: cross, encounter, face, get over, meet, negotiate, overcome, surmount ~

A: dangerous, daunting, formidable ~

HYPOTHESIS
V: accept, advance, agree with, bear out, challenge, confirm, construct, erect, favour, form, formulate, invalidate, oppose, propound, prove, put forward, raise objections to, refute, reject, rule out, set up, strengthen, support, test ~

A: audacious, bold, controversial, false, fanciful, mistaken, novel, plausible, tentative, unlikely, useful, wild, working, wrong ~

I

IDEA
V: abandon, absorb, accept, adjust to, advocate, amplify, advance, back, be against, be committed/dedicated/drawn to, be obsessed with, be struck by, borrow, cherish, clarify, cling to, come out/up with, confirm, conjure up, consider, contemplate, convey, debate, debunk, defend, demonstrate, develop, deny, dismiss, dispel, disprove, distort, drop, eliminate, encourage, endorse, entertain, explode, explore, expound, express, favour, fit, fit in with, follow up, form, formulate, foster, get, get accustomed/used to, get rid of, give up, go along with, grasp, hammer out, have, hit upon, hold, implement, imply, impose ~ on sb, incorporate, inculcate, instil, jot down, keep to, launch, meet, modify, negate, oppose, pick up, pioneer, plant, play with, popularise, present, promote, propose, put an end to, put forward, put ~ into practice, raise, refute, reinforce, reject, relish, resist, respond to, revive, ridicule, rule out, spread, squash, stick to, subscribe to, suggest, support, take to, take up, test, tinker with, toy with, turn down, warm to ~

V: ~ appeals to (me), arose, came to me, caught on, cropped up, emerged, evolved, fell through, flourished, grew, is incompatible with, occurred to (me), spread, took root, took shape, won support

A: abstract, absurd, advanced, ambitious, arresting, basic, bizarre, bold, bright, brilliant, classical, clear, common, commonsense, confused, controversial, convincing, crazy, diabolical, disconcerting, elusive, enlightened, entrenched, exaggerated, extravagant, extreme, false, familiar, fantastic, far-fetched, feasible, feeble, fixed, flexible, foolish, grotesque, hazy, heretical, imaginative, inflated, ingenious, ingrained, innovative, instinctive, intriguing, irresponsible, mad, misconceived, mistaken, monstrous, new-fangled, novel, original, old-fashioned, outdated, out-of-date, outrageous, peculiar, persuasive, preconceived, preposterous, prevalent, provocative, (un)real, (un)realistic, remarkable, revolutionary, ridiculous, risky, sensible, silly, splendid, strange, striking, superficial, untenable, useful, vague, valid, well-defined ~

P: embodiment of, germ of, spread of ~; give sb an ~ of sth; association/chain/exchange/set of *ideas*

IDEAL
V: conform to, correspond to, emulate, fall short of, match, measure up to, recognise, set up ~

IDEALS (aims)
V: betray, cling to, defend, die for, embody, fight for, give up, have, hold, keep, keep to, live up to, lose, match, preserve, pursue, put ~ into practice, shatter ~

V: ~ inspire sb

A: high, lofty, noble, precious, romantic, unattainable ~

IDENTITY
V: admit, assume, claim, conceal, deny, discover, disguise, establish, find out, lose, maintain, prove, reveal, seek, take on, trace ~
A: corporate, different, distinct, false, mistaken, national, new, real, secret, true ~
P: ~ bracelet, card, crisis, tag

IGNORANCE
V: be the result of, betray, demonstrate, display, exhibit, plead, show ~
A: abysmal, blissful, complete, gross, sheer, startling, total, unpardonable, widespread ~

ILLITERACY
V: abolish, eliminate, fight, stamp out, wipe out ~
A: widespread ~

ILLNESS
V: cure, diagnose, fight, get over, go through, have, overcome, recover from, succumb to, suffer from, survive, treat ~
A: brief, dangerous, debilitating, (near-)fatal, imaginary, mysterious, nasty, obscure, painful, psychosomatic, recurrent, serious, severe, short, sudden, terminal, terrible, tragic, untreatable ~
P: after-effects of, onset of, turning-point in sb's ~

ILLUSION
V: cherish, cling to, create, dispel, have, labour under, suffer from ~
P: under the ~ that; under no ~

ILLUSIONS
V: abandon, cling to, destroy, have few/no, lose, shatter ~

ILLUSTRATION
V: give, offer, provide ~
A: clear, colourful, excellent, good, graphic, perfect, remarkable, vivid ~

IMAGE
V: acquire, adopt, assume, boost, build up, change, conjure up, create, cultivate, damage, develop, fit, form, have, improve, maintain, match, offer, present, preserve, project, promote, protect, reinforce, reject, shatter, shed, show, spoil, suggest, tarnish, update ~
V: ~ appeared, arose, faded
A: attractive, better, clear, convincing, credible, crude, daunting, dazzling, different, dynamic, exaggerated, false, familiar, (un)favourable, (un)flattering, forward-looking, glamorous, glitzy, idealised, imposing, likeable, mental, misleading, modern, new, old-fashioned, outdated, out-of-date, pleasing, popular, potent, powerful, precise, public, (un)realistic, romantic, seductive, spurious, stock, striking, sympathetic, traditional, true, wholesome ~

IMAGE (likeness)
A: identical, perfect, real, spitting, true, very ~
P: he's the spitting ~ of his (father)

IMAGINATION
V: appeal to, attribute sth to, capture, catch, excite, exercise, feed, fire, fuel, give (full) rein to, grip, have, rouse, stir, use ~
V: ~ has dried up, is running away with (you), wandered
A: active, colourful, creative, fertile, lively, powerful, vivid, wild ~
P: figment of (your), powers of ~

IMBALANCE
V: cause, correct, create, redress ~
A: dangerous, enormous, glaring, increasing, obvious, ridiculous, serious, severe, slight ~

IMITATION
V: do, give, learn by ~
A: cheap, clever, convincing, excellent, good, pale, perfect, poor ~
IMMIGRANTS
V: admit, deport, expel, vet, welcome ~
A: early, first-generation, illegal, prospective ~
P: flow of, tide of, trickle of ~
IMPACT
V: add to, assess, cushion, diminish, exaggerate, exert, feel, have, make, lessen, offset, realise,
   reduce, resist, soften, take into consideration, weigh ~
A: actual, considerable, decisive, direct, disturbing, evident, extensive, familiar, full, great,
   horrifying, immediate, initial, limited, major, marked, massive, maximum, minimal,
   negligible, painful, potential, powerful, real, revolutionary, serious, severe, slight, strong,
   terrific, tremendous, widespread ~
IMPARTIALITY
V: demonstrate, display, insist on, maintain, preserve, question, show ~
A: absolute, complete, strict, total ~
IMPATIENCE
V: conceal, control, curb, disguise, hide, show ~
A: considerable, growing, increasing ~
IMPLICATION
V: accept, carry, deny, examine, give rise to, have, ignore, point out, realise, reject, see, suggest,
   take into consideration, work out ~
A: apparent, awkward, basic, damaging, devastating, far-reaching, full, general, grave,
   immediate, inevitable, long/short-term, obvious, ominous, profound, real, serious,
   significant, strong, underlying, unfortunate, unlikely, unpleasant ~
IMPORTANCE
V: acknowledge, acquire, add to, appreciate, assess, assume, attach, attest to, be aware of, deny,
   emphasise, estimate, exaggerate, gain in, highlight, indicate, lose, magnify, maximise,
   minimise, overestimate, overrate, play down, point out/to, realise, recognise, stress, take on,
   underestimate, underline, undermine ~
V: ~ declined, fluctuated, grew, increased
A: comparative, considerable, crucial, disproportionate, essential, exceptional, excessive, full,
   fundamental, great, international, intrinsic, key, major, marginal, minor, outstanding, overall,
   overriding, paramount, real, relative, secondary, slight, special, supreme, true, undoubted,
   undue, unique, utmost, vital ~
IMPORTS
V: ban, block, keep ~ down, protect, reduce, regulate, restrict ~
V: ~ fell, rose, went down/up
A: annual (monthly, etc), cheap, essential, growing, Third World ~
P: ban on, restrictions on ~
IMPRESSION (effect)
V: convey, counteract, create, dispel, give, leave, make, produce, spoil, wipe out ~
A: blurred, damaging, decided, deep, definite, delightful, distinct, excellent, faint, false,
   (un)favourable, fleeting, forceful, formidable, great, identical, indelible, initial, lasting,
   marked, momentary, overriding, overwhelming, passing, powerful, profound, slight, strong,
   transient, vague ~
P: get/give the wrong ~

IMPRESSION (belief)

V: come away with, confirm, derive, dispel, form, gain, gather, get, have, labour under, overcome, reinforce ~

V: ~ crystallized, emerged, faded, outweighs, persists, remains

A: clear, coherent, first, general, hazy, misleading, mistaken, overall, overriding ~

IMPROVEMENT

V: achieve, bring about, call for, demand, discern, effect, envisage, expect, keep up, look for, make, perceive, see, show, strive for, undergo ~

V: ~ came about, took place

A: all-round, considerable, continuous, decided, definite, distinct, enormous, general, genuine, gradual, great, huge, immense, lasting, major, marked, material, negligible, noticeable, obvious, perceptible, radical, real, remarkable, significant, slight, steady, substantial, tremendous, undoubted, vast, visible ~

P: room for, signs of ~; programme of *improvements*

IMPULSE

V: feel, do sth on, give way to, have, repress, resist ~

A: creative, foolish, fresh, generous, hasty, inexplicable, initial, instinctive, natural, selfish, strange, strong, sudden, violent ~

INCENTIVE

V: act as, be motivated/tempted by, hold out, offer, provide, remove ~

A: additional, attractive, big, direct, effective, extra, financial, important, main, powerful, real, strong, tempting, tremendous ~

INCIDENT

V: be involved in, be responsible for, cause, cover ~ up, deal with, disregard, exaggerate, give rise to, handle, hold sb responsible for, hush up, ignore, lead to, look into, prevent, provoke, recall, record, report, spark off, suppress, witness ~

V: ~ happened, occurred, took place

A: alarming, amusing, bizarre, brief, chilling, colourful, curious, deplorable, embarrassing, frightening, funny, horrific, humorous, intimidating, ludicrous, macabre, memorable, ominous, painful, nasty, regrettable, remarkable, ridiculous, scandalous, shocking, strange, tragic, trivial, ugly, unexpected, unfortunate, unpleasant, untoward, unusual ~

P: series of, spate of *incidents*

INCLINATION

V: curb, feel, give way to, have, resist ~

A: natural, powerful, strong, sudden ~

INCOME

V: add to, augment, boost, bring in, build up, derive, earn, get, have, increase, produce, receive, reduce, yield ~

V: ~ comes from ... , diminished, fell, fluctuated, grew, increased, rose, shrank, varied, went down/up

A: (in)adequate, annual (monthly, etc), average, basic, comfortable, considerable, disposable, erratic, excellent, good, high, large, low, main, meagre, moderate, modest, regular, reliable, satisfactory, small, steady, substantial, total, vast ~

P: drop in, loss of, rise in, source of ~

INCOMPETENCE

V: be accused of, be guilty of, be sacked for, reveal, show, uncover ~

A: colossal, complete, grave, gross, professional, sheer, total ~

INCREASE

V: ask for, bring about, calculate, demand, forecast, get, grant, maintain, measure, notice, observe, offset, plan, predict, prevent, produce, propose, refuse, reject, request, sanction, show, stop, want, welcome ~

A: alarming, annual (monthly, etc), average, basic, colossal, considerable, continuous, corresponding, dramatic, enormous, enviable, excessive, frightening, full, further, huge, marked, maximum, minimum, moderate, modest, negligible, noticeable, overall, perceptible, rapid, real, reasonable, satisfactory, sharp, slight, slow, staggering, steady, steep, substantial, tiny, total, vast, visible, welcome ~

INCONVENIENCE

V: apologise for, cause, put sb to, put up with, suffer ~

A: considerable, enormous, further, great, slight, terrible ~

INDEPENDENCE

V: achieve, assert, be given, claim, declare, defend, demand, deprive sb of, fight for, gain, get, lose, preserve, proclaim, safeguard, threaten, value, want, win ~

A: complete, full, hard-won, immediate, partial, total ~

P: ~ of mind/spirit

INDEX

V: appear in, compile, find sth in, make, look sth up in, refer to, turn to ~

A: alphabetical, author, card, comprehensive, helpful, numerical, subject ~

INDICATION

V: find, give, have, provide, require, see ~

A: added, clear, definite, (in)direct, faint, favourable, firm, general, little, obvious, possible, prior, reliable, significant, slight, strong, true, unambiguous, undeniable, unmistakable, valid, weak ~

P: give every/some ~ that ...

INDICTMENT

V: answer, face, issue, make, prove ~

A: clear, damning, devastating, serious, strong, sweeping ~

INDIFFERENCE

V: feel, feign, show, treat sb with ~

A: cold, complete, cool, marked, sheer, total, utter, wholesale ~

INDIGNATION

V: arouse, be filled with, blaze with, cause, contain, control, explode with, express, feel, show, voice ~

A: mounting, righteous, strong, widespread ~

P: chorus/storm of ~

INDISCRETION

V: be guilty of, commit, forgive, overlook, reprimand sb for ~

A: foolish, minor, serious, stupid, youthful ~

INDUCEMENT

V: accept, hold out, offer, provide, refuse ~

A: attractive, irresistible, modest, powerful, strong, suitable ~

INDUSTRY

V: build up, close down, cripple, destroy, develop, encourage, re-establish, expand, finance, invest in, manage, modernise, nationalise, privatise, promote, run, run down, stimulate ~

V: ~ came to a standstill, collapsed, developed, expanded, flourished, grew, is at a standstill, is in difficulties, is stagnating, is thriving, prospered, was brought to a standstill

A: ailing, dynamic, efficient, growth, healthy, heavy, light, modern, nationalised, obsolete, old-fashioned, primary, privatised, prosperous, secondary, state, underdeveloped, up-to-date, well-run

P: the (food, car, steel, ship-building etc) ~

INEQUALITY

V: abolish, cause, encourage, eradicate, fight, lead to, make for, oppose, prevent, reduce ~

A: blatant, glaring, great, gross, growing, marked, widespread ~

INFLATION

V: aggravate, beat, bring down, bring ~ under control, cause, combat, conquer, control, cope with, curb, cure, cut, deal with, defeat, fight, fuel, get ~ down, keep a tight rein on, keep ~ under control, lead to, prevent, push up, reduce, squeeze, stop, suffer from ~

V: ~ came down, crept up, declined, dropped, fell, got out of hand, got worse, grew, is out of/under control, levelled out, rose, soared, went up

A: escalating, galloping, high, incipient, low, rampant, rising, runaway, severe, spiralling ~

P: battle against, decline of, fight against, resurgence of ~

INFLUENCE

V: acknowledge, acquire, assert, bring one's ~ to bear, come under, consolidate, constitute, counteract, counterbalance, detect, (re-)establish, exercise, exert, feel, fight against, gain, lessen, lose, maximise, minimise, neutralise, offset, oppose, reassert, represent, resist, trace, use, wield ~

V: ~ affected sb, declined, faded, spread, waned

A: all-pervading, beneficial, benign, big, civilising, considerable, decisive, destructive, direct, dominant, enormous, evil, extensive, far-reaching, formative, full, general, great, growing, harmful, (un)healthy, immense, key, lifelong, malign, marked, moderating, negative, overpowering, overriding, overwhelming, pernicious, persuasive, pervasive, positive, powerful, profound, real, significant, slight, steadying, strong, subtle, superior, transient, tremendous, unprecedented, unsettling, widespread ~

INFORMATION

V: absorb, access, accumulate, analyse, assemble, assimilate, believe, censor, (cross-)check, classify, collate, collect, compile, conceal, contribute, copy, demand, derive, dig out, disclose, disseminate, distort, distribute, divulge, evaluate, exchange, extract, feed, feed in, file, filter, furnish, gather, get, get hold of, get the ~ out of sb, give, glean, hand over, handle, have, have access to, hold back, impart, interpret, leak, make ~ available, need, obtain, part with, pass on, possess, process, produce, provide, receive, record, release, request, require, retrieve, reveal, seek, set out, share, sieve, sift, solicit, sort, sort through, spread, store, study, summarise, sum up, supply, supply sb with, suppress, transmit, (mis)use, verify, volunteer, withhold, yield ~

A: (in)accurate, additional, (in)adequate, alarming, authoritative, awkward, (un)biased, classified, comprehensive, confidential, detailed, embarrassing, essential, exact, exhaustive, extensive, extra, factual, false, first-hand, further, genuine, impartial, important, indispensable, inside, interesting, invaluable, latest, misleading, necessary, objective, official, partial, precise, private, public, recent, relevant, (un)reliable, restricted, (un)satisfactory, scant, (top-)secret, sensitive, sketchy, timely, true, trustworthy, up-to-date, useful, useless, valuable, vital, written ~

P: access to, bits of, channels of, crumbs of, dearth of, dissemination of, flow of, fund of, items of, lack of, mine of, piece of, scraps of, snippets of, source of, stream of, supply of, surfeit of, trickle of, wealth of ~

INGREDIENTS
V: add, mix, prepare, select, stir ~
A: artificial, basic, essential, exotic, main, natural, optional, principal, proper, remaining, secret, vital, wholesome ~

INHERITANCE
V: claim, come into, get, give up, lose, receive, squander ~
A: huge, modest, vast, worthless ~

INITIATIVE
V: call for, demonstrate, display, exercise, have, lack, launch, lose, seize, show, take ~
A: admirable, bold, exceptional, final, great, immediate, independent, latest, outstanding, radical, sole, successful ~
P: act on (your) own ~

INJURY
V: cause, do sb, get over, have, inflict, meet with, receive, recover from, succumb to, suffer, sustain, treat ~
A: fatal, horrible, internal, nasty, serious, severe, slight, terrible ~

INJUSTICE
V: compensate sb for, do sb an, encounter, expose, fight, prevent, redress, remedy, suffer ~
A: blatant, glaring, great, serious, widespread ~

INNOCENCE
V: corrupt, destroy, lose, maintain, protest, prove, recapture, regain, show ~
A: childhood, child-like, complete, lost, pure, simple, total, wide-eyed ~

INNOVATION
V: adopt, apply, come out with, develop, design, exploit, introduce, make, popularise ~
A: attractive, handy, latest, popular, recent, remarkable, successful, useful ~

INSIGHT
V: give, have, show ~
A: deep, fresh, great, profound, rewarding, remarkable, sharp, shrewd, unpleasant, vivid ~
P: flash of ~

INSINUATION
V: defend oneself against, deny, make, (dis)prove, reject ~
A: horrible, nasty, serious, unfair ~

INSPECTION
V: carry out, conduct, make, order, pass ~
A: annual (monthly etc), careful, close, cursory, detailed, meticulous, quick, regular, rigorous, routine, thorough ~

INSPIRATION
V: derive, draw, find ~ in ..., get, give, lack, look for, offer, provide, seek ~
A: divine, fresh, real, sudden, true, unexpected ~
P: flash of, source of, spark of ~

INSTANCE
V: cite, constitute, give, provide, quote, represent ~
A: characteristic, clear, glaring, isolated, particular, rare, significant, typical, unique ~

INSTINCT
V: act on, appeal to, arouse, be born with, curb, follow, give way to, have, obey, resist, satisfy, suppress ~
A: aggressive, basic, deep-rooted, human, maternal, natural, rare, remarkable, strong, sure, uncanny, unerring ~

INSTITUTION
V: do away with, preserve ~
A: antiquated, archaic, charitable, cumbersome, educational, financial, fragile, mental, national, outmoded, out-of-date, permanent, political, powerful, time-honoured, traditional, unique, valuable ~

INSTRUCTIONS
V: carry out, check, follow, give, ignore, issue, keep to, (dis)obey, read, stick to ~
A: careful, (un)clear, definite, detailed, elaborate, exact, explicit, firm, minute, precise, simple, step-by-step, written ~
P: set of ~

INSTRUMENT
A: appropriate, best, effective, efficient, handy, indispensable, ingenious, proper, sensitive, suitable, superb, useful, valuable ~

INSULT
A: cruel, deadly, deliberate, studied, terrible, unforgivable ~
P: an ~ to sb's intelligence

INSURANCE
V: be covered by, cancel, carry, claim (for sth) on, fiddle, offer, provide, renew, sell, take out, underwrite ~
A: (in)adequate, comprehensive, extra, home, mandatory, motor, optional, personal, private, third-party, travel ~
P: ~ policy, premium

INTEGRATION
V: achieve, bring about ~
A: close, full, loose ~

INTELLECT
V: appeal to, challenge ~
A: exceptional, formidable, keen, sharp, superior ~

INTELLIGENCE
V: assess, demonstrate, estimate, have, measure, show, test, use, waste ~
A: above/below-average, formidable, innate, keen, normal, outstanding, poor, remarkable, sharp, superior ~

INTENTION
V: abandon, announce, assert, carry out, change, conceal, declare, defeat, discover, disguise, form, give up, have, interpret, keep to, make clear, misconstrue, pursue, realise, repeat, reveal, state, suspect, (mis)understand ~
A: basic, clear, definite, firm, future, honourable, immediate, main, obvious, original, real ~
P: with the best of *intentions*

INTEREST
V: arouse, awake, catch, develop ~ in ... , encourage, express, feel, feign, focus, foster, generate, have, keep up, lose, profess, raise, retain, revive, show, stimulate, sustain, take, whip up ~
V: ~ declined, dwindled, flagged, focused on sth, grew, peaked, picked up, waned
A: abiding, absorbing, academic, active, brief, burning, close, common, compelling, considerable, consuming, deep, detached, enduring, exceptional, fading, feverish, fleeting, general, great, human, intense, intensive, keen, lively, marked, morbid, mounting, natural, obsessive, passing, passionate, persistent, personal, profound, renewed, scientific, serious, slight, strong, sustained, tremendous, universal, wide-ranging, worldwide ~
P: flicker of, flurry of, lack of, surge of ~

INTEREST (hobby)

V: develop, take up ~

A: absorbing, chief, main ~

INTEREST (money)

V: accumulate, add, calculate, charge, earn, live off, pay, pay back with, receive, work out ~

V: ~ accrues, accumulates

A: compound, simple, substantial ~

P: ~ rate

INTEREST (advantage, gain or benefit)

V: champion, defend, further, have ~ in, jeopardize, promote, protect, safeguard, support, threaten ~

A: basic, business, common, financial, fundamental, joint, legitimate, paramount, vested, vital ~

P: ~ groups; in the national ~; not in your own best, conflict of, look after (British), oil/farming/fishing etc *interests*

INTERFERENCE

V: guard against, permit, prevent, protect sb from, put a stop to, put up with, resent, resist, stop, suffer, tolerate ~

A: blatant, constant, frequent, intolerable, malicious, outside, powerful, shocking, unjustifiable, unprovoked, unwarranted, unwelcome, unwise, well-meant ~

INTERPRETATION

V: give, make, place ~ on sth, put ~ on sth

A: different, free, generous, liberal, loose, narrow, political, strict, unusual ~

INTERRUPTION

V: apologise for, be responsible for, cause, deal with, ignore, resent, silence ~

A: awkward, inconvenient, lengthy, noisy, rude, serious, sudden, tactless, temporary, unexpected, unfortunate ~

INTERVENTION

V: prevent, risk ~

A: armed, military, unwarranted, unwelcome ~

INTERVIEW

V: attend, be called for, conduct, get, give, grant, have, seek ~

A: abrasive, amusing, brief, dramatic, entertaining, exclusive, fascinating, frank, hurried, in-depth, painful, polite, rare, revealing, rewarding, successful ~

INTIMIDATION

V: be subjected to, submit to, suffer, surrender to ~

A: blatant, continued, humiliating ~

P: wave of ~

INTRIGUE

V: carry on, discover, get mixed up in, see through, start ~

A: complicated, nasty, political ~

P: web of ~

INVASION

V: call off, carry out, launch, mount, plan, postpone, prevent, repel, resist, risk, spearhead, start, stop, threaten ~

A: full/large-scale, imminent, massive ~

P: ~ of privacy

INVENTION

V: come up with, make, market, patent, promote, register ~

A: amazing, exciting, incredible, ingenious, marketable, marvellous, novel, revolutionary, successful, unique, wonderful ~

INVESTIGATION

V: aid, be engaged in, be under, call for, carry out, close, conduct, (dis)continue, co-operate with, demand, drop, embark on, hold, hush up, impede, initiate, instigate, make, (re)open, order, press for, pursue, shelve, start, subject sb to, undertake, wind up ~

V: ~ brought sth to light, is under way

A: careful, cautious, close, comprehensive, detailed, exhaustive, frank, full, full-length/scale, internal, laborious, lengthy, official, on-the-spot, painstaking, police, protracted, rough, scientific, searching, thorough, wide, worldwide ~

INVESTMENT

V: attract, channel ~ into sth, cut, cut back, discourage, encourage, increase, inhibit, lose, make, plan, reduce, step up, stifle, stimulate ~

V: ~ bore fruit, gives a return of (7%), yields (7%)

A: careful, cautious, foolish, heavy, important, large-scale, long/short-term, massive, modest, profitable, risky, secure, sound, substantial, successful, wise ~

INVITATION

V: accept, extend, get, give, issue, offer, owe, receive, refuse, respond to, send (out), take up ~

A: casual, cordial, exciting, (in)formal, kind, official, open, personal, pressing, (long-)standing, tempting, welcome ~

INVOICE

V: check, deal with, handle, issue, make out, pay, query, receive, send (out), settle, submit ~

ISLAND

A: desert, exotic, idyllic, isolated, lonely, offshore, remote, tropical, unexplored, uninhabited ~

ISSUE

V: address, approach, argue, attack, avoid, bring up, broach, champion, clarify, complicate, concentrate on, confront, confuse, deal with, debate, decide, defer, delay, discuss, dispute, dodge, evade, examine, exclude, explore, face, fight, force ~ into the open, fudge, gloss over, handle, ignore, inflame, keep ~ open, leave aside, mishandle, mismanage, obscure, raise, resolve, settle, sidestep, (over)simplify, skirt round, solve, study, tackle, take up, touch on, wrestle with ~

V: ~ arose, came up, caused concern, cropped up, divided sb and sb, faded

A: contemporary, controversial, dangerous, debatable, economic, environmental, political, real, serious, single, specific, thorny, topical, tricky ~

ITINERARY

V: announce, change, depart from, fix, follow, keep to, plan, prepare, stick to ~

A: detailed, exact, fixed, flexible, gruelling ~

J

JAIL

V: be released from, break out of, escape from, go to, send sb to, serve time in ~

JOB
V: apply for, be out of a, be put out of, be sacked from, create, find (sb), get, give up, have, hold, hold down, hunt for, leave, look for, lose, offer, resign from, take, take up ~
V: ~ is at stake/in jeopardy
A: absorbing, badly-paid, boring, casual, challenging, cushy, dangerous, dead-end, (un)demanding, difficult, easy, exacting, full/part-time, good, hard, (un)important, interesting, menial, modest, monotonous, (un)pleasant, plum, prestigious, (ir)regular, responsible, routine, satisfying, secure, stable, steady, summer, undistinguished, unpaid, well-paid ~
JOB (task)
V: botch, bungle, do, put off, tackle, take on, undertake, work on ~
A: back-breaking, difficult, hard, laborious, thankless, unenviable, unpleasant ~
JOKE
V: be the butt of, carry ~ too far, crack, tell, make a ~ of sth, play a ~ on sb, see/get the ~
V: ~ backfired
A: blue, dirty, old, pathetic, practical, sick, silly, stale ~
JOURNEY
V: break, commence, complete, embark on, end, go on, make, plan, send sb on, set off on, set out on, start, undertake ~
A: adventurous, arduous, dangerous, dreadful, (un)eventful, exciting, exhausting, hazardous, homeward, long, outward, (un)pleasant, return, safe, short, strenuous, tiring, triumphant ~
P: on the ~ home
JOY
V: be overcome with, dance for, express, feel, jump for ~
A: boundless, great, sheer ~
JUDGEMENT
V: (dis)agree with, affect sb's, arrive at, back sb's, cloud/colour (your), comply with, display, dispute, endorse, exercise, express, form, give, have confidence/faith in sb's, impair, make, offer, overrule, pass ~ on ..., rely on, show, suspend, trust, use, vindicate, withhold ~
A: balanced, (un)biased, considered, correct, excellent, (un)fair, faultless, faulty, final, good, impartial, poor, rational, reasonable, shrewd, sound, valid, unanimous, wrong ~
P: error of ~; against (my) better ~
JUDGEMENT (court decision)
V: appeal against, comply with, deliver, dispute, enforce, give, hand down ~, issue, overturn, pass ~ on sb, pronounce, suspend ~
JURY
V: charge, dismiss, instruct, serve on, swear in ~
V: ~ convicted sb of (burglary), is (still) out, returned a (guilty) verdict, found sb guilty/not guilty
P: members of, trial by ~
JUSTICE
V: administer, deal out, dispense, escape, mete out, obstruct ~
A: impartial, natural, rough, summary, swift ~
P: miscarriage of, pervert the course of ~
JUSTIFICATION
V: find (no), give, have, invent, offer, produce, put forward, see ~
A: convincing, elaborate, moral, plausible, proper, rational, real, reasonable, (in)sufficient ~
P: There is every/no ~ for ...

K

KING
V: crown, depose, proclaim ~
V: ~ abdicated, came to the throne, inherited the throne, reigned, ruled, was crowned
A: cruel, foolish, popular, proud, strong, tyrannical, weak, wise ~
KISS
V: give sb, have, steal ~
A: goodbye, goodnight, passionate, tender ~
P: give sb the ~ of life
KNOWLEDGE
V: absorb, accumulate, acquire, apply, add to, build up, develop, disseminate, soak up, draw on, have, imbibe, impart, improve, lack, possess, seek, spread, store up, use ~
A: advanced, all-round, comprehensive, common, considerable, deep, detailed, encyclopaedic, exact, excellent, extensive, fair, first-hand, inadequate, inside, intimate, invaluable, outstanding, phenomenal, poor, profound, routine, rudimentary, slight, sufficient, superficial, wide, widespread ~
P: body of, boundaries of, branch of, quest for, search for, store of, thirst for ~; disclaim all ~ of, have a working ~ of ...

L

LABOUR (workers)
V: employ, engage, exploit, hire, need, recruit, require, take on, transfer, use ~
A: additional, casual, child, extra, migrant, mobile, (un)skilled, slave, surplus ~
P: ~ relations; (free) movement of ~
LABOUR (work)
A: forced, hard, manual, physical, tiring, unnecessary, wasted ~
LACK
V: draw attention to, excuse, experience, feel, make up for, overlook, point out, suffer ~
A: conspicuous, desperate, general, lamentable, painful, serious, severe ~
LAND
V: clear, cultivate, irrigate, live off, reclaim, work ~
A: agricultural, arable, barren, farming, fertile, grazing, parched, prime, waste ~
P: piece of, plot of ~
LANGUAGE
V: acquire, brush up, choose, control, develop, enrich, have a good command of, improve, learn, master, pick up, pollute, share, speak, standardise, teach, use ~
A: ancient, artificial, bad, classical, coarse, colloquial, colourful, common, complex, correct, crude, dead, difficult, elegant, emotive, everyday, filthy, first, flowery, foreign, (in)formal, foul, inflammatory, international, living, modern, native, natural, obscene, official, plain, poetic, primitive, offensive, racist, refined, second, sexist, sign, simple, spoken, strong, technical, universal, vulgar, written ~

LAUGH
V: get, give, raise, stifle, suppress ~
A: belly, bitter, cruel, good, hearty, loud, mischievous, nervous ~

LAUGHTER
V: break out into, give rise to, provoke, roar with ~
V: ~ broke out
A: convulsive, cruel, derisive, hearty, infectious, innocent, lighthearted, loud, mocking, nervous, scornful ~
P: burst of, gales of, peals of, shout of, shrieks of, tears of ~

LAW
V: abide by, administer, apply, be against, be above, break, change, clarify, codify, comply with, contravene, defy, depart from, endorse, enforce, establish, face, fall foul of, flout, go against, ignore, impose, invoke, keep to, maintain, modify, (dis)obey, observe, offend, rebel against, recognise, resist, respect, revise, stay within, strengthen, tighten, uphold, violate ~
V: ~ operates, stipulates/states that ...
A: (in)effective, just, oppressive, powerful ~
P: body of, breach of, breakdown of, code of, infringement of, loophole in, respect for, supremacy of, violation of ~

LAW (an Act)
V: amend, apply, bring in, change, contravene, draft, enact, enforce, formulate, frame, ignore, implement, infringe, introduce, issue, make, observe, pass, repeal, revoke, suspend ~
V: ~ applies, bans ... , came into effect/force, establishes ... , takes effect
A: draconian, oppressive, strict, unenforceable, unworkable ~

LAW AND ORDER
V: enforce, keep, maintain, preserve, respect, restore ~
P: breakdown in, establishment of, maintenance of ~

LEAD
V: assume, contest, challenge, establish, follow, give, give up, go into the, have, hold, increase, keep, lose, maintain, move into the, narrow, take, take over, whittle away, wipe out ~
A: clear, decided, magnificent, narrow, slight, substantial, unassailable ~

LEADER
V: appoint, choose, elect, select ~
A: born, charismatic, convincing, forceful, formidable, inspired, natural, strong, undisputed ~

LEADERSHIP
V: assume, exercise, exert, relinquish, surrender, take on, take over ~
A: resolute, strong ~
P: ~ contest, qualities; bid for ~

LECTURE
V: attend, deliver, give ~
A: absorbing, brief, brilliant, closing, fascinating, informative, instructive, interesting, introductory, lucid, memorial, opening, witty ~

LEGISLATION
V: adopt, apply, bring in, call for, dodge, draft, enact, introduce, issue, lay down, look up, make, obstruct, pass, prepare, press for, push through, put through, repeal, speed up, veto, vote down ~
V: ~ covers sth, is overdue, is pending, provides for sth
A: effective, far-seeking, harsh, inadequate, liberal, strict, tough ~
P: loophole in, package of ~

LESSON
V: attend, cancel, give, go to, miss, sit in on, skip, (fail to) turn up to ~
A: advanced, beginners', bitter, difficult, enjoyable, first, harsh, important, intermediate, painful, salutary, useful, valuable, vital ~

LETTER
V: deliver, dictate, drop ~ in the post, get, mail, open, post, receive, seal, send, stamp, take ~
A: anonymous, brief, business, chain, covering, detailed, follow-up, long, love, open, personal, poison-pen, rambling ~
P: ~ of application, of complaint, of resignation

LEVEL
V: aim at, aspire to, establish, exceed, fall below, keep up, maintain, reach, surpass, sustain ~
V: ~ deteriorated, improved, remained steady
A: abysmal, advanced, amateur, ambitious, average, elementary, good, high, mediocre, modest, normal, overall, poor, professional, proper, reasonable, required, satisfactory, superior, uniform, usual ~

LEVEL (physical)
V: alter, assess, bring down, come up to, estimate, exceed, fall below, fix, gauge, keep up, lower, maintain, raise, reach, regulate, rise above, set ~
V: ~ fell, remained the same, rose, sank, went down
A: critical, current, recommended, record, safe ~

LIABILITY
V: accept, acknowledge, admit, assume, deny, incur ~
A: full, limited ~

LIAR
V: call sb ~
A: accomplished, bad, born, compulsive, good, inveterate, pathological ~

LIBERTY
V: be at, deprive sb of, enjoy, fight for, grant, obtain ~
P: infringement of, loss of ~

LIBRARY
V: accumulate, add to, compile, endow ~
A: extensive, fine, impressive, massive, priceless, superb, valuable, unique, vast ~

LICENCE
V: apply for, get, grant, issue, lose, receive, renew, revoke, suspend sb's ~
V: ~ has become invalid, is out of date, lapsed
A: driving, export, permanent, renewable, special, temporary, (in)valid ~

LIE
V: believe, spread, tell ~
A: absolute, barefaced, blatant, definite, deliberate, downright, evident, monstrous, obvious, out-and-out, plausible, pointless, shameless, white, whopping ~
P: pack of, tissue of, web of *lies*

LIFE (way of life)
V: disrupt, enjoy, hanker after, lead, live, pursue, ruin, spoil ~
A: active, adventurous, blameless, boisterous, busy, dangerous, dull, eccentric, exciting, exemplary, frivolous, full, hard-working, hectic, humdrum, idyllic, industrious, lazy, lonely, placid, quiet, secluded, sedentary, selfish, sociable, solitary, strenuous, useful, useless, varied, virtuous ~
P: pleasures of, quality of, university of, way of ~

LIFE (life history)
V: blight, enrich, have, ruin ~
A: agreeable, (un)comfortable, decent, difficult, dull, easy, (un)eventful, fascinating, frustrating, good, hard, harsh, idyllic, (un)interesting, miserable, narrow, obscure, (un)pleasant, rewarding, satisfactory, satisfying, sheltered, wretched ~
P: fabric of, turning-point in ~
LIFE (physical)
V: claim, cling to, cut ~ short, end, go through, lay down, live, lose, prolong, put an end to, risk, save, shorten, spend, take ~
V: ~ was cut off
P: quality of, right to ~
LIGHT
V: dim, extinguish, put on/out/off, shine, switch off/on, turn off/on/out ~
V: ~ (dis)appeared, blazed, blinded sb, dazzled sb, flickered, gleamed, glimmered, glowed, illuminated ... , is visible, shone, twinkled, went out
A: blazing, blinding, bright, brilliant, candle, dazzling, diffuse, dim, (in)direct, electric, fading, faint, false, flashing, fluorescent, full, gas, hard, harsh, poor, powerful, pure, radiant, shimmering, shining, silvery, soft, translucent ~
LIMIT
V: approach, break through, come within, disregard, exceed, fix, go beyond/outside/over/past, impose, keep below/to, lay down, mark, observe, pass, pass beyond, place, put, raise, reach, recognise, remain within, remove, set, stick to, stretch, surpass, violate, watch ~
A: absolute, flexible, lower, outside, permitted, precise, reasonable, rigid, strict, upper ~
P: be bounded by, extend, fall within, go outside, take/test sth to its, work within *limits*
LIMITATIONS
V: acknowledge, impose, know my own, recognise ~
LINE (policy)
V: adopt, advocate, applaud, develop, draw, follow, pursue, reject, take ~
A: conciliatory, consistent, definite, distinct, firm, independent, rigid, strong, tough ~
P: toe the party ~
LINK
V: break, create, cut, establish, forge, form, keep, maintain, preserve, retain, sever, shatter ~
V: ~ binds sth, connects sth
A: close, direct, existing, fragile, lasting, loose, missing, permanent, reliable, strong, tenuous, unique, vital ~
LIST
V: add to, assemble, circulate, close, compile, consult, cross sb off, cut down, delete sth from, draw up, exhaust, extend, go down, go through, head, include sth in, make, prune, put sth in, rattle off, reduce, reel off, revise, submit, supply, swell, update, whittle down ~
A: additional, complete, comprehensive, exhaustive, expanding, extensive, final, formidable, full, impressive, long, mailing, never-ending, provisional, restricted, short, tentative ~
LIVING
V: earn, get, make, scrape ~
A: adequate, comfortable, good, honest, modest, precarious ~
LOAD
V: carry, deliver, lessen, lighten, shed, take on, transport ~
A: capacity, dangerous, enormous, full, light, hazardous, heavy, maximum, precarious, substantial ~

LOAN
V: apply for, approve, arrange (for), get, give, grant, negotiate, obtain, pay back/off, raise, receive, repay, reschedule, secure, service, take on, take out ~
A: bank, generous, huge, large, long/short-term ~

LOCATION
V: choose, decide on, discover, establish, fix, pinpoint, settle ~
A: excellent, good, ideal, perfect, poor, (un)suitable ~

LOGIC
V: apply, argue against, defy, follow, grasp, see, use ~
A: cold, hard, harsh, inner, plain, pure, sheer, simple, strict ~

LOOK
V: get, give sb, have ~
A: angry, anxious, blank, cold, dirty, disapproving, faraway, filthy, frosty, gentle, grave, hard, hostile, inquiring, intense, knowing, nasty, puzzled, quizzical, searching, strange, thoughtful, vacant, withering, worried ~

LOSS (emotional)
V: bear, compensate for, experience, get over, make up for, mourn, reconcile oneself to, recover from, suffer ~
A: bitter, cruel, great, heavy, keen, painful, sad, severe, tragic, tremendous, unbearable ~

LOSSES (financial)
V: announce, assess, calculate, count, cover, estimate, incur, make, make good, minimise, offset, recoup, recover, reduce, run up, sustain, underwrite, write off ~
V: ~ amount to ... , climbed, mounted up
A: catastrophic, combined, considerable, crippling, disastrous, heavy, huge, irreversible, negligible, serious, severe, spectacular, steady, substantial, tremendous, unavoidable, worrying ~

LOVE
V: fall in/out of, find, look for, inspire, send ~
V: ~ cooled, endured, grew
A: blind, burning, deep, everlasting, intense, mutual, obsessive, platonic, profound, puppy, pure, secret, tender, true, undying, unrequited, young ~

LOYALTY
V: claim, command, count on, earn, forfeit, give, merit, rely on sb's, reward, show, strain, swear ~ to sb, test ~
A: absolute, total, true, undying, unswerving ~

LUCK
V: be down on one's, be out of, bring, have, push, try one's ~
V: ~ deserted sb, improved, ran out, smiled on sb, took a turn for the worse, turned
A: bad, good, hard, pure, rotten, sheer, tough ~
P: beginner's, bit of, run of bad/good, slice of (good), stroke of ~

LUGGAGE
V: check in, collect, label, pick up ~
A: heavy, light ~

LUNCH
V: book, eat, get, go out to/for, have, make, prepare ~
A: 3-course, early, heavy, late, light, liquid, picnic, packed ~
P: ~ break

M

MACHINE
V: activate, operate, run, service, shut down, start, work ~
A: antiquated, bulky, efficient, foolproof, ingenious, intricate, obsolete, old-fashioned, revolutionary, simple, sophisticated, versatile, worn-out ~

MACHINERY
V: create, mobilise, provide, put ~ in motion, set up, use ~
A: complicated, effective, efficient, flexible, ingenious, modern, obsolete, old-fashioned, sophisticated, state-of-the-art, up-to-date, useful ~

MAIL
V: check, deliver, do, forward, go through, send by/out/through, sort (out) ~

MAJORITY
V: aim at, cut, enhance, gain, get, have, hold onto, increase, obtain, preserve, push up, receive, reduce, retain, secure, win ~
V: ~ grew, shrank, slipped, was cut, went down/up
A: absolute, clear, comfortable, decisive, definite, existing, generous, handsome, large, massive, overall, overwhelming, powerful, respectable, safe, secure, simple, slender, slight, slim, solid, straight, substantial, sweeping, thumping, tiny, unprecedented, vast, workable, working ~

MALNUTRITION
V: die of, suffer from, treat sb for ~
A: serious, severe, widespread ~

MANAGEMENT (control)
A: aggressive, brilliant, careful, day-to-day, (in)efficient, general, inspired, intelligent, poor, skilled, sound, strategic, strong, weak ~

MANAGEMENT (people)
A: junior, middle, senior, top ~
P: be under new, change of ~; a ~ team

MANIFESTO
V: draw up, issue, publish, sign, support ~

MANNER
V: adopt, affect, assume, display, maintain ~
A: abrupt, aggressive, (dis)agreeable, arrogant, assertive, attractive, austere, autocratic, authoritative, avuncular, awkward, bluff, blunt, bossy, brisk, brusque, brutal, bullying, businesslike, callous, careful, careless, casual, caustic, cavalier, charming, cheerful, civilised, clear-headed, clever, clumsy, coarse, cold, cordial, deliberate, determined, diffident, direct, discreet, domineering, down-to-earth, earnest, easygoing, ebullient, effective, efficient, elaborate, emphatic, exaggerated, firm, flamboyant, flippant, forbidding, forceful, forthcoming, frank, friendly, frigid, frivolous, furtive, gentle, gracious, grand, grandiose, haphazard, hearty, high-handed, hostile, humane, impressive, inconsistent, indecisive, ingratiating, kindly, majestic, matter-of-fact, methodical, meticulous, nasty, obsequious, offensive, off-hand, off-putting, organised, peremptory, persuasive, (un)pleasant, polite, pompous, provocative, quiet, relaxed, retiring, rude, sarcastic, secretive, self-confident, sharp, shy, sloppy, sociable, stealthy, stiff, stupid, subtle, systematic, tactful, timid, traditional, underhand, unfortunate, usual, vague, vivacious, vulgar, warm, welcoming, ~
P: behave in a/an (adjective) ~

MANUSCRIPT
V: accept, edit, proofread, read sth in, reject, revise, submit ~
A: authentic, extant, final, original, precious, (un)publishable, unpublished ~
MAP
V: check, compile, consult, draw, follow, look sth up on, make, mark sth on, plot sth on, produce, read, use ~
A: accurate, contour, detailed, excellent, field, large/small-scale, poor, relief, road, sketch, up-to-date, weather ~
MARGIN (financial)
A: comfortable, considerable, handsome, large, narrow, safe, slender, slim, small, wide ~
MARK (characteristic)
V: bear, show ~
A: distinguishing, noticeable, permanent, unmistakable ~
MARK (impression)
V: leave, make, remove ~
A: deep, definite, indelible, permanent, visible ~
MARKET
V: be driven out of, be pushed out of, be squeezed out of, break into, capture, come onto, corner, damage, discover, dominate, enter, expand, explore, extend, find, flood, kill, look for, lose, misjudge, open up, operate, penetrate, research, ruin, saturate, seek, segment, study, take over, tap, unsettle, withdraw from, woo ~
V: ~ is booming, declined, disappeared, dried up, flourished, fluctuated, is vulnerable to sth, plummeted, shrank
A: black, buyers', competitive, declining, domestic, expanding, export, extensive, falling, flat, good, growing, healthy, huge, international, lucrative, narrow, new, overseas, potential, profitable, ready, restricted, sensitive, sluggish, specialist, stable, static, vast, volatile, worldwide, wide ~
P: ~ research, researcher, segmentation, survey
MARRIAGE
V: announce, annul, arrange, break up, consummate, end, enter into, get out of, preserve, put an end to, rescue, ruin, save, spoil ~
V: ~ broke down/up, collapsed, endured, lasted, survived, was a failure/a success, went downhill
A: arranged, contented, disastrous, early, foolish, (un)happy, hasty, lasting, late, loveless, mixed, perfect, shotgun ~
P: ~ of convenience; breakdown of, break-up of ~
MARTIAL LAW
V: declare, impose, lift, suspend, violate ~
P: easing of, imposition of, relaxation of ~
MATERIAL (information etc)
V: accumulate, acquire, arrange, check, classify, collate, collect, come across, compile, examine, gather, get hold of, handle, hand over, index, look over/through, marshal, organise, provide, question, release, sift, study, supply, suppress, use, withhold ~
V: ~ came to light, shed light on sth
A: abundant, (in)adequate, ample, contemporary, documentary, factual, fascinating, first-hand, pertinent, previously unknown/unpublished, relevant, up-to-date, useful ~
P: abundance of, lack of, shortage of ~

MATTER

V: air, attend to, bring ~ to an end, bring up, brush ~ aside, clear up, clinch, complicate, consider, cope with, deal with, decide, drop, elucidate, examine, get to the bottom of, go into, ignore, inquire into, investigate, pursue, raise, remedy, report, resolve, settle, simplify, take up, weigh up ~

V: ~ arose, came to a head/to the fore, came up, cropped up, dragged on

A: awkward, complicated, controversial, delicate, difficult, domestic, grave, (un)important, incidental, insignificant, intimate, intricate, legal, mundane, outstanding, pressing, serious, specific, trivial, unpleasant, unusual, urgent ~

P: (no) consensus on the ~ of ...; core/crux/gist/heart of ~

MEAL

V: cook, enjoy, fix, invite sb out/over for, miss, order, prepare, serve, sit down to, skip ~

A: (3-)course, decent, evening, frugal, hearty, heavy, lavish, light, main, midday, simple, square, sumptuous, vegetarian ~

MEANING

V: clarify, communicate, conceal, convey, deduce, discover, elucidate, explain, express, extend, grasp, guess, ignore, misconstrue, mistake, probe, seek, take in, uncover, understand ~

A: abstruse, accepted, ambiguous, basic, broad, clear-cut, conventional, current, distinct, elusive, fundamental, general, literal, narrow, obscure, profound, real, sinister, specific, true ~

MEANS

V: apply, decide upon, discover, employ, exhaust, find, justify, make use of, take, try, use ~

A: (in)adequate, appropriate, available, best, brutal, clever, cunning, devious, (in)direct, dishonest, doubtful, effective, (un)fair, foul, handy, indefensible, ingenious, novel, obvious, overt, reprehensible, satisfactory, straightforward, subtle, suitable, underhand, useful ~

MEANS (financial)

V: have, live beyond/within ~

A: adequate, ample, independent, limited, modest, private, sufficient ~

MEASURES

V: adopt, advocate, apply, carry out, implement, institute, introduce, oppose, outline, prepare, propose, put ~ in hand, resort to, take, tighten up, use, work out ~

V: ~ are called for, are in force, have been put into operation, take effect

A: (in)adequate, appropriate, conciliatory, comprehensive, desperate, detailed, drastic, effective, emergency, energetic, extreme, firm, forceful, harsh, immediate, important, impracticable, interim, obstructive, practical, preliminary, preventive, prudent, remedial, repressive, sensible, stern, strict, stringent, strong, temporary, tough, unprecedented, urgent ~

P: package of, series of, set of ~

MEAT

V: barbecue, boil, braise, carve, cure, cut, (stir-)fry, grill, (spit-)roast, slice, tenderise ~

A: chewy, cold, cooked, dark, fatty, juicy, lean, leathery, raw, red, tender, tough, white ~

P: cut of, joint of, piece of, slice of ~

MECHANISM

V: make use of, set in motion ~

V: ~ broke down, worked

A: clumsy, complicated, crude, elaborate, flexible, simple, sophisticated, unique, useful ~

MEDICATION

V: administer, be off/on, come off, continue with, discontinue, give, go on, need, order, prescribe, take, take sb off ~

A: effective, mild, strong ~

124

MEETING (formal)

V: address, adjourn, arrange, attend, ban, break up, bring ~ forward, cancel, call, call off, chair, close, conduct, convene, disrupt, fix, have, hold, interrupt, open, organise, postpone, preside over, put off, skip, turn up at, wind up, wreck ~

V: ~ broke up, ended, ended in deadlock

A: ad hoc, amicable, annual (monthly, etc), brief, casual, emergency, enthusiastic, friendly, fruitful, heated, high-level, historic, hostile, impending, initial, international, key, lengthy, long, noisy, (dis)orderly, packed, preliminary, prolonged, protracted, rowdy, short, stormy, successful, summit, tense, urgent, useful ~

MEMBER

A: active, associate, card-carrying, founding, full, honorary, leading, life, retired ~

MEMORY

V: banish, blot out, bring back, cherish, commit sth to, evoke, haunt, have, jog, lose, obliterate, perpetuate, preserve, reawaken, recover, refresh, speak from, stick in the, stimulate, tarnish ~

V: ~ faded, haunts sb, lingers, lives on, rankles

A: accurate, amazing, bitter, bitter-sweet, clear, confused, dim, enduring, excellent, faulty, fond, frightening, good, happy, hazy, infallible, keen, long, long-term, painful, (im)perfect, (un)pleasant, poignant, poor, phenomenal, photographic, powerful, prodigious, retentive, sad, sentimental, short, short-term, terrible, vague, visual, vivid ~

P: feat of, loss of, recovery of ~

MERCHANDISE

V: carry, display, examine, order, purchase, ship, stock ~

A: assorted, first-class, general, high-quality, top-quality ~

P: choice of, range of ~

MESS (dirty state)

V: clean away/up, clear away/up, get into, leave, leave sth in, make, sort out, sweep up ~

A: absolute, awful, dreadful, real, shocking, terrible, total ~

MESS (confused state)

V: clear up, get into/out of, leave, leave sb/sth in, make, sort out ~

A: absolute, awful, dreadful, fine, proper, real, shocking, terrible, total ~

MESSAGE

V: acknowledge, announce, broadcast, carry, collect, contain, convey, decipher, decode, deliver, explain, get, give, intercept, interpret, leave, mix up, pass on, receive, record, relay, release, report, (un)scramble, send, stop, take, take down, take note of, transmit, (mis)understand ~

V: ~ arrived, got through

A: blunt, clear, coded, complicated, confused, desperate, frantic, friendly, garbled, genuine, important, kind, mysterious, personal, private, right, special, stark, urgent, wrong ~

METHOD

V: adopt, apply, be familiar with, change, choose, decide on, describe, develop, devise, discard, discover, employ, endorse, evolve, explain, follow, give up, improve, introduce, invent, keep to, know of, look for, outline, pioneer, popularise, produce, recommend, resort to, stick to, study, use, test, try, try out ~

V: ~ failed, worked

A: antiquated, common, complex, controversial, (un)conventional, costly, crude, dubious, effective, efficient, existing, (un)familiar, fashionable, feasible, handy, infallible, ingenious, innovative, legitimate, modern, novel, obsolete, old-fashioned, (un)orthodox, out-of-date, practicable, practical, proven, reliable, risky, sophisticated, straightforward, strange, traditional, tried-and-tested, unique, unscrupulous, up-to-date, useful, (un)usual ~

MIND
V: bear in, bring sth to, change (your), clog, come to, cultivate, develop, dominate, keep in, make (your) ~ up, speak (my), train ~
V: ~ boggles, deteriorated, drifted, failed, strayed, turned to ..., wandered, works
A: active, acute, agile, alert, analytical, astute, brilliant, calculating, clear, closed, coarse, creative, critical, cunning, devious, dirty, (un)disciplined, disorganised, dull, first-class, flexible, fresh, good, great, incisive, inquiring, inquisitive, inventive, keen, lazy, limited, lively, logical, lucid, methodical, muddled, nasty, one-track, orderly, original, outstanding, penetrating, powerful, quick, sharp, shrewd, sophisticated, superior, suspicious, systematic, tough, unbalanced, versatile, vulgar, warped, well-trained, whole, woolly ~
P: apply/put/set (your) ~ to ... ; have a good/quick, keep an open, it slipped (my) ~; take (your) ~ off ...

MIND (conscience)
V: disturb, ease, get sth off (your), have sth on (your), put (my) ~ at rest, relieve, trouble ~

MIND (mental health)
V: cloud, restore ~
V: ~ deteriorated, failed, gave way
A: disturbed, twisted, unbalanced ~

MINUTES (of a meeting)
V: accept, circulate, draw up, edit, keep, pass, read, reject, sign, take ~

MISCHIEF
V: cause, do, get into, keep oneself out of, make, stay out of ~

MISCONCEPTION
V: avoid, prevent ~
V: ~ arose, occurred
A: popular, unfortunate, widespread ~

MISCONDUCT
V: accuse sb of, be guilty of, charge sb with, complain of ~
A: gross, persistent, professional, serious ~

MISDEMEANOUR
V: be guilty of, commit ~
A: foolish, petty, serious ~

MISERY
V: alleviate, bring, cause, relieve, suffer ~
A: abject, sheer, untold, utter ~

MISFORTUNE
V: get over, have, suffer ~
A: appalling, great, overwhelming, serious, terrible, tragic ~

MISGIVINGS
V: allay, conceal, express, feel, overcome, voice ~
A: grave, serious, strong ~

MISSION
V: accept, accomplish, carry out, complete, embark on, fulfil, perform, send sb on, undertake ~
A: clandestine, delicate, dangerous, fact-finding, goodwill, hazardous, humanitarian, hush-hush, important, rescue, secret, suicide ~

MISTAKE
V: admit, clear up, commit, correct, cover up, excuse, forgive, make, make good, overlook, rectify, remedy ~

V: ~ appeared, crept in, occurred

A: appalling, bad, basic, big, careless, catastrophic, colossal, common, costly, crucial, disastrous, fatal, foolish, fundamental, ghastly, glaring, grave, huge, laughable, serious, silly, slight, typical, unfortunate ~

MISTRUST

V: add to, feel, increase, overcome ~

A: deep, instinctive, profound, strong ~

MISUNDERSTANDING

V: cause, clear up, lead to, prevent ~

A: appalling, basic, fundamental, genuine, serious, slight, unfortunate ~

MIXTURE

V: concoct, invent, produce, try ~

A: bizarre, complex, curious, dangerous, extraordinary, fascinating, heady, obscure, poisonous, strange ~

MOB

V: address, control, disperse, harangue, incite, inflame, rouse, subdue ~

V: ~ collected, dispersed, fled, got out of control, scattered

A: angry, dangerous, disorderly, howling, large, rampaging, rowdy, undisciplined, unruly, violent ~

MOMENT

V: choose, judge, mark, pick, savour ~

A: anxious, appropriate, apt, awkward, bleak, convenient, critical, crowning, crucial, embarrassing, favourable, good, historic, last, memorable, odd, opportune, proper, rare, right, sad, solemn, subtle, suitable, uncomfortable, vital, worrying, wrong ~

MOMENTUM

V: (re)gain, gather, increase, keep up, lose, maintain, pick up, slow down, work up ~

MONEY

V: advance, bank, borrow, bring in, deposit, change, earn, extort, fritter ~ away, hoard, invest, launder, lend, make, pay out, print, provide, put ~ into, put up, raise, recover, refund, repay, return, run out of, save, set aside, sink ~ into, spare, spend, squander, tie up, transfer, withdraw ~

V: ~ circulates, loses its value, ran out

A: counterfeit, easy, hush-, monopoly, pocket-, prize, ready, sound, spending, worthless ~

MONOPOLY

V: abolish, acquire, break, create, do away with, end, enjoy, establish, exercise, gain, have, hold ~

A: lucrative, state-run, (near) total ~

MONUMENT

V: build, erect, put up, unveil ~

V: ~ commemorates sb, stands ...

A: ancient, historic, historical, imposing, national ~

MOOD

V: affect, analyse, create, disperse, feel, get into, gauge, generate, have, know, read, reflect, sense ~

V: ~ changed, lasted, passed, persisted, prevailed, vanished

A: angry, bad, benign, bitter, black, buoyant, cheerful, confident, depressed, ebullient, euphoric, extravagant, foul, gloomy, good, happy, jovial, mellow, optimistic, passing, pensive, pessimistic, sombre, suspicious, ugly ~

MOON
V: cover, obscure ~
V: ~ hung, rose, set, shone, waned, waxed
A: crescent, full, harvest, new, orange, pale, silvery ~

MORALE
V: be bad/good for, boost, damage, destroy, keep up, lift, lower, maintain, raise, recover, sap, strengthen, undermine ~
V: ~ collapsed, improved, was at a low ebb
A: good, high, low, shattered ~
P: boost to, decline in, revival of ~

MORALS
V: corrupt, improve, inculcate, protect, safeguard ~
A: lax, loose, low, rigid, strict ~

MORTGAGE (loan for a house)
V: apply for, arrange, get, give, offer, pay off, repay, take out ~

MOTION (proposal)
V: adopt, agree to, carry, defeat, discuss, examine, introduce, lose, move, oppose, pass, propose, put forward, reject, second, support, table, vote against/for/on, withdraw ~
A: emergency, (un)popular ~
P: ~ was carried/defeated/passed

MOTIVATION
V: have, find, improve, increase, lack, look for, misunderstand, seek, strengthen ~
A: good, poor, strong, weak ~

MOTIVE
V: applaud, be guided/influenced by, confess, doubt, establish, explain, have, impugn, pinpoint, question, suspect, understand ~
V: ~ drove sb to do sth, induced sb to do sth, is behind sth, is suspect, lay behind sth, made sb do sth, prompted sb to do sth
A: altruistic, clear, clear-cut, disinterested, genuine, hidden, highest, mysterious, noble, obscure, powerful, pure, selfish, selfless, sinister, strong, subconscious, ulterior, ultimate, unconscious, underhand, underlying ~

MOTOR
V: burn out, operate, repair, replace, run, service, start, stop, switch off/on, wear out, wreck ~
V:~ functions, operates, overheated, runs, wore out, works
A: electric, noisy, powerful ~

MOVE
V: applaud, back, be involved in, block, counter, decide on, follow, initiate, instigate, make, prevent, risk, stop short of, thwart, veto ~
V: ~ fell flat, is under consideration, paid off, went ahead/on
A: astute, audacious, bad, bold, brave, brilliant, careful, careless, cautious, clever, conciliatory, correct, costly, cunning, dangerous, daring, decisive, deliberate, disastrous, discreet, drastic, expensive, false, fatal, generous, imminent, important, inept, inevitable, irresponsible, irrevocable, judicious, masterly, pre-emptive, political, prudent, rash, right, sensible, shrewd, significant, smart, spontaneous, suspicious, tactful, tactless, tentative, unprecedented, wily, (un)wise, wrong ~

MOVEMENT
V: control, direct, execute, hamper, make, observe, regulate, repeat, restrict, slow down, speed up, stop ~

A: agile, aggressive, awkward, brisk, clumsy, constant, economical, flowing, graceful, hesitant, incessant, involuntary, jerky, large-/small-scale, leisurely, nervous, purposeful, quick, rapid, regular, restless, rhythmic, sharp, significant, slow, smooth, steady, swaying, swift, sudden, twisting, uncontrolled, unexpected, unhurried, violent ~

MOVEMENT (political, social)

V: back, ban, finance, form, fund, found, head, infiltrate, join, lead, organise, penetrate, popularise, put down, run, split, stamp out, start, support, suppress, work for ~

V: ~ aims to, is calling/fighting for ... , expanded, gained momentum, grew, lost its popularity, split, spread

A: active, democratic, fringe, fundamentalist, growing, (un)important, left-wing, militant, narrow, opposition, (un)popular, powerful, radical, religious, revolutionary, right-wing, strong, underground, weak, widespread ~

MURDER

V: be guilty of, commit, cover up, investigate, uncover ~

A: brutal, callous, cold-blooded, deliberate, grisly, indiscriminate, mindless, motiveless, multiple, premeditated, sensational, vicious ~

P: ~ trial, victim

MUSCLE

V: contract, develop, flex, move, pull, relax, strain, tear, tense, wrench ~

MUSIC

V: compose, make, perform, play, read, set sth to, write ~

V: ~ blared out, blasted out, played

A: background, ballet, church, classical, country, country and western, deafening, early, folk, gentle, gorgeous, guitar/piano etc, haunting, lively, loud, modern, moving, orchestral, piped, pop, popular, relaxing, repetitive, romantic, slow, soft, soothing, sublime, sweet, uplifting ~

MYSTERY

V: be shrouded in, clear up, explain, solve, unravel ~

A: baffling, deep, insoluble, intriguing, real, unfathomable, unsolved ~

P: air of, aura of ~

MYTH

V: cherish, create, destroy, dispel, establish, explode, propagate ~

A: ancient, complete, popular, total ~

N

NAME

V: acquire, clear, deserve, establish, fill in (your), get, have, live up to, make a ~ for yourself, omit, print (your,) put down/forward, sign (your), submit, use ~

A: assumed, Christian, code, common, family, first, given, household, maiden, married, middle, pet, professional, real, second, stage ~

NATION

V: address, appeal to, build, lead, mobilise, rally, represent, rouse, rule, save, speak for, touch ~

A: ancient, brave, civilised, divided, friendly, great, important, independent, oppressed, peace-loving, proud, sovereign, united ~

P: birth of, emergence of ~

NATURE (people)

A: aggressive, agreeable, adventurous, ambitious, austere, beautiful, cheery, cold, cruel, determined, dominating, easy-going, excitable, fiery, friendly, generous, gentle, gloomy, happy, happy-go-lucky, helpful, human, impetuous, impulsive, likeable, loving, mean, moody, nice, obsessive, obstinate, outgoing, overbearing, passionate, petty, placid, pliable, quiet, retiring, selfish, shy, sly, stubborn, sunny, sweet, timid, volatile, warm ~

P: defects in, flaws in ~; It's second ~ to (her); appeal to (your) better ~

NATURE (essential quality)

V: ascertain, conceal, determine, disclose, discover, examine, find out, investigate, probe, study, test, (mis)understand, verify ~

A: ambitious, artificial, changing, economic, ephemeral, essential, fictitious, financial, historical, human, insubstantial, material, medical, permanent, physical, political, psychological, real, religious, scientific, spiritual, superficial, surface, true, urgent, worrying ~

P: the (adjective) ~ of the problem

NATURE (natural phenomena)

V: be against, be contrary to, go back to, harness, let ~ take its course

P: forces of, freak of, laws of, the wonders of ~

NECESSITY

V: admit, anticipate, be conscious of, be driven by, perceive, see ~

V: ~ arose

A: absolute, basic, dire, immediate, inherent, sheer, sudden, tiresome, urgent, vital ~

NECESSITIES (of life)

V: be deprived of, lack, provide ~

A: bare, basic, elementary, essential ~

NECK

V: break, crane, twist, wring sb's ~

P: ~ ache

NEED

V: acknowledge, answer, be aware of, cope with, cover, create, cut out, detect, develop, do away with, establish, experience, feel, fill, fulfil, grapple with, ignore, meet, obviate, recognise, reduce, relieve, respond to, satisfy, see, show ~

V: ~ (dis)appeared, arose, diminished, evolved, increased, vanished

A: basic, burning, common, compulsive, crying, daily, definite, desperate, dire, everyday, existing, fundamental, glaring, great, growing, heartfelt, identifiable, immediate, insatiable, long-felt, marked, obvious, overriding, overwhelming, painful, paramount, pressing, real, special, strong, urgent, vital, widespread ~

NEEDS

V: attend to, cater for, look after, meet, minister to, satisfy ~

A: basic, distinct, immediate, material, modest, separate, special, specific ~

P: serve/supply the ~ of ...

NEGLECT

V: be guilty of ~

A: appalling, deliberate, disgraceful, dreadful, serious, shameful, sheer, shocking, terrible, wholesale, wilful ~

NEGLIGENCE

V: be caused by, be guilty of ~

A: appalling, criminal, culpable, glaring, gross, sheer ~

NEGOTIATIONS

V: abandon, agree to, be engaged/involved in, be in charge of, break off, call for/off, carry on, chair, conduct, cut off, defer, enter into, hold, hold up, interrupt, jeopardize, open, postpone, prejudice, renew, resume, speed up, start, suspend, take part in, torpedo, wreck ~

V: ~ broke down, broke up, came to nothing, dragged on, failed, floundered, got under way, are nearing completion, reached a climax, reached deadlock, stalled, succeeded, took place

A: acrimonious, behind-the-scenes, bilateral, brief, complex, complicated, constructive, delicate, difficult, direct, face-to-face, friendly, fruitful, heated, high-level, immediate, intensive, joint, lengthy, open-ended, patient, (un)productive, prolonged, protracted, round-table, (un)successful, tedious, top-level, tough, tricky, urgent ~

P: breakdown in, breakthrough in, resumption of, round of, set of, starting-point for, sticking-point in ~

NEGOTIATOR

A: cautious, experienced, flexible, seasoned, shrewd, skilled, tough, wily ~

NEIGHBOURHOOD

V: be brought up in, grow up in, move into/out of ~

A: bad, dangerous, friendly, good, middle-class, nice, pleasant, poor, posh, rich, rough, run-down, working-class ~

NERVES

V: calm, strain, suffer from ~

V: ~ are in a bad state, are stretched to breaking point, got the better of (him)

A: bad, frayed, tense ~

P: ~ of steel; bag of, bundle of ~

NETWORK

V: build up, clog, destroy, develop, discover, operate, set up, smash ~

A: complicated, efficient, extensive, international, nationwide, old-boy, wide, worldwide ~

NEUTRALITY

V: declare, infringe, maintain, preserve, respect, violate ~

NEWS

V: announce, break, bring, broadcast, catch up with, censor, collect, confirm, cover, gather, get, give, give out, leak, learn, pass on, receive, send, spread, suppress, tell, withhold ~

V: ~ alarmed sb, arrived, broke, is coming in/through, flooded in, leaked out, reached sb, slipped out, spread, trickled through, was delayed

A: advance, alarming, contradictory, dramatic, encouraging, first-hand, fresh, glad, gloomy, grave, great, happy, heartening, important, joyful, latest, long-awaited, ominous, recent, sad, sensational, shattering, shocking, stale, startling, surprising, thrilling, tragic, unbelievable, unexpected, unsettling, up-to-the-minute, welcome ~

P: ~ flash; bit of, dissemination of, flow of, piece of, scraps of, snippets of ~

NEWSPAPER

V: edit, print, publish, work for ~

V: ~ came out

A: daily, evening, in-house, local, morning, quality, tabloid, underground, weekly ~

NIGHT (darkness)

V: ~ closed in, came, is drawing in, is falling, passed

A: clear, cloudy, dark, moonlit, peaceful, starry, still, stormy, summer, windy, winter ~

NIGHT (sleep)

V: have, spend, stay ~

A: bad, early, dreadful, late, peaceful, restless, sleepless, terrible ~

NOISE ·
V: cut down, drown, emit, keep ~ down, make, produce, reduce ~
V: ~ died down, grew, increased, reverberated
A: background, buzzing, constant, continual, continuous, crackling, crashing, creaking, deafening, distant, dull, faint, frightening, hissing, irritating, loud, piercing, rude, rumbling, scraping, scuffling, sharp, slight, strange, suspicious, terrible, terrific, throbbing, thudding, unpleasant, wailing ~

NOMINATION
V: accept, get, lose, put forward, reject, seek, win ~

NONSENSE
V: dismiss sth as, make a ~ of sth, put up with, talk, tolerate ~
A: absolute, complete, pure, sheer, silly, total, utter ~

NORM
V: adhere to, agree on, deviate from, establish, fix, keep to, set, violate ~
A: basic, established ~

NOSE
V: blow, break, pick, wipe ~

NOTE
V: add, address, append, draft, make, prepare, receive, send ~
A: brief, careful, cautionary, explanatory, full, important, marginal, quick, stiff, succinct ~

NOTICE
V: affix, attract, bring sth to sb's, cancel, come to sb's, escape sb's ~, issue, put up, take/tear down ~
P: take (no) ~ of sth

NOTION
V: abandon, be hostile to, clarify, conceive, derive, dismiss, dispel, disseminate, emphasise, explain, expound, flirt with, formulate, have, illustrate, invent, maintain, put forward, reject, ridicule, stick to, subscribe to, support ~
A: basic, complex, false, far-fetched, foolish, new-fangled, pleasing, odd, overriding, strange, superficial, tentative, uncomfortable, unlikely, untenable, vague, widespread ~

NOVEL
A: allegorical, amusing, (semi-)autobiographical, boring, brilliant, cheap, classic, crime, detective, entertaining, exciting, fast-moving, historical, obscene, picaresque, popular, prize-winning, riveting, romantic, science-fiction, trashy ~

NUISANCE
V: be, cause, create ~, make a ~ of oneself
A: absolute, confounded, damned, thorough, wretched ~

NUMBER
V: add, assess, augment, calculate, determine, figure out, fix, increase, maintain, raise, reduce, restrict, whittle down, work out ~
V: ~ climbed, declined, dropped, dwindled, fell, grew, mounted, picked up, remained steady, spiralled, swelled, went down/up
A: amazing, astonishing, colossal, declining, enormous, exaggerated, excessive, fair, growing, huge, impressive, incredible, indeterminate, infinite, infinitesimal, large, negligible, phenomenal, significant, sizeable, tiny, unbelievable, unprecedented, vast ~
P: reduction in, rise in *numbers*

O

OATH
V: be on/under, put sb under, swear, take ~
P: ~ of allegiance, of loyalty
OBEDIENCE
V: demand, expect, insist on, instil, pledge, promise, show, swear ~
A: absolute, blind, complete, instinctive, strict, unquestioning ~
OBJECT (aim)
V: abandon, achieve, give up, pursue, reach, seek, strive for, work for ~
A: chief, immediate, long-term, main, principal, sole, ultimate ~
OBJECTION
V: brush aside, deal with, dismiss, disregard, express, face, have, ignore, lodge, make, meet, overcome, overrule, put forward, raise, record, remove, resolve, see the force of, sustain, sweep aside, take, voice, withdraw ~
A: justifiable, (un)reasonable, rooted, serious, strong, trivial, valid, violent ~
OBJECTIVE
V: abandon, (fail to) achieve, aim at, bear in mind, clarify, fall short of, gain, give up, have ~ in mind, keep ~ in sight, move towards, pursue, reach, realise, set, set up, stick to ~
A: clear, common, covert, distant, final, immediate, important, initial, joint, long/short-term, main, modest, original, primary, principal, sole, stated, ultimate, worthwhile ~
P: in pursuit of (our) ~
OBLIGATION
V: accept, acknowledge, assume, be aware/conscious of, be bound by, be saddled with, burden sb with, carry out, discharge, enter into, escape, face, feel, free sb from, fulfil, get out of, have, honour, impose, keep to, meet, neglect, owe, place ~ on sb, recognise, repay, run away from, shift ~ onto sb, shirk, shoulder, take ~ on/upon oneself
A: contractual, financial, formal, great, heavy, huge, mutual, overwhelming, sole, solemn ~
OBSERVATION
V: come under, escape, keep sb under, make, put sb under, record ~
A: acute, astute, careful, casual, close, constant, intelligent, penetrating, perceptive, round-the-clock, shrewd, strict, witty ~
P: powers of, under ~
OBSERVER
A: accredited, astute, careful, casual, detached, experienced, impartial, independent, neutral, official, seasoned, shrewd ~
OBSESSION
V: become an ~ with sb, border on, cure, have an ~ with, suffer from ~
A: fatal, overpowering, powerful, strange, total, weird ~
OBSTACLE
V: circumvent, come across, confront, constitute, cope with, create, deal with, destroy, encounter, face, get over, get rid of, get round, meet, overcome, place/put ~ in sb's way, remove, run up against, set up, surmount, sweep aside ~
V: ~ arose, disappeared, emerged
A: daunting, difficult, formidable, great, immovable, important, insurmountable, insuperable, main, major, serious, slight, tremendous, unexpected ~

OCCASION (special time)

V: attend, be present at, celebrate, mar, mark ~

A: auspicious, dramatic, enjoyable, festive, formal, glittering, gloomy, grand, great, happy, joyful, joyous, magnificent, memorable, rare, sad, solemn, special, unique ~

OCCUPATION (job)

V: follow, have, look for, pursue, state ~

A: agreeable, (un)congenial, dangerous, demanding, full/part-time, hazardous, manual, (un)profitable, regular, rewarding, risky, safe, (un)skilled, suitable, unusual, useful ~

OCCURRENCE

V: lead to, note, observe, prevent ~

A: common, daily, distressing, everyday, (in)frequent, rare, regular, repeated, single, unexpected, unforeseen, unfortunate, unique, unprecedented, unusual ~

ODDS (probability)

V: beat, lengthen, shorten, work out ~

V: ~ are against/in favour of sth, are stacked against sb

A: considerable, formidable, great, heavy, hopeless, long, overwhelming, short ~

P: the ~ are that ... , the ~ are (5 to 1) in favour/against

ODOUR

V: detect, emit, get rid of, give off, produce, remove ~

V: ~ disappeared, lingered

A: disgusting, distinct, faint, penetrating, powerful, pungent, slight, strong, unpleasant ~

OFFENCE

V: accuse sb of, charge sb with, commit, convict sb of, plead guilty to, punish sb for, sentence sb for ~

A: capital, criminal, grave, indictable, minor, petty, punishable, serious, trivial ~

P: gravity of, guilty of, innocent of, seriousness of ~

OFFENDER

V: catch, clamp down on, deal with, imprison, lock up, punish ~

A: first-time, hardened, juvenile, minor, persistent, repeat, serious, vicious, violent, young ~

OFFENSIVE

V: crush, go on the, launch, mount, repel, repulse ~

A: air, huge, major, military ~

OFFER

V: accept, consider, decline, grab at, hold out, jump at, keep to, make, place, put forward/in, receive, refuse, reject, spurn, suggest, take, turn down, withdraw ~

V: ~ stands

A: astounding, attractive, definite, exclusive, fair, firm, flattering, generous, good, inadequate, initial, kind, low, lucrative, magnanimous, modest, original, poor, rash, reasonable, ridiculous, satisfactory, serious, tempting, tentative, unacceptable ~

P: (I'm) open to *offers*

OFFICE (position)

V: accept, appoint sb to, be given, be put out of, be relieved of, cling to, fall from, hang on to, hold, lose, obtain, occupy, resign from, run for, seek, stand for, take, take up ~

A: high, (un)important, minor, prestigious ~

OMISSION

V: correct, make good, notice, overlook, rectify, repair ~

A: glaring, grave, notable, regrettable, sad, serious, startling, stupid, unfortunate ~

P: sins of ~

OPERATION (military etc)

V: be engaged in, be in charge of, bungle, call off, cancel, carry out/through, complete, conduct, direct, hamper, handle, manage, mastermind, mount, obstruct, organise, plan, run, sanction, set in motion, support, take part in, undertake, wind up ~

V: ~ collapsed, dragged on, ended in failure, got bogged down, succeeded, went smoothly/wrong

A: brilliant, clandestine, complex, covert, critical, dangerous, disastrous, effective, efficient, extensive, formidable, integrated, joint, large/small-scale, major, precarious, precautionary, risky, secret, subsidiary, (un)successful, undercover, vast ~

OPERATION (surgical)

V: carry out, have, perform, recover from, survive, undergo ~

A: dangerous, emergency, exploratory, major, minor, risky, routine, serious ~

OPINION

V: accept, agree with, air, ask, ask for, change, confirm, convey, discount, dissent from, endorse, express, form, give, have, impose ~ on sb, influence, modify, mould, offer, seek out, state, stick to, sway, trust, venture, voice ~

V: ~ changed, coincides with sth, differs from sth, influences sb, spread

A: arbitrary, (un)biased, considered, critical, definite, eccentric, emphatic, erroneous, (un)favourable, firm, fixed, general, honest, informed, mistaken, moderate, negative, popular, positive, prejudiced, prevalent, public, rational, unfashionable, wise, wrong ~

P: a matter of, shades of, tide of, in my humble ~; conflicting, divergent *opinions*; range of *opinions*

OPPONENT

V: beat, challenge, come up against, convince, defeat, encounter, face, get the better of, meet, outwit, overcome, silence, thrash, trick ~

A: able, crafty, cunning, dangerous, daunting, fanatical, fearsome, fierce, firm, formidable, implacable, strident, strong, unrelenting, vociferous, weak, wily, worthy ~

OPPORTUNITY

V: afford, appreciate, avail oneself of, await, be on the lookout for, benefit from, come across, create, decline, demand, embrace, encounter, enjoy, exploit, find, get, give, grab, grant, grasp, have, let ~ slip, look for, lose, make, make the most of, miss, offer, overlook, recognise, relish, seek, seize, take, take advantage of, throw away, use, wait for, waste ~

V: ~ arose, came up, cropped up, emerged, occurred, opened up, passed, presented itself, recurred, remains, slipped by

A: excellent, fantastic, favourable, fleeting, fortunate, fresh, golden, good, great, heaven-sent, lost, lucky, magnificent, marvellous, missed, priceless, promising, rare, splendid, tempting, unexpected, unforeseen, unique, unprecedented, unrivalled ~

P: at the first/earliest/slightest ~; take every ~ to; equality of, a window of ~

OPPOSITION (resistance)

V: arouse, break down, brush aside, bypass, come up against, confront, conquer, create, crush, curtail, deal with, defeat, defend oneself against, demolish, destroy, encounter, experience, express, face, fight, generate, keep up, meet (with), mobilise, neutralise, offer no, overcome, provoke, put up, set up, show, smash, spearhead, stir up, suffer, sustain, voice, wear down ~

V: ~ collapsed, continued, disappeared, evaporated

A: all-out, determined, dogged, ferocious, fierce, firm, furious, great, marked, outright, prolonged, serious, stiff, strong, substantial, sudden, token, total, unexpected, vehement, vociferous, weak ~

OPPOSITION (opponents)

V: beat, crush, deal with, defeat, defend oneself against, drive back, identify, meet, overcome, rout, scatter, smash, take on ~

OPTIMISM

V: express, feel, retain, show ~

A: cautious, great, growing, guarded, light-hearted, premature, steady, tremendous ~

P: full of, room for ~

OPTION

V: accept, consider, exercise, have, hold out, offer, refuse, reject, suggest, take up, turn down ~

A: attractive, favourable, realistic, tempting ~

P: have no/little ~ but to ...

ORATOR

A: accomplished, convincing, eloquent, fine, gifted, inspired, inspiring, natural, passionate, persuasive, skilled ~

ORDEAL

V: come through, endure, face, get over, go through, subject sb to, suffer, survive, undergo ~

A: appalling, devastating, distressing, dreadful, harrowing, incredible, long, painful, severe, terrible ~

ORDER (sequence)

V: arrange sth in, establish, put sth in ~

A: alphabetical, ascending, chronological, descending, hierarchical, numerical, proper ~

P: ~ of precedence, seniority; in the right/wrong ~

ORDER (discipline)

V: destroy, establish, impose, insist on, keep, maintain, restore, upset ~

A: good, ideal, perfect, strict ~

ORDER (command)

V: cancel, carry out, comply with, countermand, defy, disregard, enforce, execute, get, give, ignore, issue, misunderstand, (dis)obey, oppose, put ~ into effect, receive, revoke, take, wait for ~

A: ambiguous, authoritative, categorical, clear, explicit, final, harsh, precise, strict ~

ORDER (for goods)

V: accept, authorise, cancel, change, chase, check, confirm, compete for, consolidate, delay, despatch, duplicate, fax (through), fill, fulfil, get, give sb, go after, hold, increase, lose, make out, meet, place, process, put in, receive, release, send, ship, sit on, take, win ~

V: ~ came in, has gone astray, went out

A: back, bulk, initial, new, potential, regular, repeat, rush, special, stock, urgent, wholesale ~

P: *orders* dried up, flooded in, piled up

ORGANISATION (body with *a/an*)

V: ban, belong to, build, create, cripple, crush, direct, disband, dissolve, enlarge, establish, finance, form, found, head, infiltrate, join, manage, reinforce, run, set up, split, sponsor, strengthen, wind up ~

V: ~ came into being/into existence, functions, operates

A: broad-based, clandestine, close-knit, complex, effective, efficient, government, grass-roots, huge, international, large/small-scale, massive, nationwide, respectable, rival, secret, sinister, solid, underground, unwieldy, vast, vital, voluntary, weak, well-run, wonderful, worldwide ~

ORGANISATION (organising)

A: careful, chaotic, clumsy, day-to-day, detailed, (in)efficient, excellent, good, meticulous, overall, poor ~

ORIGIN

V: check, determine, discover, explain, go into the ~ of, have, hide, identify, investigate, reveal, study, trace ~

A: doubtful, dubious, foreign, humble, local, mysterious, real, remote, supposed, true, unknown ~

OUTCOME

V: ascertain, decide, discover, doubt, guess, know, lead to, measure, predict, produce, seek, settle ~

A: advantageous, beneficial, (un)certain, desirable, desired, disappointing, disastrous, (un)expected, favourable, final, (un)fortunate, (un)happy, indecisive, inevitable, likely, lucky, possible, probable, prospective, real, strange, (un)successful, tragic, unexpected ~

OUTLINE

V: discern, draw, give, make out, offer, present, produce, provide, sketch, supply ~

A: blurred, broad, clear, feint, general, precise, rough, vague ~

OUTLOOK

V: adopt, change, have, spoil ~

A: alarming, balanced, (un)biased, black, bleak, blinkered, bright, broad, cheerful, cheerless, depressing, dismal, fanatical, fresh, gloomy, grim, healthy, hopeful, hopeless, jaundiced, narrow, negative, optimistic, pessimistic, poor, positive, sensible, wise ~

OUTPUT

V: assess, cut down, estimate, expect, guarantee, improve, increase, maintain, obtain, produce, raise, reduce, restrict, step up, stimulate ~

V: ~ diminished, edged upwards, has fallen/grown, is down/stagnant, is lagging behind ... , has picked up, recovered, rose, has slipped behind ... , has slackened, slumped, soared, totals (10,000 units), went down/up,

A: annual, big, current, expected, high, huge, imposing, initial, low, mass, monthly (etc), potential, present, regular, satisfactory, steady, total ~

P: fall in, rise in ~

OUTRAGE

V: be filled with, express, feel, provoke ~

A: absolute, moral ~

P: feeling of, sense of ~

OUTRAGE (act of extreme violence)

V: commit, condemn, deplore, perpetrate ~

A: latest ~

OVERCROWDING

V: alleviate, prevent, relieve, suffer from ~

A: bad, great, serious ~

P: consequences of, effects of ~

OWNERSHIP

V: dispute, pass into, seize, take (over) ~

A: collective, common, dual, joint, partial, private, public, sole, total ~

P: proof of, under new ~

P

PACE
V: dictate, go at, increase, keep ~ with sth, keep up, lose, maintain, proceed at, regulate, set, slacken, slow down, step up ~
V: ~ accelerated, increased, quickened, remains steady, slackened, slowed down
A: brisk, even, frantic, furious, good, hectic, increasing, leisurely, moderate, rapid, regular, slow, sluggish, snail's, steady, surprising, swift ~

PACT
V: break, enforce, enter into, make, sign ~
V: ~ expired

PAIN
V: bear, cause, endure, feel, inflict, kill, soothe, stand, suffer, take ~
V: ~ has worn off
A: constant, great, grievous, incessant, intense, intermittent, intractable, nagging, severe, steady, terrible, terrific, unbearable ~
P: gasp of, stab of ~

PAINT
V: apply, burn off, daub, mix, scrape off, spill, splash, spread, stir, strip, thin ~
V: ~ dried, is peeling (off)
A: fresh, gloss, matt, peeling, wet ~
P: coat of, lick of ~

PAINTING
V: authenticate, damage, date, deface, do, exhibit, hang, purchase, put ~ on show, restore, sign ~
V: ~ depicts, portrays, shows
A: abstract, controversial, dynamic, figurative, fine, huge, modern, monumental, priceless, religious, striking, traditional, valuable, worthless ~

PANIC
V: cause, create, feel, fill (me) with, give way to, prevent, spread ~
V: ~ broke out, gripped/seized (me), spread, subsided
A: acute, blind, irrational, severe, sheer, slight ~

PAPER (academic)
V: deliver, give, prepare, present, produce, publish, read, submit, summarise, write ~
V: ~ argues ... , covers ... , deals with ... , describes ... , discusses ... , refers to ...
A: brief, brilliant, comprehensive, concise, excellent, lengthy, lucid, masterly, scholarly, scientific, seminal, short, technical ~

PAPER (newspaper)
V: ban, close down, edit, found, glance at, join, look through, order, own, print, publish, revamp, run, scan, sue, take, take over, work for ~
V: ~ changed hands, comes out, expresses sth, folded, goes to press, has a circulation of (2 million), merged with ...
A: daily, downmarket, evening, in-house, local, morning, national, popular, profitable, provincial, quality, reputable, rubbishy, Sunday, tabloid, underground, weekly ~

PARADOX
V: explain, perceive, see, solve ~
A: apparent, inherent, obvious, seeming, strange, striking, worrying ~

PARALLEL
V: draw, find, observe, see ~
A: close, distinct, obvious, striking ~

PARCEL
V: address, deliver, open, post, receive, send, (un)wrap ~

PARENTS
V: defy, obey, please, take after ~
A: adoptive, birth, doting, foster, loving, proud, natural, single, unfit ~

PARLIAMENT
V: address, adjourn, attend, dissolve, elect, enter, open, recall, stand for, summon ~
V: ~ broke up, is in session, meets, re-assembles, rose, sat, voted on ... , went into recess
P: dissolution of, lifetime of, Member of, opening of ~

PART
V: constitute, form, make ~
A: basic, component, constituent, essential, fundamental, important, indispensable, indivisible, inseparable, integral, intrinsic, major, principal, separate, significant, vital ~

PARTS
V: break sth (down) into, divide sth into, fall into, split sth into ~
A: equal, interchangeable ~

PART (acting)
V: have, learn, play, take, understudy ~
A: active, bit, decisive, (un)important, key, leading, minor, speaking, subordinate, walk-on ~

PARTICIPANT
A: active, eager, regular, reluctant, (un)willing ~

PARTNERSHIP
V: dissolve, enter into, forge, form, go into, set up, undermine ~
V: ~ broke up, collapsed, flourished, foundered, lasted, split up
A: close, equal, loose, profitable, solid, unlikely ~

PARTY (political)
V: ban, be a member of, belong to, crush, defeat, dissolve, divide, do damage to, establish, form, found, join, launch, legalise, outlaw, purge, rally, reform, reorganise, represent, resign from, revitalise, run, set up, split, support, unite, vote for, weaken, work for ~
V: ~ came to power, closed ranks, collapsed, disintegrated, did well, lost, rallied, split, was returned to power
A: centre, Communist, conservative, democratic, divided, dominant, fledgling, green, influential, Islamic, left-/right-wing, liberal, losing, opposition, outgoing, powerful, progressive, radical, rebel, rival, ruling, small, socialist, strong, (un)successful, traditional, united, victorious, weak ~
P: ~ conference, rally; break-up of, demise of, disintegration of, echelons of, rift in, split in ~

PARTY (social)
V: arrange, gatecrash, give, go to, have, hold, invite sb to, throw ~
A: all-night, bring-a-bottle, cocktail, dinner, fabulous, fancy-dress, farewell, garden, going-away, hen, lavish, stag, surprise ~

PASSENGERS
V: carry, drop off, pick up, take on ~
V: ~ boarded, disembarked, got on/off

PASSION
V: arouse, be filled with, curb, excite, have a ~ for sth, inflame, restrain, satisfy, stir up ~
A: animal, burning, consuming, deep, dreadful, enduring, fatal, frenzied, lifelong, real, short-lived, terrible, uncontrollable, wild ~
P: crime of ~

PASSPORT
V: apply for, confiscate, forge, issue, renew, show, stamp, surrender ~
V: ~ has expired
A: false, valid, temporary ~

PAST
V: belong to, break with, delve into, destroy, forget, go over, ignore, obliterate, piece together, preserve, recall, reconstruct, relive, remember, wipe out ~
A: dim and distant, distant, recent ~

PAST (of a person)
A: chequered, colourful, exciting, impeccable, murky, notorious, shadowy, shady, violent ~

PATENT
V: apply for, grant, hold, infringe, issue, take out ~
V: ~ expired, runs (out)
A: ~ pending

PATH
V: follow, go down/up, keep to, stay on, stray from ~
A: gravel, muddy, narrow, steep, treacherous, tree-lined, well-marked, well-trodden, winding ~
P: (our) *paths* converged, crossed, diverged, met

PATIENCE
V: call for, exercise, exhaust, have, lose, run out of, show, summon up, try sb's ~
V: ~ is at an end, is exhausted, has run out, is wearing thin
A: boundless, endless, enormous, great, incredible, marvellous, tremendous ~

PATIENT
V: cure, discharge, examine, hospitalise, interview, look after, nurse, operate on, release, see, treat ~
V: ~ got better/worse, recovered (from sth), suffered a relapse
A: cancer, difficult, good, ideal, model, out-, private ~

PATTERN
V: break, conform to, continue, copy, create, destroy, detect, deviate from, discern, distinguish, establish, fit into, follow, form, imitate, perceive, trace, upset ~
V: ~ appears, emerged, repeats itself
A: accepted, changing, clear, coherent, confused, definite, dull, familiar, intrinsic, meaningful, natural, recurrent, recurring, shifting, traditional, underlying, unique, (un)usual, well-known ~

PATTERN (design)
V: form, invent, make, match, trace ~
A: complex, complicated, geometric, intricate, original, overall, (ir)regular, simple, subtle, traditional, unique, unusual ~

PAY
V: draw, earn, get, receive, stop ~
A: back, decent, equal, good, low, regular, sick, strike, take-home ~
P: ~ rise

PAYMENT
V: defer, make, stop, suspend ~
V: ~ is (over)due
A: annual (monthly, weekly etc), cash, final, immediate, initial, lump-sum, nominal, partial, (ir)regular, quarterly, token ~
P: ~ in cash, in kind
PEACE
V: achieve, bring about, destroy, disturb, guarantee, keep, maintain, make, make ~ with sb, negotiate, preserve, restore, safeguard, secure, strive for, work for ~
A: fragile, lasting, secure, short-lived, uneasy, world, worldwide ~
P: obstacle to, breach of the ~
PEACE (quiet)
V: disturb, enjoy, restore, shatter, threaten, violate ~
V: ~ prevailed, reigned
A: absolute, inner, perfect, short-lived ~
PENALTY
V: announce, demand, exact, face, impose, pay, reduce, suffer ~
A: death, draconian, harsh, heavy, huge, inescapable, severe, stiff ~
PENSION
V: be entitled to, claim, collect, contribute towards, draw, get, grant, increase, live on, lose, protect, receive, retire on ~
A: (in)adequate, comfortable, company, generous, good, insufficient, low, miserable, modest, private, reduced, regular, small, State, tiny ~
PEOPLE (nation)
A: ancient, brave, courageous, enterprising, freedom-loving, friendly, hard-working, heroic, law-abiding, peace-loving, primitive, proud, resilient, superstitious, tolerant, warlike ~
PERFECTION
V: achieve, aim for, approach, strive for ~
A: absolute, near, total, utter ~
PERFORMANCE (theatrical etc)
V: announce, applaud, arrange, attend, be disappointed with/impressed by, boycott, call off, cancel, give, interrupt, miss, postpone, put in, put on, witness ~
A: abysmal, accomplished, assured, astounding, average, bravura, breathtaking, brilliant, commanding, creditable, dazzling, disappointing, dismal, dull, excellent, exhilarating, exquisite, fabulous, farewell, faultless, final, fine, first-class, first-rate, flawed, flawless, gala, glittering, gripping, impeccable, impressive, inconsistent, indifferent, inspired, lack-lustre, lamentable, lavish, live, marvellous, masterly, mediocre, memorable, miserable, model, moving, mundane, nimble, notable, outstanding, patchy, pedestrian, perfect, polished, poor, practised, professional, remarkable, repeat, respectable, scintillating, sensational, sensitive, shaky, skilled, sparkling, special, spirited, splendid, spectacular, steady, sterling, stunning, stylish, subtle, superb, superlative, supreme, touching, thrilling, triumphant, uneven, unforgettable, unique, virtuoso, wonderful ~
PERFORMANCE (business)
V: be responsible for, improve, limit, monitor, reduce ~
V: ~ deteriorated, improved
A: abysmal, average, bad, disappointing, erratic, impressive, inconsistent, moderate, patchy, poor, (un)satisfactory, steady ~

PERFUME
V: put on, reek of, smell of, spray on, use, wear ~
A: exotic, exquisite, fragrant, intoxicating, overpowering, pleasant, powerful, sophisticated, strong, subtle ~

PERIOD
V: belong to, characterise, enjoy, experience, go through, herald, inaugurate, last for, mark, represent, suffer, usher in ~
V: ~ followed, lasted
A: barren, brief, confused, considerable, critical, crucial, decisive, demoralising, dynamic, early, fertile, flourishing, golden, initial, interim, lengthy, long, peak, (un)productive, prolonged, prosperous, short, stable, stagnant, subsequent, traditional, tragic, turbulent, typical, uneasy, unstable ~

PERMIT
V: apply for, cancel, get, grant, issue, obtain, refuse, withhold ~
A: fishing, hunting, proper, special, temporary, (in)valid ~

PERSECUTION
V: escape, suffer ~
A: bloody, continued, relentless, religious, ruthless ~
P: victim of, wave of ~

PERSONALITY
V: affect, alter, change, cramp, destroy, develop, display, harm, have, mould, project, stamp ~ on sth, stifle ~
V: ~ blossomed, changed, developed, disintegrated, has grown, has matured
A: abrasive, aggressive, aloof, assertive, attractive, balanced, brash, brilliant, bubbly, charismatic, charming, colourful, colourless, compelling, complex, creative, disordered, dominant, domineering, dull, dynamic, forceful, ebullient, eccentric, elusive, emotional, expansive, extraordinary, extrovert, flamboyant, formidable, friendly, gregarious, insipid, introvert, magnetic, many-sided, (im)mature, multiple, obstinate, outgoing, overbearing, pleasant, pleasing, quiet, retiring, rigid, serious, (un)stable, striking, strong, shy, split, unusual, vivacious, weak ~
P: ~ conflict, disorder

PERSONNEL
V: (re)deploy, employ, engage, manage, recruit, sack, take on, train ~
A: additional, key, qualified ~

PERSPECTIVE
V: appear in, consider, get sth out of, give sb, keep in, look at sth in, maintain, offer, present sth in, provide, put sth in, see sth in, show sth in ~
A: discouraging, distorted, encouraging, false, gloomy, proper, right, true, wrong ~
P: look at/see/view sth from a new/different, sense of ~

PESSIMISM
V: give way to, overcome ~
V: ~ grew, passed
A: deep, general, profound, unnecessary, unwarranted ~

PHASE
V: approach, arrive at, begin, come to, come to the end of, complete, enter (upon), get past, go through, herald, inaugurate, introduce, launch, mark, move into, near, pass through, reach ~
V: ~ has come to an end, lasted, passed
A: awkward, brief, closing, critical, crucial, decisive, developmental, difficult, early, final,

formative, hazardous, initial, important, integral, intermediate, introductory, late, long, new, penultimate, problematical, stable, stormy, tranquil, transitory, turbulent, violent ~

P: is in/at the (developmental) ~

PHENOMENON

V: come across, discover, encounter, explain, investigate, keep track of, observe, perceive, record, study, trace, watch, witness ~

A: amazing, baffling, common, extraordinary, inexplicable, isolated, mysterious, natural, recent, remarkable, singular, strange, supernatural, unexplained, unique, unpleasant, unusual ~

PHOTO(GRAPH)

V: blow up, crop, develop, enlarge, mount, take, touch up ~

V: ~ is in/out of focus, is over-/under-exposed

A: aerial, blurred, clear, (un)flattering, grainy, press, sharp, spectacular, stunning, wonderful ~

PHRASE

V: invent, repeat, utter ~

V: ~ comes to mind, sticks in (your) mind

A: apt, banal, colourful, common, cryptic, eloquent, empty, expressive, familiar, handy, meaningless, memorable, neat, odd, popular, striking, telling, useful, well-chosen, well-worn ~

P: a (strange) turn of, to coin a ~

PICTURE (situation)

V: arrive at, build up, conjure up, convey, create, darken, draw, gain, get, give, grasp, paint, present, produce, project, put sb in the ~

A: (in)accurate, alarming, balanced, (un)biased, bleak, bright, broad, clear, coherent, comforting, comprehensive, confused, consistent, convincing, depressing, detailed, distorted, disturbing, elaborate, exaggerated, fair, faithful, false, fantastic, flattering, frightening, fuzzy, gloomy, glowing, grim, hazy, hopeful, intimate, lop-sided, memorable, moving, optimistic, overall, pessimistic, plausible, realistic, reassuring, reliable, rosy, rough, rounded, stark, striking, tragic, true, unforgettable, vague, vivid, whole ~

PICTURE (painting)

V: acquire, auction, clean, damage, exhibit, forge, frame, hang, paint, restore, show ~

A: beautiful, grand, huge, imposing, impressive, magnificent, priceless, religious, sombre, striking, superb, valuable, world-famous ~

PITY

V: arouse, be full of, be moved to, feel, have, show ~, take ~ on sb

P: object of, sense of ~

PLACE

V: allocate, assign, deprive sb of, get, give (up), indicate, keep, locate, mark, occupy, relinquish, reserve, take (your), vacate, win ~

A: agreeable, empty, excellent, forbidding, holy, (in)hospitable, magical, particular, popular, proper, sacred, special, splendid, suitable, tiny, usual, vacant ~

PLACE (in society)

V: carve out, create, fill, know one's, occupy, win ~

A: appropriate, central, distinguished, foremost, important, influential, modest, prominent, proper, rightful ~

PLAN

V: abandon, accept, adhere to, adopt, alter, announce, approve (of), axe, back, block, cancel, carry out, change, conceal, conceive, concoct, conform to, devise, disclose, dismiss, divulge, draft, draw up, endorse, evolve, execute, finalise, foil, form, formulate, frustrate, fulfil, go ahead with, implement, initiate, invent, jeopardize, jettison, keep to, launch, make, nurture, oppose, outline, postpone, prepare, press ahead with, proceed with, pursue, put forward, put ~ in motion, put ~ into operation/practice, ratify, reject, scrap, scrutinize, scupper, shelve, stick to, submit, thwart, torpedo, unveil, upset, veto, work on/out, wreck ~

V: ~ broke down, came to fruition, collapsed, comes into effect, crystallized, entails ... , got approval, hit a snag, involves ... , is under discussion, is under way, miscarried, provides for ..., ran into trouble, requires approval, was dogged by sth, went awry/wrong, works

A: abortive, accurate, aggressive, ambitious, audacious, bold, brilliant, calculated, clever, complex, complicated, comprehensive, concrete, contingency, controversial, cunning, definite, desperate, detailed, devious, diabolical, draft, drastic, effective, elaborate, emergency, far-sighted, feasible, final, fixed, flexible, ideal, ill-conceived, immediate, impracticable, ingenious, intricate, judicious, large-scale, long-range, long/short-term, master, original, poor, practical, precise, premature, reckless, sinister, tentative, unworkable, up-to-date, urgent, useful, vast, viable ~

PLANT
V: feed, grow, water ~
A: climbing, exotic, flowering, indoor, outdoor, potted, tropical ~

PLANT (industrial)
V: build, close, close down, erect, locate, maintain, manage, open, operate, run, run down, set up, shut down, take over ~
V: ~ manufactures ... , produces ...
A: (in)efficient, giant, huge, (ultra-)modern, obsolescent, obsolete, old-fashioned, up-to-date, wasteful ~

PLAY (drama)
V: act in, adapt, ban, broadcast, commission, cut, direct, perform, present, produce, put on, rehearse, review, revive, scrap, stage, write ~
V: ~ came off, closed, flopped, folded, opens on ..., ran, was panned
A: amusing, boring, disturbing, dull, entertaining, enthralling, fascinating, interesting, serious, thoughtful ~

PLEA
V: answer, be deaf to, consider, listen to, make, refuse, respond to ~
A: emotional, humble, humiliating, impassioned, moving, passionate, statesmanlike, straightforward, strong, urgent ~

PLEA (legal)
V: enter, offer, put forward, reject, respond to, submit ~

PLEASURE
V: add to, derive, enhance, feel, find, get ~ from/out of ... , give, have, pursue, savour, share, spoil, take ~ in sth, take away ~
A: brief, doubtful, dubious, genuine, great, innocent, rare, real, tremendous, undisguised, vicarious ~
P: pursuit of ~; deprive sb of the ~ of ...ing; have (great) ~ in ...ing

PLEDGE
V: abandon, break, carry out, extract ~ from sb, fulfil, give, go back on, honour, make, offer ~
A: firm, solemn ~

PLOT
V: bungle, come upon, discover, engineer, expose, foil, hatch, make, stop, take part in, uncover, unearth ~
V: ~ came to light, fell through
A: devious, diabolical, infamous, mysterious, secret, sinister ~

POEM
V: commission, compose, learn ~ by heart, memorise, read (out), recite, scan ~
A: brilliant, charming, delightful, epic, famous, haunting, humorous, little-known, love, lyric, magnificent, marvellous, moving, narrative ~

POINT
V: agree to differ on, agree with, appreciate, argue, arrive at, bear ~ in mind, clarify, clear up, come to, concede, consider, cover, deal with, develop, discuss, dismiss, elaborate, emphasise, expand, explain, forget, get to, ignore, illustrate, introduce, investigate, keep to, labour, make, mark, mention, miss, overlook, raise, reach, return to, stick to, stress, stretch, take, underline, wander from/away from/off ~
A: apt, clear, controversial, crucial, curious, decisive, devastating, different, difficult, eloquent, essential, fundamental, general, good, identical, important, intriguing, irrelevant, key, main, moot, obvious, personal, pivotal, preliminary, puzzling, real, reasonable, ridiculous, salient, separate, significant, similar, sore, sticking, strong, subtle, surprising, telling, vital, weak ~

POLICE
V: assist, baffle, call in, clash with, contact, help, obey, report to, respect, summon, support ~
V: ~ arrested sb, caught sb, charged sb, cordoned off (the area), dealt with sth, held sb, interrogated sb, intervened, are investigating, made an arrest, are making enquiries, patrolled ... , questioned sb, are standing by, have taken sb into custody
P: ~ constable, force, officer

POLICY
V: abandon, adhere to, administer, adopt, advocate, agree on, announce, apply, approve, attack, back, call for, carry out, challenge, change, comply with, condemn, conduct, (re)consider, criticise, debate, decide on, defend, define, defy, deplore, design, develop, deviate from, devise, dictate, direct, discredit, dismantle, distance oneself from, dominate, draw up, embark on a ~ of, embrace, employ, endorse, enforce, establish, evolve, favour, finance, follow, formulate, frame, give up, implement, initiate, instigate, introduce, jeopardize, jettison, justify, launch, maintain, make, moderate, modify, need, oppose, produce, pursue, put forward, put a ~ into operation, reaffirm, reform, reject, relax, reverse, review, revise, revoke, revolutionise, sanction, settle on, (re)shape, shelve, state, stick by/to, support, suspend, switch, try, undermine, veto, work out ~
V: ~ bore fruit, broke down, calls for ... , collapsed, emerged, entails ... , failed, is aimed at/geared to ... , paid off, prevailed, resulted in ... , succeeded, survived, triumphed, worked
A: active, aggressive, alternative, biased, bold, broad, cautious, clear, coherent, common, comprehensive, confused, (in)consistent, constructive, co-ordinated, courageous, credible, cunning, current, deliberate, despicable, disastrous, doctrinaire, (in)effective, expansionist, far-reaching, firm, flexible, foolish, futile, future, generous, hard-line, humanitarian, inadequate, independent, influential, long-range, long/short-term, major, misconceived, misguided, obstructive, persistent, popular, present, provocative, radical, rational, restrictive, rigid, risky, selfish, sensible, set, settled, short-sighted, shrewd, simple, sound, steady, straightforward, strict, tough, vigorous, wise ~
P: agreement on, architect of, backing for, basis of, breach of, change of, consensus on, cornerstone of, direction of, easing-up of, evolution of, hardening of, inconsistencies of, indictment of, keystone of, pursuit of, realignment of, reversal of, shift in, substance of, support for, switch in, turn in, vindication of ~

POLITICIAN
A: able, astute, cautious, crafty, distinguished, experienced, (dis)honest, left-/right-wing, noted, outspoken, power-hungry, respected, seasoned, senior, shrewd, skilful, tough-minded ~

POLITICS
V: abandon, be involved in, dabble in, engage in, enter, go into, take part in, take up ~
A: local, international, national, office, party ~
P: rough and tumble of, understanding of, watershed in, web of ~

POLLUTION
V: cause, clean up ~
A: air, chemical, environmental, noise, oil, toxic ~

POPULARITY
V: acquire, enjoy, ensure, forfeit, gain, jeopardize, lose, seek, win ~
V: ~ dwindled, fell, grew, increased, slumped, soared
A: brief, great, immediate, immense, new-found, widespread ~

POPULATION
V: count, decimate, estimate, evacuate, expel, exploit, exterminate, feed, harass, house, move, oppress, relocate, resettle, shift, transfer, wipe out ~
V: ~ consists of ... , declined, decreased, dwindled, expanded, fell, fled, grew, increased, left, moved, remained static/steady, rose, shrank, soared, starved, suffered
A: active, ageing, civilian, dense, floating, heterogeneous, homogeneous, huge, indigenous, large, local, mixed, native, original, rural, scattered, shifting, sparse, stable, tiny, urban ~
P: ~ explosion; density of, drop in, increase in ~

PORTRAIT
V: commission, draw, give, paint, pose for, produce, provide, sit for ~
A: accurate, candid, charming, convincing, excellent, exaggerated, family, fascinating, first-hand, frank, full-length, group, imposing, lifelike, lively, realistic, rounded, striking, vivid ~

POSITION
V: accept, adopt, alter, assess, assume, back down from, be aware of, change, clarify, confirm, declare, defend, discuss, emphasise, establish, explain, express, find oneself in, jeopardize, maintain, make the ~ clear/plain, misunderstand, move closer to, outline, place sb in, put sb in, question, realise, remain in, resign oneself to, size up, state, sum up, take, take up ~
A: advantageous, anomalous, awkward, conciliatory, critical, dangerous, delicate, desperate, difficult, embarrassing, extreme, (un)favourable, firm, hopeless, humiliating, (un)official, paradoxical, precarious, radical, real, risky, satisfactory, tough, tricky, true, unassailable, unavoidable, uncertain, unenviable, unique, unpopular, untenable, unusual ~

POSITION (physical)
V: abandon, adopt, ascertain, assume, attack, find oneself in, give away/up, hold onto, keep, keep to, move, move to, occupy, reach, remain in, reveal, shift, strengthen, take (up) ~
A: awkward, central, (un)comfortable, cramped, crouching, dominant, exposed, fixed, forward, impregnable, key, kneeling, lotus, reclining, sitting, unassailable, upright, vulnerable ~

POSITION (job or office)
V: abuse, accept, achieve, apply for, appoint sb to, attain, fill, give up, have, hold, keep, lose, occupy, offer sb, reach, refuse, remove sb from, resign from, retain, rise to, take up ~
A: desirable, eminent, exalted, exposed, illustrious, influential, key, leading, lucrative, modest, permanent, prestigious, prominent, responsible, secure, temporary, vacant ~

POSSIBILITY
V: accept, admit, allow for, assess, come to terms with, deal with, demonstrate, deny, discount, dismiss, eliminate, entertain, envisage, exaggerate, examine, exclude, exploit, explore, face, guard against, ignore, investigate, limit, look into, make use of, maximise, minimise, miss, neglect, offer, open up, overestimate, overlook, pre-empt, raise, reduce, reject, restrict, rule out, see, take ~ into account/consideration, underestimate, use, waste, weigh up ~
V: ~ arose, is (no longer) there, materialised, presented itself

A: challenging, definite, distinct, excellent, exciting, faint, grim, growing, obvious, real, remote, slight, splendid, strong, theoretical, unexpected, unique, unpleasant ~

POSSIBILITIES

V: explore, limit, make the most of, open up, review ~

A: available, extensive, limited, vast ~

POST (job)

V: accept, advertise, apply for, appoint sb to, dismiss sb from, create, earmark sb for, fill, get, give, have, hold, occupy, offer sb, quit, refuse, resign from, take over/up, turn down ~

A: demanding, exacting, permanent, prestigious, prominent, responsible, temporary, well-paid ~

POTENTIAL

V: develop, fulfil, increase, reach, realise, recognise, see, use, waste ~

A: enormous, entire, greatest, highest, latent ~

P: make full use of (your) ~

POVERTY

V: abolish, alleviate, cause, live in, reduce, relieve, sink into, struggle against, suffer ~

A: abject, acute, extreme, great, grinding, growing, severe, widespread ~

POWER

V: abolish, abuse, acquire, aspire to, assume, bestow, break, challenge, come to, consolidate, curb, curtail, decentralise, delegate, deprive sb of, destroy, diminish, enjoy, entrust, erode, establish, exercise, exert, (re)gain, give, give up, grab, grant, grasp, hand over, harness, have, hold onto, increase, jostle for, misuse, possess, recognise, reduce, relinquish, resist, respect, restore, restrict, retain, return to, seize, share, sweep back to, take, threaten, transfer, undermine, use, usurp, wield ~

V: ~ changed hands, corrupts, declined, faded, increased, lies in sth, spread

A: absolute, autocratic, effective, enormous, excessive, great, growing, irresistible, limitless, magic, new-found, real, relentless, secular, superior, supernatural, supreme, tremendous, ultimate, undiminished, undisputed, unlimited, unparalleled, unprecedented, unrestricted, unrivalled, vast ~

P: accession to, acquisition of, assumption of, balance of, bid for, exercise of, fall from, handover of, loss of, lust for, scramble for, taste of, thirst for, trappings of, last vestige of ~

POWERS (authorisation)

V: abuse, define, delegate, exceed, exercise, give, grant, have, invest sb with, limit, restrict, use ~

A: advisory, discretionary, effective, emergency, excessive, extensive, full, mandatory, statutory, sweeping, undefined, wide ~

POWERS (personal faculties)

V: awaken, blunt, develop, draw on, exercise, lose, misuse, restore, tax, use ~

A: declining, diminishing, exceptional, extraordinary, fading, failing, formidable, remarkable, unimpaired, waning ~

P: decline in, height of his/her ~

PRACTICE (custom)

V: abandon, abhor, abolish, adopt, avoid, condemn, denounce, deplore, discourage, encourage, eradicate, follow, give up, go in for, introduce, recommend, revert to, stamp out, start ~

V: ~ died out, flourished, persisted, survived

A: abhorrent, accepted, admirable, antiquated, common, corrupt, customary, desirable, devious, discreditable, discredited, dubious, former, fraudulent, harmful, long-standing, mysterious, normal, previous, primitive, shady, standard, strange, underhand, unfair, usual, well-established, widespread ~

PRAISE
V: deserve, earn, get, heap ~ on sb, lavish ~ on sb, look for, merit, receive, win ~
A: enthusiastic, fulsome, generous, glowing, great, high, indiscriminate, sincere, unqualified, warm ~
P: damn with faint ~
PRAYER
V: answer, kneel in, offer, say, utter ~
A: ceaseless, communal, fervent, frequent, private, silent ~
P: power of ~
PRECAUTIONS
V: adopt, ignore, take ~
A: basic, careful, elaborate, elementary, proper, rigorous, simple, strict, wise ~
PRECEDENT
V: avoid, break, cite, create, establish, follow, invoke, mark, set ~
A: bad, dangerous, regrettable, undesirable, unfortunate, useful, (un)welcome ~
PRECISION
A: absolute, amazing, cool, great, perfect, tremendous, unerring, utmost ~
PREDICAMENT
V: avoid, extricate oneself from, face, find/seek a way out of, get into/out of, have, land oneself in, run up against, solve ~
A: awkward, embarrassing, foolish, hopeless, serious, severe ~
PREDICTION
V: make ~
V: ~ came true, proved right/wrong, turned out to be true
A: (in)accurate, alarming, confident, correct, dire, false, gloomy ~
PREFERENCE
V: acknowledge, admit, demonstrate, display, express, have, show ~
A: decided, individual, marked, natural, personal, sexual, slight, special, strong, vague ~
PREJUDICE
V: admit to, be free from/guilty of, cause, develop, dispel, display, do away with, encourage, express, feel, get over, have, hide, overcome, remove, run up against, share, show, swallow, voice ~
A: deep, entrenched, ingrained, innate, ludicrous, nasty, petty, racial, ridiculous, strong, stupid, unjust, violent ~
P: set of *prejudices*
PREMISE (logical)
V: abandon, accept, base sth on the ~ that, challenge, follow from, keep to, put forward, question, reject, start from, state, test, uphold ~
A: basic, fundamental, justifiable, main, major, mistaken, unacceptable, underlying, unlikely, untenable ~
PREPARATIONS
V: be in the middle of, be involved in, begin, break off, commence, complete, delay, finalise, get on with, give up, halt, hasten, intensify, interrupt, make, neglect, postpone, put ~ in hand, speed up, start, take part in, undertake ~
V: ~ are in hand, are going ahead/on, proceed, stopped
A: (in)adequate, careful, detailed, elaborate, extensive, final, haphazard, hasty, intensive, last-minute, lengthy, meticulous, painstaking, proper, serious, systematic, thorough ~

PRESS

V: be reported in, censor, censure, control, muzzle ~

A: free, financial, gutter, local, national, tabloid ~

P: ~ conference, report, statement; freedom of the ~

PRESSURE

V: apply, be subject to, be under, be vulnerable to, bear, build up, come under, cope with, ease, escape, exert, face, generate, give in to, give way to, increase, keep up, lessen, maintain, measure, oppose, put ~ on, reduce, relieve, remove, renew, resist, respond to, subject sb to, submit to, succumb to, sustain, stand, take ~ off, use, withstand ~

V: ~ became less, built up, eased, fell, increased, let up, mounted, rose, was brought to bear

A: constant, continuous, enormous, external, extreme, frantic, gentle, great, growing, increasing, internal, overwhelming, relentless, remorseless, steady, strong, unbearable, unrelenting, unremitting ~

PRESTIGE

V: boost, bring, build up, damage, enjoy, gain, give, lose, maintain, restore, seek, win ~

PRICE

V: accept, adjust, agree on/to, arrive at, ask, boost, bring down, control, cut, determine, drop, establish, fix, force down, freeze, get, guarantee, haggle over, hold down, increase, lower, maintain, mark up, match, name, negotiate, obtain, offer, pay, push down/up, put up, quote, raise, reduce, set, settle, slash, work out ~

V: ~ collapsed, declined, dropped, drifted down, escalated, fell, fluctuated, held, is tied to sth, jumped, kept/remained steady, outstripped ... , plummeted, plunged, ranged from ... to ... , rose, rocketed, shot up, slumped, soared, spiralled, stands at (320p), tumbled, varied, went down/up, went through the floor/roof

A: advantageous, attractive, average, bargain, competitive, cost, excessive, exorbitant, extortionate, extravagant, fair, fantastic, good, high, huge, inflated, keen, knock-down, list, low, moderate, modest, mounting, normal, official, outrageous, real, reasonable, recommended, regular, respectable, retail, ridiculous, right, selling, special, stable, static, steady, top, wholesale, world ~

P: drop in, fall in, reduction in, rise in, fetch the asking ~; boom in, curb on, cut in, jump in, range of, reduction in *prices*, house/food/hotel *prices*

PRIDE

V: be a blow to (my), feel/take a ~ in ... , hurt, injure, soothe, swallow your, wound (your) ~

A: false, great, justified, overweening, singular, unabashed ~

PRINCIPLE (in logical thinking)

V: accept, apply, base sth on, consider, contradict, define, deny, establish, examine, explain, fulfil, implement, put forward, raise, set out, study, underline, work out ~

V: ~ applies to ... , governs ... , holds good

A: basic, elementary, explicit, fundamental, general, governing, simple, sound, standard, universal ~

P: approach sth from first *principles*; based on historical/scientific etc *principles*

PRINCIPLE (in moral behaviour)

V: abandon, accept, adhere to, adopt, agree with, be opposed to, believe in, follow, infringe, invoke, keep to, lay down, live up to, obey, object to, observe, quarrel with, reaffirm, recognise, remain true to, respect, subscribe to, support, uphold, violate ~

A: basic, dearest, deepest, doubtful, firm, first, foremost, fundamental, implicit, inflexible, key, main, old-fashioned, outdated, overriding, sacred, safe, sound, strict, universal, wise ~

PRINCIPLE (on which sth works)
V: adopt, discover, grasp, study, understand, use, work on/out ~
V: ~ holds good, operates, works
A: basic, complicated, common, ingenious, key, novel, revolutionary, simple, sound, underlying, universal, useful, well-known ~
PRINCIPLES (moral)
V: abandon, betray, defend, go against, have, inculcate, lack, sacrifice, set out, share, stick to ~
A: high, noble, rigid, solid, sound, strict, worthy ~
P: set of ~; against (my), have strong ~
PRIORITY
V: accord, acknowledge, admit, claim, concede, dispute, establish, get, give, have, insist on, lose sight of, recognise, take ~
A: basic, first, high, low, (un)official, overriding, real, top ~
PRISON
V: break out of, come out of, do time in, escape from, go to, release sb from, send sb to, sentence sb to (7 years) in, spend time in ~
A: maximum-security, open, overcrowded ~
P: ~ governor, population, reform, system
PRIVACY
V: invade, protect, respect ~
P: breach of, intrusion on, invasion of ~
PRIVILEGE
V: abolish, abuse, attack, claim, cling to, confer, curb, decline, deprive sb of, do away with, earn, enjoy, exercise, give, grant, guard, have, inherit, insist on, lose, obtain, protect, recognise, refuse, reject, relinquish, retain, seek, surrender ~
A: enviable, exclusive, great, important, rare, sole, statutory, uncommon, unique, unusual ~
P: abuse of ~
PRIZE
V: award, carry off, covet, deserve, donate, get, give, miss, nominate sb for, qualify for, receive, share, win ~
A: booby, consolation, fabulous, first/second etc, glittering, grand, star, substantial ~
PROBABILITY
V: assess, discount, enhance, estimate, gauge, judge, lessen, measure, overlook, reduce, rule out, take into account ~
A: great, infinitesimal, little, slight, strong ~
P: in all ~
PROBLEM
V: address, aggravate, alleviate, apply oneself to, appreciate, approach, assess, attack, bring ~ to a head, brush aside, burden sb with, cause, circumvent, combat, come across, come to grips with, come up against, concentrate on, confront, consider, cope with, crack, create, deal with, decide, define, detect, dispose of, dodge, ease, elucidate, encounter, erase, escape from, evade, exacerbate, exaggerate, examine, experience, explain, explore, face (up to), fight, focus on, foresee, formulate, get to grips with, grapple with, grasp, handle, identify, ignore, lose sight of, magnify, master, overcome, overlook, pinpoint, perceive, pose, precipitate, predict, present, raise, recognise, rectify, relieve, represent, resolve, rise above, run into, run up against, see, settle, share, shirk, shy away from, solve, sort out, state, straighten out, struggle with, tackle, think over/through, thrash out, throw up, tinker with, touch upon, transform, trigger (off), unravel, wrestle with ~

V: ~ arose, baffled sb, boils down to ... , came to a head, cleared up, cropped up, disappeared, emerged, exists, got out of hand, haunted sb, hinges on ... , hit sb, involves ... , occurred, originates in ... , perplexed sb, persisted, preoccupied sb, recurred, remains, resolved itself, stems from ... , vanished, was made worse, worried sb

A: actual, acute, appalling, awesome, awkward, baffling, basic, central, chief, common, complex, complicated, constant, contemporary, contentious, continual, continuing, crucial, current, daunting, delicate, depressing, difficult, disgusting, endemic, enormous, explosive, familiar, formidable, fundamental, glaring, hypothetical, immediate, important, incipient, insoluble, insuperable, insurmountable, intractable, intricate, key, knotty, long-standing, long-term, main, major, marginal, minor, mundane, nasty, obvious, outstanding, painful, perennial, perpetual, perplexing, personal, potential, practical, present, pressing, principal, profound, recent, recurrent, recurring, related, real, routine, sensitive, serious, severe, simple, special, striking, subtle, tangible, tangled, tantalising, tedious, timeless, touchy, tough, tricky, trivial, troublesome, typical, underlying, unexpected, unforeseen, unique, unmanageable, unpleasant, urgent ~

P: (a whole) host of, range of, set of *problems*

PROCEDURE

V: abide by, adopt, agree on, alter, amend, apply, carry out, change, curtail, decide on, discuss, establish, examine, follow, go through, involve, keep to, observe, overhaul, scrap, settle, shorten, simplify, stick to, use, work out ~

A: accepted, basic, bureaucratic, complicated, clumsy, costly, cumbersome, (in)effective, entire, faulty, fixed, formal, general, humiliating, lengthy, long, normal, official, ordinary, regular, reverse, simple, standard, straightforward, strange, time-consuming, tortuous, usual, whole ~

PROCESS

V: accelerate, adopt, apply, arrest, check, complete, control, develop, employ, encourage, evaluate, examine, facilitate, favour, follow, further, go through, halt, hasten, help, hold back, improve, initiate, instigate, interrupt, introduce, invent, investigate, keep track of, master, modify, monitor, observe, obstruct, plan, prevent, regulate, reverse, set ~ in motion, slow down, speed up, start, stop, streamline, study, supervise, suspend, take part in, test, trigger, try (out), use ~

V: ~ came to an end/halt, continues, gathered momentum, intensified, spread, worked

A: active, awkward, basic, beneficial, complicated, cumbersome, cumulative, dangerous, daunting, decision-making, destructive, distinct, divisive, doubtful, effective, elaborate, essential, frustrating, gradual, harmful, inevitable, inexorable, ingenious, insidious, irritating, laborious, lengthy, long-drawn-out, natural, nerve-racking, noticeable, original, painful, perceptible, rapid, reliable, risky, salutary, slow, steady, step-by-step, swift, tiresome, tricky, valuable, wasteful, whole ~

P: by a ~ of elimination

PRODUCT

V: design, develop, discontinue, distribute, export, import, improve, (re)introduce, invent, (re)launch, make, manufacture, market, modify, package, promote, sell, sell out of, upgrade, withdraw ~

V: ~ is in/out of stock, flopped, has sold badly/out/well, took off

A: best-selling, end, competitive, consumer, finished, high-quality, high-tech, household, marketable, unique, waste ~

PRODUCTION
V: boost, cripple, curtail, cut down, disrupt, estimate, go into, halt, hold up, increase, interrupt, keep up, limit, manage, maximise, monitor, organise, plan, reduce, restrict, scale down, speed up, start, step up, stop, supervise ~

V: ~ climbed, declined, dwindled, eased off, fell, increased, is down/up, leapt (up), slipped, tapered off, went above (10,000 units a week)

A: annual (monthly, etc), brisk, full, full-scale, growing, mass, overall, peak, slow, sluggish, total, uninterrupted ~

P: slump in, volume of ~

PRODUCTION (theatrical)
V: design, direct, film, finance, mount, put on, record, rehearse, review, sponsor, video ~

A: amateur, awful, controversial, dazzling, disastrous, disciplined, dreadful, experimental, full-scale, gripping, high-spirited, imaginative, inspired, magnificent, major, patchy, polished, professional, sensational, spectacular, splendid, stunning, superb ~

PRODUCTIVITY
V: boost, improve, increase, raise, step up ~

A: higher, (un)satisfactory ~

PROFESSION
V: belong to, enter, go into, leave, practise, take up, train for ~

A: exacting, glamorous, learned, legal, medical, overcrowded, teaching, theatrical, well-paid ~

P: the oldest ~ in the world

PROFIT
V: accumulate, bring in, clear, cut into, derive, distribute, earn, generate, get, guarantee, improve, increase, invest, jeopardize, make, plough back, produce, realise, share, spend, take, yield ~

V: ~ accrued, accumulated, declined, disappeared, dropped, dwindled, grew, improved, mounted, plummeted, plunged, rose, shrank, vanished, varied

A: adequate, astronomical, considerable, enormous, excellent, excess, extortionate, fair, fat, gross, handsome, huge, large, legitimate, marginal, meagre, modest, net, quick, reasonable, regular, reliable, satisfactory, slight, staggering, tremendous ~

P: ~ margin, motive; drop in, rise in ~

PROGRAMME
V: abandon, adapt, adopt, adhere to, alter, announce, approve, arrange, cancel, carry out/through, change, complete, delay, draw up, embark on, expand, follow, formulate, fulfil, implement, initiate, introduce, keep to, maintain, make, organise, postpone, prepare, push through, put ~ into effect/practice, sabotage, scrap, set out/up, slow down, speed up, stick to, supervise, terminate, tone down, undertake, upset, water down, work out ~

V: ~ has fallen behind, is under way, proceeded, is running late, took shape, went through

A: (un)acceptable, alternative, ambitious, attractive, comprehensive, crash, crowded, definite, demanding, detailed, development, difficult, dull, entertaining, excellent, extensive, far-reaching, fascinating, fixed, full, gigantic, huge, (un)imaginative, imposing, impressive, interesting, joint, limited, modest, official, original, pilot, proper, rudimentary, sensible, strict, valuable, vast, vital, worthwhile ~

PROGRESS
V: accelerate, achieve, assess, block, bring about, chart, check, encourage, expect, facilitate, halt, hamper, handicap, hinder, hold back, impede, interrupt, make, measure, monitor, obstruct, register, report, report on, resume, set back, speed up, stimulate ~

V: ~ accelerated, ceased, is dependent on ... , slowed down

A: (in)adequate, astounding, cautious, considerable, current, disappointing, erratic, excellent, fair, further, good, great, imperceptible, inexorable, marked, moderate, negligible, normal, notable, noticeable, past, painstaking, poor, rapid, record, remarkable, satisfactory, significant, slow, sluggish, steady, tremendous ~

PROJECT

V: abandon, adopt, approve, approve of, axe, back, be committed to/engaged in, begin, bring ~ to fruition, cancel, carry out/through, complete, conceive, consider, delay, design, develop, devise, embark on, finance, form, give up, halt, implement, launch, lay the groundwork for, mastermind, oppose, outline, pioneer, plan, present, propose, pursue, put forward, put ~ in hand, put ~ in jeopardy, put ~ into effect, put off, reject, revive, rule out, scrap, shelve, sponsor, start, study, submit, support, undertake, upset, veto, withdraw, work on, work out ~

V: ~ came to fruition, got off the ground, grew out of ..., went ahead

A: alternative, ambitious, attractive, clever, controversial, costly, detailed, entire, gigantic, huge, imaginative, ingenious, inventive, joint, large/small-scale, long/short-term, modest, novel, ongoing, outlandish, pet, pilot, preliminary, rash, (un)realistic, reliable, (un)satisfactory, silly, stupid, (un)successful, (un)suitable, unique, vast, viable ~

PROMISE

V: break, carry out, endorse, extract, fulfil, give, go back on, honour, implement, keep (to), make ~

A: binding, definite, empty, firm, foolish, hollow, rash, solemn, vague, wild ~

PROMOTION

V: gain, get, miss, obtain, put (sb) in for, recommend sb for, strive for, win ~

A: automatic, further, rapid, slow, unexpected, well-deserved ~

PROOF

V: ask for, call for, cast doubt on, come across/upon, constitute, demand, discover, establish, find, gather, give, have, lack, look for, manufacture, need, obtain, offer, produce, provide, question, require, seek, stumble across, supply, test, want ~

A: absolute, abundant, additional, adequate, ample, clear, clear-cut, (in)conclusive, concrete, (un)convincing, definite, doubtful, dubious, eloquent, final, firm, fresh, independent, indisputable, irrefutable, logical, mathematical, neat, obscure, overwhelming, perfect, ready-made, real, reliable, rigorous, satisfactory, shaky, (in)sufficient, supplementary, undeniable, written ~

P: ~ of identity, ownership, payment; this is ~ positive that ...; the burden of ~ rests on sb

PROPAGANDA

V: be taken in by, believe, counter, counteract, disseminate, engage in, listen to, put out, resist, spread, step up ~

A: blatant, clever, enemy, false, harmful, hostile, insidious, left-/right-wing, lying, political, powerful, religious, sheer, skilful, vicious ~

P: ~ campaign, exercise

PROPERTY

V: condemn, demolish, inherit, lease, let, own, purchase, renovate, rent, seize ~

A: abandoned, commercial, desirable, industrial, marketable, private, residential, splendid ~

P: ~ developer, management

PROPORTION

V: account for, constitute, decide on, determine, discover, establish, fix, form, keep, maintain ~

V: ~ decreased, dwindled, increased

A: best, correct, desired, diminishing, direct, equal, excessive, growing, high, inverse, large, proper, right, substantial, suitable ~

PROPORTIONS (of a building)

V: admire, alter, change, determine, distort, have, maintain, spoil, take on ~

A: awkward, beautiful, classic, correct, enormous, exquisite, fine, graceful, harmonious, huge, ideal, imposing, majestic, optimum, perfect, pleasing, ugly ~

PROPOSAL

V: accept, adopt, agree to, alter, amend, announce, approve, back, block, canvass, carry out, change, circulate, clarify, come up with, consider, counter, decide about/on, defeat, discuss, draft, elaborate on, endorse, examine, explore, implement, jettison, make, modify, offer, oppose, present, produce, publish, put forward/up, receive, recommend, refuse, reject, revise, second, set out, shelve, study, submit, support, table, take up, think about, torpedo, turn down, unveil, veto, vote down, vote on, weigh up, welcome, withdraw, work on ~

A: advantageous, alarming, alternative, amazing, ambitious, attractive, bold, concrete, controversial, definite, far-reaching, firm, helpful, imaginative, important, ingenious, interesting, interim, kind, likely, long-awaited, major, modest, novel, original, provocative, ridiculous, risky, satisfactory, sensible, serious, suitable, tempting, tentative, useful, vague ~

P: ~ of marriage; package of, series of, set of *proposals*

PROPOSITION

V: accept, consider, make, oppose, present, put forward, refer to, reject, study, submit, support, welcome, withdraw ~

A: alarming, attractive, concrete, interesting, logical, serious, tempting ~

PROPOSITION (logical)

V: accept, (dis)agree with, bear out, elaborate on, endorse, examine, prove, put forward, refute, reject, set out ~

A: basic, controversial, daring, important, interesting, intriguing, logical, novel, plausible ~

PROSPECT

V: be dismayed at/by, be faced with/perplexed by/shattered by, be wary about, consider, destroy, dread, enjoy, entertain, examine, exploit, explore, face, have, hold out, jeopardize, look forward to, offer, open up, raise, relish, revive, rule out, see, spoil, study, take advantage of, throw away, waste, weigh up ~

V: ~ appals sb, attracts sb, delighted sb, faded, haunted sb, horrified sb, opened up, receded, terrified sb, thrilled sb, upset sb, vanished, worried sb

A: alluring, bad, bleak, bright, challenging, dark, daunting, dazzling, depressing, disappointing, dismal, distant, dubious, encouraging, excellent, exciting, fascinating, gloomy, grim, hopeful, hopeless, immediate, irresistible, poor, promising, stimulating, tantalising, vague ~

PROSPERITY

V: achieve, create, destroy, enjoy, ensure, erode, maintain, regain, safeguard, spoil, threaten ~

A: comparative, general, great, lasting, modest, new-found, relative, tremendous, widespread ~

P: height of ~

PROTECTION

V: afford, give, offer, provide ~

A: absolute, additional, adequate, complete, effective, extra, partial, police, special, total ~

PROTEST

V: abandon, brush aside, cause, deal with, dismiss, do sth under, enter, ignore, issue, lodge, maintain, make, record, register, reject, show, silence, stage, voice ~

V: ~ did no good, made no difference

A: angry, categorical, feeble, firm, formal, futile, growing, indignant, loud, mild, mounting, sharp, silent, strong, vigorous, violent, vociferous, widespread, worldwide ~

P: rumble of, storm of, wave of ~; flood of *protests*

PUBLIC
V: annoy, convince, deceive, educate, fool, inform, mislead, please, shock, win over, woo ~
P: cross-section of, members of the (general) ~

PUBLIC OPINION
V: alienate, anger, antagonise, appeal to, be out of step with, change, defy, enlighten, galvanise, go against, ignore, inflame, influence, keep up with, manipulate, mollify, mould, offend, pander to, placate, play to, polarise, rally, rouse, satisfy, split, sway ~
V: ~ hardened, is against/behind/divided/split/in favour of/opposed to ... , shifted, wavered
P: shift in, tide of ~

PUBLICATION
V: distribute, edit, issue, put out, print, subsidise, withdraw ~
A: defunct, erudite, handy, imaginative, important, (un)interesting, latest, popular, recent, scholarly, useful ~

PUBLICITY
V: abhor, attract, avoid, cause, court, gain, get, give rise to, hate, seek, shun, shy away from ~
A: adverse, (un)favourable, unprecedented, unwelcome ~
P: ~ campaign, stunt; blaze of, fanfare of, flurry of, glare of, spate of, wave of ~

PUNISHMENT
V: administer, carry out, deal out, deserve, dodge, dole out, escape, hand out, impose, inflict, mete out, suffer ~
A: appropriate, brutal, capital, corporal, cruel, degrading, fit, harsh, just, lenient, mild, prompt, severe, well-deserved ~
P: cruel and unusual ~

PURPOSE
V: accomplish, achieve, carry out, conceal, defeat, divert sb from, fit, fit in with, keep to, obscure, obstruct, pursue, realise, serve, suit, understand ~
A: apparent, basic, chief, clear, common, conscious, deliberate, fixed, immediate, implicit, intrinsic, legitimate, main, major, mundane, obscure, obvious, overriding, practical, (im)proper, real, sinister, true, ultimate, underhand, underlying, useful ~
P: strength of ~

PURSUIT
V: abandon, engage in, follow in, give up, hamper, take up ~
A: avid, close, constant, diligent, dogged, frenetic, futile, hot, mad, relentless, steady, unremitting, vain ~

PURSUITS (activities)
V: be fond of, enjoy, follow, go in for, take up ~
A: agreeable, arduous, energetic, fascinating, hazardous, healthy, indoor, intellectual, interesting, leisure, leisurely, literary, outdoor, scientific, sedentary ~

Q

QUALIFICATIONS
V: add to, check, demand, get, improve, list, need, possess, recognise, require, specify ~
A: academic, appropriate, essential, excellent, good, ideal, inadequate, necessary, outstanding, poor, proper, special, suitable ~

QUALITY
V: aim at, appreciate, assess, check, control, demand, ensure, guarantee, improve, insist on, inspect, keep up, lower, maintain, measure, preserve, raise, regulate, reject, specify, stipulate, test, watch ~

V: ~ declined, deteriorated, fell, fluctuated, improved, varied, went down

A: abysmal, atrocious, average, disgraceful, excellent, first-rate, high, inferior, mediocre, patchy, perfect, poor, prime, real, (un)satisfactory, special, standard, star, sterling, superb, superior, superlative, supreme, top, uneven ~

P: ~ control; not of merchantable ~ (legal term)

QUALITY (characteristic)
V: admire, capture, discern, exemplify, have, praise, see ~

A: admirable, attractive, basic, dominant, elusive, endearing, good, inherent, intimate, intrinsic, mysterious, personal, obvious, outstanding, rare, redeeming, remarkable, special, strange, true, unique, unusual ~

QUANTITY
V: add to, check, control, cut, estimate, fix, increase, limit, measure, reduce, restrict, settle, supply ~

V: ~ diminished, dropped, grew, increased

A: additional, astounding, considerable, excessive, extra, huge, indeterminate, infinitesimal, large, limited, moderate, modest, negligible, prodigious, (in)significant, sizable, spectacular, substantial, sufficient, tiny, vague ~

QUARREL
V: avoid, cause, get drawn into/involved in, give rise to, keep out of, lead to, mend, patch up, pick, provoke, resolve, start, take part in ~

V: ~ arose, broke out

A: ancient, bitter, fierce, long-standing, nasty, serious, slight, violent ~

QUERY
V: answer, deal with, handle, put, put forward, raise, respond to ~

QUEST
V: abandon, continue, embark on, enter on, follow, give up, go off on, go on, pursue, set off on, take up, undertake ~

A: blind, fascinating, heroic, hopeful, hopeless, long, noble, unending, urgent, vain ~

QUESTION
V: address ~ to sb, answer, ask, avoid, conjure up, direct ~ to sb, dodge, draft, draw up, duck, evade, formulate, frame, handle, ignore, invite, pose, put, react to, reply to, respond to, sidestep, submit ~

A: abrupt, academic, awkward, baffling, barbed, challenging, direct, easy, embarrassing, hypothetical, impertinent, inconvenient, legitimate, loaded, nasty, oblique, penetrating, perennial, perfunctory, pertinent, plain, pointed, preliminary, provocative, recurring, rhetorical, roundabout, routine, rude, searching, set, sharp, stock, straight, straightforward, tantalising, tricky, unanswerable, unexpected, veiled, vital ~

P: barrage of, battery of, flood of, list of, series of, set of, string of *questions*

QUESTION (issue)
V: argue, avoid, bring up, brush aside, consider, deal with, debate, decide, discuss, examine, explore, go into, handle, ignore, judge, look at, pass over, pursue, put ~ into perspective, puzzle over, raise, refer to, resolve, rethink, settle, shelve, sidestep, solve, tackle, take up ~

V: ~ arose, came to a head, came up, cropped up, disturbed sb, interested sb, popped up, puzzled sb, struck sb

A: awkward, bewildering, broad, burning, complex, complicated, contentious, controversial, crucial, debatable, delicate, difficult, disturbing, fascinating, fundamental, immediate, intractable, intriguing, key, main, major, minor, philosophical, political, pressing, puzzling, real, religious, secondary, sensitive, simple, supreme, tantalising, thorny, topical, tricky, trivial, troublesome, unresolved, vexed, worrying ~

QUESTIONNAIRE
V: answer, circulate, compile, complete, construct, distribute, fill in, hand out, send out ~
A: complicated, comprehensive, detailed, extensive, lengthy, short, multiple-choice ~

QUEUE
V: form, join, jump, push into, stand in, stretch back to ..., wait in ~
V: ~ formed, got longer, moved on
A: endless, long, patient, short ~
P: back of, end of, front of, head of ~

QUORUM
V: form, get, have, obtain ~

QUOTA
V: abolish, do away with, fix, fulfil, impose, lay down, scrap ~
A: fishing/milk etc, statutory ~

QUOTATION
V: include, look up, recognise, take ~ from sth, track down, trace ~
A: apt, direct, lengthy ~

QUOTATION (financial)
V: accept, get, give, submit ~

R

RACE
V: cancel, challenge sb to, compete in, complete, drop out of, enter (for), lose, organise, run (in), sponsor, take part in, time, win, withdraw from ~
A: close, competitive, desperate, exciting, gruelling, important, tough ~

RACE (ethnic)
A: ancient, chosen, dominant, inferior, master, mixed, noble, proud, superior ~
P: ~ relations

RACISM
V: accuse sb of, combat, stamp out ~
A: blatant, rampant, vicious, widespread ~
P: accusations of, evidence of, victims of ~

RADIATION
V: be exposed to, be protected from, detect, emit, give off, measure, produce ~
A: harmful, high/low-level, lethal, nuclear ~
P: ~ leak, sickness, therapy

RAGE
V: drive sb into, fall into, fly into, get into, shake with, tremble with, work oneself up into ~
A: blind, frightening, impotent, jealous, road, sudden, terrible, towering ~
P: fit of, outburst of ~

RAID
V: carry out, go on, launch, make, take part in ~
A: abortive, armed, audacious, bold, daring, dawn, spectacular, (un)successful, surprise ~

RAIN
V: forecast, pour with, pray for, shelter from ~
V: ~ beat/poured/pelted down, came on, fell, let up, started, stopped, streamed down, soaked sb, subsided, went on (all day)
A: driving, fine, gentle, heavy, pouring, soft, steady, torrential, tropical ~

RALLY
V: address, attend, ban, disperse, hold, organise, take part in ~
V: ~ broke up, got out of hand
A: big, noisy, peace, peaceful, political, youth ~
P: an anti-(war, nuclear) ~

RALLY (car race)
V: compete in, enter for, hold, organise, take part in ~
A: annual, cross-country, exhausting, famous, important ~

RANGE (distance)
V: achieve, calculate, come into, go out of, extend, increase, keep within, measure, reach, reduce ~
A: close, fixed, limited, long, point-blank, short ~
P: is within/in/out of ~

RANGE (variety)
V: add to, cover, enlarge, exceed, expand, extend, fill, improve, increase, offer, present, provide, reduce, show, supply, update, withdraw sth from ~
A: astonishing, bewildering, broad, enormous, entire, excellent, extensive, full, good, huge, infinite, large, limited, narrow, restricted, superb, surprising, up-to-date, whole, wide ~

RANSOM
V: ask for, exact, extort, demand, hold sb to, pay ~
P: ~ demand, note

RAPE
V: accuse sb of, be convicted of, commit ~
A: attempted, brutal, date, gang, serial, violent ~
P: ~ victim

RATE (tempo)
A: accelerating, astonishing, dizzying, excessive, fantastic, fearful, great, measured, moderate, rapid, slow, steady, terrific, tremendous ~

RATE (financial)
V: boost, bring down, change, charge, cut, demand, drive up, ease, estimate, fix, increase, inflate, jack up, maintain, prop up, push up, put up, raise, reduce, set, slash ~
V: ~ came down, continued at (8%), dropped, fell, fluctuated, jumped, reached a peak, slackened, tumbled, varied, went up
A: acceptable, annual, competitive, concessionary, current, excessive, exorbitant, flat, full, good, high, initial, interest, low, moderate, modest, present, prevailing, reduced, regular, stationary, steady, unchanged ~
P: ~ of interest; pay the going, drop in, fall in, reduction in, rise in, surge in ~

RATIO
V: alter, calculate, change, determine, exceed, fix, increase, reduce ~
A: diminishing, (in)direct, high, increasing, inverse, satisfactory ~

RATIONS
V: hand out, issue ~
A: daily (weekly etc), double, emergency, extra, short, (in)sufficient ~

REACTION
V: affect, cause, encounter, expect, find, foresee, get, give rise to, hasten, lead to, observe, meet with, obtain, precipitate, predict, prevent, produce, provoke, record, result in, sense, set off, test, trigger ~
A: adverse, angry, chain, common, delayed, exaggerated, (un)expected, (un)favourable, harmful, healthy, horrified, hostile, hysterical, immediate, indirect, inexplicable, initial, instant, instantaneous, instinctive, intense, (il)logical, low-key, muted, natural, negative, (ab)normal, ominous, overdue, positive, prompt, sceptical, shocked, slight, spontaneous, standard, strange, strong, sudden, surprising, swift, typical, understandable, undesirable, unexpected, unfriendly, violent, weak ~

READER
V: address, appeal to, attract ~
A: avid, compulsive, general, great, regular, slow, voracious ~

REALITY
V: accept, become a, be blind to, bring sb back to, come down to, come to terms with, cope with, deal with, escape from, face, forget, get away from, obscure, recognise, run away from, search for ~
A: bare, concrete, grim, harsh, stark, underlying, unpleasant, unwelcome ~

REASON
V: admit, advance, ascertain, deny, demolish, discover, divulge, explain, expose, find, find out, furnish, get at, give, have, ignore, imagine, invent, justify, know, offer, point to, produce, provide, reject, seek, set forth, state, supply, tell ~
A: basic, chief, clear, cogent, compelling, complex, convincing, down-to-earth, excellent, explicit, far-fetched, forceful, frank, frivolous, fundamental, genuine, good, incomprehensible, inexplicable, irrelevant, legitimate, likely, logical, main, mysterious, obscure, obvious, odd, ostensible, overwhelming, personal, perverse, plausible, political, poor, potent, powerful, practical, rational, real, self-evident, sensible, simple, sinister, specific, straightforward, strong, sound, true, underlying, valid ~
P: for a whole host of, set of *reasons*

REASON (reasonableness)
V: appeal to, be amenable to, listen to, see, stand to ~
P: choose/do/pick/spend/take anything within, beyond all ~

REASON (mind)
V: exercise, lose, rely on, use ~
V: ~ failed sb, tells (me) ...

REASONING
V: (dis)agree with, follow, grasp, understand ~
A: complicated, confused, faulty, logical, patient, plain, sensible, simple, sound, step-by-step, tortuous ~
P: powers of ~

REBELLION
V: crush, incite sb to, lead, put down, quash, quell, spark off, squash, stir up, subdue, suppress, take part in ~
V: ~ broke out, failed, flared up, got out of hand, spread, was rife
A: abortive, armed, dangerous, full-/large-scale, incipient, open, outright, overt ~

REBUFF
V: deliver, get, give, meet with, suffer ~
A: cruel, firm, hasty, official, painful, polite, sharp, well-deserved ~

REBUKE
V: administer, deliver, deserve, get, give, merit, receive, suffer ~
A: gentle, mild, official, painful, severe, sharp, stern, stinging, strong ~

RECEIPT
V: ask for, file, give, get, keep, make out, require, sign, write, write out ~

RECEPTION
V: accord sb, face, find, get, give sb, meet with ~
A: chilly, cold, cool, cordial, emotional, (un)enthusiastic, favourable, friendly, hostile, indifferent, mixed, rapturous, rough, rousing, warm ~

RECEPTION (formal gathering)
V: attend, give, hold, host ~
A: crowded, formal, glittering, official, smart, wedding ~

RECESSION (economic)
V: aggravate, alleviate, come out of, contribute to, cope with, counter, cure, deal with, fight, find a way out of, get out of, go into, head for, prevent, recover from, reverse, suffer from, tackle ~
V: ~ bottomed out, got out of hand, got worse, hit, loomed, spread
A: current, deep, deepening, economic, frightening, global, prolonged, serious, severe, unavoidable, worldwide ~
P: onset of ~

RECOGNITION
V: accord ~ to sb, apply for, demand, get, grant, obtain, receive, refuse, seek, win ~
A: belated, full, general, growing, official, proper, public, spontaneous, universal ~
P: be given official ~

RECOLLECTION
V: ~ faded
A: clear, depressing, dim, distinct, faint, happy, hazy, horrifying, painful, (un)pleasant, precise, vague, vivid ~

RECOMMENDATION
V: accept, back, carry out, consider, do sth on sb's, draw up, endorse, follow, go against/along with, ignore, implement, make, overturn, pass on, put forward/into effect, reject, support ~
A: controversial, sensible, strong ~

RECOMMENDATION (testimonial)
V: ask for, check, give, provide, supply ~
A: excellent, fine, first-class, good, lukewarm, splendid, unqualified, useful, warm ~

RECONSTRUCTION
V: attempt, carry out, complete, undertake ~
A: careful, complete, extensive, meticulous, painstaking, partial, successful, total ~

RECORD (account of facts)
V: check, compile, consult, correct, destroy, examine, erase, falsify, give, have/keep sth on, keep, look up, make, preserve, produce, provide, refer to ~, set ~ straight
V: ~ shows that ...
A: accurate, authentic, careful, close, complete, comprehensive, confused, detailed, dubious, exact, faithful, full, lasting, meticulous, official, permanent, pictorial, precise, reliable, systematic, true, unique, valuable, written ~

RECORD (reputation)

V: conceal, check, dig up, enquire into, have, look back on, look up, spoil ~

A: abysmal, admirable, appalling, blameless, brilliant, clean, clear, deplorable, dismal, distinguished, dreadful, dubious, enviable, excellent, fine, glittering, honourable, impeccable, impressive, past, poor, reliable, remarkable, satisfactory, shameful, splendid, superb, track, unblemished, unchallenged, wartime ~

RECORD (sports)

V: achieve, beat, break, challenge, equal, establish, have, hold, improve on, lose, match, set (up), take ~

V: ~ fell, stands

A: all-time, famous, fine, great, Olympic, splendid, superb, unbeatable, unique, vulnerable, world ~

RECORD (disc)

V: cut, make, play, put on, scratch ~

RECOVERY

V: aid, bring about, delay, effect, endanger, ensure, further, hamper, hasten, help, hinder, hope for, make, predict, speed up, sustain ~

A: amazing, astounding, complete, excellent, full, gradual, hopeful, instantaneous, magic, miraculous, moderate, modest, quick, rapid, remarkable, slight, slow, spectacular, startling, steady, unexpected ~

P: wish sb a speedy ~

REDUCTION

V: achieve, agree to, bring about, call for, cause, contribute to, demand, effect, get, lead to, make, obtain, offer, oppose, propose, result in, seek ~

A: considerable, decided, definite, gradual, important, major, marked, massive, minor, real, severe, significant, slight, small, steady, substantial, unprecedented, visible ~

P: a ~ in real terms

REFERENCE (allusion)

V: contain, make ~

A: apt, brief, casual, cutting, (in)direct, important, oblique, official, vague, veiled ~

REFERENCE (testimonial)

V: ask for, check, get, give, provide, supply, take up ~

A: excellent, glowing, negative, poor, positive, satisfactory ~

REFLECTION

A: anxious, careful, cautious, deep, patient, quiet, sad, serious, sober ~

REFORM

V: accomplish, advocate, agitate for, be in need of, block, bring about, call for, carry out/through, champion, concede, cry out for, demand, endorse, halt, hold back, implement, instigate, introduce, launch, lead to, make, need, obstruct, oppose, oversee, postpone, press for, push/put through, put ~ into effect, speed up, supervise, tackle, thwart, undo, urge, work for ~

A: basic, bold, complete, comprehensive, effective, essential, extensive, far-reaching, fundamental, gradual, imaginative, immediate, inadequate, initial, key, long-term, necessary, (long-)overdue, radical, rapid, revolutionary, step-by-step, successful, sweeping, tentative, thorough, urgent, wide-ranging ~

P: architect of ~

REFUGE

V: discover, find, give, grant, offer, provide, seek, take ~

A: comfortable, perfect, safe, secure ~

REFUGEES
P: flood of, influx of, tide of, wave of ~
REFUND
V: ask for, be entitled to, claim, demand, get, give, obtain, offer sb, pay, receive ~
A: full, partial ~
REFUSAL
V: accept, issue, send ~
A: abrupt, adamant, blank, blunt, brusque, definite, determined, final, firm, flat, immediate, indignant, obstinate, point-blank, polite, rough, steadfast ~
REGIME
V: back, bolster up, bring down, create, destabilize, destroy, establish, fight (against), oust, overthrow, prop up, rebel against, remove, replace, serve, set up, strengthen, support, tear down, topple, undermine, uphold ~
V: ~ came into power, collapsed
A: authoritarian, brutal, Communist, corrupt, cruel, despotic, dictatorial, discredited, inept, interim, liberal, oppressive, puppet, repressive, rigid, strict, totalitarian, tottering, tyrannical ~
P: overthrow of ~
REGRET
V: express, feel, show ~
A: bitter, deep, keen, lasting, profound, sincere ~
REGULATIONS
V: abide by, act against, adopt, apply, break, bring in, comply with, defy, draw up, enforce, flout, go against, ignore, impose, introduce, issue, keep to, lay down, modify, obey, observe, relax, scrap, suspend ~
V: ~ apply to ... , come into force, govern, lay down/require/state ...
A: complicated, strict, stringent, tough ~
P: against/contrary to the, breach of, set of, tangle of ~
REHEARSAL
V: conduct, have, hold, miss, schedule, stage ~
A: dress, final ~
REJECTION
V: cope with, face, meet with, suffer ~
A: complete, massive, overwhelming, total, utter ~
P: fear of, feeling of, sense of ~
RELATIONS
V: affect, break off, build up, cement, cloud, cut off, define, develop, disrupt, ease, encourage, enjoy, ensure, establish, expand, foster, govern, handle, have, impair, improve, jeopardize, keep, maintain, mend, normalise, nurture, patch up, poison, promote, renew, restore, resume, sever, sour, spoil, stabilize, strain, strengthen ~
V: ~ deteriorated, improved, plummeted, prospered, slumped, turned sour, worsened
A: amicable, close, cold, cool, cordial, current, diplomatic, excellent, friendly, international, lukewarm, mutual, normal, peaceful, reasonable, reciprocal, relaxed, sensitive, sexual, sour, smooth, stormy, strained, tense, trade, troubled, warm ~
P: breakdown in, cooling of, thaw in, worsening of ~
RELATIONSHIP (between people)
V: break, break off, build, cement, come out of, create, cultivate, damage, destroy, develop, develop into, endanger, enhance, establish, forge, form, foster, go into, have, jeopardize, poison, sever, sour, spoil, strain, sustain, undermine ~

V: ~ blossomed, deteriorated, endured, flourished, lasted (20 years), rests on ... , survived, went wrong, withered

A: adult, ambivalent, budding, business, casual, civilised, close, confidential, constructive, cosy, dangerous, deep, delicate, difficult, discordant, distant, doomed, easy-going, enduring, enigmatic, enriching, excellent, extramarital, fragile, friendly, generous, hostile, idealistic, incestuous, intimate, lasting, love-hate, loving, lukewarm, mature, meaningful, platonic, prickly, professional, relaxed, rewarding, romantic, (un)satisfactory, sexual, solid, special, spiritual, strange, tortured, trusting, uneasy, warm ~

P: have a good working ~

RELATIONSHIP (between things, ideas)

V: affect, analyse, clarify, compare, contrast, define, describe, discern, dissect, establish a ~ between A and B, evaluate, examine, exaggerate, explain, explore, express, highlight, look at, outline, perceive, probe, see, review, specify, study, understand, work out ~

A: ambiguous, arbitrary, broad, causal, cause-and-effect, clear, clear-cut, close, complicated, crucial, (in)direct, distant, distinct, incongruous, inexplicable, (no) necessary, obvious, paradoxical, straightforward, strong, symbiotic, tenuous, unique ~

P: bear some/no/a close ~ to; the ~ between cause and effect

RELATIVE

A: blood, close, distant, near(est) ~

RELEASE of sb

V: bring about, call/campaign for, demand, engineer, obtain, order, push for, secure, work for ~

A: conditional, early, immediate, prompt ~

RELEVANCE

V: deny, emphasise, establish, point out, see, stress, underline ~

A: clear, close, definite, great, immediate, slight ~

P: is of no/little ~ to ... ; has little/little or no/no ~ to ...

RELIABILITY

V: have confidence/faith in the ~ of, question, test, trust ~

A: complete, questionable, total, utter ~

RELIEF (from pain or worry)

V: breathe/heave a sigh of, bring, experience, express, feel, give, provide, seek ~

A: comic, enormous, great, immediate, immense, instant, permanent, slight, temporary, tremendous, welcome ~

P: a moment of light, feeling of, sigh of, surge of ~

RELIEF (help)

V: bring, call for, expect, provide, refuse, send, summon ~

A: immediate, tangible, unexpected, welcome ~

P: ~ fund, famine ~

RELIGION

V: give up, practise, renounce, turn to ~

A: ancient, austere, Christian, official, organised, primitive, state ~

P: comfort of, consolations of, defence of, persecution of, practice of, tenets of ~

RELUCTANCE

V: display, do sth with, overcome, show ~

A: extreme, great, marked, slight ~

P: to show some/a certain ~ to

REMARK

V: come out with, dissociate (myself) from, let slip, make, overhear, pass, qualify, resent, utter ~

V: ~ caused offence, slipped out

A: acrimonious, apt, blunt, casual, caustic, conciliatory, conventional, critical, cruel, cryptic, cutting, defamatory, defiant, disparaging, enigmatic, facetious, facile, flippant, frivolous, hypocritical, impersonal, impertinent, impetuous, inconsiderate, indelicate, insulting, jocular, naive, nasty, odd, offensive, off-hand, off-the-cuff, oft-quoted, outrageous, pithy, polite, profound, provocative, revealing, rude, sarcastic, scathing, snide, stupid, tactful, tactless, tantalizing, trenchant, trite, uncalled-for, unguarded, unkind, witty ~

P: closing, introductory, opening *remarks*

REMEDY

V: apply, prescribe, provide, recommend, resort to, seek, supply, use ~

V: ~ failed, succeeded, worked

A: common, desperate, drastic, effective, excellent, immediate, lasting, long-term, painful, poor, powerful, practical, radical, satisfactory, speedy, successful, (un)usual ~

REMINDER

V: act as, bring, constitute, form, issue, offer, send sb ~

A: awesome, bitter, final, gentle, gloomy, grim, salutary, sombre, timely ~

REMORSE

V: express, feel, show ~

A: acute, bitter, deep, genuine ~

RENOWN

A: great, international, wide, worldwide ~

RENT

V: be behind with, charge, collect, owe, pay, put up, raise ~

A: fair, high, low, market ~

REPAIRS

V: carry out, do ~

A: emergency, extensive, lengthy, major, minor, necessary, superficial ~

REPERCUSSIONS

V: avoid, be afraid of, be followed by, cause, have, lead to, prevent, produce ~

A: damaging, devastating, far-reaching, important, lasting, serious, sinister, unforeseen, unfortunate, widespread ~

REPLY

V: await, delay, elicit, expect, fax, get, give, ignore, insist on, issue, make, postpone, produce, publish, put off, receive, send, submit, wait for ~

A: (un)ambiguous, appropriate, audible, blunt, brief, brisk, cheerful, confused, decisive, definite, detailed, early, (un)equivocal, evasive, exhaustive, explicit, favourable, firm, flippant, forceful, forthright, frank, frosty, full, immediate, impertinent, impudent, laconic, long-winded, neat, non-committal, outspoken, pointed, polite, prompt, provocative, rude, (un)satisfactory, straight, terse, truthful, vague, witty ~

REPORT

V: act upon, adopt, advise on, alter, amend, analyse, bring out, challenge, change, circulate, cite, commission, compile, confirm, consider, contradict, criticise, cut, deliver, deny, digest, dismiss, draft, draw up, edit, endorse, examine, file, get, give, ignore, implement, issue, launch, leak, make, make ~ public, prepare, present, produce, publish, quote, receive, reject, release, scrutinize, send in, shelve, study, submit, suppress, welcome, work on, write ~

V: ~ advocates sth, appeared, calls for sth, claims sth, came out, condemns sth, covers sth, criticises sth, deals with sth, describes sth, discloses sth, draws attention to sth, endorses sth, exposes sth, highlights sth, hints ..., identifies ..., implies sth, indicates sth, makes clear that ..., notes sth, pinpoints sth, points out that ..., raises questions, reaches the conclusion that ..., recommends sth, reveals sth, shows sth, states sth, stresses sth, suggests sth, tackles sth ~

A: accurate, adverse, alarmist, annual/monthly etc, authoritative, baffling, balanced, (un)biased, bleak, candid, cautious, clear, complacent, confidential, critical, damaging, damning, definite, detailed, disappointing, disquieting, dissenting, disturbing, draft, encouraging, exhaustive, eye-witness, factual, fair, (un)favourable, final, first-hand, forthcoming, garbled, gripping, illuminating, instructive, interim, intriguing, libellous, long-awaited, majority, minority, monumental, negative, objective, (un)official, optimistic, police, positive, preliminary, recent, reliable, revealing, scathing, tendentious, top-secret, true, unambiguous, unanimous, unconfirmed, verbatim ~

REPRESENTATIVE
V: appoint, dismiss, elect, name, nominate, send ~
A: elected, exclusive, official, sole ~

REPRIMAND
V: administer, give sb, issue, receive ~
A: harsh, mild, severe, sharp, stern, stiff ~

REPRODUCTION
A: accurate, brilliant, exact, excellent, faithful, (im)perfect, poor, superb ~

REPUBLIC
V: establish, form, proclaim, set up ~
A: autonomous, banana, breakaway, democratic, federal, independent, socialist ~

REPULSION
V: conceal, feel, get over, overcome ~
A: instinctive, overwhelming, strong ~

REPUTATION
V: add to, advance, build (up), clear, cultivate, damage, defend, destroy, diminish, enhance, establish, gain, get, guard, harm, improve, injure, keep up, live up to (his), lose, make, preserve, protect, recover, rescue, restore, ruin, salvage, save, stake ~ on sth, tarnish, uphold, vindicate ~
V: ~ declined, improved, lies in ruins, rests on ... , rose, suffered, went down/up
A: bad, blameless, brilliant, considerable, deserved, dubious, enviable, established, exaggerated, excellent, flawless, formidable, good, grim, hard/well-earned, high, impeccable, intact, international, long-standing, notorious, posthumous, scandalous, secure, shady, shocking, solid, spotless, unassailable, unblemished, unrivalled, untarnished, well-established, widespread, worldwide ~
P: have/win a ~ for; (my) ~ was at stake; (his) ~ was founded on ...

REQUEST
V: accede to, answer, carry out, comply with, consider, deny, file, fulfil, grant, honour, ignore, issue, listen to, make, put in, refuse, reject, respond to, submit, turn down, withdraw ~
A: awkward, earnest, embarrassing, formal, important, modest, official, polite, (un)reasonable, repeated, serious, urgent, written ~

REQUIREMENTS
V: catalogue, come up to, comply with, conform to, describe, fit in with, fulfil, identify, impose, lay down, list, match, (fail to) meet, satisfy, set, specify ~
A: demanding, difficult, exact, exacting, full, minimum, precise, pressing, strict, urgent ~

RESCUE
V: arrange (for), attempt, carry out, come to (sb's), effect, organise, take charge of ~
A: daring, dramatic, heroic, successful ~

RESEARCH
V: back, be engaged in, carry out, conduct, co-ordinate, cut back on, develop, do, expand, finance, fund, initiate, intensify, proceed with, promote, publish, put money into, sponsor, start, undertake, work on ~
V: ~ bore fruit, concludes that ..., covers ..., deals with ... , demonstrated ... , draws attention to ..., established ..., indicates ..., is aimed at ..., is based on ..., led to ..., means ..., proved ..., raises questions about ..., revealed ..., shows ..., suggests ...
A: academic, advanced, basic, brilliant, cancer/Aids etc, confidential, continuing, controversial, detailed, encouraging, field, fundamental, historical, important, independent, intensive, joint, laborious, latest, market, official, ongoing, original, outstanding, painstaking, pioneering, preliminary, recent, scientific, serious, substantial, systematic, thorough, up-to-date, vital ~
P: development of, expansion of ~

RESEMBLANCE
V: bear, have, show ~
A: close, disconcerting, faint, family, marked, remote, slight, striking, strong, uncanny, vague ~

RESENTMENT
V: aggravate, arouse, cause, get over, express, feel, hide, lead to, smother, suppress, voice ~
V: ~ lingered, simmered
A: bitter, deep, great, justified, marked, mounting, pent-up, profound, smouldering, strong ~

RESERVATIONS
V: express, have, overcome, voice ~
A: considerable, deep, grave, hidden, important, initial, major, minor, profound, serious, strong ~

RESERVES (resources)
V: accumulate, amass, build up, dent, deplete, dip into, draw on, exhaust, fall back on, have, hoard, keep up, maintain, make use of, replace, replenish, squander, swell, use up, waste ~
V: ~ diminished, disappeared, dwindled, ran down/out, went down
A: abundant, adequate, ample, enormous, gold, huge, important, limited, limitless, massive, meagre, unlimited, vast ~

RESIDENCE
V: apply for, be granted, take up ~
A: country, desirable, family, official, permanent, private, temporary ~

RESIGNATION
V: accept, consider, hand in, offer, receive, refuse, reject, send in, submit, tender, withdraw ~

RESISTANCE
V: break sb's, break down, come across, crush, destroy, encounter, face, meet, offer, overcome, put down, put up, smash, soften, stiffen, strengthen, wear down ~
V: ~ broke down, collapsed, crumbled, weakened
A: armed, brave, considerable, courageous, determined, fierce, heroic, magnificent, passive, remaining, steady, stiff, strong, stubborn, useless, violent, weak ~

RESOLUTION (formal proposal)
V: adopt, carry, debate, defeat, draft, frame, implement, make, oppose, pass, present, propose, put forward, reject, submit, support, table, veto, vote against/in favour of ~
V: ~ calls for sth
A: draft, formal, joint, New Year's, UN ~

RESOLVE

V: abandon, break, give up, maintain, shake, stiffen, test, weaken ~

V: ~ remains firm, wavered

A: firm, immediate ~

RESOURCES

V: allocate, build up, channel, concentrate, deploy, develop, discover, dispense, dissipate, distribute, divert, drain, draw on, employ, exhaust, exploit, fall back on, find, harness, hold onto, husband, lack, look for, lose, make the most of, make use of, pool, protect, recover, release, rely on, safeguard, share, squander, spare, strain, survey, take advantage of, tap, transfer, (mis)use, utilise, waste ~

V: ~ disappeared, dwindled, lasted, ran out

A: abundant, additional, (in)adequate, ample, available, basic, enormous, existing, failing, formidable, great, hidden, infinite, joint, (un)limited, limitless, massive, meagre, natural, plentiful, remaining, rich, scarce, slender, substantial, (in)sufficient, untapped, vast ~

RESPECT

V: accord, command, deserve, develop, earn sb's, enjoy, feel, keep, lose, lower, maintain, owe, retain, show, win ~

A: deep, due, exaggerated, great, grudging, healthy, mutual, profound, total, universal, warm ~

P: hold sb in great ~

RESPONSE

V: bring (about/forth), call for, come out with, delay, draw up, elicit, evoke, get, give, inhibit, lead to, make, meet with, obtain, offer, prepare, produce, provoke, receive, solicit ~

V: ~ arrived, came, was forthcoming

A: aggressive, amazing, angry, automatic, awful, brisk, cool, desperate, detailed, devastating, direct, discouraging, disproportionate, emotional, encouraging, (un)enthusiastic, favourable, feeble, firm, (un)friendly, frigid, full, generous, hasty, hostile, immediate, inept, instantaneous, instinctive, intelligent, intuitive, mechanical, mild, negative, overwhelming, phenomenal, positive, prompt, rapid, ready, rude, (un)satisfactory, sceptical, (in)sensitive, sharp, slow, staggering, strange, swift, tremendous, ugly, unexpected, united, violent, warm, wholehearted ~

RESPONSIBILITY

V: absolve sb from, accept, acknowledge, admit, assume, attribute, avoid, be aware of/conscious of, bear, carry out, claim, cover up, delegate, deny, discharge, disclaim, divide, entrust, evade, exercise, face, feel, fix, fulfil, get out of, have, meet, place/put ~ on sb, shake off, share, shift ~ onto sb, shirk, shoulder, shrug off, shun, take on ~

V: ~ falls on sb, rests with sb

A: added, additional, awesome, awful, basic, big, collective, corporate, daunting, direct, enormous, entire, extra, full, further, grave, great, growing, heavy, huge, increasing, joint, main, overall, partial, personal, (un)pleasant, prime, proper, public, sole, total, tremendous, ultimate, whole ~

P: I accept full ~

REST

V: deserve, earn, have, stop for, take ~

A: complete, thorough, welcome, well-earned ~

RESTAURANT

V: go (out) to, manage, open (up), run ~

A: busy, crowded, decent, family-run, famous, fancy, fast-food, fish, local, noisy, popular, posh, quiet, seafood, superb, traditional, vegetarian, wonderful ~

RESTRAINT (reserve)

V: advise, behave with, counsel, exercise, exhibit, free oneself from, get rid of, impose, place ~ on ... , remove, shake off, show, throw off ~

A: admirable, commendable, great, important, powerful, remarkable ~

RESTRICTIONS

V: abolish, adopt, avoid, be subject to, bypass, cancel, defy, do away with, ease, eliminate, flout, impose, lay down, lift, place/put ~ on ..., relax, remove, tighten ~

V: ~ are in force, (still) hold

A: awkward, effective, further, harsh, heavy, painful, (un)reasonable, rigid, severe, tight, unfair, unnecessary, unpleasant, widespread ~

P: relaxation of ~

RESULT

V: achieve, announce, avoid, be satisfied with, bring about, cancel, contribute to, describe, destroy, dread, fear, foresee, get, give, hope for, jeopardize, lead to, measure, misconstrue, observe, outline, predict, (re-)produce, scrutinize, see, spoil, take ~ in account, welcome, yield ~

A: astonishing, astounding, beneficial, catastrophic, common, concrete, confusing, deadly, desired, devastating, dire, (in)direct, disastrous, discouraging, dramatic, encouraging, end, excellent, (un)expected, far-reaching, favourable, final, frequent, fruitful, (un)fortunate, gratifying, happy, hopeful, hopeless, immediate, important, impressive, inevitable, lasting, main, major, marvellous, net, obvious, phenomenal, pleasing, poor, positive, potential, practical, principal, profound, prospective, quick, regrettable, remarkable, sad, (un)satisfactory, sensational, (in)significant, splendid, staggering, (un)successful, tangible, tragic, unavoidable, unexpected, unforeseen, unpalatable, visible, worthwhile ~

RESULTS (research)

V: apply, assess, bias, challenge, check, collate, collect, come out with, confirm, criticise, disseminate, dismiss, duplicate, evaluate, examine, exclude, falsify, get, give, go over, have confidence in, interpret, invalidate, lead to, make ~ available, obtain, outline, present, (re)produce, publish, question, record, reveal, study, take into account, tamper with, trust, yield ~

V: ~ are based on ..., challenge ..., confirm ..., corroborate ..., demonstrate ..., indicate ..., prove ..., raise questions about ..., reveal ..., rule out ..., show ..., suggest ...

A: astonishing, astounding, clear, conflicting, confusing, controversial, definite, disappointing, discouraging, dramatic, dubious, early, encouraging, fascinating, fruitful, hopeful, inconclusive, inconsistent, invaluable, negative, phoney, positive, preliminary, promising, puzzling, (un)reliable, startling, surprising, trustworthy, unequivocal, unexpected, unexplained, (in)valid, valuable ~

RESULTS (election)

V: announce, comment on, discuss, falsify, forecast, get, guess, predict, question, scrutinize, tamper with, trust, wait for, watch, welcome ~

A: decisive, disappointing, dramatic, early, final, overall, preliminary, sensational, staggering ~

RESULT (mathematical)

V: arrive at, calculate, check, get, obtain, produce, work out ~

A: (in)accurate, correct, (un)expected, improbable, wrong ~

RESULT (sport)

V: announce, await, celebrate, confirm, predict, produce ~

A: disappointing, dramatic, exciting, fantastic, final, fine, good, grand, marvellous, mediocre, poor, shock, surprise ~

RETIREMENT
V: approach, come out of, enjoy, go into, look forward to ~
A: active, enjoyable, happy, peaceful ~
P: take early ~

RETREAT
V: carry out, cover, end in, make, sound ~
A: forced, headlong, (dis)orderly, rapid, strategic, tactical ~
P: beat a hasty ~

RETURN (profit)
V: aim at, derive, expect, get, look for, want ~
A: disappointing, excellent, falling, good, healthy, high(er), low(er), poor, (un)satisfactory, steady ~
P: a ~ of (5%); a ~ on capital

REUNION
V: have, hold, organise ~
A: class, dramatic, ecstatic, emotional, family, happy, joyful, tearful, touching ~

REVELATIONS
V: bring out, make ~
A: amazing, astonishing, astounding, damaging, incriminating, lurid, scandalous, shocking, startling, stunning ~

REVENGE
V: be intent on, call for, demand, exact, get, inflict, seek, take, thirst for ~
A: awful, bitter, bloody, cold-blooded, cruel, fitting, grim, hideous, horrible, immediate, painful, sickening, spiteful, suitable, swift, terrible ~

REVENUE
V: collect, cut off, depend on, derive, draw, erode, estimate, generate, get, improve, increase, lose, obtain, overestimate, produce, raise, receive, reduce, secure ~
A: considerable, enormous, good, huge, large, modest, satisfactory, small, substantial, sufficient ~
P: tax *revenues*

REVIEW (book etc)
V: get, produce, publish, receive, write ~
A: adverse, bad, balanced, (un)biased, brief, critical, cutting, damning, detailed, dismissive, encouraging, entertaining, fabulous, favourable, good, hostile, important, impressive, informative, long, poor, rave, rotten, scathing, venomous, witty ~

REVIEW (survey)
V: carry out, undertake ~
A: comprehensive, detailed, sweeping, thorough, timely, urgent ~

REVOLT
V: crush, deal with, face, handle, head, inspire, instigate, join, lead, plot, provoke, raise, stage, stimulate, stir up, suppress, take part in, whip up ~
V: ~ broke out, collapsed, failed, flared up, grew, occurred, petered out, spread, was put down
A: armed, dangerous, desperate, fierce, open, spontaneous, widespread ~

REVOLUTION
V: call for, crush, face, foment, join, incite sb to, keep ~ at bay, lead, lead to, mastermind, plot, preach, precipitate, put down, spark off, spearhead, stage, start, stir up, support, suppress, take part in ~
V: ~ broke out, erupted, failed, gathered momentum, spread, took place
A: bloodless, bloody, budding, imminent, impending, peaceful, victorious, violent ~

REWARD

V: announce, claim, deserve, get, give, merit, offer, pay, present, reap, receive, refuse ~

A: adequate, attractive, big, fair, financial, generous, glittering, huge, just, large, massive, meagre, miserable, modest, monetary, poor, (un)satisfactory, sizeable, splendid, substantial, tangible, tempting, token, visible, well-earned ~

P: ... brings its own *rewards*

RHETORIC

A: eloquent, empty, harsh, impassioned, passionate, powerful ~

RHYTHM

A: constant, frenzied, gentle, heavy, hypnotic, insistent, monotonous, pulsating, steady, strong, subtle, syncopated, undulating, wild ~

P: sense of ~

RICHES

V: accumulate, acquire, amass, bring, give away, hoard, spend, store up ~

A: fabulous, great, undreamed of, untold, vast ~

RIDE (short journey)

V: give sb ~, go for, hitch, offer sb, take ~

A: bumpy, comfortable, enjoyable, hair-raising, pleasant, rough, smooth ~

RIDICULE

V: hold sb up to, lay oneself open to, subject sb to ~

RIGHT

V: abandon, abolish, acknowledge, acquire, assert, assign, assume, campaign for, challenge, claim, contest, convey, curtail, declare, defend, demand, deny, deprive sb of, dispute, divest sb of, do away with, earn, encroach on sb's, enjoy, establish, exercise, extend ~ to sb, forfeit, give, give up, grant, have, inherit, justify, limit, lose, maintain, override, possess, preserve, proclaim, protect, protest, question, recognise, refuse, register, relinquish, renounce, restrict, safeguard, secure, seize, sign away, suspend, take advantage of, take away, throw away, transfer, violate, waive, win ~

A: absolute, automatic, basic, broad, clear, definite, divine, exclusive, fundamental, hereditary, inalienable, indisputable, inherent, legal, moral, natural, obvious, (un)official, paramount, perfect, prior, sole, statutory, superior, supreme, undeniable, undoubted, unqualified ~

P: the ~ of free speech; have/reserve the ~ to; know/stand up for your *rights*; within (your) *rights*; animal, human, women's *rights*; the Declaration of Human *rights*

RIOT

V: avert, cause, deal with, join, put down, spark off, start, suppress, take part in, trigger ~

V: ~ broke out, got out of hand, started

A: dangerous, race, violent ~

RIOTING

P: aftermath of, spread of, upsurge of ~

RISE

V: advocate, bring about, cause, check, cope with, curb, hold down, lead to, observe, prevent, propose, result from/in, reverse, stem, stimulate, trigger, witness ~

A: alarming, all-round, considerable, consistent, constant, continuous, dramatic, excessive, gradual, imperceptible, important, inevitable, irreversible, marginal, marked, massive, meteoric, moderate, modest, phenomenal, rapid, relentless, serious, sharp, significant, slight, slow, steady, steep, substantial, sudden, temporary, tremendous ~

RISK

V: accept, anticipate, avoid, be aware of, calculate, constitute, eliminate, encounter, enhance, entail, estimate, face, foresee, gauge, guard against, justify, lessen, magnify, minimise, mitigate, outweigh, pose, realise, reduce, represent, run, spread, take, take on ~

V: ~ diminished, grew, receded

A: appalling, apparent, attendant, calculated, colossal, dangerous, daunting, faint, full, great, high, horrifying, huge, immediate, imminent, incalculable, infinitesimal, (un)justifiable, (un)justified, low, negligible, obvious, overwhelming, perceptible, remote, serious, significant, slight, substantial, terrible, tremendous ~

P: it's worth the ~

RITUAL

V: celebrate, go through, hold, perform, take part in ~

A: elaborate, extravagant, pagan, religious, sacred, solemn ~

RIVAL

V: beat, confound, defeat, eliminate, get the better of, get rid of, oust, warn off ~

A: bitter, close, conspicuous, keen, serious ~

RIVALRY

V: cut out, encourage, enter into, foster, intensify ~

V: ~ broke out, developed, grew up, lasted, ran high, sprang up

A: bitter, fierce, friendly, intense, internecine, keen, serious, sibling ~

RIVER

V: bridge, cross, dam, dredge, ford, navigate ~

V: ~ dried up, forks, flooded, flows, meanders, overflowed/broke its banks, rose, runs, winds

A: broad, deep, navigable, salmon, shallow, sluggish, swift, tidal, wide ~

ROAD

V: block, build, clear, close, dig ~ up, follow, repair, (re)surface, turn into ~

V: ~ climbs, curves, descends, goes, leads to ... , runs, twists and turns, winds

A: bumpy, country, excellent, impassable, main, major, minor, private, public, ring, straight, trunk, wide, winding ~

P: ~ block, junction, side, system

ROLE

V: adopt, assign, assume, cast off, define, deviate from, give up, overestimate, play, reduce, resume, strengthen, take on, transform, underestimate, undertake, usurp ~

A: active, ambiguous, ambivalent, back-room, beneficial, challenging, commendable, conspicuous, critical, decisive, dual, effective, essential, hidden, identifiable, (un)important, indispensable, influential, key, leading, main, major, minor, parental, permanent, pivotal, praiseworthy, principal, prominent, secondary, shadowy, (in)significant, sinister, strange, subordinate, subsidiary, substantial, tangible, true, unique, vital ~

ROLE (theatrical)

V: cast sb in, fill, give up, have, interpret, perform, play, take, take over, understudy ~

A: ambitious, demanding, important, leading, principal, starring, subordinate, supporting, title ~

ROMANCE

A: holiday, secret, teenage, whirlwind ~

ROOM

V: decorate, furnish, let (out), occupy, rent (out), tidy (up) ~

A: adjoining, adjacent, changing, charming, cheerful, common, conference, consulting, cosy, dark, delightful, depressing, dining, double, draughty, drawing, dreary, light, living, meeting, poky, single, sitting, spacious, spare, stuffy, waiting ~

ROUTE

V: follow, map out, mistake, plan, take ~

A: circuitous, difficult, (in)direct, easy, long-haul, normal, picturesque, roundabout, scenic, spectacular, straight, tough, tourist, winding ~

ROUTINE

V: abandon, adapt oneself to, break, deviate from, disturb, fall into, follow, get into/out of, have, impose, keep to, lay down, obey, observe, set, settle into, stick to ~

A: daily, day-to-day, dull, established, exact, exhausting, harsh, monotonous, punishing, regular, relaxed, sedate, strict, usual ~

ROW (disagreement)

V: be embroiled in, be mixed up in, cause, develop into, get into, get involved in, have, spark off, stop, trigger off ~

V: ~ blew up, broke out, is brewing, developed, erupted, flared up, upset sb

A: blazing, ferocious, fierce, full-blown, furious, mighty, pointless, scandalous, serious, simmering, terrible, tremendous, violent ~

RUINS

V: be (left) in, be reduced to, lie in, pick/sift through ~

A: ancient, charred, crumbling, smoking, smouldering ~

RULE

V: accept, adhere to, break, come under, establish, follow, get out of, impose, keep to, overthrow, rebel against, relax, waive ~

A: alien, authoritarian, foreign, general, home, invariable, mob, stable, strict, tribal, totalitarian, unvarying, usual ~

P: the ~ of law; exception to the ~; the exception that proves the ~

RULER

V: install, overthrow ~

A: absolute, benign, (in)decisive, despotic, dictatorial, (un)just, rightful, self-styled, strong, weak, wise ~

RULES

V: abide by, abolish, accept, amend, apply, approve, be acquainted with, be bound by, be ignorant of, bend, breach, break, cancel, change, circumvent, codify, comply with, conform to, contravene, create, define, deviate from, devise, dictate, do away with, enforce, establish, explain, flaunt, flout, follow, form, formulate, go by, ignore, impose, infringe, interpret, introduce, invent, issue, keep to, lay down, make, (dis)obey, observe, rebel against, relax, respect, revive, satisfy, scrap, set, simplify, stick to, suspend, transgress, violate, waive ~

V: ~ apply to ..., cover ..., fell into disuse, govern ..., mean that ..., operate, state ...

A: basic, binding, broad, complicated, elastic, existing, explicit, (un)fair, firm, fundamental, ineffective, narrow, obscure, official, oppressive, pointless, proper, (un)reasonable, restrictive, rigid, severe, standard, strict, stringent, unjust, unpopular ~

P: breach of, contravention of, infringement of, interpretation of, loophole in, set of ~

RULING

V: accept, apply, ask for, follow, ignore, interpret, make, pronounce ~

A: definite, definitive, fair, final, firm, unbiased ~

RUMOUR

V: believe, check, come across, confirm, deny, discount, dismiss, dispel, encounter, feed, follow up, hear, invent, investigate, pass on, repeat, scotch, spread, start, trace, verify ~

V: ~ arose, is circulating, is going about/around, persists, points to ... , proved unfounded, reached sb, spread, started, subsided

A: cruel, curious, dangerous, disturbing, harmful, insistent, latest, nasty, scurrilous, silly, strong, ugly, unconfirmed, unfounded, unlikely, unpleasant, vague, wild ~

RUMOURS

V: ~ abound, are rife, are circulating/flying

A: contradictory, extravagant, persistent, wild ~

S

SACRIFICE

V: call for, make, offer up ~

V: ~ was in vain, was rewarded, was worthwhile

A: great, heroic, huge, human, noble, personal, ritual, supreme, tremendous, ultimate, willing ~

P: at great personal ~; a ~ worth making

SADNESS

V: conceal, express, feel, hide, show ~

A: deep, indescribable, overwhelming, profound ~

SAFETY

V: endanger, ensure, guarantee, jeopardize, provide, reach, seek, threaten ~

A: absolute, complete, relative ~

SALAD

V: garnish, make, toss ~

A: Caesar's, crisp, fruit, green, limp, mixed, potato, side, Waldorf ~

SALARY

V: boost, command, cut, draw, earn, get, increase, negotiate, pay, raise, receive, reduce ~

A: annual, attractive, average, index-linked, high, modest, monthly, starting, substantial ~

SALE

V: agree to, ban, cancel, complete, conduct, consent to, decide on, delay, halt, handle, make, necessitate, negotiate, order, permit, postpone, prevent, recommend, stop ~

A: annual, car boot, clearance, closing-down, compulsory, end-of-season, forced, immediate, profitable, satisfactory, spring, urgent, winter ~

SALES

V: affect, boost, bump up, estimate, hit, increase, promote, push up ~

V: ~ are down/up, dropped (off), fell, increased, leapt, picked up, recovered, rocketed, slumped, soared, went down/up

A: brisk, disappointing, domestic, encouraging, export, gross, heavy, increased, net, phenomenal, poor, satisfactory, sluggish, stagnant, steady ~

P: ~ area, campaign, force, manager, team; boom in, fall in, slump in ~

SANCTIONS

V: apply, call for, ease, extend ~ to sth, get round, impose, lift, put ~ into effect, relax ~

V: ~ came into effect

A: economic, immediate, sweeping, tight, tough, trade, wide-ranging ~

SANITY

V: keep, lose, maintain, preserve (your) ~

SATISFACTION

V: add to, cause, derive, experience, express, feel, find, gain, get, give, increase, lessen, look for, obtain, take ~

A: considerable, deep, doubtful, genuine, great, growing, inner, lasting, perfect, personal, profound, pure, quiet, real, supreme, total, tremendous, unexpected, unique, utmost, widespread ~

P: feeling of, glow of ~; deprive sb of the ~ of ...

SAVINGS

V: deposit, dip into, invest, lose, squander, withdraw ~

A: considerable, life, personal ~

SCALE

V: appreciate, cut, estimate, increase, measure, reduce, step up ~

A: ambitious, astronomical, broad, colossal, diminishing, enormous, generous, gigantic, grand, heroic, huge, immense, large, lavish, massive, minute, moderate, modest, monumental, small, staggering, stupendous, unprecedented, vast ~

SCANDAL

V: avoid, be implicated in/involved in/(un)touched by, cause, cover up, create, defuse, expose, face, get mixed up in, give rise to, hush up, listen to, play down, prevent, reveal, spread, uncover ~

V: ~ broke out, came out, died down, erupted, grew, persisted, rocked ... , ruined sb, surrounded sb, threatened/touched sb

A: full-scale, impending, major, notorious, worldwide ~

P: breath of, risk of, whiff of ~

SCAR

V: bear, carry, leave ~

A: hideous, noticeable, permanent, prominent, ugly ~

SCARCITY

V: cause, cope with, lead to ~

V: ~ affected sb, came about, developed, was caused by ...

A: marked, seasonal, serious, sudden, temporary ~

SCENE

V: culminate in, depict, describe, give an account of, recall, record, watch, witness ~

V: ~ horrified sb, presented itself, shocked sb

A: alarming, amazing, appalling, awful, awkward, confusing, convivial, death-bed, depressing, disgraceful, distressing, disturbing, dramatic, embarrassing, emotional, exhilarating, extraordinary, fascinating, final, harrowing, heart-rending, horrible, horrific, horrifying, ludicrous, painful, stirring, terrifying, ugly, unforgettable ~

SCENT

A: exotic, faint, familiar, heady, heavy, pungent, sweet, thick ~

SCHEDULE

V: adhere to, disrupt, draw up, fix, follow, have, interrupt, keep to, make, make a mess of, plan, put together, revise, stick to, upset ~

A: busy, demanding, fixed, full, gruelling, heavy, hectic, punishing, rigid, strict, tight ~

SCHEME

V: abandon, administer, adopt, amend, apply, axe, back, be engaged/involved/mixed up in, benefit from, boycott, cancel, carry out, concoct, create, design, develop, devise, discover, draw up, drop, embark on, endorse, envisage, examine, finance, fit into, float, foil, follow, form, frustrate, get involved in, give up, go in for, halt, hamper, hatch, implement, improve, initiate, invent, join, launch, modify, monitor, operate, oppose, opt out of, outline, phase out, pioneer, plan, promote, propose, pursue, put forward, put ~ in hand/in motion/into effect/into operation, reject, run, see through, shelve, sponsor, start, stop, study, submit, suggest, support, tailor, take part in, take up, think up, thwart, try out, turn down, undermine, use, welcome, work out ~

V: ~ became operational, calls for ... , came to light, came to nothing, came up against ... , collapsed, failed, fell flat/through, foundered, got off the ground, involves ... , provides for sth, went ahead/wrong, worked

A: adventurous, ambitious, audacious, bizarre, bold, brilliant, clandestine, clear, complicated, convincing, crack-pot, crazy, deplorable, devious, diabolical, dishonest, effective, elaborate, exciting, foolish, get-rich-quick, giant, gigantic, grandiose, hazardous, huge, ill-conceived, imaginative, impetuous, ingenious, mad, mind-boggling, novel, pet, pilot, pioneering, (im)practical, rash, (un)realistic, sensible, sinister, sound, timely, underhand, unrealistic, vast, viable, well-thought-out, wicked, wild, (un)workable, worldwide ~

SCHOOL
V: attend, change, drop out of, enrol sb in, finish, go to, leave, play truant from, skip, start ~
A: art, boarding, (all) boys, business, Catholic/Muslim etc, comprehensive, dancing, day, dental, drama, driving, elementary, evening, exclusive, finishing, first, (all) girls, grammar, high, infant, junior, language, law, medical, middle, mixed, night, nursery, primary, private, public, riding, secondary, single-sex, state, summer, Sunday, technical, vocational ~
P: ~ bus, fees, friend, holidays, leaver, meals, report, rules, system, uniform; of ~ age

SCIENCE
V: advance, foster, invest in, popularise, promote ~
A: applied, basic, behavioural, natural, physical, popular, social ~
P: advance of, branch of, field of, frontiers of, fruits of, progress of, pursuit of, role of ~

SCOPE
V: adjust, assess, be outside, come within, create, define, enhance, enlarge, exceed, expand, extend, give, lie outside, limit, narrow, offer, outline, provide, restrict, widen ~
A: ample, broad, comprehensive, excellent, great, limited, moderate, narrow ~

SCRUPLES
V: discard, get rid of, have, ignore, lose, overcome, respect ~
A: lingering, serious, strong ~

SCRUTINY
V: call for, demand, need, require, subject sth to, survive, undergo ~
A: careful, constant, detailed, meticulous, official, painstaking, public, rigorous, strict ~
P: doesn't stand up to/bear close ~

SEA
V: cross, drift out to, go to, put out to ~
A: calm, choppy, dangerous, deep, open, rough, smooth, stormy, treacherous ~
P: heavy, high, mountainous, rough *seas*

SEARCH
V: abandon, break off, call off, carry on with/out, conduct, continue, embark on, give up, lead, leave off, make, order, organise, pursue, resume, set off on, start, step up, take up, undertake ~
V: ~ covered (a wide area), ended in ... , failed, got under way, included ... , led nowhere/to ..., produced ... , resulted in ... , revealed ... , showed ... , took in ... , yielded ...
A: careful, cursory, desperate, exhaustive, extensive, frenetic, fruitful, fruitless, furtive, half-hearted, hopeful, hopeless, house-to-house, intensive, methodical, meticulous, painstaking, persevering, relentless, street-by-street, (un)successful, systematic, thorough, vain, wide ~

SEASON
V: close, inaugurate, open, spend, start, usher in, wind up ~
V: got under way, is in full swing, was a failure/a success
A: busy, full, high, holiday, hunting, low, poor, shooting, slack, tourist ~
SECRECY
V: ensure, preserve, swear sb to ~
A: strict, total ~
P: breach of, curtain of, veil of ~
SECRET
V: be privy to, betray, come across, disclose, discover, divulge, give away, guard, guess, have,
    impart, keep, know, let out/sb into, preserve, protect, reveal, safeguard, share, stumble on,
    tell, uncover ~
V: ~ came out
A: closely-guarded, dark, guilty, important, open, state, trade, ugly ~
SECURITY
V: compromise, endanger, enjoy, ensure, guarantee, impose, improve, lack, maintain, provide,
    safeguard, seek, step up, strengthen, threaten, tighten, undermine ~
A: (in)adequate, complete, foolproof, increased, internal, lax, massive, maximum, national,
    overall, personal, strict, tight, top ~
P: breach in, lapse in ~
SELECTION
V: carry out, have, make, offer ~
A: careful, choice, comprehensive, dazzling, interesting, judicious, narrow, poor, rigorous,
    staggering, unrivalled, wide, wise, wonderful ~
SELF-CONFIDENCE
V: acquire, boost, build up, get, have, lose, restore, undermine ~
P: blow to, boost to ~
SENSATION
V: aggravate, alleviate, cause, feel, give rise to, have, heighten, intensify, lack, lessen, lose,
    magnify, reduce, relieve, remove ~
A: agreeable, burning, buzzing, cold, continuous, dull, eerie, faint, familiar, funny, humming,
    invigorating, marked, peculiar, permanent, (un)pleasant, sharp, slight, strange, strong,
    tangible, tingling, unique, vague, warm, weird ~
SENSATION (excitement)
V: cause, create, make, produce ~
A: great, terrific, unparalleled, worldwide ~
SENSE
V: arouse, be filled with, deaden, dispel, dull, enjoy, experience, foster, get rid of, have,
    increase, intensify, reinforce, relieve, sharpen ~
A: abiding, confused, deep, delicious, haunting, keen, mild, new-found, overpowering, rare,
    renewed, strange, strong, unique, vague ~
P: feel a real ~ of achievement
SENSE (of smell, sight)
V: deaden, destroy, dull, have, heighten, lose, numb, recover, regain, sharpen, stimulate, use ~
A: acute, keen, poor, sharp ~
SENSE (of duty, responsibility)
V: acquire, appeal to, awaken, blunt, develop, distort, foster, inculcate, instil, reinforce, rouse ~
A: clear, confused, deep, developed, distorted, marked, profound, strong, underdeveloped ~

SENSE (of humour)

V: demonstrate, display, have, show ~

A: delightful, dry, great, irreverent, lively, outrageous, quiet, subtle, warped, weird, wicked ~

SENSE (meaning)

V: alter, change, convey, distort, get, grasp, understand ~

A: basic, figurative, literal, old-fashioned, proper, real, strict, superficial, traditional, true, underlying, usual ~

P: used in the loose/strict ~ (of the word)

SENTENCE (judicial)

V: carry out, commute, defer, execute, get, hand out, impose, pass, postpone, pronounce, reduce, remit, review, serve, suspend, uphold, waive ~

A: custodial, death, exemplary, fair, harsh, heavy, lenient, life, light, long, mandatory, reduced, savage, severe, stiff, suspended, (three-)year ~

SENTIMENT

V: appeal to, arouse, be governed by/guided by/ruled by, display, express, feel, have, ignore, show, stir up, suppress, voice ~

A: growing, heartfelt, hostile, lingering, loyal, mixed, patriotic, prevailing, public, real, strong, tender, true, (un)worthy ~

SEQUENCE

V: arrange in, break, continue, end, interrupt, start ~

A: chronological, continuous, correct, endless, logical, natural, numerical, rapid, unbroken ~

P: a ~ of events; in/out of ~

SERIES

V: continue, end, inaugurate, interrupt, launch, repeat, run, start ~

A: brief, lengthy, long, short ~

P: a ~ of problems, disasters, difficulties etc (most often negative ideas)

SERIOUSNESS

V: add to, appreciate, be aware of, comprehend, emphasise, exaggerate, heighten, realise, stress, take into consideration, underestimate ~

A: absolute, awful, deadly, great, real, true ~

SERVANT

A: devoted, domestic, dutiful, faithful, humble, loyal, personal, trusted ~

SERVICE

V: call for, complain about, demand, get, give, offer, perform ~

A: awful, careless, dreadful, erratic, excellent, first-class, first-rate, good, great, immense, marvellous, polite, poor, professional, prompt, public, quick, shocking, slow, superb, terrible, top-quality, (in)valuable, vital, wonderful ~

SERVICE (public transport)

V: axe, cut back on, cut out, disrupt, do away with, extend, have, improve, keep, maintain, lay on, make use of, operate, provide, restore, run, run down, suspend, trim, use ~

V: ~ broke down, deteriorated, improved

A: (in)adequate, (in)efficient, erratic, essential, existing, (in)frequent, intermittent, limited, poor, reduced, regular, (un)reliable, scheduled ~

P: disruptions to, run-down of ~

SESSION

V: adjourn, attend, call, cancel, chair, close, convene, fix, hold, inaugurate, postpone ~

A: ad-hoc, annual, brief, briefing, closed, closing, emergency, extraordinary, full, general, joint, lively, marathon, open, opening, plenary, regular, special ~

SETBACK

V: come up against, encounter, face, get over, lead to, mark, meet (with), overcome, recover from, run into, suffer ~

A: awkward, daunting, difficult, disastrous, huge, important, major, minor, serious, slight, sudden, temporary, unexpected ~

SETTING (venue)

A: appropriate, attractive, colourful, cosy, delightful, dramatic, exotic, idyllic, majestic, natural, peaceful, splendid, suitable, superb, tranquil, unlikely, unusual ~

SETTLEMENT

V: abide by, accept, agree on, arrive at, breach, come to, discuss, engineer, find, move towards, negotiate, reach, seek, work out, work towards ~

A: amicable, comprehensive, fair, final, just, lasting, out-of-court, permanent, reasonable, satisfactory, separate ~

P: basis for, grounds for, hope of ~

SETTLEMENT (village)

V: build, discover, establish, excavate, find, form, found, make, uncover ~

V: ~ dates from (the 7th century BC)

A: ancient, human, isolated, native, prehistoric, primitive, remote, tiny ~

SHADE (colour)

A: bright, dark, deep, delicate, delightful, dreadful, horrible, light, magnificent, pale, pastel, soft, vivid ~

SHAME

V: acknowledge, admit, bring ~ on sb, confess to, experience, express, face, feel, forget, get rid of, get over, hide, live with, overcome, rid oneself of ~

A: awful, bitter, deep, eternal, everlasting, indelible, lasting, profound ~

P: It's a(n) awful/crying/dreadful/real/terrible ~

SHAPE

V: acquire, alter, assume, change, have, identify, lose, modify, take, take on ~

A: attractive, curved, definite, different, distinct, elegant, familiar, final, former, ghostly, graceful, huge, indistinct, indistinguishable, monstrous, original, peculiar, pleasing, (ir)regular, round, square, strange, tall, ugly, unusual, vague ~

SHARE

V: accept, allocate, assess, assume, claim, contribute, decide, demand, deny sb, determine, estimate, exceed, get, give, give up, have, own, reduce, refuse, reject, take ~

A: appropriate, diminishing, disproportionate, due, equal, excessive, (un)fair, full, generous, good, growing, (un)important, (ever-)increasing, inordinate, large, major, moderate, modest, part, proper, rightful, small, tiny ~

P: the lion's ~

SHARES (in a company)

V: buy (up), deal in, hold, issue, offer, sell (off) ~

A: ordinary, preference ~

SHIFT

V: bring about, call for, cause, make, necessitate, produce ~

A: abrupt, alarming, belated, big, decisive, definite, dramatic, fundamental, important, irreversible, marked, massive, noticeable, profound, rapid, sudden, unexpected ~

P: a ~ in public opinion

SHIP

V: abandon, board, break up, build, captain, charter, disembark, from, fit out, jump, launch, (un)load, man, name, own, navigate, pilot, refit, register, repair, requisition, rescue, sail, salvage, scuttle, sink, take ~ out of service, tie up, torpedo, tow ~

V: ~ berthed, carried ... , docked, entered port, foundered, heaved, is laid up, heeled over, keeled over, was leaking, listed, pitched, proceeded, rolled, ran aground, sailed, sank, was lost/wrecked, went aground/down

A: beautiful, fine, huge, sailing ~

SHOCK

V: cause, feel, get, give sb, have, receive, recover from, suffer from, survive ~

A: awful, bad, dreadful, electric, great, mild, nasty, painful, profound, rude, severe, sharp, slight, sudden, terrible, violent ~

P: ~ result, tactics

SHOES

V: (un)buckle, do up, lace up, mend, polish, put on, repair, scuff, slip off/on, take off, try on ~

A: ballet, comfortable, court, fashion, fashionable, flat, golf, high/low-heeled, ill-fitting, platform, running, sports, suede, tight, walking ~

SHOP

V: close, extend, manage, open, refit, refurbish, re-organise, run, staff, stock ~

V: ~ carries, changed hands, closed down, is situated, offers, sells, stocks, went bankrupt

A: book, busy, clothes, corner, decent, duty-free, exclusive, expensive, fashionable, gift, local, secondhand, smart, specialist, trendy, unusual, well-stocked ~

P: ~ assistant, doorway, window; chain of *shops*; ~ front

SHORTAGE

V: account for, alleviate, avoid, cause, cope with, ease, feel the effect of, get over, lead to, make up for, prevent, relieve, suffer, suffer from ~

V: ~ continued, is caused by sth, is due to sth, occurred

A: acute, alarming, appalling, bad, big, catastrophic, chronic, constant, critical, current, desperate, disastrous, long, painful, permanent, perpetual, prolonged, serious, severe, slight, temporary, worrying ~

SHOW (theatrical)

V: direct, finance, give, launch, produce, promote, put on, see, sponsor, stage, take in ~

V: ~ came off, has been running for (5 years)

A: brilliant, colourful, delightful, entertaining, fabulous, great, magnificent, masterly, polished, sophisticated, spectacular, witty ~

SIGHT

V: avoid, hate, see, wait for, welcome, witness ~

V: ~ appalled, astounded, comforted, frightened, impressed (me)

A: agreeable, amazing, awe-inspiring, awesome, awful, beautiful, comforting, comical, common, daunting, disturbing, dreadful, everyday, (un)familiar, fearsome, gruesome, horrible, horrifying, imposing, impressive, incongruous, intimidating, lovely, memorable, moving, pitiful, (un)pleasant, rare, remarkable, sad, shocking, terrible, terrifying, unusual, uplifting, welcome, woeful, wonderful ~

P: be used/accustomed to the ~ of, catch/lose ~ of ...; see the *sights*

SIGHT (one of the senses)

V: affect sb's, have, look after, lose, ruin, recover, spoil, test ~

V: ~ deteriorated, improved

A: bad, excellent, failing, good, keen, long, near, normal, poor, sharp, short ~

SIGN
V: carve, erect, follow, give, ignore, interpret, look out for, make, miss, notice, obey, observe, offer, provide, put up, read, receive, see, watch for ~
V: ~ indicates ..., means ..., shows ..., tells (you) to/that ...
A: cautious, clear, comforting, definite, discreet, distinct, exit, hopeful, huge, mysterious, negative, obscure, ominous, outward, overhead, plain, plus/minus/equals etc, positive, prominent, rudimentary, sacred, secret, solemn, strong, sure, tangible, tell-tale, unmistakable, visible, warning ~
P: ~ language, of the Cross, of the times; detect/show no ~ of life
SIGNAL
V: emit, get, give, intercept, (mis)interpret, lose, obtain, pick up, put out, receive, see, send, transmit ~
V: ~ disappeared, faded, means ...
A: clear, confusing, faint, intermittent, mysterious, poor, strong, unmistakable, urgent, warning ~
SIGNIFICANCE
V: accept, acquire, admit, appreciate, assess, attach, be aware of, carry, deny, dispute, emphasise, exaggerate, explain, give, grasp, have, ignore, miss, play down, realise, recognise, reveal, see, stress, understand ~
V: ~ became apparent/clear, dawned on (me), escaped (me), hit (me), lies in the fact that ... , remains unclear, sank in
A: added, apparent, basic, deadly, deep, due, exceptional, far-reaching, full, fundamental, general, great, hidden, little, long/short-term, limited, major, mysterious, mystical, obvious, overriding, overwhelming, (no) particular, practical, profound, rare, real, slight, small, special, superficial, supreme, tremendous, true, ultimate, underlying, unfortunate, vast, wide, worldwide ~
P: be of no/little/great ~
SILENCE
V: break, disturb, impose, interrupt, keep, maintain, observe, pierce, reduce sb to ~
V: ~ dragged on, lasted, prevailed, reigned
A: absolute, awkward, bored, dead, deep, discreet, eerie, heavy, horrified, hushed, impenetrable, long, ominous, oppressive, pained, pregnant, profound, prolonged, stony, suspicious, total, uncanny ~
SIMILARITY
V: observe, perceive, see ~
A: apparent, close, distinct, faint, great, marked, obvious, slight, striking, strong, superficial, uncanny, vague ~
SIN
V: ask forgiveness for, commit, confess (to), forgive, pardon, repent ~
A: deadly, grave, mortal, venial ~
P: ~ of omission
SITE
V: build on, buy, choose, decide on, develop, earmark, exploit, establish, purchase, take over, use ~
A: attractive, central, convenient, expensive, exposed, huge, ideal, perfect, prime, (un)suitable ~
SITE (archaeological)
V: abandon, discover, excavate, find, investigate, locate, loot, mark, ruin, spoil ~
A: ancient, important, iron-/bronze-age, key, prehistoric ~

SITUATION

V: accept, affect, alleviate, analyse, arrive at, assess, avoid, be in command of, bring about, change, control, cope with, create, deal with, ease, exploit, get out of, gloss over, grasp, handle, imagine, land in, lead to, make the best of the ~, make ~ worse, manage, meet, misconstrue, outline, precipitate, produce, prolong, reach, recognise, re-create, rectify, result in, retrieve, sabotage, save, set up, size up, (de)stabilize, summarise, sum up, take account of, take advantage of, take charge of, take in, take stock of, transform, (mis)understand, view, weigh up ~

V: ~ arose, deteriorated, developed, emerged, evolved, got/was out of hand, got better/worse, is out of control, worsened

A: (un)ambiguous, anomalous, (in)auspicious, astonishing, astounding, awkward, basic, bewildering, calm, clear, complex, complicated, compromising, critical, current, dangerous, delicate, desperate, difficult, disagreeable, embarrassing, emergency, existing, explosive, extraordinary, farcical, fluid, (un)fortunate, grave, grim, hazardous, hopeful, hopeless, hypothetical, immediate, inflammable, intolerable, laughable, life-and-death, ludicrous, no-win, odd, ominous, original, painful, plain, (un)pleasant, precarious, promising, real, remarkable, ridiculous, risky, serious, simple, (un)stable, strange, tense, terrible, traumatic, tricky, true, trying, typical, ugly, unhappy, unique, unnecessary, unprecedented, volatile, win-win, worrying ~

SIZE

V: estimate, exaggerate, increase, measure, reckon, reduce, scale down ~

A: average, big, enormous, fair, giant, huge, impressive, manageable, middling, moderate, modest, ordinary, relative, tremendous, vast ~

SKILL

V: acquire, apply, demonstrate, develop, hone, learn, master, perfect, possess, practise, show, take, use ~

A: amazing, basic, considerable, consummate, effortless, expert, extraordinary, great, growing, manual, marketable, marvellous, professional, rare, real, remarkable, special, specialist, specific, technical, unbelievable, unique, wonderful ~

SKIRT

V: hem, lengthen, shorten ~

A: divided, flared, full, mini-, pleated, slit, straight, wrap-around ~

SKY

V: light up, obscure ~

V: ~ cleared, clouded over, darkened

A: bright, brilliant, clear, cloudless, cloudy, heavy, night, overcast, starry, stormy, threatening ~

SMELL

V: detect, give off, leave, notice ~

A: acrid, appetizing, distinct, distinctive, faint, foul, funny, horrible, nasty, nice, noxious, overpowering, powerful, pungent, refreshing, sickening, sickly, slight, strong, sweet, unmistakable, unpleasant ~

SMILE

V: give, hide, raise, switch on/off ~

A: amused, appreciative, approving, benevolent, bland, bright, broad, charming, cheerful, cold, confident, contented, cool, dazzling, disarming, enigmatic, faint, false, fixed, forced, friendly, frozen, happy, indulgent, insincere, nervous, open, (un)pleasant, radiant, ready, satisfied, shy, sly, smug, superior, supercilious, tolerant, triumphant, wan, warm, watery, welcoming, wry ~

SMOKE
V: ~ (dis)appeared, belched out, billowed out, rose, spiralled up, suffocated sb
A: acrid, billowing, heavy, light, thick ~
P: clouds of, column of, pall of, trail of, wisp of ~

SOCIETY
V: belong to, be part of, bind together, build, change, create, defend, endanger, fit into, live in, overturn, polarise, reform, threaten, undermine, unite ~
V: ~ broke down, collapsed, crumbled, evolved, existed, flourished, survived
A: advanced, affluent, backward, barbaric, caring, (un)civilised, classless, class-ridden, close-knit, cohesive, compassionate, competitive, corrupt, decadent, divided, egalitarian, equitable, fashionable, flexible, free, (un)happy, healthy, high, humane, just, law-abiding, liberal, multi-racial, open, ordered, peaceful, (im)perfect, polite, primitive, prosperous, puritanical, repressive, sick, smart, stable, stressful, tolerant, trouble-free, violent ~
P: backbone of, dregs of, (highest) echelons of, fabric of, foundations of, higher reaches of, pillar of, structure of ~

SOCIETY (association)
V: ban, belong to, disband, establish, form, found, join, organise, resign from, run, set up ~
V: ~ exists to ... , flourished, was moribund
A: active, charitable, eminent, exclusive, illustrious, learned, literary, scientific, secret, self-governing ~

SOLUTION
V: accept, achieve, adopt, advocate, agree on, aim at, apply, arrive at, call for, come up with, defy, demand, favour, find, formulate, hit upon, look for, offer, oppose, prevent, produce, propose, provide, put forward, reach, reject, require, rule out, seek, stumble on, work out ~
V: ~ cropped up, emerged, gained acceptance, presented itself
A: (un)acceptable, clever, comprehensive, concrete, crude, drastic, early, easy, effective, equitable, excellent, feasible, final, foolish, happy, honourable, immediate, inadequate, ingenious, just, lasting, logical, neat, novel, obvious, overall, painful, partial, permanent, poor, possible, (im)practical, predictable, prompt, proper, quick, realistic, reasonable, right, satisfactory, sensible, simple, speedy, standard, straightforward, stupid, suitable, temporary, unworkable, viable, wise, wrong ~

SORROW
V: cause, express, feel, share (in) sb's, show ~
A: deep, genuine, great, inexpressible, personal, profound ~

SOUND
V: detect, drown, emit, give out, hear, imitate, make, produce, utter ~
A: appalling, beautiful, buzzing, cheerful, crashing, creaking, discordant, distant, distinctive, dull, faint, grating, harsh, high-pitched, hissing, hollow, mysterious, ominous, (un)pleasant, recurrent, rumbling, rustling, sharp, shrill, sinister, soft, sudden, sweet, terrific, tiny, tremendous, unexpected, weird, welcome ~

SOURCE
V: (re)check, come from, constitute, cut off, discover, explore, find, find out, get sth from, give, have, identify, investigate, pinpoint, provide, quote, refer to, rely on, tap, trace, use ~
V: ~ confirms that ... , dried up, revealed ..., says ..., tells (us) that ...
A: additional, authoritative, available, basic, cheap, chief, common, constant, continual, deep, dependable, (in)direct, doubtful, endless, excellent, external, first-class, frequent, fruitful, great, immediate, impartial, impeccable, important, independent, inevitable, inexhaustible, informed, lasting, (un)limited, main, never-ending, obscure, official, original, perennial,

plentiful, prime, principal, private, rare, reasonable, recent, regular, (un)reliable, remote, reputable, rich, secret, superb, tremendous, true, ultimate, unattributable, unbiased, undisclosed, unfailing, unique, unknown, unnamed, unrivalled, untapped, well-known, wonderful ~

P: a ~ close to the Minister; a ~ of information; Government *sources*

SOUVENIR
A: cheap, official, perfect, special, unique ~

SOVEREIGNTY
V: cede, claim, erode, establish, (re)gain, give up, grant, infringe, restore, threaten, violate ~
A: full, joint ~
P: infringement of, loss of, transference of, violation of ~

SPACE
V: allocate, apportion, arrange, clear, close, devote, divide, enter, fill (in/up), find, have, leave, limit, occupy, patrol, reserve, save, take over, take up, waste, widen ~
A: adequate, ample, available, big, blank, empty, enough, extra, free, handy, inconvenient, large, (un)limited, minute, narrow, open, remaining, restricted, small, sufficient, tiny, whole, wide ~

SPACE (cosmic)
V: be lost in, conquer, disappear into, enter, explore, orbit in, travel through ~
A: infinite, outer ~
P: ~ age, shuttle, station, suit, travel

SPEAKER
A: able, compelling, concise, effective, eloquent, engaging, entertaining, experienced, fine, fluent, gifted, guest, persuasive, poor, practised, public, wonderful ~

SPECIALIST
V: call in, consult, go to ~
A: eminent, well-known ~

SPECIES
V: breed, decimate, destroy, identify, preserve, produce, study, wipe out ~
V: ~ has become extinct, died out, flourished, is threatened with extinction, multiplied, reproduced itself, survived, vanished
A: common, endangered, exotic, extinct, little-known, new, rare, unusual ~

SPECTACLE
V: mount, produce, put on, rehearse, stage, watch, witness ~
V: ~ alarmed sb, confronted sb, presented itself
A: alarming, amazing, bizarre, brilliant, colourful, dignified, dramatic, fabulous, glittering, glorious, grand, horrifying, magnificent, marvellous, moving, proud, remarkable, sad, solemn, splendid, stirring, strange, time-honoured, tragic, tremendous, unedifying, unique, unusual, wonderful ~

SPECULATION
V: confirm, discourage, foster, fuel, give rise to, heighten, indulge in, intensify, rule out, stifle ~
V: ~ is rife, mounted, spread
A: amusing, anxious, bold, dangerous, disturbing, endless, far-fetched, general, idle, interesting, irresponsible, (un)justified, mere, mild, pointless, premature, pure, sheer, unfounded, uninformed, well-founded, widespread, wild ~

SPECULATION (financial)
V: encourage, engage in, frown on, lead to, stamp out, wipe out ~
A: dangerous, foolish, harmful, modest, profitable, rampant, rash, risky, shady, widespread ~

SPEECH (with *a*)

V: ad-lib, applaud, boo, broadcast, cancel, change, deliver, draft, follow, give, hail, improvise, interrupt, listen to, make, postpone, prepare, publish, rehearse, report, summarise, write ~

V: ~ calls for ... , inspired ...

A: acceptance, after-dinner, amusing, boring, brief, campaign, clever, conciliatory, constructive, controversial, defiant, dignified, disastrous, eloquent, excellent, farewell, fascinating, final, forceful, hard-hitting, historic, impassioned, important, impromptu, inaugural, inflammatory, inspired, inspiring, introductory, irresponsible, key, keynote, lengthy, lively, long-winded, masterly, memorable, moving, outspoken, passionate, polite, pompous, poor, powerful, rambling, rousing, simple, splendid, statesmanlike, stirring, successful, well-argued, wide-ranging, wonderful ~

P: gist of, substance of, tone of ~

SPEECH (manner of speaking)

A: blurred, clear, clipped, defective, halting, hesitant, indistinct, poor, slurred ~

P: clarity of ~

SPEED

V: build up, check, control, exceed, go at, increase, keep to, maintain, measure, pick up, proceed at, reduce, regulate, travel at, watch ~

V: ~ exceeded ... , dropped, fell, went down/up

A: actual, breakneck, breathtaking, constant, cruising, dangerous, dizzy, excessive, frantic, full, great, high, lightning, low, maximum, minimum, moderate, reckless, regular, ridiculous, safe, sensible, slow, steady, supersonic, terrific, top ~

P: the ~ limit; burst of, spurt of ~

SPENDING

V: check, curb, curtail, cut down, limit, restrict ~

A: excessive, extravagant, foolish, indiscriminate, lavish, reckless, thoughtless, unnecessary ~

P: cuts in, freeze on ~

SPHERE (scope)

V: belong to, be outside, come within, determine, establish, expand, extend, indicate, lie outside, limit, mark, outline, restrict ~

A: appropriate, broad, exact, limited, main, narrow, ordinary, particular, proper, restricted, wide ~

P: ~ of influence

SPIRIT

V: break (sb's), have, lose, show ~

A: admirable, competitive, exemplary, fiery, fighting, great, indomitable, real, rebellious, tremendous, true, unbreakable, unconquerable ~

SPIRIT (real meaning)

V: act in accordance with, embody, epitomise, express, feel, follow, go against, keep to, match, obey, (mis)understand ~

A: true, underlying ~

SPIRITS

V: keep (your) ~ up, raise, revive ~

V: ~ drooped, fell, flagged, rose, sank, soared

A: cheerful, excellent, fine, good, high, low, poor ~

P: dampen, improve, lift, raise, restore (your) ~; in good/high ~

SPLENDOUR

A: great, incredible, lavish, magnificent, oriental, ornate, regal, unrivalled ~

SPORT
V: be fond of/keen on, go in for ~
A: amateur, competitive, contact, country, exciting, dangerous, field, individual, national, professional, gruelling, rough, spectator, summer, water ~
P: world of ~; winter *sports*
SPOT (place)
V: choose, find, mark, pick, return to ~
A: beautiful, beauty, favourite, ideal, isolated, lovely, peaceful, perfect, secluded, suitable ~
SQUABBLE
V: get mixed up in, settle, start ~
V: ~ arose, broke out
A: bitter, petty, silly, unseemly ~
STABILITY
V: achieve, affect, destroy, ensure, lend ~ to ... , maintain, preserve, promote, threaten, undermine ~
A: emotional, fragile, lasting, long-/short-term, permanent, political, remarkable, temporary, welcome ~
STADIUM
V: empty, fill, pack ~
A: crowded, huge, indoor, massive, magnificent, outdoor, packed, sports ~
STAFF
V: be in charge of, be responsible for, develop, dismiss, employ, fire, handle, have, headhunt, hire, lay off, lead, make ~ redundant, pay, poach, provide, recruit, sack, supervise, supply, take on, train ~
A: adequate, administrative, conscientious, dedicated, devoted, efficient, extra, large, loyal, mobile, permanent, pleasant, poor, (well-)qualified, reliable, seasonal, skeleton, temporary, (fully-)trained, young ~
P: ~ training; recruitment of, shortage of ~
STAGE
V: arrive at, be at, belong to, go through, pass, reach, usher in ~
A: advanced, closing, conceptual, critical, crucial, dangerous, distinct, dramatic, early, elementary, final, formative, initial, interim, intermediate, introductory, late, new, preliminary ~
STAGE (theatre)
V: appear on, be on/off, go on, leave ~
STAMP
V: issue, lick, moisten ~, put/stick ~ on sth
A: commemorative, first-/second-class, postage, rare ~
STANCE
V: adopt, modify, take ~
A: conciliatory, courageous, hard-line, realistic, supportive, tough ~
STAND
V: adopt, back, make, oppose, support, take ~
A: courageous, desperate, determined, firm, last, last-ditch, resolute, strong, tough ~
STANDARD
V: achieve, adhere to, apply, aspire to, attain, bring down, comply with, conform to, demand, drop below, expect, fall below, fix, improve, insist on, keep to, lower, maintain, (fail to) meet, raise, reach, seek, set, surpass ~

V: ~ deteriorated, fell, improved, remained the same, went down/up

A: (un)acceptable, accepted, (in)adequate, appalling, average, common, demanding, deplorable, dreadful, exacting, expected, fixed, general, high, impossible, low, minimum, normal, outdated, overall, poor, required, rigorous, rising, satisfactory, strict, stringent, usual ~

P: up to/below the required the expected ~

STANDARD OF LIVING

V: achieve, affect, aim at, create, enjoy, ensure, have, improve, keep up, lower, maintain, protect, provide, raise, reach, reduce, threaten ~

V: ~ dropped, fell, improved, remained level/steady, rose, sank, went down/up

A: (in)adequate, comfortable, enviable, high, low, luxurious, miserable, modest, poor, (un)satisfactory ~

P: fall in, improvement in, reduction in, rise in ~; enjoy a better ~

STANDPOINT

V: adopt, (dis)agree with, argue against, arrive at, change, criticise, justify, oppose, share, support ~

A: biased, clear, definite, determined, different, former, general, narrow, novel, opposite, personal, practical, (un)reasonable ~

STANDSTILL

V: be at, bring sth to, come to, grind to ~

A: absolute, complete, total, virtual ~

STAR

V: ~ glittered, shone, twinkled

A: bright, distant, evening, falling, morning, North, Pole, shining, shooting, twinkling ~

START

V: get off to, make ~

A: (in)auspicious, dreadful, early, encouraging, false, faltering, flying, fresh, late, poor, promising, quick, terrible, unhappy ~

STATE

V: ~ deteriorated, improved, worsened

A: chronic, critical, crumbling, dirty, dangerous, deplorable, desperate, disgraceful, disgusting, dreadful, embryonic, excellent, nervous, perfect, pitiful, poor, precarious, (un)satisfactory, shocking, sorry, transitional, unconscious, weakened, wretched ~

P: a (adjective) ~ of affairs

STATE (nation)

V: create, defend, establish, form, found, govern, rule, set up ~

A: authoritarian, autonomous, breakaway, democratic, (un)friendly, hostile, independent, leading, member, neighbouring, non-aligned, police, powerful, puppet, religious, satellite, sovereign, totalitarian ~

STATEMENT

V: acknowledge, add to, amend, amplify, await, bear out, come out with, confirm, contest, contradict, corroborate, deliver, deny, deplore, dismiss, draft, draw up, elaborate on, elicit, endorse, expect, extract, issue, leak, make, prepare, publish, put out, quote, read (out), receive, refute, release, repeat, report, repudiate, retract, sign, submit, substantiate, supplement, support, test, volunteer, welcome, withdraw, write ~

V: ~ accuses sb of ... , alleges ... , (re)asserts ... , clears up ... , contradicts ... , deplores ... , explains ... , makes ... clear, outlines ..., says ... , suggests ..., sums ... up, underlines ...

A: awkward, balanced, bald, bold, brief, categorical, cautious, clear, clear-cut, comforting, compassionate, conciliatory, confident, contradictory, damaging, defamatory, definite, definitive, detailed, earlier, eloquent, explicit, factual, false, final, firm, (in)formal, forthright, full, (un)guarded, helpful, inflammatory, interim, joint, lengthy, long, loose, lucid, matter-of-fact, misleading, (un)official, original, plausible, polemical, preliminary, previous, public, qualified, questionable, rash, reassuring, revealing, risky, short, solemn, strong, strongly-worded, succinct, sweeping, tentative, terse, tough, (un)true, unequivocal, vague, welcome, wild, written ~

STATESMAN
A: able, elder, eminent, famous, great, popular, prominent ~

STATISTICS
V: analyse, collect, compile, falsify, gather, issue, juggle with, produce, reel off, release, tabulate ~
V: ~ indicate ..., prove ..., reveal ..., show ..., suggest ..., support ...
A: bogus, cold, false, hard, impressive, reliable, vital ~
P: analysis of, array of, mass of ~

STATUS
V: achieve, acquire, challenge, claim, enhance, enjoy, have, keep, lose, obtain, reach, recognise, restore, threaten ~
A: celebrity, elevated, full, high, inferior, low, modest, non-aligned, obscure, official, privileged, refugee, special, superior, uncertain, unique ~

STATUS QUO
V: be in favour of, challenge, change, cling to, continue with, defend, destroy, keep, maintain, preserve, restore, retain, revert to, support, undermine, upset, violate ~

STEAK
V: barbecue, fry, grill ~
A: fillet, juicy, medium, minute, rare, rump, sirloin, T-bone, tender, tough, well-done ~

STEP (action)
V: contemplate, make, take ~
A: bold, cautious, correct, critical, dangerous, decisive, desirable, determined, disastrous, drastic, effective, elementary, energetic, false, fatal, final, initial, positive, precautionary, preliminary, prudent, silly, (un)wise ~
P: take immediate *steps*

STIMULUS
V: act as, apply, give, keep up, need, offer, provide, react to, respond to, withdraw ~
A: added, general, powerful, regular, sharp, strong ~

STOCK
V: amass, build (up), draw on, keep, (re)order, pile up, put in, reduce, replenish ~
V: ~ diminished, grew, moved, went down
A: big, entire, good, huge, initial, large ~
P: ~ check, control, report, room; in/out of ~; cereal/coal/food/oil etc *stocks*

STORM
V: avoid, be caught in, brave, face, forecast, predict, ride out, shelter from, weather ~
V: ~ blew itself out, blew over, blew up, broke, is brewing, came up, gathered, grew, hit (southern California), passed, quietened down, raged, receded, struck, threatened
A: dreadful, fierce, frightening, furious, heavy, severe, terrible, tremendous, violent ~
P: the eye of the ~

Starting from a noun

STORY
V: back up, bear out, believe, carry, change, check, circulate, come across, come out with/up with, concoct, corroborate, cover up, edit, embellish, embroider, expose, fabricate, follow up, get, go after, go back on, hear, hush up, invent, kill, liven up, make up, manufacture, narrate, piece together, print, pursue, put together, recount, relate, report, run, stick to, tell, verify, work on, (re)write ~

V: ~ broke, centres on ... , unfolded

A: amazing, amusing, apocryphal, authentic, bedtime, children's, cock-and-bull, coherent, complicated, cover, dazzling, detailed, dramatic, elaborate, enthralling, exciting, exclusive, fairy, false, fascinating, front-page, full, funny, garbled, genuine, grim, gripping, gruesome, hard-luck, human interest, improbable, inside, intriguing, love, moving, (im)plausible, ridiculous, riveting, romantic, scandalous, scurrilous, short, silly, sob, sordid, superb, tall, true, unlikely, whole ~

P: gist of, substance of, thread of ~

STRAIN
V: alleviate, bear, be aware of, be weighed down by, cause, collapse under, cope with, crack under, create, ease, experience, feel, get over, give rise to, impose, lead to, lessen, mitigate, place/put a ~ on ... , produce, relieve, reduce, relieve sb of, share, stand, suffer from, take ~, take ~ off ...

V: ~ shows, is telling

A: acute, awful, constant, continuous, great, heavy, increasing, intolerable, mental, nervous, severe, steady, terrible, terrific, tremendous ~

P: the ~ was too much for sb, be under a (lot of) ~

STRANGER
A: complete, mysterious, perfect, relative, total, virtual ~

STRATEGY
V: abandon, adopt, apply, change, co-ordinate, decide on, devise, draw up, evolve, follow, formulate, implement, invent, map out, plan, pursue, reappraise, undermine, work out ~

V: ~ collapsed, failed, is in disarray, succeeded, worked

A: alternative, clever, coherent, consistent, cunning, global, long/medium/short-term, obsolete, overall, sound, (un)successful, workable ~

STREAM
V: be/come on, go with/against the ~

V: ~ dried up, flowed (past), rushed down/through ... , started/stopped, trickled through

A: steady, constant, continuous, mountain, shallow ~

P: ~ of consciousness, of traffic; a ~ of abuse/complaints/insults; the A/B/C ~

STREET
V: clear, cross ~

A: back, busy, congested, dead-end, deserted, lonely, narrow, quiet, side, wide ~

STRENGTH
V: acquire, build up, collect, conserve, deplete, develop, exert, exhaust, find, gain, gather, get back, give sb, have, measure, need, overtax, possess, recover, regain, renew, sap, save, test, try out, underestimate, use ~

V: ~ drained away, dwindled, ebbed, failed, grew

A: awesome, considerable, declining, existing, extra, great, immense, incredible, maximum, phenomenal, prodigious, remaining, superior, tremendous ~

P: show of, sign of ~

STRESS

V: add to, alleviate, bear, cause, control, cope with, create, ease, encounter, experience, feel, get rid of, go through, increase, live under, reduce, relieve, stand, subject sb to, suffer, survive, withstand, work under ~

A: acute, considerable, constant, continual, enormous, great, intolerable, prolonged, severe, terrible, unbearable ~

STRESS (emphasis)

V: lay, place/put ~ on sth

A: additional, considerable, (in)direct, extra, firm, general, great, heavy, immediate, main, marked, particular, principal, specific, strong ~

STRIFE

V: aggravate, avoid, cause, create ~

V: ~ broke out, died down, is endemic

A: bitter, continual, domestic, internal, serious ~

STRIKE

V: announce, avert, be engaged in, be (out) on, break, break off, break up, call, call off, cause, come out on, conduct, end, go (out) on, halt, handle, head off, hold, join, lead, lead to, organise, precipitate, prevent, prolong, put down, resolve, settle, smash, spark off, stage, support, suppress, take part in, threaten ~

V: ~ affected sb, broke out, came to an end, collapsed, cracked, dragged on, ended, escalated, extends to ... , fizzled out, lasted, spread, went ahead

A: all-out, brief, counter-productive, disastrous, general, harmful, indefinite, irresponsible, lightning, national, nationwide, (un)official, one-day, prolonged, selective, serious, spontaneous, token, wildcat ~

P: threat of ~ action; spate of, wave of *strikes*

STRUCTURE

V: alter, build, change, create, demolish, design, destroy, develop, devise, dismantle, erect, examine, expand, improve, modernise, modify, overhaul, plan, preserve, prop up, put up, repair, restore, shake, shore up, slim down, strengthen, study, support, undermine, weaken ~

A: appropriate, archaic, basic, chaotic, clumsy, colossal, compact, complex, cumbersome, damaged, dangerous, dilapidated, effective, efficient, elegant, firm, (in)flexible, flimsy, gigantic, handsome, highly developed, huge, ideal, imposing, intact, interior, intricate, lop-sided, massive, modern, molecular, monolithic, obsolete, original, permanent, relevant, revised, rotten, shaky, solid, sound, (un)stable, strong, suitable, tall, temporary, top-heavy, two-tier, unstable, unwieldy, vast, weak, whole ~

STRUGGLE

V: be caught up in/engaged in/involved in/locked in, carry on, continue, enter into, face, give up, join, pursue, put up, resolve, settle, take part in, take up, trigger off ~

V: ~ broke out, developed, escalated, was resolved, went on

A: armed, bitter, bloody, brief, courageous, desperate, determined, endless, epic, fierce, frantic, furious, global, grim, hard, hopeless, life-and-death, momentous, prolonged, protracted, serious, titanic, unending, unrelenting, unremitting, uphill, violent ~

P: culmination of, outcome of ~

STUDENT

V: enrol, examine, expel, interview, take, teach, tutor ~

V: ~ enrolled, failed, graduated, matriculated, passed

A: average, bright, brilliant, conscientious, diligent, excellent, exceptional, gifted, good, hardworking, keen, outstanding, perennial, poor, promising, talented, weak ~

STUDY

V: apply oneself to, be engaged in, carry out, commission, complete, conduct, devote oneself to, embark on, get down to, make, require, take up, undertake, work on ~

A: ambitious, careful, close, comprehensive, conscientious, constant, continuous, deep, detailed, diligent, hard, intensive, laborious, methodical, meticulous, painstaking, patient, prolonged, regular, scientific, serious, straightforward, successful, systematic, thorough, vast ~

STUDY (with *a/the*)

V: come up with, conduct, do, make, produce, publish, submit ~

V: ~ came to the conclusion that ..., concluded that ..., demonstrates ..., is based on ..., is concerned with ..., predicted sth, proves ..., shows that ..., suggests ..., supports ...

A: academic, careful, classic, clear, comprehensive, (in)conclusive, definitive, detailed, elegant, excellent, exhaustive, experimental, exploratory, famous, fascinating, flawed, ground-breaking, in-depth, initial, intensive, lengthy, ongoing, original, penetrating, perceptive, pioneering, preliminary, profound, rigorous, scientific, searching, sophisticated, thorough, thoughtful, useful, valuable, well-balanced ~

STUPIDITY

V: be due to, be guilty of, put sth down to ~

A: crass, monumental, sheer, unbelievable, utter ~

STYLE

V: abandon, adopt, alter, ape, copy, create, develop, follow, have, imitate, impose, introduce, keep to, lack, mark, perfect, polish, refine, show, use ~

V: ~ altered, became popular, came into fashion, changed, emerged, flourished, is characteristic, is derived from ..., is out of fashion, is typical of sb, spread

A: abrasive, affected, aggressive, attractive, austere, awkward, bold, characteristic, classic, classical, clear, clumsy, conventional, dazzling, delightful, derivative, diffuse, direct, distinct, distinctive, distinguished, easy, eclectic, economical, elegant, exuberant, fancy, flamboyant, flexible, florid, flowery, fluent, forceful, formal, former, heavy, idiosyncratic, impressive, laborious, lucid, mixed, modern, old-fashioned, ornate, pedantic, pedestrian, plain, pompous, ponderous, quiet, racy, refreshing, restrained, robust, self-conscious, severe, simple, smart, sober, spare, sparkling, splendid, straightforward, striking, subtle, terse, traditional, turgid, typical, unassuming, up-to-date, vigorous, vulgar ~

P: clash of, diversity of, multiplicity of, plurality of, range of *styles*

SUBJECT

V: abandon, address, approach, attack, avoid, bring up, broach, change, concentrate on, cover, deal with, debate, discuss, dismiss, dispute, drop, elaborate on, embark on, (re-)examine, exhaust, follow, go into, handle, introduce, investigate, leave, master, mention, pursue, raise, revert to, study, tackle, take up, throw light on, touch (on), treat, write about/on ~

V: ~ concerns ... , covers ... , cropped up, fascinated (me), palled, received attention

A: abstruse, ambitious, (in)appropriate, arcane, awkward, barren, boring, chief, complex, complicated, controversial, crucial, delicate, difficult, dull, entertaining, enthralling, esoteric, fascinating, general, important, (un)interesting, intricate, involved, key, low-key, main, mundane, obscure, (un)pleasant, principal, relevant, sensitive, simple, specialised, specific, taboo, touchy, tricky, trivial, troublesome, vast, vital, wide ~

P: grasp of ~

SUBJECT (course of study)

V: master, study, tackle, take (up) ~

A: academic, compulsory, core, favourite, optional, popular, required, strong, weak ~

SUBSIDY
V: apply for, cut, depend on, get, give, grant, increase, obtain, pay, phase out, provide, raise, receive, seek, withdraw ~
A: generous, good, huge, large, massive, meagre, modest, substantial ~

SUBSTANCE
V: handle, use ~
A: awkward, bulky, colourless, dangerous, fatty, fine, (in)flammable, greasy, harmful, harmless, heavy, lethal, light, mysterious, natural, oily, poisonous, slippery, spongy, sticky, synthetic, toxic, volatile, waxy ~

SUBSTITUTE
V: act as, provide, supply ~
A: adequate, good, poor, (un)satisfactory, useful, valuable ~

SUCCESS
V: acclaim, achieve, attribute ~ to sth, be assured of, be crowned with, boost, bring about, claim, deserve, end in, enhance, enjoy, ensure, guarantee, have, jeopardize, lead to, meet with, merit, owe ~ to sth, predict, prove, pursue, score, taste ~
V: ~ came (to sb), depended on ... , eluded sb, escaped sb, hinged on ... , is due to/the result of ... , stems from ...
A: big, brilliant, commercial, complete, encouraging, ephemeral, fantastic, fragile, genuine, great, heartening, huge, immediate, increasing, initial, instant, material, moderate, modest, outright, outstanding, overnight, overwhelming, partial, (un)qualified, rapid, real, resounding, runaway, sensational, spectacular, startling, stupendous, total, tremendous, triumphant, undoubted, unexpected, unmitigated, unparalleled, visible, worldly, worldwide ~
P: barrier to, chances of, key to, secret of, trappings of ~; make a ~ of sth

SUFFERING
V: add to, aggravate, alleviate, avert, bear, be inured to, be tormented by, cause, ease, eliminate, endure, experience, feel, get rid of, go through, increase, inflict, intensify, prevent, put an end to, relieve, stand, tolerate, undergo ~
V: ~ ceased, diminished, got worse, increased, lasted, went on
A: acute, chronic, considerable, constant, continuous, dreadful, extreme, great, intense, prolonged, terrible, unbearable, unnecessary, unspeakable, untold ~

SUGGESTION
V: accept, act on, adopt, advance, agree to/with, balk at, carry out, come forward with/out with/up with, consider, deny, discount, dismiss, dispute, fall in with, follow up, go along with, handle, lend weight to, make, offer, produce, put forward, rebut, refute, reject, repudiate, resist, respond to, rule out, submit, take up, turn away/down, waive ~
V: ~ found/met with support/opposition, gained support
A: absurd, amazing, appropriate, astute, bold, clever, contentious, crazy, cunning, daring, (in)direct, disgraceful, effective, fatuous, feasible, foolish, (un)fortunate, fruitful, handy, helpful, hesitant, ingenious, kind, ludicrous, malicious, mistaken, modest, novel, outrageous, pertinent, practical, preposterous, reasonable, shrewd, silly, sound, startling, straightforward, tactful, tempting, useful, useless, wise ~

SUIT
A: business, casual, checked, crumpled, dark, double-/single-breasted, flashy, lightweight, made-to-measure, off-the-peg, pin-striped, shiny, smart, summer, tailor-made, two-/three-piece ~

SUIT (legal claim)
V: bring, contest, dismiss, file, lose, press, win ~

SUM (money)

V: earmark, earn, lose, put aside, raise, save, spend, win ~

A: considerable, derisory, enormous, excessive, extravagant, huge, large, lump, nominal, small, substantial, tidy, tiny, useful, vast ~

SUMMARY

V: add, append, draw up, give, make, prepare, provide, submit, supply, write ~

A: accurate, brief, concise, detailed, long, quick, rapid, rough, short, terse, useful ~

SUN

V: bask in ~

V: ~ beat down, is high/low/overhead/up, came out, rises, sets, shone, went down

A: blazing, bright, hot, merciless, midday, pale, rising, setting, strong, summer, tropical, warm, watery, wintry ~

SUNLIGHT

V: let in, shut out ~

A: bright, brilliant ~

P: shaft of ~

SUNSHINE

V: sit in, soak up ~

A: beautiful, brilliant, glorious, lovely, warm ~

SUPERSTITION

V: believe (in), pander to ~

A: ancient, common, dangerous, deep-rooted, harmful, local, old, popular, powerful, silly, strong, widespread, weird ~

SUPERVISION

V: arrange for, be in need of, come under, escape from, exercise, keep sb under, put sb under, relax, tighten ~

A: close, constant, effective, efficient, general, lax, loose, regular, round-the-clock, strict ~

SUPPLIES

V: arrange for, ask for, augment, build up, conserve, cut down/off, disrupt, distribute, draw on, eke out, ensure, exhaust, get, guarantee, hold back/up, keep up, lay in, limit, maintain, need, obtain, order, provide, put in, receive, rely on, replenish, restrict, safeguard, secure, step up, stop ~

V: ~ arrived, came in, diminished, dried up, dwindled, are getting low, improved, lasted, are running out, went down

A: abundant, (in)adequate, additional, ample, constant, continuous, copious, current, domestic, emergency, enormous, essential, excess, existing, extra, foreign, fresh, good, huge, large, limited, local, low, meagre, normal, plentiful, poor, precarious, (ir)regular, remaining, (in)sufficient, surplus, welcome ~

P: cutback in, flow of, lack of, shortage of ~; ... is in short *supply*

SUPPORT

V: alienate, appeal for, arouse, attract, bid for, build, call for, canvass, capture, claim, collect, command, count on, declare, derive, draw, draw on, drum up, end, enjoy, enlist, express, extend, forfeit, foster, gain, gather, generate, get, give, guarantee, have, lend, look for, lose, mobilise, obtain, offer, pledge, promise, provide, rally, re-affirm, receive, rely on, retain, round up, secure, seek, solicit, undermine, win, withdraw ~

V: ~ arrived, came, dwindled, ebbed away, evaporated, faltered, grew, shrank, waned, was forthcoming

A: active, all-out, ardent, broad, chief, constant, continuous, crucial, discreet, enthusiastic, firm, frail, generous, hearty, (un)limited, little, loyal, lukewarm, mass, massive, material, moral, much, negligible, noisy, organised, overwhelming, passionate, persistent, qualified, rank-and-file, reliable, solid, staunch, strong, tacit, tepid, timely, token, total, uncritical, unequivocal, unfailing, unflinching, unqualified, unquestioning, unstinting, unwavering, warm, weak, wholehearted, wide, worldwide ~

SUPPORTERS
V: delight, disappoint, rouse, thank, win ~
A: ardent, articulate, disillusioned, enthusiastic, erstwhile, faithful, fanatical, fervent, firm, football, former, loyal, lukewarm, outspoken, regular, stalwart, staunch, strong, trusted ~

SUPPOSITION
V: bear out, confirm, corroborate, express, make, rule out, test ~
A: baseless, bold, extraordinary, likely, logical, mere, plausible, preposterous, pure, rational, ridiculous, sheer, tentative, unjustified ~

SUPREMACY
V: achieve, acknowledge, admit, aim at, assert, attain, break, challenge, claim, compete for, deny, desire, destroy, enjoy, envy, establish, fear, foster, gain, halt, have, keep, lose, maintain, oppose, question, rebel against, rival, seek, undermine, win, work for ~
A: clear, total, unchallenged, uncontested, undisputed, undoubted ~

SURFACE
V: be above/below/beneath, penetrate, polish, scratch, skim ~
A: bumpy, even, flat, hard, outer, protective, rough, sloping, slippery, smooth ~

SURGERY
V: need, perform, recommend, undergo ~
A: emergency, major, minor ~

SURPLUS
V: accumulate, build up, create, destroy, dispose of, draw on, dump, end up with, get rid of, have, hoard, keep, obtain, produce, profit from, store ~
V: ~ accumulated, disappeared, dwindled, vanished
A: enormous, huge, large, modest, slight, small, unexpected, useful ~

SURPRISE
V: arouse, cause, evoke, excite, exhibit, experience, express, get, get over, give sb, have, hide, occasion, overcome, produce, receive, show ~, spring a ~ on
A: authentic, big, complete, considerable, genuine, great, mild, nasty, nice, (un)pleasant, real, terrible, total, tremendous, widespread ~

SURRENDER
V: accept, agree to, call for, demand, discuss, force, negotiate, offer ~
A: shameful, total, unconditional ~

SURROUNDINGS
V: accept, adapt oneself to, adjust to, affect, alter, arrange, be content with, be disgusted by, be pleased with, be reconciled to, be satisfied with, become accustomed to, complain about, change, damage, enjoy, feel happy about/in, get used to, hate, ignore, improve, object to, protest about, put up with, spoil, surround oneself with, view ~
A: agreeable, (un)attractive, austere, bare, beautiful, bizarre, charming, cheerful, comfortable, current, difficult, distressing, drab, elegant, existing, familiar, gloomy, grim, horrible, ideal, idyllic, interesting, lovely, luxurious, miserable, modest, natural, nice, perfect, (un)pleasant, quiet, shabby, sombre, spartan, temporary, terrible, unaccustomed, unbelievable ~

SURVEY
V: carry out, commission, conduct, do, embark on, make, mount, undertake ~
V: ~ brought ... to light, concludes ..., confirms ..., covers ..., deals with ..., demonstrates that ...,
   disclosed ..., indicates ..., is based on ..., points to ..., reveals ..., shows ..., suggests ...
A: annual (monthly etc), aerial, brief, broad, careful, chronological, comprehensive, costly,
   exhaustive, extensive, full-scale, general, huge, impartial, impressive, in-depth,
   international, market, massive, nationwide, (un)official, overall, pictorial, preliminary,
   recent, regular, systematic, thorough, underwater, wide-ranging ~

SURVEILLANCE
V: conduct, maintain, place/put sb under ~
A: close, constant, round-the-clock, strict ~

SURVIVAL
V: ensure ~
A: basic, miraculous, remarkable ~
P: hope of, struggle for ~; the ~ of the fittest

SUSPECT
V: arrest, bring in, detain, eliminate, interrogate, interview, place ~ under surveillance, question,
   rule out ~
A: prime ~

SUSPENSE
V: break, build up, cause, create, keep sb in, lead to, maintain, relieve ~
A: constant, continual, frightening, great, increasing, terrific, unbearable ~

SUSPICION
V: aggravate, allay, alert, arouse, avert, bear out, be open to, be under, calm, come under,
   confirm, defy, disguise, divert, fall under, feed, feel, fuel, give rise to, harbour, have,
   heighten, hide, increase, investigate, lay oneself open to, overcome, prove, provoke, put
   aside, reinforce, register, remove, share, show ~
V: ~ arose, centres on ... , fell on sb, formed in (my) mind, grew, lingered, turned out to be
   true/false, vanished, was justified/proved right/unfounded
A: awkward, dark, deep, distinct, dull, faint, fleeting, gnawing, grave, increasing, lingering,
   lurking, mounting, nagging, nasty, secret, shrewd, smouldering, sneaking, strong, ugly,
   uncomfortable, uneasy, unpleasant, widespread ~
P: (my) worst *suspicions* were confirmed

SWEATER
A: crew-neck, heavy, round-neck, V-neck, polo-neck, thick, turtle-neck, warm ~

SYMBOL
V: adopt, recognise, use ~
V: ~ means sth, signifies sth
A: enduring, eternal, familiar, hackneyed, lasting, potent, powerful, sacred, widespread ~

SYMPATHY
V: accept, alienate, arouse, attract, capture, command, convey, deserve, enlist, express, extend,
   extract, feel, gain, get, give, have, look for, provoke, reject, share, show, solicit ~
A: deep, great, heartfelt, profound, sincere, warm ~
P: please accept my deepest ~; I have every ~ with

SYMPTOMS
V: alleviate, come across, conceal, cure, describe, develop, disguise, ease, examine, exhibit,
   feign, find, get rid of, have, identify, ignore, look for, mask, notice, observe, recognise,
   relieve, remove, report, reveal, see, show, treat, (mis)understand, watch out for ~

V: ~ (dis)appeared, got worse, manifested themselves, recurred, vanished, went away
A: acute, alarming, chronic, classic, clear, common, definite, distressing, distinct, early, faint, incipient, latent, marked, obvious, puzzling, rare, similar, specific, strange, tell-tale, typical, (un)usual, withdrawal ~

SYSTEM
V: abandon, abolish, adapt, adopt, advocate, alter, apply, back, beat, be part of, break, build, bypass, change, clog (up), constitute, construct, control, create, defend, destroy, devise, dislocate, disrupt, do away with, employ, establish, exploit, follow, give up, improve, improvise, install, institute, introduce, invent, keep to, make use of, manage, manipulate, monitor, operate, (re)organise, overhaul, overthrow, patch up, perfect, perpetuate, produce, provide, rebel against, reform, reinforce, replace, restore, restructure, run, scrap, set up, slip through, smash, streamline, support, switch over to, tailor ~ to fit ... , tinker with, transform, undermine, upset, use, weaken, work out, wreck ~
V: ~ is bankrupt/geared to/in operation/in jeopardy/near to collapse, became operational, broke down, collapsed, flourished, functions, operates, rests on ... , works
A: absurd, accounting, advanced, anachronistic, analogous, antiquated, archaic, authoritarian, automatic, awkward, back-up, balanced, bureaucratic, Byzantine, (de)centralised, closed, clumsy, coherent, compact, complex, complicated, comprehensive, computer, computerised, confusing, controversial, co-ordinated, costly, cumbersome, disastrous, effective, (in)efficient, elaborate, enlightened, equitable, evil, excellent, existing, expensive, extensive, fair, flexible, foolproof, healthy, humane, independent, inequitable, ingenious, iniquitous, intimidating, intricate, latest, makeshift, (ultra-)modern, monolithic, normal, obsolete, old-fashioned, oppressive, (un)orthodox, outdated, out-of-date, over-regulated, (im)perfect, permanent, pernicious, piecemeal, political, poor, popular, powerful, questionable, (un)reliable, repressive, repugnant, rigid, simple, smooth-running, sophisticated, sound, special, specific, (un)stable, standard, straightforward, support, tailor-made, temporary, top-heavy, traditional, two-tier, unique, unwieldy, up-to-date, usual, valid, viable, vulnerable, widespread, workable ~
P: doubts about, defects in, flaws in, shortcomings in/of ~; administrative *systems*

T

TACT
V: display, exercise, have, show ~
A: considerable, great, rare ~
TACTICS
V: adopt, employ, use ~
V: ~ are useless, failed, worked
A: aggressive, bullying, clever, cunning, delaying, devious, disruptive, imaginative, recognised, ruthless, scare, sinister, standard, strong-arm, stonewalling, underhand ~
TALE
V: believe, come out with, concoct, embellish, invent, make up, produce, spin, tell ~
A: absurd, astounding, bizarre, convincing, extraordinary, fanciful, foolish, frightening, graphic, grizzly, hair-raising, harrowing, haunting, imaginative, legendary, moving, (im)plausible, poignant, rambling, remarkable, sad, shocking, sorry, true, unlikely, weird, wild ~

TALENT

V: cultivate, demonstrate, develop, display, encourage, exploit, have, hide, inherit, make good use of, nurse, ruin, show, squander, waste ~

A: budding, enormous, fine, formidable, genuine, great, inherited, innate, natural, prodigious, outstanding, rare, remarkable, special, unique ~

TALENT (talented people)

V: discover, encourage, foster, spot ~

A: home-bred, local, native, real ~; ~ scout

TALK

A: brief, confidential, dangerous, encouraging, fascinating, frank, heart-to-heart, high-minded, hopeful, idle, interesting, intimate, loose, private, profitable, quiet, serious, silly, stimulating, useful, vague ~

TALK (lecture)

V: follow, give, prepare ~

A: amusing, boring, brief, controversial, entertaining, fascinating, helpful, informal, informative, instructive, interesting, provocative, short, stimulating ~

TALKS (negotiations)

V: adjourn, begin, break off, call off, complete, conduct, enter into, hold, initiate, interrupt, jeopardize, resume, sabotage, start, suspend, take part in, wreck ~

V: ~ broke down, came to nothing, continue, dragged on, ended in (failure), failed, foundered, got under way, reached an impasse, resumed, started, succeeded, took place, went on ~

A: abortive, approaching, critical, exploratory, (in)formal, fresh, fruitful, future, high-/top-level, intensive, last-minute, (un)productive, wide-ranging ~

P: round of ~

TARGET

V: abandon, achieve, aim at, be committed to, concentrate on, depart from, deviate from, establish, exceed, fix, lower, meet, miss, overshoot, pick, raise, revise, set, specify, stick to, work towards ~

A: ambitious, distant, flexible, immediate, key, long/short-term, original, prime, principal, real, (un)realistic, sales ~

TASK

V: abandon, allot ~ to sb, assign sb, attempt, attend to, avoid, be faced with, carry out, complete, cope with, delegate, do, embark on, entrust ~ to sb, execute, face, fulfil, get down to/on with/out of, give ~ to sb, give up, impose ~ on sb, overlook, perform, put off, return to, set, set about, tackle, take on/up, undertake ~

A: absorbing, arduous, challenging, colossal, crucial, daunting, delicate, demanding, difficult, easy, embarrassing, essential, exacting, fearsome, final, formidable, fruitless, grim, gruelling, hard, heavy, herculean, heroic, hopeless, huge, (un)important, impossible, insuperable, laborious, mammoth, meaningless, menial, monumental, onerous, painstaking, (un)pleasant, primary, prodigious, reasonable, (un)rewarding, routine, sad, self-imposed, simple, tedious, thankless, time-consuming, tremendous, tricky, unenviable, ungrateful, uphill, worthwhile ~

TASTE

V: disguise, have (got), spoil ~

A: acquired, bitter, discriminating, distinct, excellent, exquisite, foul, fruity, ghastly, horrible, impeccable, lingering, mild, nasty, nice, odd, peculiar, personal, (un)pleasant, refined, salty, simple, sophisticated, sour, strange, sugary, sweet, terrible, unique, weird ~

P: be in good/bad ~, a matter of (personal) ~

TAX
V: abolish, avoid, collect, cut, evade, impose, increase, levy, lift, lower, pay, put a ~ on, put up, raise, reduce, remove ~

A: company, corporation, (in)direct, excessive, heavy, income, property, sales, swingeing, unfair, unjust ~

P: ~ allowance, avoidance, base, bracket, burden, credit, evasion, exile, haven, incentive, inspector, loss, relief, return, threshold, year

TEACHER
V: become, train as ~

A: born, (in)competent, excellent, (in)experienced, French/maths etc, (un)inspiring, painstaking, primary/secondary school, strict, student, superb, supply, typical ~

TEAM
V: be dropped from, break up, captain, choose, coach, develop, field, form, manage, organise, pick, select, split up ~

A: adventurous, committed, dedicated, disciplined, effective, exciting, fine, first, football/basketball etc, home, integrated, national, opposing, poor, representative, reserve, rival, school, special, successful, unique, visiting, well-knit, winning, youth ~

TEARS
V: be reduced to, burst into, choke back, shed, weep ~

V: ~ flowed/rolled/streamed down sb's cheeks, welled up in sb's eyes

TECHNIQUE
V: acquire, apply, develop, devise, evolve, improve, invent, learn, perfect, test, try out, use, work on/out ~

A: advanced, complicated, contemporary, controversial, effective, efficient, familiar, individual, ingenious, (ultra-)modern, novel, obsolete, old-fashioned, out-of-date, (un)reliable, sophisticated, special, state-of-the-art, successful, well-known ~

TECHNOLOGY
V: apply, create, develop, employ, export, have access to, import, promote, transfer ~

A: advanced, basic, complicated, contemporary, effective, efficient, high-level, ingenious, modern, novel, obsolete, out-of-date, (un)reliable, sophisticated, special, state-of-the-art ~

TEETH
V: brush, cap, clean, clench, drill, extract, fill, gnash, grind, grit, pull ~

A: back, discoloured, false, front, milk, perfect, rotten ~

TELEPHONE
V: answer, (dis)connect, install, pick up, speak to sb on/over, tap ~, take/leave ~ off the hook

A: cordless, mobile, public, push-button ~

TEMPER
V: fall/fly/get into, keep, lose ~

A: bad, dreadful, explosive, ferocious, fierce, fiery, filthy, foul, furious, gloomy, good, hot, nasty, quick, sharp, short, terrible, uncontrollable, violent ~

P: display of, fit of ~

TEMPERAMENT
A: aggressive, amiable, artistic, calm, cautious, difficult, easy-going, equable, even, excitable, explosive, fiery, nervous, passionate, quiet, sensitive, volatile, wild ~

TEMPERATURE (weather)
V: ~ dropped, fell, plummeted, remained constant/steady, rose, soared, went down/up

A: average, constant, high, low, maximum, mild, minimum, normal, pleasant, record, steady ~

P: fall/rise in ~

TEMPO
V: increase, keep up, keep to, maintain, mark, match, quicken, reduce, regulate, set, slow down, speed up, step up, upset ~
V: ~ gathered pace, quickened, slowed down
A: brisk, dramatic, even, fast, feverish, fierce, lively, measured, normal, quick, rapid, slow, steady, vigorous ~

TEMPTATION
V: face, feel, give in to, give way to, keep away from, overcome, put ~ in sb's way, resist, succumb to, withstand, yield to ~
A: constant, dangerous, great, irresistible, overwhelming, slight, strong ~

TENACITY
V: demonstrate, exhibit, show ~
A: commendable, dogged, great, persistent, remarkable, strong, stubborn ~

TENDENCY
V: aggravate, check, curb, demonstrate, discern, display, encourage, have, modify, note, observe, overcome, perceive, reinforce, resist, reverse, see, show ~
A: alarming, common, (un)desirable, distinct, general, growing, harmful, increasing, marked, nasty, natural, obscure, pronounced, regrettable, slight, steady, strong, unfortunate, unhealthy, universal ~

TENSION
V: add to, aggravate, alleviate, break, cause, create, defuse, diminish, dissolve, ease, exacerbate, feel, generate, give rise to, heighten, increase, induce, keep down/up, lead to, lessen, maintain, produce, reduce, relax, release, relieve, remove, resolve, suffer from, whip up ~
V: ~ built up, eased, grew, increased, mounted, rose
A: agonizing, acute, dangerous, diminishing, great, mounting, rising, unbearable, unresolved ~
P: build-up of, heightening of, sense of ~

TERM
V: coin, use ~
A: abstract, apt, blunt, clear, descriptive, disparaging, general, generic, glowing, legal, literary, medical, pejorative, scientific, technical, useful ~
P: ~ of abuse; describe sth in abstract/blunt/clear/general/glowing *terms*, in no uncertain *terms*

TERMS (conditions)
V: accept, agree, arrive at, be bound by, break, comply with, dictate, disagree about, fix, keep to, lay down, name, negotiate, obtain, offer, reject, set out, settle, spell out ~
A: agreed, attractive, (un)favourable, flexible, generous, harsh, political, rigid, (un)satisfactory, stiff, strict, tough ~

TERRAIN
V: cross, enter, traverse ~
A: difficult, harsh, hilly, inhospitable, marshy, mountainous, rough ~

TERRITORY
V: acquire, administer, annex, capture, cede, conquer, cover, defend, expand, explore, gain, give up, govern, mark, occupy, take over ~
A: adjacent, common, dangerous, disputed, enemy-occupied, large, (un)occupied, uncharted, unexplored, vast, wide ~

TERROR
V: experience, feel, inspire, instil, live in, overcome ~, strike ~ into sb
A: abject, sheer, sickening ~
P: campaign of, reign of ~

TERRORISM
V: combat, curb, fight, oppose, stamp out ~
A: organised, state, urban ~
P: act of, fight against, outbreak of, wave of ~

TERRORIST
V: capture, harbour, imprison, kill, punish, release ~
V: ~ blew up ... , bombed ... , demanded ... , gave himself up, hijacked sb, is holding sb hostage, kidnapped sb, killed sb, shot sb, stormed ... , threatened sb
A: armed, urban ~

TEST
V: apply, carry out, come through, construct, devise, do, fail, get through, give, have, mark, pass, put sb through, score, set, sit, take ~
V: ~ shows ...
A: accurate, acid, aptitude, blood, complicated, demanding, difficult, driving, easy, effective, end-of-term, exacting, final, good, hard, infallible, intelligence, key, mid-term, painful, poor, pregnancy, preliminary, real, regular, reliable, revealing, rigorous, rough, spelling, standard, stiff, strict, stringent, supreme, thorough, useful, valid ~
P: ~ of endurance, stamina

TESTS (trials)
V: cancel, come/go through, endure, face, fail, hold, pass, put sth through, suspend, undergo ~
V: ~ confirm ..., cover ..., demonstrate ..., establish ..., indicate ..., mean ..., prove ..., reveal ..., show ..., suggest ...
A: critical, exhaustive, exploratory, extensive, initial, laboratory, medical, nuclear, periodic, preliminary, regular, rigorous, routine, scientific, severe, standard, stiff, stringent, thorough, vital ~
P: series of ~

TEXT
V: add to, alter, amend, annotate, change, check, correct, edit, produce, refer to, revise, supply ~
A: (un)abridged, academic, (in)accurate, authentic, concise, contemporary, detailed, full, illustrated, literary, original, set ~

THANKS
V: accept, express, give (one's), say, receive ~
A: genuine, heartfelt, sincere, warmest ~

THEATRE
A: amateur, classical, contemporary, experimental, fringe, legitimate, live, mainstream, street ~

THEME
V: adopt, be familiar with, borrow, choose, continue, deal with, develop, draw on, elaborate on, embroider, expand, follow, handle, introduce, invent, keep harping on, keep to, launch out into, outline, pick, pick up, pursue, recognise, repeat, revert to, select, stick to, take up, try out, use, work on, write about ~
V: ~ comes in, keeps repeating itself, occurs (again), runs through ...
A: accustomed, basic, central, clear, common, commonplace, constant, contemporary, contrasting, controversial, difficult, disturbing, dominant, dull, eternal, entertaining, familiar, fashionable, fascinating, favourite, graceful, haunting, historical, identical, important, interesting, main, major, minor, moving, novel, original, persistent, popular, principal, recurrent, recurring, rich, rousing, sentimental, serious, similar, strange, subsidiary, tricky, underlying, uplifting, unusual, weird, well-known, well-tried ~
P: variations on ~

THEORY

V: abandon, accept, adopt, advance, argue against, attack, base sth on, build, challenge, come down in favour of, confirm, construct, corroborate, defend, develop, discount, discredit, dispute, eliminate, espouse, evolve, examine, explode, expound, favour, fit in with, form, formulate, hold, invalidate, invent, launch, lend support to, outline, overthrow, overturn, present, propose, propound, (dis)prove, put forward, put ~ to the test, question, reverse, revise, rule out, shake, subscribe to, substantiate, suggest, support, test, try out, undermine, uphold, upset, vindicate, work out ~

V: ~ accounts for ... , applies to ... , breaks down, explains ... , fits the facts, gained favour/ground/support, holds good, implies ... , rests on ... , suggests ...

A: acceptable, adequate, alternative, bold, brilliant, cherished, coherent, contemporary, controversial, convenient, convincing, crack-pot, credible, current, daring, elaborate, fanciful, far-fetched, fashionable, imaginative, intriguing, latest, logical, major, modern, novel, original, pet, plausible, preconceived, preposterous, revolutionary, sophisticated, stimulating, (un)tenable, unique, unlikely, unorthodox, valid ~

P: basis of ~

THESIS

V: present, submit, (re)write ~

A: doctoral, excellent, Masters, PhD, poor, weak, well-presented, well-researched ~

THINKER

A: clear, creative, great, lateral, logical, muddled, original ~

THINKING

A: clear, fresh, hard, independent, lateral, logical, precise, quick, rapid, straight, wishful, woolly ~

THIRST

V: die of, quench, slake, suffer from, work up ~

A: raging, terrible, unquenchable ~

THOUGHT

V: accept, admit, be deep in, be lost in/sunk in, be tempted by, call for, devote ~ to ... , encourage, exercise, entertain, express, facilitate, give some ~ to ... , have, hinder, need, prevent, reject the ~ of ... , require, shudder at, stimulate ~

V: ~ alarmed (me), came into (my) head/mind, came to (me), crossed (my) mind, occurred to (me) that ... , rankled, unnerved (me)

A: advanced, anxious, brilliant, careful, clever, considerable, considered, deep, frightening, happy, hard, inspiring, intriguing, modern, passing, preliminary, profound, progressive, prolonged, radical, recurrent, serious, sobering, splendid, strange, sudden, tempting, upsetting, up-to-date, worrying ~

P: clarity of, food for, independence of, line of, pattern of, school of, train of ~

THOUGHTS

V: collect (your), dispel, gather (your), marshal (your), share (my/a few) ~

A: anxious, innermost, sad, sombre, stray, troubling, uneasy ~

THREAT

V: avoid, be alerted to/confronted with, be intimidated, be terrified by, carry out, combat, cope with, constitute, counter, counteract, deter, dispel, dodge, face, give into, head off, ignore, implement, issue, lift, live under, make, pay (no) attention/heed to, pose, present, receive, remove, repel, represent, resist, take ~ seriously, utter ~

V: ~ decreased, diminished, disappeared, fizzled out, hangs over sb, increased, looms, receded, remains, vanished

A: constant, continual, continuing, dangerous, deadly, death, dire, distinct, effective, emerging, empty, ever-present, explicit, external, fierce, frightening, genuine, grave, great, imminent, impending, implicit, implied, important, internal, loud, noisy, ominous, open, potential, real, serious, severe, significant, sole, strong, tremendous, veiled, violent ~

THUNDER
V: ~ boomed, reverberated, roared, rumbled
P: clap of, crash of, peal of, roll of ~

TIES (links)
V: create, destroy, develop, form, have, maintain, sever, strengthen, weaken ~
V: ~ became closer/stronger, link sb
A: close, friendly, strong ~

TIME
V: agree on, allocate, allot, arrange, begrudge, be pressed for, change, devote ~ to ... , fix, fritter away, gain, have, invest, kill, limit, lose, make a note of, mark, pass, play for, restrict, run out of, save, set, spare, specify, spend, take, take up, waste, while away ~
V: ~ dragged, elapsed, expired, flew, passed, ran out, was taken up with ... , went quickly/slowly
A: ample, certain, free, leisure, proper, set, spare, specific, sufficient ~
P: length of, march of, matter of, passage of, space of ~; living on borrowed ~

TIME (with *a/the*)
V: foresee, go through, have, long for, look back on/forward to, remember, spend ~
A: amusing, anxious, bewildering, busy, critical, delightful, depressing, difficult, dreadful, easy, entertaining, exciting, grim, gruelling, happy, hard, harrowing, horrible, marvellous, miserable, painful, (un)pleasant, rough, sad, trying, worrying, wretched ~
P: at the allotted/appointed ~

TIMES (circumstances)
V: be characteristic of, be typical of, experience, go through, have, live in, live through, long for, look back on, look forward to, recall, survive ~
A: affluent, dangerous, depressing, difficult, former, happy, hard, momentous, normal, past, prehistoric, prosperous, recent, troubled, worrying ~

TIMETABLE
V: consult, disrupt, draw up, follow, keep to, look sth up in, produce, set, upset, wreck ~
A: bus, busy, cramped, crowded, flexible, loose, railway, regular, rigid, strict, tight ~

TITLE
V: acquire, assert, claim, dispute, get, give up, have, inherit, possess, renounce ~
A: ancient, courtesy, hereditary, honorary, (un)official ~

TOLERANCE
V: display, show ~
A: admirable, benign, great, incredible ~

TOLL
V: exact, reduce, take ~
A: death, devastating, heavy, sad, tragic ~

TONE
V: adopt, alter, change, modify ~
A: affectionate, angry, apologetic, arrogant, avuncular, bullying, calm, cheerful, conciliatory, condescending, cynical, dry, emphatic, fatherly, flippant, friendly, gentle, gloomy, harsh, impartial, jocular, level, light, matter-of-fact, nasty, objective, ominous, patronizing, peremptory, petulant, plaintive, (un)pleasant, pompous, reflective, sarcastic, serious, sharp, sober, soothing, stern, strident, subdued, sulky, threatening, triumphant, urgent, welcoming ~

TOPIC
V: approach, avoid, bring up, broach, change, cover, embark on, deal with, develop, discuss, drop, dwell on, elaborate on, embark on, examine, go into, ignore, keep off/to, pursue, raise, return to, stick to, study, suggest, tackle, take up, touch on ~
A: absorbing, abstruse, awkward, boring, common, controversial, current, dangerous, difficult, dull, everyday, familiar, fascinating, fashionable, favourite, fresh, heavy, important, interesting, key, light, main, major, original, overworked, (un)pleasant, political, popular, principal, risky, safe, sensitive, sole, taboo, unlikely, vital ~
P: (main) ~ of conversation

TORTURE
V: employ, inflict, resort to, subject sb to, undergo, use ~
P: victims of ~

TOUCH (physical)
A: delicate, gentle, light, slight, soft, tender ~

TOUCH (feature)
A: attractive, bright, colourful, finishing, happy, interesting, personal, woman's ~

TOUR
V: conduct, go on, operate, organise ~
A: concert, conducted, guided, lecture, lightning, sightseeing, whirlwind ~

TOURISM
V: develop, promote ~
V: ~ is booming/flourishing/thriving

TOWN
V: ~ declined, flourished, grew (up), spread
A: ancient, (un)attractive, boom, busy, coastal, crowded, depressing, dilapidated, dormitory, dull, fortified, ghost, important, industrial, large, market, mediaeval, medium-sized, mining, modern, neighbouring, one-horse, picturesque, pleasant, pretty, prosperous, quaint (little), satellite, shanty, ugly ~
P: on the outskirts of ~; in the ~ centre

TRACE
V: discern, find, follow, leave, lose, pick up, see, show, wipe out ~
A: clear, distinct, faint, infinitesimal, obvious, slight, strong, visible ~

TRADE
V: build up, carry on, conduct, develop, encourage, engage in, foster, harm, help, look for, promote, restrict, ruin, spoil, stimulate, welcome ~
V: ~ declined, disappeared, grew, flourished, is bad/good/poor/slack/slow/sluggish/steady, picked up, prospered, shrank, stagnated, stopped
A: booming, brisk, busy, free, growing, healthy, illegal, illicit, lively, lucrative, mutual, overseas, profitable, prosperous, reciprocal, world ~
P: ~ agreement, association, deficit, directory, dispute, fair, figures, gap, mark, name, press, price, restrictions, secret, surplus, terms, union; control of, increase in, slump in, volume of ~

TRADE (job)
V: follow, have, learn, take up ~
A: ancient, dying, useful ~

TRADITION
V: abandon, abolish, adopt, break with, build up, carry on, continue, create, destroy, encourage, establish, follow, foster, give up, hand down, have, ignore, keep up, kill, maintain, neglect, observe, pass on, preserve, reject, respect, revive, stick to, turn one's back on, uphold ~

V: ~ dates back to ... , died out, disappeared, exists, goes back to ... , is (still) alive, lingers on, survives ~

A: accepted, age-old, ancient, cherished, classical, colourful, dead, dying, famous, folk, glorious, hallowed, living, local, long, old, oral, popular, powerful, rigid, sacred, strict, universal, vanishing, widespread ~

TRAFFIC

V: ban, be closed to, block, carry, control, cope with, direct, divert, follow, get lost in/stuck in, get through, halt, hold up, obstruct, reduce, regulate, slow down, speed up, stop ~

V: ~ built up, crawled, flowed, increased, is congested/stuck, moved, passed

A: busy, chaotic, congested, dense, fast, heavy, light, local, merging, moderate, one-way, slow-moving, through, well-behaved ~

P: ~ control, island, lights; control of, density of, intensity of ~

TRAGEDY

V: avert, bring about, cause, experience, heighten, increase, lead to, witness ~

V: ~ struck

A: great, impending, personal, terrible ~

TRAIN

V: board, catch, derail, get off/on, hold, leave, miss, take ~

V: ~ is approaching, arrived, departed, pulled in/out

A: commuter, (semi-)direct, express, freight, non-stop, slow, stopping, through ~

TRAINING

V: apply for, do, get, go through, provide ~, put ~ to use

A: basic, demanding, formal, full-/part-time, intensive, lengthy, rigorous ~

TRANSACTION

V: break off, conclude, conduct, make, stick to ~

A: binding, (il)legal, (un)profitable, shady, valid ~

TRANSFORMATION

V: see, undergo, witness ~

A: amazing, complete, personal, radical, total, unbelievable ~

TRANSITION

V: accomplish, bring, carry through, complete, effect, go through, hamper, hasten, herald, hinder, mark, oppose, plan, prepare for, prevent, propose, reject, resist, signal, speed up ~

A: abrupt, complete, early, easy, gradual, immediate, rapid, smooth, speedy, swift, sudden, traumatic, violent ~

P: period of ~

TRANSLATION

V: check, correct, do, go over, polish, produce, revise ~

A: close, direct, exact, excellent, faithful, free, literal, loose, poor, reliable, rough, satisfactory, word-for-word ~

TRAVELLER

A: experienced, frequent, indefatigable, intrepid, seasoned, unwary ~

TREASURE

V: come across, hoard, hunt for, loot, recover, salvage, seize, steal ~

A: ancient, buried, lost, priceless, sunken, valuable ~

TREATMENT

V: be exposed to, be given, be subject to, count on, expect, get, mete out, receive, suffer ~

A: atrocious, brutal, cruel, (un)fair, generous, harsh, humiliating, inhumane, kind, lenient, preferential, sensitive, shabby, shocking, soft, terrible, unexpected, unjust, unlawful ~

TREATMENT (medical)

V: administer, get, give, propose, provide, receive, recommend, respond to, try, undergo ~

V: ~ affected (me), did (me) good, failed, helped (me), worked

A: drastic, effective, hospital, out-patient, painful, radical, regular, (un)successful ~

P: outcome of, result of ~

TREATY

V: abide by, acknowledge, breach, break, conclude, confirm, draw up, endorse, enter into, infringe, initial, jeopardize, make, negotiate, ratify, repudiate, sign, tear up, violate, withdraw from, work out ~

V: ~ came into force ~

A: binding, peace, valid ~

P: breach of, ratification of, signing of ~

TREE

V: chop down, climb, cut down, fell, plant, prune, shelter under, uproot ~

V: ~ bore fruit, blossomed, fell down, grew, swayed

TREND

V: accelerate, accentuate, aggravate, analyse, anticipate, check, combat, counter, counteract, create, curb, defy, deplore, detect, encourage, establish, exaggerate, follow, halt, hasten, intensify, mirror, observe, oppose, overcome, perceive, recognise, reflect, resist, resume, reverse, see, set, slow, start, strengthen, study, sustain, underline, weaken ~

A: clear, common, continuing, dangerous, definite, distinct, downward, encouraging, fashionable, favourable, general, gradual, growing, incipient, increasing, marked, modern, noticeable, novel, obvious, perceptible, popular, powerful, real, recent, rising, slight, steady, strong, surprising, regrettable, underlying, undesirable, unfortunate, upward, (un)welcome, worrying ~

P: reversal of ~

TRIAL

V: adjourn, attend, bring sb to, come up for, conduct, face, fix, follow, go to, hold, postpone, preside over, put off, put sb on, rig, set, set up, stage, stand ~

A: early, fair, immediate, impartial, lengthy, mock, open, public, secret, sensational, show, spectacular, summary ~

P: ~ by jury; (can't) get a fair ~

TRIBE

V: belong to, lead ~

A: exotic, indigenous, lost, nomadic, primitive, remote, wandering, warlike ~

P: member of ~

TRIBUTE

V: express, offer, receive ~

A: extravagant, fitting, generous, glowing, heartfelt, hollow, ironic, lavish, moving, sincere, touching, warm ~

TRICK

V: foil, play ~ on sb, resort to, see through ~

V: ~ came off, failed, worked

A: clever, cunning, dirty, familiar, mean, mischievous, nasty, underhand ~

TRIP

V: arrange, cancel, embark on, go for/on, have, make, organise, plan, postpone, take ~

A: business, day, disastrous, enjoyable, extended, holiday, long, (un)pleasant, round-the-world, short, (un)successful, tiring, weekend ~

TRIUMPH

V: announce, celebrate, claim, detract from, end in, engineer, enjoy, experience, feel, glory in, have, proclaim, score ~

A: early, final, glorious, great, hollow, important, latest, notable, recent, resounding, short-lived, tremendous, well-deserved ~

TROOPS

V: bring in, commit, deploy, despatch, lead, review, send in, station, use, withdraw ~

A: armoured, crack, defeated, demoralised, ground, raw, (ir)regular, seasoned, shock, victorious ~

TROUBLE

V: anticipate, avert, avoid, be in, be involved in, cause, cope with, curb, deal with, encounter, experience, get into/out of, have, instigate, invite, land in, look for, make, spark off, start, steer clear of, stir up, suppress, take, wriggle out of ~

V: ~ arose, broke out, is brewing, came to a head, ended, ensued, flared up, loomed

A: potential, real, serious, sudden, violent ~

P: cause of, outbreak of, root of the, worth the ~; went to a great/good deal of ~; financial, serious *troubles*

TROUSERS

V: button up, do up, pull up, put on, take off, unbutton, unzip, zip up ~

A: baggy, flared, short, tight ~

TRUCE

V: agree on, arrange, break, call, declare, negotiate, violate, work out ~

A: uneasy ~

TRUST

V: betray, deserve, enjoy, forfeit, give, have, lose, place, put, spoil, strain, undermine ~

A: absolute, blind ~

P: abuse of, lack of ~

TRUTH

V: arrive at, ascertain, assess, believe, blurt out, bring out, check, close one's eyes to, conceal, confirm, confront sb with, convey, defend, demonstrate, deny, discover, disentangle, disguise, distort, doubt, establish, expose, express, face, find out, grasp, hide, ignore, keep to, pursue, question, reveal, search for, seek, speak, stick to, stretch, suppress, tell, uncover, value ~, vouch for ~ of

V: ~ came out, dawned on (me), prevailed

A: absolute, awful, bare, bitter, gospel, hard, harsh, important, incontrovertible, inescapable, literal, naked, obvious, plain, real, sad, sheer, sober, solemn, stark, uncomfortable, unvarnished, universal, unpalatable, unpleasant, unvarnished, unwelcome, whole ~

P: travesty of the ~; germ of, glimmer of, grain of, not one iota of, pursuit of, ring of ~; the ~ the whole ~ and nothing but the ~

TUNE

V: carry, compose, hum, sing, whistle, write ~

A: catchy, familiar, lively, memorable, merry, popular, simple, unforgettable, well-known ~

TURNING-POINT

V: arrive at, come to, pass, reach, signal ~

A: crucial, important, irreversible, significant ~

TYPE

V: belong to, choose, come across, define, denote, determine, deviate from, differentiate, distinguish, encounter, exemplify, follow, identify, recognise, represent, revert to, select, single out, specify, stick to ~

V: ~ (dis)appeared, has become extinct, died out, occurs, has vanished

A: antiquated, archaic, broad, common, distinct, exotic, familiar, fine, interesting, main, old-fashioned, out-of-date, particular, peculiar, quaint, rare, specific, standard, strange, traditional, (un)usual, unique, widespread, well-defined, well-known ~

P: classify sth into, segregate sth into *types*

TYRANNY

V: abolish, escape from, free sb from, put down, rebel against, rescue sb from, suffer under ~

P: overthrow of ~

U

ULTIMATUM

V: deliver, give, get, ignore, issue, present, receive, withdraw ~

UNCERTAINTY

V: add to, cause, dispel, express, get rid of, increase, intensify, lead to, relieve ~

V: ~ prevailed, surrounds sth

UNDERSTANDING

V: arrive at, be based on, bring about, come to, develop, promote, reach, rule out, seek, show, work towards ~

A: basic, better, broad, clear, complete, deep, firm, full, mutual, real, tacit, working ~

UNDERTAKING (scheme)

V: abandon, decide on, embark on, give up, take on ~

A: ambitious, colossal, dangerous, difficult, foolhardy, formidable, futile, hopeless, important, major, massive, noble, risky, serious, worthwhile ~

UNDERTAKING (promise)

V: break, carry out, fulfil, give, honour ~

A: secret, solemn ~

UNEMPLOYMENT

V: banish, bring down, cause, check, combat, conquer, contain, cope with, counteract, create, curb, cure, cut, deal with, ease, eliminate, find a cure for, give rise to, hold down, lead to, push up, reduce, relieve, tackle ~

V: ~ climbed, declined, doubled, escalated, got out of hand, grew, increased, occurs, persists, remains high/steady, rose, rocketed, soared, spiralled, stands at (2 million), went down/up

A: chronic, falling, high, large/small-scale, long-/short-term, low, mass, massive, mounting, permanent, record, rising, seasonal, serious, soaring, sustained, widespread ~

P: drop in, fall in, fight against, level of, rise of, tide of ~

UNION (trade union)

V: create, dissolve, form, join, outlaw, set up, split ~

V: ~ broke away, are holding a ballot

P: ~ leaders, members, officials

UNITY

V: achieve, appeal for, break, call for, destroy, endanger, enhance, harm, jeopardize, lead to, live together in, lose, maintain, preserve, promote, protect, reinforce, safeguard, shatter, threaten, undermine, win, work for ~

A: complete ~

UNIVERSE
V: create, explore ~
A: alternative, expanding, known, orderly ~
P: centre of, origin of, secrets of ~

UNIVERSITY
V: apply to, attend, be at, be thrown out of, establish, found, go (up) to, leave, start ~
A: ancient, famous, modern, prestigious, top ~

UNREST
V: quell, spark off ~
P: wave of (violent) ~

UPBRINGING
A: careful, cloistered, close, conservative, (un)conventional, disciplined, harsh, narrow, ordinary, puritanical, religious, restricted, strict ~

UPHEAVAL
V: cause, end in, lead to, prevent ~
A: great, internal, political, social, tremendous ~

UPRISING
V: commemorate, crush, lead, lead to, organise, put down, quell, start, suppress, take part in ~
V: ~ broke out, collapsed, took place
A: armed, full-scale, heroic, peasant, popular, violent ~

URGE
V: awaken, be driven by/moved by/prompted by/tempted by, control, experience, feel, give in to, give way to, have, overcome, repress, resist, satisfy, stifle, succumb to, suppress ~
V: ~ came over (me), made me ...
A: faint, fatal, fierce, generous, instinctive, irresistible, natural, overpowering, powerful, primitive, strong, sudden, uncontrollable, violent ~

URGENCY
V: realise, stress ~
A: great, special, utmost ~
P: matter of (great) ~; the ~ of the situation

USAGE
V: abandon, adhere to, adopt, follow, go along with, go by, keep to ~
A: accepted, common, current, general, normal, official, traditional, well-established ~

USE
V: abandon, abhor, advise, advocate, authorise, avoid, ban, be against, be in favour of, bring sth into, complain about, continue, criticise, encourage, ensure, extend, give up, justify, object to, oppose, permit, plan, prevent, prohibit, promote, recommend, reject, restrict, secure, stop, threaten ~
A: adroit, appropriate, common, constant, constructive, continuous, controversial, correct, current, defensive, deft, devastating, discerning, domestic, effective, efficient, everyday, excessive, extravagant, familiar, frequent, future, general, generous, habitual, heavy, imaginative, immediate, immoral, important, industrial, ingenious, iniquitous, intermittent, internal, irresponsible, large-scale, lavish, liberal, limited, main, major, medical, military, moderate, narrow, obvious, odd, ordinary, personal, popular, practical, principal, profligate, (im)proper, real, reckless, (ir)regular, resourceful, ridiculous, ruthless, secondary, secret, senseless, sensible, sophisticated, special, standard, traditional, unauthorised, unique, universal, unorthodox, unusual, wide, widespread, wise ~
P: ban/limitations/regulations/restrictions on the ~ of

V

VACUUM
V: create, fill, leave, live in, produce ~
A: perfect, total, virtual ~

VALUE
V: acquire, add to, admit, agree on, appreciate, arrive at, assess, attach, be aware of, enhance, establish, exceed, fix, get, give, have, hold, judge, keep, lose, maintain, overestimate, overrate, place, play down, preserve, put a ~ on sth, realise, reckon, recognise, reduce, underestimate ~
V: ~ accrued, declined, diminished, fell, grew, remains constant/steady, went down/up
A: approximate, current, exact, face, full, great, incalculable, inestimable, intrinsic, market, nominal, precise, real, slight, tremendous, true ~

VALUES (standards)
V: believe in, cherish, defend, have, hold, keep to, recognise, reject, respect, subscribe to ~
A: basic, family, fundamental, idealistic, lasting, materialistic, moral, spiritual, traditional ~
P: set of, system of ~

VARIETY
V: add, explore, lend, offer, provide, seek ~
A: amazing, bewildering, dazzling, enormous, extraordinary, fascinating, great, immense, infinite, large, profuse, rich, tremendous, weird, wide ~

VEGETABLES
V: boil, chop, dice, grow, stir-fry ~
A: crisp, fresh, frozen, green, home-grown, mixed, organic, raw, root, seasonal, steamed ~

VENGEANCE
V: exact, seek, swear, take, vow, wreak ~
A: cruel, full, horrible, swift, terrible ~
P: thirst for ~

VERDICT
V: accept, agree on, announce, appeal against, arrive at, bring in, consider, deliver, give, hand down, issue, oppose, overturn, proclaim, produce, pronounce, question, reach, read out, seek, uphold ~
A: confident, fair, final, majority, open, questionable, sensational, surprise, unanimous ~

VERSION
V: accept, believe, bring out, cast doubt on, challenge, come forward with/up with, complete, create, develop, get, give out, hear, invent, offer, peddle, piece together, play, popularise, produce, put about/forward, put on, put out, substantiate, use ~
V: ~ agrees with ...
A: abbreviated, abridged, acceptable, accepted, amended, bowdlerised, colourful, concise, condensed, contradictory, credible, customised, current, definitive, distorted, draft, edited, exaggerated, expanded, false, final, garbled, genuine, highly-coloured, improved, modern, novel, one-sided, original, persuasive, pirate, plausible, politically correct, popular, preliminary, primitive, proper, revised, shortened, simplified, special, straightforward, tailor-made, true, unique, updated, up-to-date, watered-down ~

VESTIGE
A: last, last remaining ~

VICTIM

V: attack, choose, destroy, find, finish off, go after, harm, kill, lure, mark sb out as, pursue, seek, stalk, trail ~

A: chance, easy, helpless, inevitable, innocent, intended, pathetic, potential, sole, unfortunate, unintended, unsuspecting, unwitting ~

VICTORY

V: be assured of, bring off, celebrate, claim, consolidate, declare, end in, follow up, gain, go on to, grasp, hail, lead to, score ~ over sb, secure, seize, snatch, spearhead, throw away, win ~, wrest ~ from sb

V: ~ eluded sb, was within (their) grasp

A: amazing, brilliant, certain, clear, clear-cut, convincing, costly, decisive, definite, empty, famous, glorious, great, hard-fought/-won, hollow, landslide, lasting, major, massive, narrow, outright, overwhelming, painful, Pyrrhic, renowned, resounding, short-lived, splendid, stunning, substantial, surprise, sweeping, total, ultimate, unexpected, unprecedented ~

VIEW

V: accept, adopt, advocate, (dis)agree with, argue, bear out, be opposed to, canvass, challenge, change, cling to, come round to, confirm, corroborate, defend, dismiss, dispute, disregard, dissent from, echo, encourage, endorse, espouse, expound, express, foster, give up, go along with, have, hold, incline to/towards, justify, modify, oppose, overcome, preclude, promote, put (forward), quarrel with, reach, reflect, reinforce, reiterate, reject, repudiate, resist, share, stick to, strengthen, subscribe to, substantiate, support, sympathise, take, uphold ~

V: ~ emerged, gained ground, is based on ...

A: acceptable, balanced, benign, bleak, broad, broadminded, candid, caustic, comforting, (un)common, commonsense, consensus, constructive, contemporary, contentious, controversial, conventional, cool, critical, cynical, detached, different, dim, dispassionate, dissenting, distorted, erroneous, (un)fair, false, firmly-held, fresh, frivolous, general, generous, gloomy, grim, harsh, helpful, heretical, honest, independent, jaundiced, lenient, level-headed, liberal, magnanimous, minority, mistaken, naive, normal, objective, obscure, old-fashioned, one-sided, opposite, optimistic, outrageous, overall, perverse, pessimistic, philosophical, poor, popular, pragmatic, predominant, preposterous, prevailing, prevalent, primitive, radical, realistic, reasonable, revolutionary, ridiculous, romantic, sensible, simplistic, smug, sober, standard, stereotyped, strange, superficial, surprising, tentative, unacceptable, unanimous, unequivocal, unique, universal, untenable, unusual, wide, widespread ~

VIEW (physical)

V: block, cut off, give, have, obscure, offer, restrict, spoil ~

A: beautiful, bird's eye, breathtaking, panoramic, restricted, splendid, superb, uninterrupted ~

VIEWS (opinions)

V: air, ascertain, discover, divulge, elicit, enquire into, exchange, express, have, hold, make ~ plain, obtain, parade, respect, solicit, spell out ~

V: ~ carry weight, diverged

A: authoritarian, (un)biased, broad, clear, complex, conflicting, confusing, conservative, contradictory, decided, deplorable, dissenting, divergent, dogmatic, eccentric, enlightened, explicit, extreme, foolish, forthright, frank, identical, irreconcilable, liberal, lucid, mistaken, moderate, naive, narrow, old-fashioned, opposing, (un)orthodox, outdated, out-of-date, outmoded, outspoken, plain, progressive, radical, reactionary, real, romantic, sceptical, sensible, sound, strange, strict, strong, tenacious, tolerant, wide-ranging ~

VIOLENCE

V: abhor, avert, avoid, become accustomed to, bring ~ under control, combat, condemn, condone, contain, control, crack down on, curb, deal with, defeat, degenerate into, denounce, deplore, eliminate, employ, end, erupt into, incite sb to, inflame, meet, oppose, precipitate, prevent, provoke, put down, reduce, renounce, resort to, stamp out, suppress, tackle, threaten, use ~

V: ~ broke out, died down, erupted, escalated, flared up, got out of hand, got worse, increased, spread, subsided, was confined to ...

A: communal, continuing, endemic, excessive, habitual, isolated, local, mindless, mounting, prolonged, random, renewed, sporadic ~

P: act of, catalogue of, eruption of, outbreak of, spiral of, use of, victim of, wave of ~

VIRTUE

V: display, exemplify, extol, possess ~

A: admirable, chief, common, great, much-prized, old-fashioned, rare, remarkable, solid, traditional, valuable ~

P: paragon of ~

VISA

V: apply for, cancel, deny sb, extend, get, grant, issue, overstay (your), receive, renew ~

A: entry, exit, transit, valid ~

VISION

V: conjure up, create, have, pursue, see ... in, share ~

V: ~ (dis)appeared, came true, faded, haunted sb, materialised, vanished, was realised

A: apocalyptic, blurred, bright, clear, clear-cut, clouded, confused, convincing, defective, distorted, double, elusive, excellent, far-sighted, frightening, glorious, great, hazy, ideal, idealistic, impaired, inspired, messianic, misleading, mysterious, narrow, nightmare, normal, optimistic, peripheral, perfect, poor, realistic, remarkable, restricted, romantic, simple, strange, tempting, tunnel, uncompromising, unrealistic, wide, wonderful ~

P: loss of ~

VISIT

V: announce, arrange, call off, cancel, cut short, pay, postpone, put off, return, schedule, welcome ~

A: brief, ceremonial, courtesy, disappointing, enjoyable, exciting, flying, formal, friendly, fruitful, impending, (un)official, pleasant, pointless, prolonged, return, (un)scheduled, state, stormy, successful, unexpected, useful, (un)welcome ~

VISITOR

A: (in)frequent, mysterious, regular, surprise, unexpected, weekend, (un)welcome ~

VISTA

V: ~ opens out before sb

A: attractive, broad, endless, imposing, open, pleasant, wide ~

VOCABULARY

V: build (up), develop, employ, enlarge, expand, use ~

A: basic, enormous, extensive, huge, limited, massive, restricted, rich, specialist, technical ~

VOICE

V: change, have, lose, lower, raise, shout at the top of (your) ~

V: ~ broke, changed, cracked, dropped, trembled

A: aggressive, angry, anxious, arrogant, booming, calm, decided, deep, distinct, distorted, dull, failing, faint, faltering, faraway, firm, flat, (un)friendly, frightened, fruity, gentle, grating, gruff, harsh, hesitant, high-pitched, hoarse, hollow, husky, insincere, level, loud, low, monotonous, nasty, patient, quiet, raucous, rich, rough, severe, sharp, shrill, small, soft, soothing, squeaky, (un)steady, stern, strange, strident, strong, subdued, tense, threatening, thunderous, tiny, trembling, warm ~

P: tone of ~; at the top of (your) ~; the ~ of experience

VOTE

V: be entitled to, call for, cancel, cast, count, count on sb's, get sb's, give sb, have, influence, lose, overturn, pass, propose, put sth to, receive, record, secure, swing, switch, take, win ~

V: ~ shifted, slumped, was split

A: big, casting, close, crucial, deciding, decisive, majority, massive, nationwide, overwhelming, popular, unanimous ~

P: ~ of (no) confidence

VOTES

V: ask for, bring in, canvass for, capture, count, get, lose, receive, switch, win ~

VOTERS

V: antagonise, attract, bribe, canvass, influence, intimidate, put off, win, win over, woo ~

A: disaffected, floating, loyal ~

VOW

V: break, keep, make, take ~

P: ~ of celibacy, of silence

W

WAGE

V: bring in, earn, get, pay ~

A: decent, excessive, fair, high, honest, living, low, minimum, miserly, modest, nominal, proper, regular, ridiculous, small, steady, weekly ~

P: ~ packet, levels

WAGES

V: cut, demand, depress, earn, freeze, get, guarantee, increase, keep down, lower, negotiate, pay, push up, put up, raise, restrain, withhold ~

V: ~ fell, remained level, rose, shot up, went down/up

WALK

A: brisk, country, leisurely, lonely, long, pleasant, quiet, short, solitary ~

WALL

V: build, climb, demolish, erect, knock down/through, paint, paper, put up, strip, tear down ~

A: bare, blank, crumbling, damp, high, low, retaining, solid, (dry-)stone, supporting, thick ~

WAR

V: avoid, bring ~ to an end, cause, conduct, declare, end, enter, fight (in), get through, go to, lead to, live through, lose, make, put an end to, precipitate, prevent, prolong, provoke, resort to, spark off, start, stop, survive, take part in, wage, win ~

V: ~ broke out, came to an end, dragged on, ended, erupted, escalated, raged, spread, went on

A: all-out, civil, conventional, cruel, devastating, disastrous, full-scale, global, guerrilla, holy, imminent, just, limited, nuclear, open, phoney, (un)successful, total, world ~

P: ~ of attrition; aftermath of, brink of, conduct of, declaration of, horrors of, outbreak of, state of, theatre of ~

WARFARE
A: biological, chemical, conventional, gang, guerrilla, jungle, modern, psychological ~
WARNING
V: deliver, dismiss, disregard, do sth without, get, give sb, heed, ignore, issue, pay attention to, receive, reinforce, require, send, shout, take heed of ~
V: ~ came too late, failed to stop ... , fell on deaf ears, had no effect, went unheeded
A: adequate, advance, awesome, blunt, clear, dire, early, effective, final, forcible, frantic, powerful, previous, serious, solemn, stern, sufficient, timely, written ~
P: (we) had very little ~ of
WASTE
V: abolish, cause, cut down on, cut out, detect, eliminate, eradicate, put a stop to, reduce ~
A: complete, dreadful, foolish, incredible, needless, senseless, sheer, terrible, unnecessary ~
WATCH
V: ~ gained/lost five minutes etc, is fast/slow, keeps (good) time, has stopped, ticked
A: designer, digital, pocket, quartz, shockproof, waterproof, wrist ~
WATER
V: boil, contaminate, distil, draw, drink, filter, pollute, pour, purify, run, sip, soften, spill, splash, sprinkle, squirt, sterilise ~
V: ~ boiled, bubbled, dripped, evaporated, flowed, froze, gushed, leaked, overflowed, poured, ran, soaked ... , sparkled, splashed, surged, trickled
A: boiling, brackish, (crystal-)clear, deep, fast-flowing, fresh, hard, lukewarm, mineral, muddy, murky, running, salt, shallow, soft, sparkling, stagnant, tepid ~
WAVES
V: ~ broke, came over/crashed onto/engulfed/pounded/swallowed ... , subsided
A: big, giant, huge, mountainous ~
P: tidal *wave*; on the crest of a *wave*
WAY (method of doing sth)
V: affect, adopt, choose, demonstrate, devise, discover, explain, explore, find, follow, have, indicate, invent, lead, look for, reject, show, take, use, work out ~
A: acceptable, amusing, appropriate, bold, careful, charming, cheapest, considerate, convenient, cost-effective, dangerous, devious, difficult, (in)direct, discriminating, easy, easy-going, effective, efficient, fair, funny, haphazard, honest, ingenious, interesting, long, main, neat, normal, novel, off-putting, odd, ordinary, particular, persuasive, practical, principal, proper, quick, ridiculous, right, risky, roundabout, sensible, short, silly, simple, standard, straightforward, strange, thoughtless, traditional, useful, (un)usual, violent, wrong ~
P: get (your) own ~, variety of *ways*
WAY (possibility, with *the*)
V: open ~ for ..., pave/smooth ~ for, point the ~ to
WAYS (habits)
A: disgusting, eccentric, mysterious, old-fashioned, strange ~
WEAKNESS
V: have, rectify, remedy, reveal, show, suffer from ~
A: apparent, basic, crucial, distinct, essential, fatal, fundamental, glaring, great, inherent, marked, obvious, regrettable, serious, structural, unfortunate ~
WEALTH
V: accumulate, acquire, amass, bring, come into, confiscate, flaunt one's, inherit, possess ~
A: enormous, fabulous, fantastic, great, new-found, tremendous, untapped, untold, vast ~
P: ~ tax; redistribution of ~

WEAPONS
V: accumulate, ban, brandish, bristle with, carry, conceal, decommission, employ, give up, improve, invent, issue, manufacture, put aside, release, smuggle, stockpile, supply, surrender, throw down, use ~
A: awesome, biological, chemical, conventional, costly, dangerous, deadly, lethal, modern, nuclear, offensive, primitive, short-/long-range, sophisticated, strategic, tactical, useful ~
P: array of, arsenal of, assortment of, cache of, proliferation of, stock of, stockpile of ~

WEATHER
V: brave, depend on, enjoy, expect, experience, face, forecast, have, meet, predict, rely on, run into ~
V: ~ affected (me), is approaching, changed, deteriorated, got better/worse, improved, is on the way, lasted
A: agreeable, appalling, atrocious, awful, beautiful, changeable, cold, deplorable, disappointing, dreadful, dry, fabulous, fair, fine, foul, freakish, horrible, hot, ideal, inclement, indifferent, mild, nasty, oppressive, (un)pleasant, terrible, typical, unpredictable, warm ~

WELCOME
V: arrange, be certain of/sure of, extend a ~ to sb, find, get, give sb, organise, outstay (your), overstay (your), prepare, receive ~
A: ceremonial, cheerful, cordial, (un)enthusiastic, frosty, great, impressive, magnificent, moving, official, proper, rapturous, real, rousing, strange, tremendous, tumultuous, warm ~

WEIGHT
V: carry (a lot of), gain, lose, put on, take off ~
V: ~ dropped off, fell off
A: average, excess, ideal, normal ~
P: ~ problem

WHEEL
V: oil, rotate, spin, turn ~
V: ~ locked, rotated, spun, turned

WHIM
V: do sth on, give in to, gratify, pander to, satisfy ~
A: idle, sudden ~

WILL
V: bend, break, impose one's, strengthen, undermine ~
A: implacable, iron, strong ~
P: ~ power; (sheer) force of ~

WIND
V: ~ abated, blew, blew up, changed, died down, disappeared, dropped, freshened, got up, howled, increased in force, picked up, subsided, veered, went down
A: biting, favourable, following, gale-force, gentle, gusty, icy, light, moderate, north, northerly,/easterly etc, prevailing, slight, soft, strong, trade ~
P: breath of, gust of ~

WINE
V: bottle, make, produce, taste ~
A: classic, crisp, cooking, country, dessert, (medium-)dry, fruit, fruity, full-bodied, German/Italian etc, heavy, home-made, house, light, mulled, New World, red, robust, rosé, rough, smooth, sparkling, (medium-)sweet, table, vintage, white ~

WINNER
A: clear, eventual, final, indisputable, outright, overall, potential, sure, ultimate, unexpected ~

WINTER
A: bitter, bleak, cruel, hard, harsh, long, severe, terrible, tough ~

WISDOM
V: challenge, doubt, question ~
A: conventional, worldly ~

WISH
V: conceal, deny, entertain, express, feel, fulfil, get, grant, have, make, respect, satisfy, share ~
V: ~ came true
A: dearest, declared, dying, fervent, genuine, last, secret, strong ~
P: (I) haven't the slightest ~ to ...

WISHES
V: act contrary to, act in accordance with, comply with, disregard, ignore, impose ~ on sb, interpret, make ~ clear, meet, oppose, override, pander to ~

WIT
V: display, show ~
A: acid, caustic, razor-sharp, ready ~

WITHDRAWAL
V: carry out, complete, make ~
A: complete, humiliating, mass, orderly, panic-stricken, rapid, strategic, swift, tactical ~

WITNESS
V: badger, (re-)call, dismiss, (cross-)examine, discredit, interrogate, interview, lead, question, swear in ~
A: character, excellent, expert, hopeless, hostile, key, poor, reliable, trustworthy ~

WORDS
V: be at a loss for, choose, distort sb's, exchange, find, juggle with, lack, pick, play on/with, use ~
A: angry, appropriate, apt, brave, choice, eloquent, empty, fighting, harsh, kind, meaningless, proper, right, sharp, soft, stirring, suitable, sympathetic, well-chosen ~
P: (he) didn't mince his ~

WORK
V: arrive at, be engaged in, be in/out of, be off, carry out, come home from, complete, concentrate on, criticise, devote oneself to, do, embark on, find, fling oneself into one's, get, get to, have, involve, leave, (dis)like, look for, lose, need, neglect, produce, put ~ into sth, require, resign from, resume, seek, start (on), tackle, take on, take time off, take (up) ~
A: backbreaking, badly/highly/poorly paid, boring, careful, casual, competent, conscientious, creative, dull, easy, effective, efficient, essential, excellent, exhausting, extraordinary, first-class, free-lance, full-/part-time, gruelling, hack, hard, heavy, important, intensive, interesting, intricate, laborious, light, manual, menial, meticulous, (un)necessary, original, outstanding, painstaking, patchy, piece, polished, real, regular, repetitive, responsible, routine, seasonal, shoddy, sloppy, solid, sophisticated, sterling, strenuous, stupendous, superfluous, time-consuming, tiring, tremendous, useful, valuable ~
P: capacity for, piles of, progress of ~

WORK (artistic, literary, musical with *a/the*)
V: admire, alter, ban, censor, compose, conduct, create, criticise, damage, display, edit, exhibit, hang, improvise, (dis)like, perform, play, polish, produce, unveil, vandalise, write ~
V: ~ went on show

A: accomplished, avant-garde, beautiful, breathtaking, classic, classical, competent, contemporary, controversial, creative, difficult, early, erudite, excellent, extraordinary, first-class, gloomy, great, handsome, idiosyncratic, important, impressive, influential, innovative, inspired, inspiring, interesting, inventive, late, lengthy, literary, lyrical, magnificent, major, (im)mature, melodious, minor, misunderstood, modern, momentous, monumental, moving, mysterious, naive, notable, outstanding, peculiar, principal, (un)publishable, radical, (un)readable, scholarly, seminal, shocking, short, sophisticated, splendid, stupendous, tedious, transitional, tremendous, tuneful, unique, valuable ~

P: ~ of art; his/her life's ~; the *works* of (Shakespeare)

WORKERS

V: employ, lay off, make ~ redundant, reinstate, sack, suspend, take on ~

WORLD

V: be transported into, belong to, (re)build, circumnavigate, create, destroy, enter, inhabit, plan, plan for, save, see, shut out, take over, travel ~

V: ~ collapsed, disintegrated, vanished

A: aesthetic, austere, brutal, busy, (fast-)changing, chaotic, circumscribed, civilised, closed, cruel, dangerous, desolate, different, divided, dream, everyday, fairy-tale, fantastic, fantasy, frivolous, harsh, hostile, ideal, magic, make-believe, modern, narrow, natural, new, orderly, outside, peace-loving, (im)perfect, philistine, private, protected, real, remote, secret, secretive, shadowy, small, strange, war-torn, western, whole ~

P: creation of, end of, four corners of ~

WORRY

V: avoid, cause ~

A: constant, incessant, persistent, unnecessary ~

WORRIES

V: be beset by, cope with, deal with, forget, have, put (your) ~ behind (you), suppress ~

A: dreadful, growing, nagging, niggling, serious ~

WOUND

V: attend to, cauterise, clean, dress, heal, inflict, receive, recover from, stitch, sterilise ~

V: ~ festered, got better, healed, opened up

A: bullet, deep, difficult, fatal, gaping, gunshot, knife, lasting, mortal, painful, permanent, self-inflicted, serious, severe, stab, superficial ~

WOUND (figurative)

V: deal sb, get over, give, heal, inflict, soften, suffer ~

A: lasting, painful, permanent, serious ~

WRITER

A: award-winning, brilliant, budding, dissident, distinguished, eminent, famous, (non-)fiction, freelance, gifted, little-known, obscure, professional, prolific, promising, skilled, sophisticated, struggling, talented, well-known ~

Y

YEAR

V: begin, cover, have, last for, lose, make up for, mark, miss, spend, take ~

V: ~ passed, slipped past, started off

A: academic, busy, calendar, coming, crowded, current, difficult, dreadful, entire, eventful, exciting, final, financial, fiscal, following, full, heavy, important, last, leap, memorable, momentous, next, past, preceding, present, previous, prosperous, record, (un)satisfactory, school, (un)successful, tax, vintage, whole ~

YEARS

V: last, look back on, look forward to, make up for, pass, span, spend, take ~

V: ~ follow one after the other, fly past, go by, roll on, slip past

A: advanced, advancing, barren, childhood, coming, consecutive, creative, dangerous, declining, early, eventful, fertile, formative, former, fruitful, future, happy, later, lean, lost, middle, past, post-/pre-war, previous, productive, recent, tender, turbulent, twilight, useful, wasted ~

P: passage of ~; the best ~ of (my) life

YIELD

V: expect, get, give, improve, increase, obtain, produce, provide, reduce ~

A: annual (monthly etc), average, bumper, disappointing, encouraging, fair, fine, good, high, low, normal, poor, (un)satisfactory ~

P: a ~ of (7%)

YOUTH

V: idle away, look back on, pass, spend, waste ~

A: carefree, early, (un)happy, lost, misspent ~

Z

ZEAL

V: dampen, lose, maintain, match ~

V: ~ diminished

A: admirable, commendable, crusading, customary, great, missionary, mounting, old-fashioned, patriotic, religious, revolutionary, true ~

ZONE

V: approach, avoid, delineate, designate, differentiate, enlarge, enter, establish, extend, fence off, guard, keep out of, mark (off), occupy, patrol, reach, set up ~

A: adjacent, border, buffer, central, contiguous, danger, demilitarised, exclusion, extensive, forbidden, inner, large, neutral, (un)occupied, outer, prohibited, restricted, safe, time, undefined, war ~

THE ADVERB SECTION

Using the adverb section

This section helps you to add one-word adverbs – *extremely, carefully* – and multi-word adverbial expressions – *to and fro, in good faith* – to verbs and adjectives.

Place of adverbs

Adverbial expressions almost always follow the verb – *agree with some reluctance*. Single adverbs usually follow the verb – *drive dangerously*. Sometimes they either can or must come before the verb – *I strongly suggest ..., We sincerely wish ..., I hardly know what to think*. The lists show you the most usual position.

Adverbs of time and place

There are an enormous number of adverbs and adverbials which can be used with many different verbs.

Adverbs of time   I met/rang/told her – *yesterday/last week/the other day*.
Adverbs of place   We drove/hurried/wandered – *back/into town/down to the beach*.

Some adverbs can be used to make almost any adjective stronger or weaker:

   a bit/rather/very/quite different, difficult, dangerous

You probably know many of these already so we do not list examples like these. To help you choose the best adverb when, for example, you are writing an essay, we only include the strongest and most frequent collocations.

Adverbs of manner

These words – *carefully, quickly* – and expressions – *in detail* – explain how the action was done. There are some adverbs of manner which can occur with many different verbs:

   He spoke/walked/explained/parked *quickly*. (but not *He waited *quickly*.)

We do not list these general words, but only strong collocations of the verb.

Modifiers

There is a special group of adverbs which are used to make adjectives stronger or weaker. The most common of these (see above) can be used with a huge number of adjectives. Some others – *completely, totally, utterly, relatively, comparatively* – can be used with many gradable adjectives, but some collocations are more common than others. The lists guide you to what is most probable. Remember many adjectives are ungradable when used literally, but are gradable when used metaphorically.

A

ABANDON
abandon sb/sth altogether, completely, totally, utterly
hastily, reluctantly, subsequently, suddenly *abandon*
ABANDONED
completely, totally, utterly *abandoned*
ABLE TO
hardly, perfectly, scarcely *able to ...*
ABSENT
conspicuously, mysteriously, noticeably, rarely, strangely *absent*
ABSORBED
completely, thoroughly, totally *absorbed* by/with sth
ABSORBING
completely, totally *absorbing*
ABSURD
absolutely, clearly, completely, patently, totally *absurd*
ABUSE
abuse sb cruelly, shamefully
constantly, habitually *abuse*
ACCEPT (a gift)
accept sth eagerly, gladly, graciously, gratefully, humbly, reluctantly, willingly
ACCEPT (a decision)
accept sth cheerfully, grudgingly, philosophically, reluctantly, tacitly, tentatively, unconditionally, unhesitatingly, with a good grace, without question
wholeheartedly *accept*
ACCEPT (believe)
accept sth automatically, uncritically, unquestioningly, unreservedly, without question
cheerfully, readily, tacitly, tentatively, uncritically, unhesitatingly, wholeheartedly *accept*
ACCEPTABLE
mutually, perfectly, totally, widely *acceptable*
ACCOMPLISH
accomplish sth easily, in record time, smoothly, successfully, without much trouble
ACCUMULATE
accumulate easily, gradually, over a long period (of time), over the years, steadily, systematically, rapidly
ACCURATE
amazingly, consistently, extremely, incredibly, insufficiently, remarkably, not strictly, surprisingly, totally, unbelievably *accurate*
ACCUSED
falsely, repeatedly, rightly, unjustly, wrongfully *accused* of sth
ACHIEVE
achieve sth easily, effortlessly, somehow, with difficulty, with great effort
ACKNOWLEDGE
acknowledge gratefully, immediately, promptly
finally, freely, fully, openly, privately, publicly, readily, reluctantly *acknowledge* sth

ACQUIRE
acquire sth dishonestly, by accident, by chance, fraudulently, (il)legally, recently

ACQUIRED
newly, recently *acquired*

ACT
act cautiously, correctly, decisively, fast, foolishly, freely, hastily, (dis)honestly, honourably, illegally, impulsively, independently, in good faith, in haste, instinctively, promptly, quickly, (un)reasonably, (ir)responsibly, sensibly, strangely, swiftly, unconstitutionally, under duress, unethically, unilaterally, unwisely

> **ACT**
> Verbs which describe an action – for example, *act, smile, walk* – can be used with many different adverbs of manner which tell you how the person did the action. You can 'walk' *thoughtfully, carefully, distractedly*. These collocations are correct, but are not strong enough or frequent enough to be listed here. To help you with questions you may have when, for example, writing an essay, we include only the most useful collocations.

ADD
add as an afterthought, flippantly, hastily, hopefully, jokingly, quickly, thoughtfully
add appreciably, slightly, substantially to sth

> **ADD**
> *Add* is similar to other verbs which describe how we speak, for example, *answer, speak, reply*. Because they also describe an action, they collocate, like *act* above, with many different adverbs of manner.

ADDICTED
hopelessly, strongly *addicted* to sth

ADEQUATE
barely, hardly, perfectly, *adequate*

ADHERE
adhere closely, strictly to sth

ADJUST
adjust automatically, easily, effortlessly, smoothly

ADJUSTED
automatically, easily, quickly, soon *adjusted*

ADMIRE
admire sb enormously, greatly, secretly, tremendously
genuinely, greatly *admire*

ADMIRED
greatly, secretly, widely *admired* (for sth)

ADMIT
admit sth afterwards, at once, straightaway
cheerfully, finally, frankly, freely, grudgingly, honestly, openly, readily, reluctantly, tacitly *admit* sth

ADORNED
lavishly, richly *adorned*

ADVANCE
advance carefully, cautiously, fearlessly, inexorably, quickly, rapidly, slowly, steadily, step-by-step, warily

ADVISE
seriously, strongly *advise* sb to do sth

ADVISED
badly, ill-, well-*advised*

AFFECT
affect adversely, considerably, (in)directly, greatly, significantly

AFFECTED
adversely, badly, deeply, (in)directly, greatly, not remotely, profoundly, seriously, severely, significantly, strongly, visibly *affected* by sth

AFFECTIONATE
openly *affectionate* towards sb

AFFIRM
definitely, repeatedly, strongly, wholeheartedly *affirm* (that) sth

AFFLICTED
badly, seriously, severely *afflicted* with/by (an illness)

AFFORD
ill-, hardly, scarcely, well-*afford* sth/to do sth

AGE
age prematurely, rapidly

AGREE
agree (un)conditionally, enthusiastically, eventually, reluctantly, wholeheartedly to do sth
agree to do sth at once, in the end, straightaway
absolutely, (not) /completely/ fully, entirely, rarely, readily *agree*
not *agree* at all that ...
I don't altogether *agree* with (you)

AGREED
unanimously *agreed*

ALLOCATE
allocate equitably, fairly

ALTER
alter a great deal, completely, dramatically, fundamentally, (very) little, out of all recognition, radically, slightly, substantially, totally

ALTERNATE
alternate rapidly, regularly

AMAZED
absolutely, totally, truly, utterly *amazed*

AMAZING
absolutely, truly, utterly *amazing*

AMEND
amend extensively, radically, slightly, substantially

AMUSED
easily, highly *amused*

AMUSING
extremely, highly *amusing*

ANALYSE
analyse sth carefully, closely, exhaustively, in detail, objectively, systematically, thoroughly

ANNOUNCE
announce sth (in)formally, officially, proudly, publicly, unexpectedly, with great pleasure, with great satisfaction

ANNOYED
extremely *annoyed* (by sth/with sb)

ANNOYING
extremely *annoying*

ANSWER
answer (sb/sth) at length, bluntly, confidently, curtly, defiantly, fully, in detail, in full, hesitantly, politely, truthfully

> **ANSWER**
> *Answer* is similar to other verbs which describe how we speak, for example, *add, speak*. They also describe an action, so they collocate with many different adverbs of manner.

ANTAGONISTIC
privately, publicly, openly, violently *antagonistic* to sb/sth

ANTICIPATE
cleverly, confidently, fully *anticipate* sth

ANTICIPATED
eagerly, keenly *anticipated*

ANXIOUS
extremely, morbidly, over-, terribly *anxious*

APOLOGISE
apologise profusely, unreservedly
sincerely *apologise*

APPALLED
absolutely, utterly *appalled* (by sth)

APPALLING
absolutely, utterly *appalling*

APPARENT
clearly, increasingly, painfully *apparent*

APPEALING
extremely, instantly *appealing*

APPEAL
appeal to sb greatly, instantly, strongly

APPEAR (arrive)
appear briefly, in full view, magically, momentarily, out of nowhere, out of the blue
appear as arranged, as expected, at the appointed time, promptly

APPEAR (seem)
appear (un)likely, odd, probable, strange

> **APPEAR**
> Notice the words used in this structure are adjectives, not adverbs. *Appear* is used in a similar way like this: *He appears tired. It appears expensive.* See also *seem* and *look*.

APPLAUD
  applaud enthusiastically, loudly, warmly, wildly
APPLICABLE
  generally, universally *applicable*
APPLY
  apply early, in advance, in person, in plenty of time, in writing
  apply (paint) carefully, evenly, generously, gently, smoothly, sparingly
  apply in principle, in some cases, particularly, solely, strictly to sth
  basically, generally *apply* to sth
APPOINTED
  newly, recently *appointed* to (a job)
APPRAISE
  appraise sb/sth coolly, critically
APPRECIATE
  appreciate sth enormously, immensely
  fully, rarely, seldom *appreciate* sth
  genuinely, greatly, sincerely, thoroughly *appreciate* ...
APPRECIATED
  generally, properly, universally, widely *appreciated*
APPROACH
  approach (sth) silently, stealthily, warily
  approach sth calmly, carefully, from a new/different angle
  rapidly *approaching* (40)
APPROVE
  approve of sth in general, in principle, on the whole
  basically, definitely, enthusiastically, formally, strongly, thoroughly, unanimously,
  wholeheartedly *approve* of sth
ARBITRARY
  completely, purely, somewhat *arbitrary*
ARGUE
  argue constantly, convincingly, furiously, persuasively that ...
ARISE
  arise naturally, suddenly, unexpectedly
ARRANGE
  arrange sth at the last minute, beforehand, carefully, efficiently, (well) in advance, in plenty
  of time
ARRANGED
  arranged alphabetically, haphazardly, in order of size/weight etc, neatly, systematically,
  thematically
  beautifully, carefully, hastily *arranged*
ASHAMED
  dreadfully, thoroughly *ashamed*
ASK
  ask aggressively, anxiously, calmly, casually, doubtfully, hopefully, impatiently,
  incredulously, innocently, point-blank, (im)politely, repeatedly, rhetorically, straight out,
  suspiciously, thoughtfully
  constantly, legitimately, reasonably *ask* ...

> **ASK**
> *Ask* is similar to other verbs which describe how we speak, for example, *answer, speak, reply.* Because they also describe an action, they collocate with many different adverbs of manner.

ASSERT
   boldly, confidently, positively *assert* sth
ASSESS
   assess sb/sth accurately, carefully, coolly, properly
ASSIST
   actively, gladly, greatly, kindly, willingly *assist* sb
ASSISTED
   generously, greatly *assisted* by sb/sth
ASSOCIATE
   automatically, commonly, generally, inevitably, invariably, subconsciously, usually, vaguely *associate* ...
ASSOCIATED
   briefly, closely, inextricably, intimately, loosely *associated* with sb/sth
ASSORTED
   richly *assorted*
ASSUME
   automatically, confidently, correctly, generally, immediately, innocently, naively, naturally, rightly, safely, wrongly *assume* sth
ASTONISHED
   absolutely, totally, utterly *astonished*
ASTONISHING
   absolutely, utterly *astonishing*
ATTACHED
   extremely *attached* to sb/sth
   firmly, loosely, securely *attached* to sth
ATTACK
   attack sb scathingly, vigorously, violently, vociferously, without provocation/warning
ATTACKED
   bitterly, brutally, fiercely, mercilessly, publicly, repeatedly, ruthlessly, savagely, viciously, violently *attacked*
ATTEMPT
   attempt again and again, desperately, foolishly, in vain, time and again to do sth
ATTEND
   attend sth conscientiously, faithfully, occasionally, regularly, religiously
ATTRIBUTED
   commonly, (in)correctly, erroneously, generally, mistakenly *attributed* to sth
AUTHENTIC
   absolutely, completely, totally *authentic*
AVAILABLE
   easily, freely, generally, ordinarily, readily, universally, widely *available*
AVERT
   narrowly *avert* (a disaster)

AVOID
  avoid sth at all costs
  carefully, cleverly, deliberately, instinctively, narrowly, scarcely, scrupulously, skillfully, studiously, successfully, wisely *avoid* sb/sth
AWAITED
  eagerly, long- *awaited*
AWARE
  acutely, dimly, fully, keenly, painfully, perfectly, uncomfortably, vaguely *aware* of sth
AWFUL
  absolutely, indescribably, truly, unbelievably *awful*

B

BAD
  dreadfully, extremely, incredibly, notoriously, unbelievably *bad*
BALANCE
  balance dangerously, precariously on sth
  balance sth carefully on sth
  carefully *balance* (factors/considerations)
BALANCED
  delicately, evenly, perfectly, precariously *balanced*
BAN
  ban completely, outright
  effectively, totally *ban* sth
BANNED
  banned altogether, forever
  permanently, temporarily, totally *banned*
BASED
  entirely, mainly, originally, partly, soundly *based* on ...
  firmly, medically, reliably, scientifically, theoretically *based*
BEAT
  beat sb by a wide/narrow margin, convincingly, easily, narrowly
BEATEN
  savagely, severely, soundly, mercilessly *beaten*
BEAUTIFUL
  amazingly, breathtakingly, exceedingly, exquisitely, extremely, incredibly, outstandingly, stunningly *beautiful*
BECOME
  become imperceptibly, increasingly (adj)
  become sth in the end
  eventually, gradually, inevitably, steadily, suddenly, swiftly *become* sth
BEGIN
  begin seriously to do sth
  begin afresh, (all over) again, in earnest, late, on time, promisingly, right away, shortly, straightaway

BEHAVE

behave abominably, appallingly, atrociously, badly, childishly, disgracefully, properly, (ir)responsibly

> **BEHAVE**
>
> Verbs which describe an action – for example, *behave, smile, walk* – can be used with many different adverbs of manner which tell you how the person did the action. You can 'behave' *thoughtfully, arrogantly, altruistically*. These collocations are not strong enough or frequent enough to be listed here. To help you with questions you may have when, for example, writing an essay, we include only the most useful collocations here.

BELIEVE

firmly, fully, genuinely, honestly, passionately, readily, rightly, scarcely, sincerely, strongly, truly, wrongly *believe* that ...

deeply, fervently, firmly, passionately, strongly *believe* in sth

BENEFIT

benefit a great deal, enormously, greatly, immensely, significantly, substantially, tremendously from sth

BETTER

a bit, a little, little, a lot, marginally, much, no, rather, significantly, slightly, somewhat *better*

BLAME

blame sb completely, entirely

entirely, largely to, partly to *blame*

BLAMED

rightly, wrongly *blamed*

BLEED

bleed heavily, profusely, slightly, to death

BOAST

boast openly, rashly

BOOST

boost sth greatly, substantially

BORED

bored stiff, to tears

completely, thoroughly, totally *bored*

BORING

deadly, excruciatingly, incredibly, terribly *boring*

BORROW

borrow heavily

BOUND UP WITH

closely, inextricably *bound up with* sth

BREAK OFF

break off sth abruptly, for good, for no reason, suddenly

BREATHE

breathe deeply, evenly, gently, hard, heavily, rapidly, regularly, softly, with difficulty

BRIGHT

dazzlingly, extremely *bright* (light)

extremely, incredibly *bright* (person)

Starting from a verb or adjective

BRIGHTEN UP
brighten up considerably
BROUGHT UP
badly-, strictly, well- *brought up*
BROADCAST
broadcast (sth) live
BROKEN
badly, completely, irreparably *broken*
BUILT
badly-, newly-, solidly-, well- *built*
BURN
burn brightly, easily, fiercely, furiously, steadily, vigorously
BUSY
always, extremely, forever, incredibly, ridiculously, terribly, unbelievably *busy*
BUY
buy anonymously, at auction, cheaply, in bulk, on impulse, on the spur of the moment, outright, secondhand, wholesale

C

CALCULATE
calculate accurately, approximately, carefully, roughly
CALL
call loudly, quietly, softly
CALM
amazingly, completely, perfectly, totally *calm*
CAMPAIGN
campaign effectively, energetically, hard, tirelessly, vigorously
CANCEL
cancel sth altogether, at the last minute/moment, completely, hurriedly, regretfully, reluctantly, unexpectedly, without warning
CANCELLED
promptly, suddenly, unexpectedly *cancelled*
CARE
care deeply, passionately about ...
CARRY ON
carry on bravely, resolutely
CARRY OUT
carry out (a policy) as planned, systematically, (instructions) to the letter
CARVED
delicately, exquisitely, intricately, richly, roughly *carved*
CAUSE
accidentally, generally, inadvertently, inevitably, invariably, unfortunately *cause* sth
CAUTIOUS
particularly, relatively, specially, unnecessarily *cautious*

CELEBRATE
celebrate noisily, quietly

CENSORED
heavily, officially, severely, strictly *censored*

CERTAIN
absolutely, completely, totally *certain* (about/of sth)

CHALLENGE
implicitly, openly, publicly, seriously *challenge* sb/sth

CHANGE
change (sth) a great deal, abruptly, completely, dramatically, drastically, for the better/worse, fundamentally, gradually, immediately, imperceptibly, irrevocably, materially, out of all recognition, overnight, quickly, radically, rapidly, significantly, slightly, slowly, substantially, subtly, suddenly, totally, unpredictably

CHECK
check sth again and again, automatically, carefully, closely, meticulously, over and over again, painstakingly, properly, quickly, regularly, repeatedly, thoroughly

CHEER
cheer ecstatically, enthusiastically, loudly, madly, wildly

CHOOSE
choose badly, blindly, carefully, deliberately, wisely

CHOSEN
arbitrarily, carefully, cleverly, ill-, well- *chosen*

CIRCULATE
circulate freely, openly, widely

CLAIM
confidently, falsely, honestly, justifiably, legitimately, reasonably, rightfully, seriously *claim*

CLAP
clap enthusiastically, in unison, loudly, wildly

CLASH
clash angrily, head-on, sharply, violently

CLEAR
absolutely, abundantly, comparatively, completely, crystal, fairly, not altogether, not entirely, perfectly, totally *clear*

CLEAN
spotlessly *clean*

CLIMB
climb steadily

CLING
cling desperately to sth

CLOSE
close (a door etc) firmly, properly, quietly

CLOSE (adj)
dangerously, extremely, fairly, perilously, uncomfortably *close*

CO-EXIST
co-exist happily, peacefully

COINCIDE
coincide exactly with sth
roughly *coincide* with sth

COLD
bitterly, freezing *cold*

COLLAPSE
collapse all of a sudden, at any time, in a heap
collapse completely, eventually, inevitably, suddenly, totally

COLLECT
collect avidly, enthusiastically, indiscriminately, laboriously

COLLIDE
collide head on

COLOURED
brightly *coloured* (room), highly *coloured* (account)

COME ABOUT
come about by chance/good fortune, quite naturally

COME OUT
come out strongly, unanimously, against/in favour of sth

COMMENT
comment at length, briefly, (un)favourably, in detail on ...

COMMIT
commit oneself completely, enthusiastically, fervently, tentatively, totally, wholeheartedly, wholly to sth

COMMITTED
absolutely, completely, deeply, fully, passionately, totally *committed* to sth

COMPARE
compare badly, (un)favourably, well with sth

COMPENSATED
compensated (in)adequately, fairly, generously for sth

COMPETE
compete eagerly, fiercely, vigorously

COMPETITIVE
fiercely *competitive*

COMPILED
carefully, painstakingly *compiled*

COMPLAIN
complain bitterly, constantly, forcefully, loudly, noisily, strongly, vociferously

COMPLAINING
constantly, forever *complaining* about sth

COMPLETE
complete sth ahead of schedule/time, as planned, early, in record time, on time, satisfactorily

COMPLICATE
complicate sth further, unnecessarily

COMPLY
comply with sth promptly, readily, reluctantly

COMPREHEND
fully, hardly, scarcely *comprehend* sth

CONCEALED
barely, carefully, cleverly, completely, cunningly, easily, hastily, partially, partly *concealed*

CONCEDE
finally, readily, reluctantly *concede* that ...

CONCENTRATE
concentrate largely, mainly, solely on sth
concentrate on sth to the exclusion of everything else
CONCERNED
closely, seriously, slightly *concerned* about sth
intimately, mainly, primarily, principally *concerned* with sth
CONCLUDE
reasonably, regretfully, wrongly *conclude* that ...
CONDEMN
condemn out of hand, unfairly
roundly, strongly, totally, unequivocally *condemn* sb/sth
CONDEMNED
bitterly, unfairly, unjustly *condemned* for sth
CONFIDENT
completely, extremely, fairly, supremely, totally *confident*
CONFIDENTIAL
highly, strictly, totally *confidential*
CONFINED
largely, mainly, mostly, narrowly, strictly *confined* to sth
CONFIRM
broadly, definitely *confirm* sth
CONFLICT
conflict directly, markedly, sharply with sth
CONFUSED
altogether, completely, decidedly, hopelessly, horribly, particularly, pretty, somewhat, totally *confused* about sth
CONFUSING
terribly, notoriously, totally, unbelievably, utterly *confusing*
CONGRATULATE
congratulate sb most sincerely, warmly on sth
CONNECTED
closely, loosely, not remotely, vaguely *connected* with sth
CONSCIOUS
deeply *conscious* of (the situation)
fully *conscious*
CONSENT
eventually, finally, gladly, reluctantly *consent* to sth
CONSIDERED
generally, legitimately, rightly, usually *considered* to be...
CONSIDER
actively, briefly, carefully, seriously *consider*
consider objectively, urgently
CONSISTENT
amazingly, completely, remarkably, surprisingly *consistent*
entirely, logically, perfectly, roughly, totally, wholly *consistent* with sth
CONSTRUCTED
badly, carefully, poorly, solidly *constructed*

CONTEMPLATE
 contemplate sth with equanimity
 calmly, quietly *contemplate* sth
CONTEMPTUOUS
 faintly, openly, privately, totally *contemptuous* of sb/sth
CONTEST
 contest sth fiercely, strongly
CONTESTED
 closely, fiercely, hotly, keenly *contested*
CONTINUE
 continue ad infinitum, indefinitely
 continue calmly, happily, steadily, stubbornly to do sth
CONTRADICT
 apparently, directly, flatly *contradict* sth
CONTRAST
 contrast favourably, markedly, sharply, starkly, strongly, vividly with sth
CONTRIBUTE
 contribute (money) generously, handsomely, regularly, significantly, unwittingly
 greatly, largely *contribute* to sth
CONTRIVED
 carefully, cleverly, skillfully *contrived*
CONTROL
 control carefully, effectively, expertly, firmly, properly, rigidly, rigorously, ruthlessly, strictly
CONTROVERSIAL
 deliberately, extremely, highly, notoriously, relatively, somewhat *controversial*
CONVERTED
 easily, successfully *converted* into/to sth
CONVINCED
 absolutely, almost, easily, half-, more or less, not altogether, not entirely, practically, totally
 convinced about/of ...
COPE
 cope adequately, beautifully, brilliantly, effectively, magnificently, skillfully, successfully
 barely *cope* with sth
COPY
 copy sth carefully, exactly, faithfully
CORRECT
 correct sb discreetly, gently, politely, sympathetically, tactfully, tactlessly
CORRESPOND WITH
 correspond closely, exactly *with* sth
COURTEOUS
 unfailingly *courteous*
COVER
 cover sth carefully, completely, evenly, gently, loosely, neatly, totally
CRASH
 crash head on, heavily, to the ground
CREATE
 create sth from scratch, jointly, single-handedly

CREDIBLE

entirely, hardly, perfectly, scarcely *credible*

CRITICAL

fiercely, mildly, openly, sharply, strongly *critical* of sb/sth

CRITICISE

criticise bitterly, fiercely, harshly, justly, mildly, openly, publicly, rightly, strongly, unfairly

CRITICISED

openly, rightly, severely, unfairly *criticised*

CRUEL

deliberately, needlessly, notoriously, terribly *cruel* to sb/sth

CRY

cry bitterly, oneself to sleep, openly, softly

CRY OUT

cry out in agony, in despair, in fear, in pain

CURIOUS

intensely, mildly *curious* about sb/sth

CUT

cut sth dramatically, drastically, heavily, severely

CUT BACK/DOWN

drastically *cut back/down*

CUT OUT

cut out (sugar) altogether

D

DAMAGED

damaged beyond repair

badly, extensively, seriously, severely, slightly *damaged*

DANGEROUS

extremely *dangerous*

DEAD

absolutely, almost, completely, nearly *dead*

DEAL WITH

deal with sth adequately, at length, effectively, efficiently, fairly, harshly, in detail, privately, promptly, ruthlessly, straightaway, successfully, swiftly

DEBATED

hotly *debated*

DECIDE

decide arbitrarily, belatedly, calmly, foolishly, immediately, instantly, once and for all, on moral/practical grounds, on the spot, on the spur of the moment, reluctantly

deliberately, finally, rashly, ultimately, wisely *decide*

DECLARE

declare boldly, categorically, confidently, defiantly, emphatically, firmly, openly, resolutely, unequivocally

solemnly *declare*

DECLINE
decline abruptly, alarmingly, dramatically, gradually, markedly, noticeably, progressively, rapidly, sharply, significantly, steadily, steeply, suddenly, visibly

DECLINE (refuse)
politely, regretfully, reluctantly *decline*

DECORATED
lavishly, luxuriously, ornately, richly, sumptuously, tastefully *decorated*

DECREASE
decrease abruptly, alarmingly, dramatically, gradually, markedly, noticeably, progressively, rapidly, sharply, steadily, suddenly, visibly

DEDICATED
absolutely, totally, wholly *dedicated* to sth

DEFEATED
heavily, narrowly, thoroughly, utterly *defeated*

DEFEND
defend sb/sth at all costs, bravely, courageously, fiercely, passionately, successfully, to the last, valiantly, vigorously

DEFINED
broadly, clearly, narrowly, precisely, strictly, well- *defined*

DEFY
openly *defy* sb

DELAY
delay sth deliberately, until it was too late

DELAYED
considerably, seriously, temporarily, unavoidably *delayed*

DELIBERATE
clearly, obviously *deliberate*

DELIGHTED
absolutely, highly *delighted*

DELIVER
deliver on time, promptly, regularly, safely, to the door

DEMAND
angrily, persistently, promptly *demand*

DEMONSTRATE
demonstrate beyond all shadow of a doubt, clearly, conclusively, convincingly, graphically adequately, vividly *demonstrate*

DEMORALISED
absolutely, badly, completely, thoroughly, utterly *demoralised*

DENOUNCE
angrily, bitterly, fiercely, furiously, openly, strongly, vigorously *denounce* sb/sth

DENY
absolutely, categorically, consistently, emphatically, explicitly, fiercely, persistently, strenuously, totally, vigorously *deny* sth/that...

DEPART
depart abruptly, hastily, hurriedly, in a hurry, on time, punctually, reluctantly, unexpectedly

DEPEND
depend crucially, mainly, partly, solely on ...

DEPICT
   dramatically, faithfully, vividly *depict* sth
DEPRESSING
   deeply, extremely *depressing*
DEPRIVE
   deprive sb of sth altogether, completely
   cruelly, totally *deprive* sb of sth
DERIVED
   (in)directly, largely, originally *derived* from sth
DESCEND
   descend steadily, steeply
DESCRIBE
   describe sth accurately, at length, briefly, brilliantly, carefully, euphemistically, evocatively,
   exactly, fully, graphically, in (minute) detail, precisely, vividly
   (not) adequately *describe*
DESCRIBED
   loosely, roughly *described* as sth
DESERVED
   fully, richly, truly, well- *deserved*
DESIGNATED
   clearly, roughly *designated*
DESIGNED
   badly, basically, beautifully, brilliantly, cleverly, exquisitely, mainly, originally, poorly,
   primarily, specially, specifically, well- *designed*
DESIRABLE
   eminently, highly *desirable*
DESIRE
   genuinely, sincerely *desire* sth/to do sth
DESPERATE
   absolutely *desperate* to do sth
DESTROY
   destroy sb/sth by accident, by fire, by mistake
   carelessly, completely, deliberately, methodically, ruthlessly, systematically, thoughtlessly,
   totally, utterly, wilfully *destroy* sb/sth
DETAILED
   beautifully, carefully, finely, extremely, fairly, fully *detailed*
DETERIORATE
   deteriorate alarmingly, badly, rapidly
DEVELOP
   develop gradually, naturally, (ab)normally, gradually, rapidly, satisfactorily, systematically
DEVISED
   cleverly, ingeniously, specially *devised*
DEVOTE
   devote (oneself) entirely, exclusively to sth
DEVOTED
   absolutely, deeply, fanatically, genuinely, utterly, wholeheartedly *devoted* to sb/sth
DEVOUR
   devour avidly, greedily

DIE
> *die* bravely, in agony, in poverty, in tragic/suspicious circumstances, needlessly, peacefully, prematurely, tragically

DIFFER
> *differ* fundamentally, greatly, marginally, markedly, noticeably, radically, sharply, significantly, totally from sb/sth

DIFFERENT
> completely, crucially, markedly, notoriously, radically, substantially, totally, widely *different*

DIFFERENTIATE
> *differentiate* carefully, clearly, easily, sharply between sth and sth

DIFFICULT
> exceptionally, exceedingly, extraordinarily, fiendishly, notoriously, (not) particularly, relatively *difficult*

DIMINISH
> greatly, progressively, seriously, visibly *diminish*

DISAGREE
> absolutely, basically, flatly, fundamentally, passionately, profoundly, strongly, vehemently, violently *disagree*

DISAPPEAR
> *disappear* altogether, completely, for ever, from sight, from the scene, from view, into thin air, mysteriously, suddenly, without trace

DISAPPEARING
> fast *disappearing*

DISAPPOINTED
> bitterly, deeply, dreadfully, terribly, tremendously *disappointed* about/with ...

DISAPPROVE
> mildly, strongly, thoroughly *disapprove* of sb/sth

DISCOVER
> *discover* sth afresh, anew, bit by bit, by accident/chance, eventually, fortuitously, gradually, recently, unexpectedly

DISCUSS
> *discuss* sth at (great) length, briefly, calmly, openly, rationally, seriously, thoroughly
> freely, fully *discuss* sth

> **DISCUSS**
> *Discuss* is similar to other verbs which describe how we speak, for example, *add, speak, reply*. Because they also describe an action, they collocate with many different adverbs of manner.

DISFIGURED
> appallingly, badly, shockingly *disfigured*

DISGRACED
> publicly, utterly *disgraced*

DISGRACEFUL
> absolutely, downright, utterly *disgraceful*

DISGUISED
> cleverly, cunningly, heavily, poorly, thinly *disguised*

DISHONEST
downright, notoriously, thoroughly *dishonest*

DISILLUSIONED
completely, somewhat, thoroughly, totally *disillusioned*

DISLIKE
dislike sb/sth intensely, strongly, thoroughly

DISLIKED
generally, greatly *disliked*

DISMISS
dismiss sth angrily, contemptuously, glibly, instantly, out of hand, scornfully

DISORGANISED
hopelessly, thoroughly, utterly *disorganised*

DISPATCH
dispatch sth by air, by carrier, by courier, by (registered) post, by return, immediately, promptly, straightaway

DISPEL
dispel effectively, quickly

DISPERSE
disperse quickly

DISPLAY
display sth proudly
openly *display*

DISPLAYED
displayed to the best advantage
attractively, beautifully, frankly, openly, prominently *displayed*

DISPUTED
fiercely, hotly, vigorously *disputed*

DISQUALIFIED
temporarily, permanently *disqualified*

DISREGARD
disregard sb/sth completely, entirely, totally
conveniently, deliberately, flagrantly *disregard* sb/sth

DISRUPT
seriously, severely *disrupt* sth

DISTASTEFUL
extremely, faintly, mildly *distasteful*

DISTINGUISH
distinguish clearly, sharply between sth and sth

DISTORTED
distorted out of all recognition/proportion
badly, dangerously, deliberately, grossly, grotesquely, seriously, wildly *distorted*

DISTRIBUTE
distribute sth evenly, fairly, generously

DISTURBED
deeply, not unduly, profoundly, seriously *disturbed*

DISTURBING
deeply, profoundly *disturbing*

DIVERGE
  diverge considerably, greatly, radically, significantly
DIVIDE
  divide sth equally, equitably, fairly
DIVIDED
  (un)equally, roughly *divided*
DO
  do sth badly, competently, perfectly, promptly, properly, reluctantly, single-handedly, well

> **DO**
> Verbs which describe an action – for example, *do, smile, walk* – can be used with many different adverbs of manner which tell you how the person did the action. You can 'do something' *thoughtfully, carefully, distractedly*. Here we include only the most useful collocations. *Do* is one of the important verbs which have hardly any meaning on their own, but which are part of many fixed expressions. You should find these in your ordinary dictionary.

DOCUMENTED
  amply, carefully, fully, scrupulously *documented*
DOMINATE
  absolutely, completely, totally, utterly, wholly *dominate* sb/sth
DOOMED
  inescapably *doomed*
DOUBT
  seriously *doubt* ...
DRESSED
  appropriately, attractively, badly, beautifully, conservatively, casually, (not) correctly, eccentrically, elegantly, extravagantly, fashionably, (in)formally, fully, impeccably, modestly, neatly, poorly, quietly, shabbily, smartly, soberly, suitably *dressed*
DRIFT
  drift helplessly, lazily, peacefully, quietly, slowly but surely towards sth
DRINK
  drink far too much, heavily, in moderation, to excess
DRIVE
  drive badly, carefully, dangerously, erratically, furiously, like mad, recklessly
DROP
  drop alarmingly, dramatically, gradually, markedly, noticeably, rapidly, sharply, steadily, suddenly
DROP (fall)
  drop sth accidentally, carelessly, clumsily, inadvertently
DUBIOUS
  extremely, highly *dubious* about ...
DUE
  entirely, partly, presumably, supposedly, wholly *due* to sb/sth
DULL
  excruciatingly, incredibly, terribly *dull*

E

EASE
ease sth greatly, marginally, slightly, somewhat
EASY
comparatively, dead, deceptively, fairly, perfectly, relatively, ridiculously *easy*
EAT
eat heartily, noisily, ravenously, voraciously
ECCENTRIC
a little, somewhat, totally *eccentric*
ECHO
echo faintly, hollowly, loudly, ominously
EDITED
edited brilliantly, carefully, carelessly, scrupulously, thoughtfully
EFFECTIVE
brilliantly, devastatingly, extremely, highly, immensely, remarkably, surprisingly, tremendously *effective*
EFFICIENT
exceptionally, extremely, highly, reasonably, ruthlessly, tremendously *efficient*
EJECT
eject forcibly, unceremoniously
ELIMINATE
eliminate sth altogether, completely, totally
EMBARRASSED
acutely, dreadfully, extremely, painfully, visibly *embarrassed*
EMBARRASSING
deeply, extremely, dreadfully, highly, most, potentially *embarrassing*
EMERGE
emerge briefly, clearly, cautiously, gradually
eventually, finally, rapidly, soon *emerge*
EMPHASISE
repeatedly, strongly *emphasise* sth
EMPLOYED
casually, currently, fully, gainfully, permanently, regularly, temporarily, under- *employed*
ENCOUNTER
frequently, generally, occasionally, regularly *encounter* sb/sth
ENCOURAGE
actively, deliberately, discreetly, gently, strongly *encourage* sb/sth to do sth
ENCOURAGED
greatly *encouraged*
ENCOURAGING
extremely, mildly *encouraging*
END
end abruptly, at last, badly, decisively, disastrously, eventually, finally, happily, in deadlock, in disaster, in failure, in success, in triumph, in victory, predictably, prematurely, successfully, suddenly, traumatically, tragically, unexpectedly

ENDANGERED
seriously *endangered*
ENDLESS
seemingly *endless*
ENDURE
endure sth bravely, patiently, philosophically, stoically, without complaint
ENFORCE
legally, rigorously, strictly *enforce* sth
ENGINEERED
cleverly *engineered*
ENHANCED
greatly *enhanced*
ENJOY
enjoy oneself enormously, immensely, quietly, tremendously
clearly, greatly, thoroughly *enjoy* oneself
ENJOYABLE
enormously, extremely, thoroughly, tremendously *enjoyable*
ENQUIRE
enquire cautiously, discreetly, eagerly, tactfully, quietly
anxiously, formally, politely *enquire* about sb/sth
ENSUE
inevitably *ensue*
ENTANGLED
deeply, hopelessly, thoroughly *entangled* in sth
ENTER
enter by the back door, discreetly, illegally, unannounced, without permission
ENTERTAIN
entertain lavishly, on a grand scale
ENTERTAINING
consistently, extremely, highly, unfailingly, wonderfully *entertaining*
ENTRUST
confidently, foolishly, naively, safely *entrust* sb with sth/sth to sb
EQUAL
absolutely, approximately, exactly, more or less, notionally, precisely, roughly *equal*
EQUIPPED
(in)adequately, badly, fully, ideally, ill-, poorly, properly, suitably, uniquely, well- *equipped*
ERUPT
erupt suddenly, violently, without warning
ESCALATE
escalate dramatically, rapidly
ESCAPE
escape by the skin of (my) teeth, under cover of darkness
ESCAPED
finally, narrowly *escaped*
ESTABLISH
establish sth beyond all (reasonable) doubt, conclusively, finally, unequivocally that ...
ESTIMATE
estimate sth accurately, correctly, roughly, tentatively

EVADE
cleverly, successfully *evade* sth

EVERY
absolutely, almost, nearly, virtually *every*

EVICT
forcibly *evict* sb

EVIDENT
clearly, readily *evident*

EVIL
fundamentally, thoroughly, totally, truly *evil*

EVOCATIVE
powerfully, strangely, subtly *evocative*

EVOKE
brilliantly, powerfully, readily, vividly *evoke*

EXAGGERATE
exaggerate sth out of all proportion, slightly, somewhat

EXAGGERATED
enormously, greatly, grossly, highly, ridiculously, slightly, somewhat *exaggerated*

EXAMINE
examine briefly, carefully, closely, critically, fully, in (minute) detail, intently, minutely, properly, reverently, rigorously, thoroughly

EXCEED
far, fractionally, greatly, marginally, slightly, substantially *exceed* sth

EXCEPTIONAL
absolutely, completely, totally, utterly *exceptional*

EXCITABLE
highly *excitable*

EXCITED
easily, highly, over-, wildly *excited*

EXCITING
extremely, incredibly, tremendously, wonderfully *exciting*

EXCLAIM
exclaim excitedly, indignantly, loudly

EXCLUDE
absolutely, completely, deliberately, effectively, partially, totally *exclude* sb/sth

EXECUTED (done)
badly, beautifully, carefully, carelessly, flawlessly, perfectly, poorly, well- *executed*

EXEMPT
(not) completely, fully, partially, totally, wholly *exempt* from sth

EXHAUSTED
absolutely, completely, practically, totally, utterly, well-nigh *exhausted*

EXPAND
expand cautiously, continually, dramatically, fast, indefinitely, piecemeal, rapidly, significantly, steadily, step-by-step, tremendously

EXPANDED
gradually, greatly *expanded*

EXPANDING
continually, rapidly *expanding*

EXPECT
anxiously, confidently, definitely, eagerly, fully, half-, intuitively, realistically, seriously, reasonably *expect*

EXPECTED
generally, widely *expected*

EXPENSIVE
dreadfully, extremely, far/much too, not too, outrageously, prohibitively, ridiculously, terribly *expensive*

EXPERIENCE
experience sth directly, personally, recently
actually *experience*

EXPERIENCED
highly, widely *experienced*

EXPLAIN
explain apologetically, at length, briefly, clearly, completely, gently, helpfully, in detail, laboriously, patiently, politely, simply, satisfactorily
adequately, broadly, fully, hardly, neatly, partly, partially, readily *explain*

EXPLAINED
easily, simply *explained*

EXPLOIT
fully, ruthlessly, shamefully, shamelessly *exploit*

EXPLORE
explore sth carefully, fully, in depth, systematically, thoroughly

EXPOSE
cruelly, inadvertently, mercilessly, needlessly, publicly, ruthlessly, *expose* sb

EXPRESS
express sth awkwardly, beautifully, candidly, clearly, coherently, crudely, elegantly, eloquently, forcefully, freely, openly, publicly, strongly, tangibly, vigorously, vividly

EXPRESSED
frankly, powerfully, vividly *expressed*

EXPRESSIVE
wonderfully *expressive*

EYE
eye sth doubtfully, enviously, jealously, suspiciously, with interest

F

FACE
face sth squarely, with confidence/courage/equanimity

FAIL
fail sth abysmally, altogether, badly, completely, dismally, lamentably, miserably, utterly
completely, consistently, conspicuously, entirely, invariably, never, narrowly, persistently, hardly, seldom, wholly *fail*

FAIR
absolutely, hardly, scrupulously *fair*

FALL

fall awkwardly, from a great height, headfirst, headlong, heavily, like a stone

FALL (decrease)

fall dramatically, gradually, rapidly, significantly, sharply, slightly, steadily, steeply, substantially

FALL (in love)

fall deeply, head over heels, hopelessly, madly, passionately *in love*

FALSE

absolutely, clearly, completely, entirely, obviously, palpably, patently, totally, wholly *false*

FAMILIAR

curiously, depressingly, distressingly, increasingly, only too, painfully, reassuringly, strangely *familiar*

FANCIFUL

wildly *fanciful*

FASCINATING

absolutely, endlessly, utterly *fascinating*

FASHIONABLE

currently, highly *fashionable*

FASTEN

fasten sth firmly, properly, safely, securely, tight

FEASIBLE

no longer, perfectly, scarcely *feasible*

FEATURE

feature regularly, prominently in sth

FEEL

feel all right, bad, (un)comfortable, dreadful, fine, good, great, ill, marvellous, poorly, sick, terrible, well, wonderful

> **FEEL**
>
> Notice the words used in this structure are adjectives, not adverbs. See also *appear, look,* and *seem.*

FEEL (think, believe)

feel deeply, strongly that...

definitely, instinctively, instantly, rightly, somehow, strongly *feel* that...

FEW

comparatively, disappointingly, pitifully, relatively, remarkably, surprisingly, very *few*

FIGHT

fight bitterly, bravely, courageously, desperately, fiercely, frantically, gallantly, hard, magnificently, relentlessly, resolutely, ruthlessly, selflessly, single-handed(ly), superbly, tenaciously, to the bitter end, to the death/finish, unsuccessfully, valiantly, viciously, vigorously

FINANCED

partially, partly, privately, publicly *financed*

FINE

exceptionally, extremely, particularly, remarkably, unusually *fine*

FINISH

finish sth hastily, hurriedly, in/on time

FIRE
  fire (guns) indiscriminately, wildly
FIT (verb)
  fit badly, beautifully, comfortably, exactly, neatly, perfectly, snugly
FIT (adj)
  extremely, fighting, not quite, perfectly, reasonably, remarkably, superbly *fit*
FIX (attach)
  fix firmly, loosely, permanently, securely
FIXED
  absolutely, definitely, provisionally, tentatively *fixed*
FLATTERING
  extremely *flattering*
FLAWED
  badly, basically, fatally, fundamentally, seriously *flawed*
FLOW
  flow easily, fast, freely, rapidly, silently, sluggishly, smoothly, steadily, swiftly
FLUCTUATE
  fluctuate alarmingly, sharply, slightly, wildly
FLUENT
  absolutely, completely, fairly, passably, remarkably, totally *fluent*
FOCUS
  focus carefully on sth
FOCUSED
  sharply *focused*
FOLD
  fold sth carefully, diagonally, in half, in three etc, lengthwise, neatly
FOLLOW (a person or idea)
  follow blindly, faithfully, slavishly, unthinkingly
FOLLOW (listen to or understand)
  follow attentively, carefully, closely, exactly, intently, perfectly, precisely, with difficulty
  hardly, scarcely *follow* sb
FOLLOW (instructions)
  follow carefully, closely, faithfully, in detail, meticulously, precisely, to the letter
FOLLOW (one thing follows another)
  immediately, inevitably, inexorably, invariably, quickly, swiftly *follow*
FOLLOWED
  closely, quickly *followed* by sb
FORBID
  absolutely, expressly, specifically, strictly *forbid*
FORGET
  completely, easily, entirely, momentarily, promptly, quickly, totally *forget*
FORGIVE
  completely *forgive*
FORGOTTEN
  completely, largely, long since *forgotten*
FORMED
  beautifully, perfectly, strangely *formed*

FORTIFIED
heavily *fortified*
FOSTER
actively, carefully *foster* sth
FRANK
absolutely, amazingly, brutally, completely, disarmingly, refreshingly, remarkably, ruthlessly, surprisingly, totally *frank*
FREE (from)
absolutely, completely, entirely, mercifully, surprisingly, thankfully, totally, utterly *free*
FRIENDLY
extremely, genuinely *friendly* to sb
FRIGHTENED
a little, extremely *frightened* of sb/sth
FRIGHTENING
extremely, really, terribly *frightening*
FROWN
frown angrily, thoughtfully, with displeasure
FRUITFUL
extremely, genuinely, immensely, potentially, unexpectedly *fruitful*
FULFIL
amply, completely, entirely, not altogether, partially, satisfactorily *fulfil*
FULL
absolutely, almost, half-, nearly, totally *full*
FUNCTION
function adequately, effectively, efficiently, normally, perfectly, properly, satisfactorily, smoothly
FUNNY
excruciatingly, extremely, hilariously, outrageously *funny*
FURNISHED
beautifully, comfortably, elegantly, expensively, fully, half-, luxuriously, poorly, sparsely, tastefully *furnished*

G

GAIN
gradually, quickly, rapidly, slowly *gain* (control, experience etc)
GAIN ON
steadily, rapidly *gain on* sb
GAMBLE
gamble heavily
GAUGE
gauge sth accurately, exactly
GAZE AT
gaze admiringly, anxiously, apathetically, blankly, fondly, gloomily, intently, longingly, pensively, sadly, steadily, sorrowfully, vacantly *at*

GENEROUS
amazingly, exceedingly, exceptionally, extremely *generous*
GESTICULATE
gesticulate angrily, excitedly, furiously, violently, wildly
GET BETTER/WORSE
get considerably, far, noticeably, progressively, slightly, significantly, somewhat, steadily *better/worse*
GIFTED
enormously, exceptionally, prodigiously, tremendously, uniquely *gifted*
GIVE
give anonymously, generously, grudgingly, promptly, reluctantly, willingly

> **GIVE**
> *Give* is one of the important verbs which have hardly any meaning on their own, but which are part of many fixed expressions, for example, *give an immediate answer, give a remarkable performance*. You should find these in your ordinary dictionary.

GIVE UP
give up sth completely, easily, entirely, for ever/good, readily, reluctantly, voluntarily, (un)willingly
GLANCE AT
glance anxiously, casually, furtively, hastily, knowingly, nervously, quickly, shyly, surreptitiously, timidly, uneasily, swiftly *at*
GLARE AT
glare at sb accusingly, angrily, defiantly, disapprovingly, fiercely, sullenly
GLIMPSE
glimpse briefly, in the distance
GLOW
glow brightly, dimly, feebly, in the dark, softly
GLOWING
glowing with health, with pride
GO
go astray, backwards, by a roundabout route, direct(ly), forward, immediately, nowhere, round in circles, sideways, straight to ...

> **GO**
> *Go* is one of the most common verbs in English. It makes many collocations with adjectives: *go quiet, go mad, go wrong*. When it means 'move', it can be followed by many adverbs of manner: *go quietly, go quickly*. It is also part of many expressions which you will find in your ordinary dictionary

GO AWAY
go away forever, for good, suddenly, without warning
GO DOWN/UP
go down/up dramatically, gradually, rapidly, significantly, slightly, steadily, substantially, suddenly, tremendously
GO ON
go on endlessly, for ever and ever, indefinitely, interminably

GO OVER

go over (the contract) carefully, in (minute) detail, line by line, methodically, patiently, systematically, with a fine toothcomb

GO THROUGH

go through smoothly, without a hitch

GOOD

good enough

exceedingly, exceptionally, extraordinarily, extremely, fairly, reasonably, remarkably, surprisingly *good*

GOOD (morally)

fundamentally, genuinely, remarkably *good*

GOOD AT

equally, exceptionally, extremely, fairly, moderately, reasonably, supremely, surprisingly, uncommonly, unusually *good at*

GOVERNED

badly, effectively, wisely *governed*

GRASP

grasp sth firmly, tightly

grasp sth clearly, easily, fully, instinctively

GRATEFUL

deeply, enormously, eternally, extremely, profoundly, sincerely, tremendously, truly *grateful*

GRATIFYING

especially, immensely, truly *gratifying*

GREAT

truly, undoubtedly *great*

GREATER

far, infinitely, significantly, substantially *greater*

GREEDY

dreadfully, incredibly, terribly *greedy*

GREET

greet sb cordially, effusively, politely, stiffly, warmly

GRIN

grin broadly, cheekily, from ear to ear, mischievously, shyly

GRIP

grip firmly, tightly

GROPE

grope blindly, feverishly

GROW

grow at a great rate, conspicuously, dramatically, fast, gradually, impressively, inexorably, (im)perceptibly, prodigiously, quickly, rapidly, significantly, slightly, steadily, substantially, suddenly, tremendously

GROW OLD

grow old before one's time, gracefully, prematurely

GUARD

guard carefully, closely, jealously, with one's life

GUESS

guess sth correctly, right(ly), wrong(ly)

H

HAMPERED
badly, greatly, seriously, severely *hampered* by sb/sth
HANDICAPPED
badly, seriously, severely *handicapped*
HANDLE
handle sth astutely, awkwardly, badly, beautifully, carefully, carelessly, cleverly, confidently, clumsily, deftly, discreetly, efficiently, expertly, firmly, gently, gingerly, roughly, sensitively, skilfully, successfully, tactfully, well, with care
HANDSOME
extremely, incredibly, ruggedly, strikingly, undeniably *handsome*
HANG
hang at an angle, limply, precariously, rigidly, straight
HAPPEN
happen by chance, suddenly, unexpectedly
actually, frequently, rarely, really, seldom *happen*
HAPPY
blissfully, completely, deliriously, not altogether, reasonably, tremendously, truly *happy*
HARD
extremely, incredibly *hard*
HARM
deliberately, intentionally, seriously *harm*
HATEFUL
absolutely, positively, utterly *hateful*

> **HAVE**
> *Have* is one of the most common verbs in English. The word itself does not usually have much meaning except in the rare case where it is a full verb: *They have three children.* Most of the uses of *have* are either part of the grammar of the language or part of fixed expressions. Different adverbs collocate with different expressions which contain *have*, so it is impossible to list them here.

HAZARDOUS
extremely *hazardous*
HEAD FOR/TOWARDS
head blindly, determinedly, immediately, straight *for/towards* sb/sth
HEAL
heal badly, beautifully, miraculously, nicely, quickly
HEALED
completely, partially *healed*
HEAR
hear clearly, (in)distinctly, faintly, in the distance, properly, vaguely
HELP
help enormously, generously, significantly, tremendously
gladly, greatly, willingly *help*

HIDE
  hide carefully, completely, discreetly, in a safe place, secretly, surreptitiously

HIGH
  abnormally, alarmingly, dangerously, exceptionally, extremely, sufficiently *high*

HIGHER
  considerably, significantly, substantially *higher*

HIERARCHICAL
  extremely, notoriously, strictly, rigidly *hierarchical*

HINDERED
  greatly, seriously *hindered*

HINT
  hint darkly, gently, ominously, tactfully

HIT
  hit again and again, badly, hard, repeatedly, softly, squarely

HOLD
  hold at a distance, at arm's length, carefully, close, down, firm, firmly, level, loosely, securely, steady, tenderly, tight(ly)

HOLD ON
  hold on desperately, grimly, tenaciously

HONEST
  absolutely, completely, scrupulously, totally, touchingly *honest*

HOPE
  hope in vain
  confidently, devoutly, fervently, naively, realistically, sincerely, very much *hope*

HORRIBLE
  absolutely, completely, unspeakably, utterly *horrible*

HOSTILE
  covertly, decidedly, definitely, implacably, increasingly, openly, overtly, persistently, plainly, violently *hostile*

HOT
  awfully, boiling, oppressively, terribly, unbearably *hot*

HOVER
  hover menacingly, overhead, protectively

HUMOROUS
  quietly, wryly *humorous*

HURT
  badly, bitterly, deeply, seriously, severely *hurt*

HYPOTHETICAL
  completely, purely, totally *hypothetical*

I

IDENTIFIABLE
  easily, immediately, instantly, readily *identifiable*

IDENTIFIED
  closely, easily, positively *identified*

IDENTIFY
identify sb/sth beyond all doubt, easily, immediately, straightaway, tentatively, without difficulty

IDENTIFY WITH
identify oneself automatically, closely, instinctively, readily, subconsciously, totally *with*

IGNORANT
absolutely, abysmally, blissfully, completely, disgracefully, incredibly, pathetically, shockingly, totally, unbelievably *ignorant*

IGNORE
ignore sb/sth altogether
blatantly, blithely, completely, conveniently, deliberately, largely, more or less, safely, studiously, totally, utterly *ignore* sb/sth

ILL
critically, dangerously, desperately, gravely, seriously, terminally, terribly *ill*

ILLUMINATE
illuminate clearly, sharply, vividly

ILLUSTRATED
attractively, badly, beautifully, clearly, colourfully, fully, generously, graphically, lavishly, marvellously, superbly, vividly *illustrated*

IMAGINARY
purely *imaginary*

IMAGINATIVE
highly *imaginative*

IMITATED
closely, perfectly, widely *imitated*

IMPAIRED
badly, seriously *impaired*

IMPEDED
badly, greatly, seriously *impeded*

IMPLEMENT
fully, systematically *implement* sth

IMPLORE
earnestly, humbly *implore*

IMPLY
clearly, obviously, seriously, strongly, subtly *imply*

IMPORTANT
all-, comparatively, crucially, extremely, overwhelmingly, particularly, relatively, supremely, vitally *important*

IMPOSE
impose arbitrarily
autocratically, rigidly, ruthlessly *impose*

IMPOSSIBLE
impossible in practice/theory, to all intents and purposes
absolutely, almost, altogether, completely, fundamentally, genuinely, logically, nearly, obviously, practically, seemingly, theoretically, totally, utterly, virtually, well-nigh, wholly *impossible*

IMPRACTICAL
completely, extremely, obviously, seemingly, totally, wholly *impractical*

IMPRESS
impress sb (un)favourably, greatly, tremendously
IMPRESSED
deeply, enormously, greatly, suitably, tremendously *impressed*
IMPRESSIVE
enormously, extremely, incredibly, tremendously *impressive*
IMPRISONED
unlawfully, wrongfully *imprisoned*
IMPROBABLE
completely, highly, wildly *improbable*
IMPROVE
improve considerably, dramatically, enormously, gradually, greatly, marginally, markedly, overnight, rapidly, significantly, slightly, steadily, substantially, suddenly, sufficiently, tremendously, unexpectedly
IMPROVED
greatly, much, noticeably *improved*
INACCESSIBLE
extremely, notoriously, totally, virtually *inaccessible*
INACCURATE
obviously, seriously, slightly, totally, wildly *inaccurate*
INADEQUATE
completely, grossly, hopelessly, ludicrously, patently, pitifully, scandalously, shamefully, totally, utterly, woefully, wholly *inadequate*
INAPPROPRIATE
clearly, completely, hopelessly, singularly, wholly *inappropriate*
INCAPABLE
physically, totally *incapable*
INCOHERENT
absolutely, almost, completely, logically, totally, utterly *incoherent*
INCOMPETENT
absolutely, completely, hopelessly, notoriously, totally, utterly *incompetent*
INCREASE
increase appreciably, considerably, dramatically, enormously, gradually, greatly, marginally, rapidly, significantly, slightly, steadily, substantially, suddenly, tremendously, visibly
INDEBTED
deeply, enormously, greatly, heavily *indebted*
INDEPENDENT
absolutely, completely, dangerously, fiercely, fully, genuinely, newly, totally *independent*
INDICATE
indicate sth beyond all doubt, by one's manner, discreetly, in a roundabout way, subtly
clearly, plainly *indicate* sth
INDICATIVE
broadly, strongly *indicative*
INDIFFERENT
callously, completely, totally *indifferent*
INDISCREET
extremely, famously, notoriously, somewhat, terribly *indiscreet*

249

INDULGE
freely, occasionally, rarely *indulge*
INEPT
appallingly, completely, hopelessly, shockingly, somewhat, totally *inept*
INEXHAUSTIBLE
absolutely, apparently, seemingly, virtually *inexhaustible*
INFILTRATE
infiltrate clandestinely, surreptitiously
cleverly, secretly *infiltrate*
INFLUENCE
influence enormously, greatly, profoundly, strongly
INFLUENCED
heavily, profoundly, slightly, strongly, tremendously, unconsciously, undoubtedly, unduly, unfairly *influenced*
INFLUENTIAL
enormously, extremely, highly *influential*
INFORM
inform belatedly, immediately, in person, in writing, personally
regretfully *inform*

> **INFORM**
> *Inform* is similar to other verbs which describe how we speak, for example, *add, speak, reply*. Because they also describe an action, they collocate with many different adverbs of manner.

INFORMED
duly, fully, immediately, (un)officially, reliably *informed*
INFORMAL
completely, extremely, purely, relatively *informal*
INFURIATING
absolutely *infuriating*
INJURED
badly, fatally, seriously, severely, slightly *injured*
INQUIRE (see ENQUIRE)
INQUISITIVE
exceedingly *inquisitive*
INSANE
absolutely, certifiably, completely, totally *insane*
INSIST
insist loudly, repeatedly, vehemently that...
absolutely, adamantly, obstinately, (quite) rightly, stubbornly *insist*...
INSOLUBLE
absolutely, basically, inherently, virtually *insoluble*
INSPECT
inspect carefully, closely, perfunctorily, thoroughly
INSTALL
install free of charge, properly

INTACT
largely, more or less, still, totally *intact*
INTELLIGENT
extremely, highly, outstandingly, relatively *intelligent*
INTELLIGIBLE
barely, hardly, perfectly, scarcely *intelligible*
INTEND
definitely, firmly, fully, genuinely, obviously, originally, seriously, vaguely *intend*
INTENT
absolutely, fully, wholly *intent* on...
INTERESTED
deeply, definitely, extremely, genuinely, intensely, keenly, mildly, most, not remotely, particularly, passionately, primarily, seriously, tremendously, vaguely *interested*
INTERESTING
consistently, extremely, fairly, intrinsically, not remotely, outstandingly, particularly, perennially, specially, thoroughly *interesting*
INTERFERE
interfere all the time, constantly, unduly
INTERFERING
always, constantly *interfering*
INTERPRET
interpret sth (quite) correctly, literally, strictly, wrongly
faithfully, roughly *interpret* sth
INTERRUPT
briefly, brutally, constantly, continually, rudely *interrupt*
INTERVENE
intervene effectively, forcefully, forcibly, personally, publicly
INTRODUCE
introduce experimentally, generally, tentatively
initially, finally *introduce*
INTUITIVE
completely, largely, purely, totally *intuitive*
INVENTIVE
amazingly, endlessly, wonderfully *inventive*
INVEST
invest foolishly, heavily, massively, modestly, prudently, rashly, (un)wisely
INVESTIGATE
investigate carefully, closely, fully, rigorously, thoroughly, urgently
INVOLVED
closely, deeply, directly, emotionally, foolishly, heavily, inadvertently, inextricably, intimately, seriously, secretly, unintentionally, unwittingly *involved*
IRRATIONAL
completely, totally, utterly *irrational*
IRRITATING
deeply, exceedingly, extremely *irritating*

J

JEALOUS
insanely, madly, obsessively *jealous*
JEOPARDIZE
needlessly, seriously *jeopardize* sth
JOIN
join eagerly, reluctantly, voluntarily, willingly
JOIN IN
join in enthusiastically, happily, reluctantly, wholeheartedly
JUDGE
judge accurately, correctly, exactly, (un)fairly, harshly, impartially, objectively, severely, sternly, wrongly
JUMP (increase)
jump dramatically, sharply
JUSTIFIED
fully, largely, perfectly, scarcely, wholly *justified*

K

KEEN
extremely, fairly, particularly *keen*
KEEP
keep sth permanently, safe(ly), securely

> **KEEP**
> *Keep* has very little meaning on its own, but it is used in many expressions – *keep warm, keep your job, keep going.* You will find these expressions in your ordinary dictionary.

KILL
kill sb accidentally, in a fit of jealousy/rage, in cold blood
KNOCK
knock gently, loudly, sharply
KNOW
know sth at once, backwards, by heart, for certain/sure, from experience, from the outset, from A to Z, full well, in detail, intuitively, instinctively, (London) like the back of (my) hand, somehow, thoroughly
know sb by name/sight/reputation, intimately, personally, professionally, since childhood, slightly, socially, vaguely
KNOWLEDGEABLE
amazingly, extremely, incredibly, surprisingly *knowledgeable*
KNOWN
hardly, internationally, little, widely *known*

L

LACK
obviously *lack* sth
LACKING
altogether, badly, conspicuously, notoriously, seriously, totally *lacking* in sth
LAUGH
laugh heartily, helplessly, loudly, nervously, openly, out loud, spontaneously, uneasily

> **LAUGH**
> Verbs which describe an action – for example, *laugh, smile, walk* – can be used with many different adverbs of manner which tell you how the person did the action. You can 'laugh' *apologetically, happily, ruefully*. These collocations are correct, but are not strong enough or frequent enough to be listed here. To help you with questions you may have when, for example, writing an essay, we include only the most useful collocations.

LAY
lay sth carefully, diagonally, evenly, flat, neatly
LAZY
downright, thoroughly *lazy*
LEAD
(in)directly, eventually, finally, gradually, inevitably, ultimately *lead* to sth
LEAP
leap athletically, boldly, excitedly, nimbly
LEARN
learn by doing, by heart, by observation, by rote, from experience, fast, gradually, naturally, the hard way
LEAVE
leave hastily, in a hurry, on time, punctually, quietly, suddenly
LEAVE BEHIND
leave sth *behind* absentmindedly, by mistake, on purpose
carelessly *leave* sth *behind*
LIABLE
personally, solely, ultimately *liable*
LIFT
lift sth carefully, effortlessly, gently, with care/difficulty
barely, hardly *lift* sth
LIKE
like enormously, tremendously
instinctively, really *like* ...
LIKE (similar to)
a bit, a little, a lot, not remotely, rather, remarkably *like* ...
LIKEABLE
extremely, instantly *likeable*
LIKELY
extremely, hardly, highly, least, (far/much) less, (far/much) more, most *likely*

LIMIT
limit drastically, strictly
LIMITED
strictly *limited*
LINGER
linger briefly
LINKED
closely, inextricably, intimately, loosely, mysteriously, secretly *linked* to/with sb/sth
LISTEN
listen attentively, carefully, closely, eagerly, hard, impassively, intently, patiently, politely, sympathetically, with interest

> **LISTEN**
> Verbs which describe an action – for example, *listen, smile, walk* – can be used with many different adverbs of manner which tell you how the person did the action. You can 'listen' *absent-mindedly, respectfully, wearily*. These collocations are correct, but are not strong enough or frequent enough to be listed here. To help you with questions you may have when, for example, writing an essay, we include only the most useful collocations.

LIT
badly, brightly, dimly, dramatically, feebly, poorly, softly *lit*
LIVE
live abroad, alone, at/by the seaside, beyond your means, by (yourself), comfortably, dangerously, downstairs, down the road/street, extravagantly, from hand to mouth, frugally, happily ever after, in peace/harmony, in comfort/luxury, in cramped/overcrowded conditions, modestly, next door, overseas, peacefully, to a ripe old age, upstairs
LOCATE
easily, precisely, roughly *locate* sth
LOCK UP
lock sth *up* properly, safely, securely
LOGICAL
completely, entirely, totally *logical*
LONG
exceedingly, extremely, fairly, incredibly, infinitely, inordinately, surprisingly, tremendously *long*
LOOK
look all right, good, fabulous, fine, great, ill, marvellous, sick, terrible, well, wonderful

> **LOOK**
> Notice most of the words used in this structure are adjectives, not adverbs. *He looks terrible. Everything looks fine.* See also *appear* and *seem*.

LOOK AFTER
look after sb/sth carefully, properly
LOOK AHEAD
look ahead anxiously, apprehensively, optimistically, pessimistically, with confidence

LOOK AROUND
 look around anxiously, frantically, helplessly, shyly

LOOK AT
 look at (things, the situation) again, carefully, calmly, dispassionately, (more) closely, from (my/another) point of view, in detail, objectively

> **LOOK AT**
> This is another case where it is almost impossible to give a general list of adverbs. You can *look at* almost anything and feel many different emotions about what you see, so the adverb depends on both what you see and how you feel. So, you can *look greedily at something to eat, look suspiciously at someone who is doing something strange, look enviously at a friend's new car etc.* A general list will not help you, but it helps if you think of the noun which follows *look at* and of how you feel.

LOOK BACK
 look back fondly, in anger, nostalgically

LOOK FOR
 look anxiously, desperately, everywhere, frantically, systematically *for ...*

LOOK FORWARD TO
 look forward eagerly, enormously, keenly *to* sth

LOOK ON
 look on calmly, coldly, helplessly, impassively

LOOK ROUND
 look round anxiously, apprehensively, cautiously

LOSE (eg a competition)
 lose by a considerable/wide margin, consistently, decisively, (sth) forever, heavily, narrowly

LOST
 completely, hopelessly, irretrievably, totally *lost*

LOVE
 love sb dearly, passionately, tenderly, to distraction, with all (my) heart
 deeply, really, truly *love* sb

LOVED
 greatly, universally *loved*

LOVELY
 absolutely *lovely*

LOW
 alarmingly, dangerously, disconcertingly, disgracefully *low*

LOWER
 a bit, a little, much, significantly, slightly, substantially *lower*

LOYAL
 absolutely, completely, fiercely, intensely, surprisingly, totally, touchingly *loyal*

LUCKY
 amazingly, astonishingly, extraordinarily, extremely, surprisingly, unbelievably *lucky*

LUCRATIVE
 amazingly, extremely, highly, potentially *lucrative*

LURK
 lurk in the background, unobtrusively, suspiciously

M

MADE

badly, beautifully, carelessly, crudely, exquisitely, poorly, roughly, solidly, sturdily, well- *made*

MAINTAIN

maintain consistently, staunchly, strongly that...

MAINTAINED

badly, beautifully, impeccably, poorly, well-*maintained*

> **MAKE**
> The word *make* on its own has almost no meaning, but it is used in many different collocations such as to *make friends, make a mistake, make a difference.* Each of these has different collocations. So, once again, it is not possible to give a helpful general list.

MANAGE

manage sth badly, (in)competently, effectively, efficiently, discreetly, prudently, well, wisely

MANIPULATE

manipulate sb cleverly, cynically, ruthlessly, skilfully

MARCH

march proudly, purposefully, stiffly

MATCH

match beautifully, exactly, perfectly

MATCHED

evenly, ill-, perfectly, well- *matched*

MATTER

matter enormously, greatly, tremendously

MEAN

actually, automatically, clearly, inevitably, obviously, really *mean* sth

MEET

meet (sb) by appointment, by arrangement, by chance, clandestinely, fortuitously, in private/secret, on a regular basis, regularly, secretly

MEMORABLE

truly *memorable*

MENTION

mention briefly, casually, in passing, obliquely, rarely, seldom, tentatively, vaguely

MERGE

gradually, imperceptibly, subtly *merge* with/into sth

MINGLE

mingle freely

MISERABLE

absolutely, rather, utterly *miserable*

MISJUDGE

badly, fatally, grossly, seriously *misjudge* ...

MISLEAD

accidentally, deliberately, (un)intentionally *mislead* sb

MISLEADING
badly, completely, notoriously, somewhat, totally, wholly *misleading*

MISREPRESENT
grossly, wilfully *misrepresent* sth

MISS
miss (the target) altogether, by a hair's breadth, by a whisker, by a wide margin, completely, consistently, narrowly
just, narrowly *miss* (the target)

MISS (bus etc)
almost, just, nearly *miss* (the bus)

MISS (home etc)
miss (home) badly, dreadfully, terribly

MISSED (after death)
badly, greatly, sadly, sorely *missed*

MISTAKE
constantly, continually, easily, readily *mistake* sth

MISTAKEN
altogether, badly, completely, sadly, seriously, totally, utterly, wholly *mistaken*

MISTRUST
deeply, instinctively *mistrust* sb/sth

MISUNDERSTAND
completely, totally *misunderstand* sb/sth

MISUNDERSTOOD
badly, completely, sadly, widely *misunderstood*

MIX (socially)
mix easily, freely, openly, socially

MOBILISED
fully, quickly, rapidly *mobilised*

MOCK
mock sb cruelly, gently, unmercifully

MOCKED
cruelly *mocked*

MODIFY
modify drastically, greatly, radically, slightly, subtly, to some extent

MONITOR
monitor actively, carefully, closely, round the clock

MONOPOLISE
effectively, totally *monopolise* sth

MOVE
move adroitly, aimlessly, awkwardly, back, backwards, briskly, cautiously, effortlessly, fast, forward, freely, gracefully, lethargically, noiselessly, purposefully, quickly, restlessly, sideways, smoothly, stealthily, swiftly

MOVE AWAY
move away discreetly, tactfully

MOVE TOWARDS
move apprehensively, cautiously, imperceptibly, inexorably, purposefully, rapidly, relentlessly, silently, slowly, steadily, unobtrusively *towards* ...

MOVED
moved to tears
deeply *moved*
MOVING
deeply, profoundly *moving*
MUDDLED
badly, completely, dreadfully, hopelessly *muddled*
MULTIPLY
multiply at a fantastic/unbelievable rate, exponentially, indefinitely, rapidly
MUMBLE
mumble distractedly, inarticulately, incoherently, indistinctly, under one's breath
MURDER
murder sb in cold blood
MURDERED
brutally *murdered*
MURMUR
murmur apologetically, confidentially, faintly, gently, in a low voice, nervously, shyly, softly
MUTTER
mutter angrily, discontentedly, inaudibly, under one's breath

N

NAIVE
amazingly, dangerously, extremely, surprisingly, terribly, touchingly *naive*
NAMED
appropriately, aptly, evocatively *named*
NASTY
downright, thoroughly *nasty*
NECESSARY
(not) absolutely, hardly, no longer, not particularly, not strictly, scarcely *necessary*
NEED
badly, definitely, desperately, obviously, really, urgently *need*
NEEDED
badly, desperately, urgently, vitally *needed*
NEGLECT
neglect badly, completely, cruelly, entirely, foolishly, seriously, shamefully, totally
sadly *neglect*
NEGOTIATE
negotiate (sth) from a position of strength, in good faith, patiently, skilfully, under duress
NERVOUS
acutely, dreadfully, extremely, terribly, unaccountably *nervous*
NEW
absolutely, almost, brand-, completely, nearly, totally *new*

NOD

nod appreciatively, approvingly, complacently, contentedly, in agreement, sagely, thoughtfully, vigorously, wearily

NOTE

note carefully, methodically, particularly

NOTICE

notice at once, in particular that ..., in passing that ...

immediately, particularly *notice* sb/sth/that ...

O

OBEY

obey blindly, dutifully, humbly, immediately, reluctantly, strictly, to the letter, unquestioningly, willingly, without question

OBJECT

object loudly, on principle, quite reasonably, strongly, violently, vociferously

OBJECTIVE

absolutely, purely, totally *objective*

OBLIVIOUS

completely, totally, utterly *oblivious*

OBSCENE

totally, utterly *obscene*

OBSCURE

extremely, incredibly *obscure*

OBSERVANT

remarkably *observant*

OBSERVE

observe at close quarters, carefully, closely, critically, from a distance, impassively

OBSERVE (rules)

observe (the rules) exactly, precisely, religiously, rigorously, to the letter

OBSOLETE

almost, completely, increasingly, totally, virtually *obsolete*

OBTAIN

obtain sth easily, freely, illicitly, improperly, legally, (quite) legitimately, on the black market, readily, unlawfully, with/without difficulty

OBTUSE

deliberately, painfully *obtuse*

OBVIOUS

absolutely, blindingly, fairly, glaringly, painfully, perfectly *obvious*

OCCUPIED

busily, fully, happily, peacefully, pleasantly, wholly *occupied*

OCCUR

occur by chance, long ago, once in a lifetime, recently, repeatedly, unexpectedly

hardly, rarely *occur*

OFFENDED
   deeply, mortally *offended*
OFFENSIVE
   deeply, deliberately, extremely, gratuitously, highly, unnecessarily *offensive*
OFFER
   offer sth at a reduced price, for free/nothing, free of charge, in exchange
   generously, kindly, nobly, politely, promptly, rashly *offer*
OLD
   extremely, incredibly, prematurely, terribly *old*
OMIT
   omit altogether, on purpose
   accidentally, carelessly, deliberately *omit*
OPEN (verb)
   open gently, inwards, outwards, suddenly, unexpectedly, wide
OPEN (adj)
   always, barely, completely, half-, wide *open*
OPERATE
   operate at a profit/loss, automatically, badly, clandestinely, continuously, covertly,
   effectively, efficiently, (il)legally, in secret, intermittently, internationally, locally, manually,
   on a wide scale, openly, profitably, publicly, seasonally, secretly, underground
   clearly, currently *operate*
OPPOSE
   oppose sth actively, fiercely, firmly, forcefully, strongly, unanimously, vehemently,
   vigorously, vociferously
OPPOSED
   adamantly, basically, bitterly, completely, diametrically, directly, implacably, strongly,
   totally, utterly, vehemently, violently *opposed* to ...
OPPOSITE
   completely, diagonally, diametrically, directly, straight *opposite*
OPPRESSIVE
   brutally, cruelly, harshly *oppressive*
OPPRESSIVE (weather)
   dreadfully, terribly *oppressive*
OPTIMISTIC
   cautiously, (un)justifiably, over-, (not) overly, guardedly, incorrigibly, naively, unduly,
   unrealistically, (not) wildly *optimistic*
ORDINARY
   perfectly *ordinary*
ORGANISED
   badly, efficiently, highly, poorly, superbly, well- *organised*
ORIGINAL
   boldly, completely, extremely, highly, startlingly, totally *original*
ORNATE
   richly *ornate*
OUTCLASSED
   completely, hopelessly, totally *outclassed*
OUTNUMBERED
   completely, easily, far, greatly, heavily, increasingly, slightly, totally, vastly *outnumbered*

OUT-OF-DATE

completely, hopelessly, increasingly, ludicrously, sadly *out-of-date*

OUTSPOKEN

extremely, fiercely *outspoken*

OVERCOME

overcome sth easily, effortlessly, finally, largely, with great effort

OVERCROWDED

badly, dangerously, dreadfully, unbelievably *overcrowded*

OVERESTIMATE

badly, consistently, dangerously, greatly, grossly, ludicrously, seriously, vastly *overestimate*

OVERRATED

greatly, seriously *overrated*

OWN

own sth completely, in perpetuity, jointly, outright, personally

P

PACK

pack hastily, neatly, safely, tidily, tightly

PAID

badly, over-, under-, well- *paid*

PAINFUL

acutely, bitterly, deeply, dreadfully, excruciatingly, extremely, terribly, unbearably *painful*

PAINTED

brightly, freshly, gaily, garishly *painted*

PARALLEL

absolutely, approximately, exactly, more or less, roughly, strictly *parallel*

PART (leave)

part acrimoniously, amicably, forever, tearfully

PASS

pass freely, without hindrance

PASS (an exam)

pass brilliantly, easily, with flying colours, without any difficulty

barely, only just *pass*

PATRONISING

extremely, mildly *patronising*

PATTERNED

beautifully, brightly, intricately *patterned*

PAUSE

pause briefly, expectantly, for an instant

PAY

pay by bank draft, by cheque, by credit card, by return, (in) cash, cash on delivery, generously, immediately, in advance, in full, in instalments, on the spot, promptly, reluctantly, through the nose, willingly

261

PECULIAR
  extremely *peculiar*
PEER
  peer anxiously, closely, inquisitively, suspiciously, uncertainly
PERCEIVE
  clearly, dimly, vaguely *perceive*
PERCEIVED
  rightly, wrongly *perceived* to be ...
PERCEPTIBLE
  barely, scarcely *perceptible*
PERCHED
  perched precariously on sth
PERFECT
  perfect in every way
  absolutely, almost, well-nigh *perfect*
PERFORM
  perform badly, brilliantly, creditably, flawlessly, poorly, (un)predictably
PERPLEXED
  greatly, rather, thoroughly, vaguely *perplexed*
PERPLEXING
  thoroughly, totally, utterly *perplexing*
PERSIST
  persist grimly, obstinately, stubbornly
PERSUADE
  persuade sb in the end
  eventually, finally *persuade* sb
PESSIMISTIC
  comparatively, deeply, extremely, relatively, somewhat, unduly *pessimistic*
PICK UP (improve)
  pick up dramatically, remarkably well, significantly, unexpectedly
PLAIN
  absolutely, fairly, perfectly, totally *plain*
PLAN
  plan ahead, beforehand, brilliantly, carefully, in detail, meticulously, secretly, systematically
PLANNED
  carefully, meticulously *planned*
PLAY
  play as a team, badly, brilliantly, competitively, freely, professionally, safely, together, well
PLAY (music)
  play badly, beautifully, brilliantly, magnificently, perfectly, poorly, too loud/quietly
PLEAD
  plead desperately, eloquently
PLEASED
  distinctly, enormously, extremely, fairly, genuinely, justifiably, not altogether, obviously, sincerely, tremendously *pleased*
PLUNGE INTO
  plunge foolishly, headlong, rashly, recklessly, thoughtlessly *into* ...

POINT OUT

point out firmly, proudly, repeatedly, smugly

POLITE

extremely, scrupulously, unfailingly *polite*

POOR

comparatively, desperately, extremely, relatively *poor*

POPULAR

enormously, extremely, generally, increasingly, incredibly, tremendously, unbelievably, undeniably, universally *popular*

POPULATED

densely, heavily, sparsely, thinly *populated*

PORTRAY

portray (un)favourably, in a/an (un)favourable light

PORTRAYED

accurately, faithfully, vividly *portrayed*

POSSESSIVE

extremely, fiercely *possessive*

POSSIBLE

basically, certainly, clearly, definitely, distinctly, eminently, entirely, hardly, just (not), (not) remotely, scarcely, theoretically *possible*

POSTPONE

postpone sth for a while, indefinitely, reluctantly, till a later date

POWERFUL

immensely, tremendously *powerful*

POWERLESS

completely *powerless*

PRACTISE

practise a lot, at home, diligently, for hours (on end), intensively, regularly

PRAISED

highly *praised*

PRECISE

absolutely, relatively, scrupulously *precise*

PREDICT

predict accurately, gloomily, precisely

confidently, consistently, correctly, safely, wrongly *predict*

PREDICTABLE

completely, easily, eminently, fairly, highly, sadly, totally *predictable*

PREFERABLE

greatly *preferable*

PREJUDICE

seriously *prejudice* sth

PREJUDICED

blatantly, deeply *prejudiced*

PREPARE

prepare (well) beforehand, carefully, meticulously, systematically, well ahead of time

PREPARED

(not) adequately, badly, carefully, fully, just not, painstakingly, skillfully, thoroughly, well-*prepared*

PREPOSTEROUS
absolutely, quite, frankly, totally *preposterous*
PRESERVE
preserve carefully, for all time, for posterity, religiously
PRETTY
exceptionally, extremely *pretty*
PREVAIL
ultimately *prevail*
prevail against the odds, in the end
PREVENT
prevent sth (from happening)/sb from doing sth altogether, as far as possible, at all costs, by all possible means, no matter what happens
completely, effectively *prevent* sth
PRICED
competitively, moderately, modestly, reasonably *priced*
PROCEED
proceed as agreed/planned/usual, reluctantly
PROCLAIM
proclaim boldly, loudly, publicly sth/that...
PRODUCE
produce abroad, artificially, automatically, cheaply, economically, efficiently, en masse, for export, for home consumption, for the domestic market, in bulk, in large quantities, locally
PROFITABLE
amazingly, barely, enormously, highly, immensely, moderately, potentially *profitable*
PROGRESS
progress satisfactorily, smoothly, steadily
PROLONG
prolong sth indefinitely, unduly, unnecessarily
PROMISE
promise faithfully, solemnly
PROMOTE
promote cleverly, energetically, enthusiastically, tirelessly
PROPHESY
prophesy accurately, confidently, gloomily, optimistically
PROPORTIONED
badly, beautifully, finely, generously, magnificently, well- *proportioned*
PROTECT
protect adequately, effectively, fiercely, from harm, fully, properly
PROTECTED
heavily *protected*
PROTEST
protest angrily, bitterly, feebly, fiercely, furiously, half-heartedly, in the strongest possible terms, in vain, loudly, publicly, strongly, vigorously, violently
PROUD
enormously, immensely, justifiably *proud*
PROVE
prove beyond all doubt/question, conclusively, decisively, definitely, easily, logically, theoretically, without a (shadow of) doubt that...

PROVIDED FOR
adequately, comfortably, generously, properly *provided for*

PROVOCATIVE
deliberately, extremely, openly, unnecessarily *provocative*

PROVOKE
deliberately, unwittingly *provoke*

PRUNED
drastically, severely *pruned*

PUBLICISED
heavily, widely *publicised*

PUBLISHED
newly, recently *published*

PULL
pull gently, hard, steadily, tight, vigorously, with all one's might

PUNISH
punish harshly, severely, unjustly

PURSUE
pursue doggedly, relentlessly, ruthlessly, single-mindedly, systematically, tenaciously, wholeheartedly
actively, systematically *pursue*

PUT IT (say)
put it admirably, bluntly, briefly, crudely, delicately, in a nutshell, mildly, plainly, politely, tactfully

> **PUT**
> *Put* has very little meaning on its own, but it is used in many expressions. For example *put the kids to bed, put the matter beyond all doubt.* You should find these expressions in your ordinary dictionary.

PUZZLED
genuinely, greatly, totally *puzzled*

Q

QUALIFIED
highly, (in)adequately, poorly, (not) properly, well- *qualified*

QUARREL
quarrel bitterly, constantly, continually, fiercely, incessantly, violently

QUESTION
question sb closely, personally

QUESTIONABLE
highly *questionable*

QUOTE
quote accurately, at (great) length, extensively, verbatim, word for word

R

RAISE
raise (prices) appreciably, considerably, dramatically, progressively, sharply, slightly, steadily

RANDOM
completely, purely, seemingly, totally *random*

RANGE
range widely

RARE
comparatively, exceedingly, extremely, fairly, increasingly, relatively *rare*

REACH
eventually, finally, ultimately *reach* ...

REACT
react angrily, atypically, badly, calmly, coldly, favourably, indignantly, instantly, instinctively, irritably, negatively, normally, positively, properly, strangely, strongly, swiftly, typically, violently, with surprise

READ
read aloud, avidly, badly, carefully, closely, convincingly, eagerly, expressively, extensively, from cover to cover, in detail, over and over again, thoughtfully, quickly (=superficially), voraciously, widely, with (great) interest

REALISE
realise at once, belatedly, clearly, in a flash, immediately, instinctively, suddenly, too late, with hindsight that...
fully, suddenly *realise* that ...

REASONABLE
completely, entirely, fairly, perfectly *reasonable*

REASONABLE (cheap)
extremely, fairly, pretty *reasonable*

REASSURED
completely, somewhat, totally *reassured*

REASSURING
oddly, pleasantly *reassuring*

REBEL AGAINST
rebel angrily, fiercely *against* ...

REBUKE
rebuke sb harshly, severely, sternly

RECALL
recall clearly, fondly, in detail, instantly, vaguely, vividly
scarcely, vaguely, vividly *recall*

RECEIVE
receive gladly, gratefully, secretly, through the post
occasionally, recently, regularly *receive*

RECEIVED
enthusiastically, (not) favourably, (not) well *received* by (the critics)

RECOGNISABLE
easily, faintly, instantly, scarcely *recognisable*
RECOGNISE
recognise sb/sth at once, easily, immediately, instantly
fully, hardly, scarcely *recognise* ...
RECOLLECT
barely, clearly, vaguely, vividly *recollect*
RECOMMEND
recommend sb/sth personally, specifically, strongly, unreservedly, warmly
confidently, strongly *recommend*
RECOMMENDED
highly *recommended*
RECONSIDER
reconsider carefully
urgently *reconsider*
RECORD
record faithfully, verbatim
RECOVER
completely, fully, gradually, miraculously *recover*
RECOVERED
fully, not entirely/quite, properly *recovered*
REDUCE
reduce sth considerably, dramatically, drastically, significantly, substantially
REDUCED
greatly, severely *reduced*
REFER TO
refer casually, contemptuously, disparagingly, in passing, jocularly, obliquely, scathingly,
vaguely *to* ...
REFLECT
reflect faithfully, for a moment, precisely
accurately, dimly, genuinely, (in)directly, strongly *reflect* ...
REFRAIN FROM
refrain from ...-ing altogether
completely, politely, wisely *refrain from* ...-ing
REFUSE
refuse angrily, consistently, outright, point-blank, politely, reluctantly
absolutely, adamantly, categorically, firmly, flatly, invariably, obstinately, pointedly,
stubbornly *refuse*
REGAIN
finally, fortunately, momentarily, partially, partly, ultimately *regain* sth
REGARDED
commonly, generally *regarded* as sth
REGRET
bitterly, deeply, sincerely, very much *regret* sth
REGULATED
carefully, strictly *regulated*
REINFORCE
greatly, strongly *reinforce* sth

REINTRODUCE
  reintroduce gradually, in stages, step by step
REJECT
  reject sth out of hand
  absolutely, completely, emphatically, firmly, totally, unanimously, utterly *reject* sth
RELATED
  closely, distantly *related*
RELAX
  relax completely, properly, totally
  safely *relax*
RELAXED
  completely, perfectly, totally *relaxed*
RELEASE
  release sb eventually, finally, immediately, promptly, unconditionally
RELEVANT
  extremely, hardly, totally *relevant*
RELIEVE
  relieve (the pain) instantly, somewhat
RELIEVED
  extremely, enormously, greatly *relieved*
RELY
  rely absolutely, completely, heavily, mainly, mostly, partly, solely, totally on sb/sth
REMAIN
  remain somewhere indefinitely, permanently, to the very end
REMARK
  remark bitterly, casually, complacently, conversationally, drily, in passing, perceptively
REMARKABLE
  absolutely, really, truly *remarkable*
REMEMBER
  remember clearly, exactly, perfectly, vaguely, vividly
  clearly, distinctly, faintly, hardly, particularly, scarcely, vaguely, vividly *remember*
REMEMBERED
  chiefly *remembered* for ...
REMIND
  remind sb gently
REMINDED
  painfully, vividly *reminded* of sth
REMINISCENT
  curiously, faintly, strangely, strongly, vaguely *reminiscent* of sth
REMOVE
  remove sth altogether, bit by bit, carefully, completely, easily, entirely, illegally, neatly, partially, promptly, totally, unceremoniously, with difficulty
  completely, gently, totally *remove*
REPAIR
  repair badly, neatly, properly, skillfully
REPEAT
  repeat sth again and again, constantly, continually, incessantly, over and over again, parrot-fashion, verbatim, word for word

REPENT
fully, sincerely, subsequently *repent*
REPETITIVE
boringly, extremely *repetitive*
REPLACE
replace sth carefully, discreetly, hurriedly, quickly
REPLY
reply abruptly, angrily, at length, by return, calmly, confidently, contemptuously, dismissively, eagerly, evasively, firmly, gently, impatiently, nonchalantly, non-committally, politely, simply

> **REPLY**
> This is a word like *speak* where there are many adverbs of manner which can occur; you can *reply gloomily, proudly, wearily*. The list above gives strong collocations of *reply*.

REPORT
report accurately, briefly, extensively, faithfully, in depth/detail, regularly, reliably, verbatim, word for word
REPORTED
extensively, reliably, widely *reported* that ...
REPRESSED
brutally, savagely *repressed*
REPRESSIVE
brutally, ruthlessly *repressive*
REPRIMAND
officially, severely *reprimand* sb
REPRODUCE
reproduce clearly, exactly, perfectly
REPRODUCED
beautifully, faithfully *reproduced*
REPUDIATE
repudiate sth altogether
firmly, strongly *repudiate* sth
REPUGNANT
completely, totally *repugnant*
REQUEST
kindly, politely, urgently *request* sth
RESEARCHED
accurately, carefully, exhaustively, laboriously, meticulously, properly, thoroughly, well-*researched*
RESEMBLE
closely, faintly, not remotely, superficially, vaguely *resemble* sb/sth
RESENT
bitterly, deeply, strongly *resent* sth
RESENTFUL
bitterly, deeply, strongly *resentful* (about sth)

RESERVED
extremely *reserved*

RESIST
resist sth blindly, bravely, courageously, determinedly, fiercely, firmly, stubbornly, vigorously

RESOLVE
resolve (the problem) immediately, properly, speedily, straightaway, quickly

RESOLVED
fully, properly *resolved*

RESPECT
fully *respect*

RESPECTABLE
eminently, highly, outwardly, perfectly, totally *respectable*

RESPECTED
greatly, highly, internationally, universally, well-, widely *respected*

RESPOND
respond eagerly, emotionally, enthusiastically, favourably, furiously, generously, immediately, instantly, instinctively, magnificently, negatively, passionately, positively, promptly, sympathetically

RESTORED
restored to its former glory, to its original condition
beautifully, faithfully, impeccably, lovingly, painstakingly, patiently *restored*

RESTRICTED
heavily, severely *restricted*

RESULT
result automatically, eventually, inevitably in ...

RETREAT
retreat in confusion/disarray/disorder/panic

RETURN
return again and again, in due course, in triumph, reluctantly, safely, unexpectedly
eventually *return*

RETURN TO
return again and again, constantly *to* (an idea)

REVEAL
reveal in detail, publicly
clearly, fully, deliberately, inadvertently, gradually, plainly, unintentionally, unwittingly *reveal*

REVERT TO
revert automatically, rapidly *to* sth

REVIEW
review (the evidence, situation) carefully, calmly, critically, in the light of ..., objectively, rigorously, systematically

REVIEWED
reviewed at length, critically, (un)favourably

REVISE
revise sth carefully, drastically, extensively, substantially, thoroughly

REWARDED
fairly, generously, lavishly, poorly, properly *rewarded*

REWARDING
  deeply, extremely, potentially, unexpectedly *rewarding*
RICH
  comparatively, enormously, fabulously, tremendously *rich*
RIDICULOUS
  absolutely, completely, faintly, slightly, totally, utterly *ridiculous*
RIGHT
  absolutely, almost, completely, exactly, morally, nearly, partly *right*
RISE
  rise alarmingly, appreciably, considerably, dangerously, dramatically, fast, enormously, gradually, inexorably, marginally, noticeably, rapidly, remorselessly, sharply, significantly, slightly, steadily, steeply, substantially, suddenly, tremendously, uncontrollably
RISK
  risk sth foolishly, recklessly, stupidly, unwisely
ROMANTIC
  extremely, hopelessly, incredibly, incurably, purely *romantic*
RUDE
  extremely, incredibly, terribly *rude*
RUIN
  completely, utterly *ruin* sth
RULE
  rule autocratically, benignly, fairly, wisely
RULE OUT
  absolutely, not entirely, totally *rule out* (the possibility)
RUN (function)
  run badly, beautifully, effectively, efficiently, like clockwork, perfectly, properly, smoothly
RUN (adj)
  competently, efficiently, faultlessly, well- *run*
RUTHLESS
  absolutely, completely, totally, utterly *ruthless*

S

SACK
  sack sb on the spot, without notice/warning
SAD
  dreadfully, extremely, terribly, tremendously *sad*
SATISFACTORY
  (not) completely, far from, not altogether, perfectly, (not) wholly *satisfactory*
SATISFIED
  absolutely, comparatively, (not) completely, (not) entirely, fully, not altogether, perfectly, relatively, thoroughly, totally *satisfied*
SATISFYING
  completely, extremely, thoroughly, wholly *satisfying*

SAVE
    save carefully, hard, systematically, weekly/monthly etc
SCEPTICAL
    deeply, profoundly, somewhat *sceptical*
SCRIBBLE
    scribble furiously, illegibly, secretly, surreptitiously
SCRUTINIZE
    scrutinize sth carefully, closely, in minute detail, keenly
SEARCH
    search anxiously, carefully, desperately, diligently, everywhere, frantically, high and low, inch by inch, in vain, methodically, systematically, thoroughly, tirelessly
SECURE
    absolutely, comparatively, completely, fairly, reasonably, perfectly, totally *secure*
SEE
    see sb/sth clearly, distinctly, faintly, in the distance
SEE (understand)
    see clearly, exactly, instinctively, intuitively, more or less, precisely (what you mean)
SEEK
    seek constantly, desperately, endlessly, in vain
SEEM
    clearly, definitely, quite frankly *seem* to be ...
SEEM (appear)
    it clearly, definitely, probably *seems* ...
    it *seems* certain, doubtful, (un)likely, plausible, possible, probable, reasonable, strange, wrong that ...

> **SEEM**
> Notice the words used in this structure are adjectives, not adverbs. *Seem* is used in a similar way like this: *He seems tired. It seems expensive. She seems efficient.* See also *appear* and *look*.

SEIZE
    seize sth by force, unlawfully
SELECT
    select sth carefully
SELECTED
    carefully, specially *selected*
SELECTIVE
    highly *selective*
SELF-CONSCIOUS
    acutely, extremely, painfully *self-conscious*
SELL
    sell at auction, at the going rate, at cost, at a loss, at a profit, cheaply, easily, like hot cakes, piecemeal, slowly, well
SELL OFF
    sell off cheaply
SEND
    send sth by air, courier, e-mail, fax, mail, messenger, post, return

SENSIBLE

extremely, eminently, thoroughly *sensible*

SENSITIVE

extremely, particularly, relatively *sensitive*

SENTIMENTAL

cloyingly, ludicrously, ridiculously, sickeningly, stupidly *sentimental*

SERIOUS

comparatively, deadly, extremely, incredibly, relatively, totally *serious*

SERVE

serve (the organisation) devotedly, faithfully, loyally

SET

Set has very little meaning on its own, but it is used in many expressions where the second part is a noun; *set the price, set objectives, set a good example*. You should find these expressions in your ordinary dictionary.

SET OFF

set off at the crack of dawn, at once, early, immediately, late, promptly

SET UP

set up initially, in the first place, originally

SETTLE

settle (there) for good, permanently

SETTLE (a dispute)

settle (a dispute) amicably, once and for all, out of court, properly, to everyone's satisfaction

SEVERE

comparatively, excessively, extremely, relatively, uncompromisingly *severe*

SHAKE

shake sb/sth energetically, gently, hard, thoroughly, vigorously, violently, well

SHAKEN

badly, seriously *shaken*

SHARE

share equally, generously, readily, (un)willingly

SHATTERED

absolutely, completely, totally, utterly *shattered*

SHIFT

shift (your views) appreciably, considerably, dangerously, noticeably, sideways, slightly, to the right/left, visibly

SHOCKED

badly, dreadfully, profoundly, terribly *shocked*

SHOCKING

absolutely, deeply, deliberately, profoundly, really, truly, utterly *shocking*

SHOUT

shout angrily, at the top of one's voice

SHOW

show beyond all doubt, clearly, conclusively, once and for all, plainly, to a certain extent, unambiguously, unmistakably, vividly that ...

SHY

desperately, dreadfully, extremely, painfully, terribly *shy*

SIGH
  sigh deeply, heavily, softly, wearily
SIGN
  sign on the dotted line, under duress, where indicated
SIGNIFICANT
  extremely, highly, profoundly, terribly *significant*
SILENT
  silent as the grave
  absolutely, completely, ominously, totally *silent*
SIMILAR
  fairly, remarkably, somewhat, strikingly, superficially *similar*
SIMPLE
  comparatively, deceptively, extremely, relatively, remarkably, unbelievably *simple*
SIMPLIFY
  simplify sth drastically, enormously, greatly, radically, somewhat
SIT
  sit upright, comfortably, quietly, still
SITUATED
  badly, beautifully, conveniently, ideally, perfectly, poorly, well- *situated*
SKILLED
  highly *skilled*
SLEEP
  sleep badly, fitfully, heavily, lightly, like a log/top, peacefully, round the clock, soundly, uneasily, well
SLIDE
  slide gently, gradually, out of control, silently
SLOW
  dreadfully, extremely, painfully, pitifully, relatively, terribly *slow*
SLUMP
  slump alarmingly, badly, disastrously, heavily, rapidly, sharply
SMALL
  comparatively, fairly, pitifully, relatively, ridiculously *small*
SMELL
  smell awful, delicious, disgusting, foul, horrible, terrible

> **SMELL**
> Notice the words used in this structure are adjectives, not adverbs. Other similar verbs are: *appear, look, seem.*

SMILE
  smile happily, pleasantly, politely, sweetly, tenderly, warmly

> **SMILE**
> Verbs which describe an action – for example, *act, smile, walk* – can be used with many different adverbs of manner which tell you how the person did the action. You can 'smile' *thoughtfully, quietly, proudly.* These collocations are correct, but are not strong enough or frequent enough to be listed here. To help you with questions you may have when writing an essay, we include only the most useful.

SOB
  sob bitterly, loudly, uncontrollably

SOLVE
  solve sth altogether, satisfactorily, single-handed(ly), together, to (my own) satisfaction
  completely, partly *solve* sth

SORRY
  dreadfully, extremely, terribly, truly *sorry*

SOUND (adj)
  absolutely, basically, fundamentally, perfectly, reasonably *sound*

SPEAK
  speak at length, calmly, clearly, confidently, eloquently, enthusiastically, in a clear/loud/shrill voice, loudly, movingly, openly, passionately, persuasively, quietly, simply, softly, with authority/confidence, with a(n) accent/lisp/stammer/stutter

> **SPEAK**
> This is another word which has a great many loose collocations – *speak arrogantly, feelingly, scathingly.*

SPEND
  spend (money) extravagantly, freely, heavily, lavishly, liberally, wisely
  easily, happily, idly *spend* (time)

SPOILT (of a child)
  completely, dreadfully, terribly, thoroughly, totally, utterly *spoilt*

SPREAD
  spread all over the world, evenly, far and wide, fast, for miles, like wildfire, out of control, quickly, rapidly, smoothly, swiftly, thickly, thinly, widely

SPRINKLE
  sprinkle sth all over, evenly, generously, lightly, sparingly (on) sth

SQUALID
  extremely, indescribably, utterly *squalid*

SQUANDER
  squander sth foolishly, irresponsibly

SQUEEZE
  squeeze sb/sth gently, hard, tight

STAINED
  badly *stained*

STAND
  stand at ease, to attention, erect, motionless, patiently, quietly, still, stock-still

STAND
  (the building) *stands* back from the street, in a prominent/exposed position, in its own grounds, on a hill/slope, on the main square

STAND OUT
  stand out clearly, plainly, prominently

STARE
  stare blankly, blindly, coldly, hard, in horror, intently

START
  start sth afresh, (all over) again, badly, disastrously, from scratch, inauspiciously, in a small way, modestly, promisingly, well

STATE
state briefly, bluntly, categorically, clearly, confidently, explicitly, officially, openly, plainly, repeatedly, specifically, unequivocally, that ...

STEP
step aside, backward, carefully, cautiously, forward

STINK
stink to high heaven

STOP
stop abruptly, altogether, dead, in (your) tracks, once and for all, straightaway
effectively *stop*

STRESS
stress as strongly as possible, constantly, in the strongest possible terms, particularly, repeatedly

STRETCH
stretch a long way, away into the distance, endlessly, for miles, on forever

STRICT
excessively, extremely, relatively, unnecessarily *strict*

STRIKE
strike sb/sth again and again, forcibly, furiously, repeatedly

STRIKE (impress)
strike (me) as odd, immediately, straightaway, suddenly that ...

STRIVE
strive conscientiously, earnestly, energetically, in vain, tirelessly

STRONG
comparatively, emotionally, extremely, relatively, unbelievably, unusually *strong*

STRUGGLE
struggle bravely, courageously, desperately, furiously, hard, helplessly, heroically, in vain, tirelessly, violently, with all (your) might

STUDY
study sth carefully, closely, conscientiously, dispassionately, in depth, in detail, minutely, objectively, properly, thoroughly, under laboratory conditions

STUPID
extremely, incredibly, unbelievably *stupid*

SUBMIT
submit finally, quietly, reluctantly to ...

SUBSIDISED
directly, heavily *subsidised*

SUBSTITUTE
easily, successfully *substitute* sth

SUCCEED
succeed admirably, beyond one's wildest dreams, brilliantly, in the end, to some extent, invariably, not altogether/entirely, partially *succeed*

SUCCESSFUL
amazingly, astonishingly, consistently, hugely, moderately, not altogether/entirely, outstandingly, phenomenally, remarkably, spectacularly, surprisingly, (not) wholly *successful*

SUFFER
suffer abominably, badly, considerably, dreadfully, economically, greatly, in silence, psychologically, terribly, unduly, unjustly, unnecessarily, visibly, without complaint

SUGGEST
  suggest diffidently, hesitantly, in good faith, obliquely, politely, repeatedly, wearily
  seriously, strongly, tentatively *suggest* sth/that...

SUIT
  suit sb admirably, down to the ground, fine, perfectly

SUITABLE
  eminently, not really, perfectly *suitable*

SUITED
  admirably, ideally, ill-, not really, well- *suited*

SUMMARISE
  summarise briefly, neatly

SUM UP
  sum sth *up* briefly, neatly

SUPERFLUOUS
  completely, totally *superfluous*

SUPERVISE
  supervise closely, properly

SUPPLIED
  adequately, amply, poorly, well- *supplied*

SUPPLY
  supply easily, regularly, secretly

SUPPORT
  support openly, strongly, vigorously, warmly, wholeheartedly
  implicitly, invariably, openly, strongly, tacitly *support*

SUPPOSE
  correctly, mistakenly, naturally, rightly, wrongly *suppose* that...

SUPPRESS
  suppress sth brutally, ruthlessly, violently

SURE
  (not) absolutely, fairly, (not) quite, totally *sure*

SURPRISED
  agreeably, extremely, genuinely, mildly, not unduly, pleasantly, somewhat *surprised*

SURPRISING
  extremely, hardly *surprising*

SURRENDER
  surrender unconditionally

SURVEY
  survey (the evidence) calmly, carefully, critically, objectively, systematically

SURVIVE
  miraculously, narrowly, only just *survive*

SUSPECT
  suspect all along, from the very beginning that ...
  dimly, rightly, seriously, vaguely, wrongly *suspect* sb/sth

SUSPEND
  suspend immediately, permanently, temporarily, until further notice, with immediate effect,
  without notice/warning

SUSPICIOUS
  deeply, definitely, extremely, highly, pretty, understandably *suspicious*

T

TACKLE
tackle (the problem) fearlessly, head-on, immediately, skillfully, successfully

TAKE
take sth badly, hard, personally, philosophically, the wrong way

> ### TAKE
> *Take* has very little meaning on its own, but it is used in many expressions where the second part is a noun; *take an opportunity, take your medicine, take French*. You should find these expressions in your ordinary dictionary.

TAKE ON
take on (the job) foolishly, readily, reluctantly, single-handedly

TAKE PART IN
take part in sth eagerly, enthusiastically, gladly, readily, willingly

TALENTED
enormously, exceptionally, extremely, incredibly, particularly, uniquely *talented*

TALK
talk all the time, animatedly, at cross purposes, at length, candidly, endlessly, frankly, freely, knowledgeably, openly, sensibly, vaguely

> ### TALK
> Verbs which describe an action – for example, *act, smile, walk, talk* – can be used with many different adverbs of manner which tell you how the person did the action. You can 'talk' *thoughtfully, carefully, distractedly*. These collocations are correct, but are not strong enough or frequent enough to be listed here.

TEDIOUS
dreadfully, extremely, terribly *tedious*

TELL
tell sb bluntly, candidly, casually, frankly, gently, in no uncertain terms, jokingly, politely, straight that ...

TEMPTED
easily, sorely, strongly *tempted* to ...

TEMPTING
enormously, extremely *tempting*

> ### TEND
> This verb is much more useful than you probably think. It is often preferred in academic writing instead of adverbs like *usually, sometimes* etc. It is used like this: *People tend to become more conservative as they get older; Unemployment tends to rise at this point in the economic cycle; These results tend to support the hypothesis that ... .*

TERMINATE
terminate abruptly, unexpectedly, without warning

TEST
   test sth carefully, experimentally, properly, repeatedly, rigorously, systematically, thoroughly, to destruction

THANK
   thank sb effusively, from the bottom of (my) heart, politely, profusely, sincerely, warmly

THANKFUL
   deeply, profoundly, truly *thankful*

THEORETICAL
   comparatively, completely, dangerously, entirely, explicitly, extremely, intrinsically, largely, mainly, purely, relatively, wholly *theoretical*

THINK
   think along the right/same lines, aloud, carefully, clearly, constantly, constructively, deeply, dispassionately, furiously, hard, idly, intensively, fast, logically, long and hard, objectively, positively, practically, seriously, with hindsight
   automatically, definitely, foolishly, mistakenly, seriously *think* that ...

THINK OUT
   think sth *out* carefully

THREATEN
   seriously *threaten* sb/sth

TIDY
   beautifully, comparatively, obsessively, remarkably, unusually *tidy*

TIE
   tie sth loosely, neatly, securely

TIRE
   tire easily, quickly

TIRED
   always, constantly, desperately, dreadfully, extremely, over-, perpetually *tired*

TOLERANT
   comparatively, extremely, increasingly, relatively *tolerant*

TOUCH
   touch accidentally, gently, reassuringly

TOUCH ON
   touch on (the figures) in passing
   barely, briefly, hardly *touch on* (the subject of ...)

TRAGIC
   absolutely, deeply *tragic*

TRAINED
   highly, legally, medically, professionally, specially, superbly, well- *trained*

TRANSFORM
   transform sth completely, dramatically, to a great/large extent, within a short space of time

TRANSLATE
   translate accurately, awkwardly, badly, literally, roughly, verbatim, word for word

TRAPPED
   completely, hopelessly *trapped*

TRAVEL
   travel abroad, by air, by road, by sea, by train, cheaply, extensively, far and wide, frequently, incognito, in comfort/luxury, light, on foot, on horseback, round the world, widely
   rarely, seldom *travel*

TREAD
tread carefully, delicately, lightly, softly, warily
TREAT
treat sb abominably, badly, carefully, condescendingly, disgracefully, (un)fairly, generously, humanely, indulgently, kindly, leniently, magnanimously, properly, reasonably, shabbily, sympathetically, well, with contempt, with respect

> **TREAT**
> Verbs which describe an action – for example, *treat, smile, walk* – can be used with many different adverbs of manner. You can 'treat somebody' *courteously, ruthlessly, benignly*. These collocations are not strong enough or frequent enough to be listed here. To help you, we include only the most useful collocations here.

TRICK
deliberately *trick* sb
TRICKY
amazingly, extremely, notoriously, relatively, unbelievably *tricky*
TRUDGE
trudge laboriously, steadily, wearily
TRUE
absolutely, basically, fundamentally, largely, not strictly, partially, partly, substantially, undoubtedly, unquestionably *true*
TRUST
trust sb absolutely, blindly, completely, implicitly, with one's life
TRY
try again and again, conscientiously, desperately, frantically, hard, in vain, once more, over and over again, repeatedly, steadily, valiantly
genuinely, half-heartedly, hastily, honestly, repeatedly, tentatively *try* to ...
TURN AGAINST
inexplicably, unaccountably *turn against* ...
TURN AWAY
turn away in disgust/horror
TURN DOWN
turn sth *down* flat, out of hand
TURN OUT
turn out all right (in the end), disastrously, marvellously

U

UGLY
amazingly, extremely, hideously, incredibly *ugly*
UNABLE
completely, physically, virtually *unable* to ...
UNACCEPTABLE
completely, culturally, morally, socially, totally *unacceptable*

UNAVAILABLE
completely, previously, totally *unavailable*
UNAWARE
blissfully, comparatively, completely, mercifully, totally, utterly *unaware* ...
UNCOMFORTABLE
dreadfully, extremely, relatively, terribly *uncomfortable*
UNDERESTIMATE
badly, consistently, constantly, grossly, seriously *underestimate* ...
UNDERRATE
constantly, greatly, seriously *underrate* ...
UNDERSTAND
understand completely, clearly, fully, immediately, instinctively, perfectly, properly, thoroughly
barely, fully, genuinely, hardly, instantly, intuitively, more or less, thoroughly, vaguely *understand* sth
UNDERSTANDABLE
completely, perfectly, totally *understandable*
UNDISTURBED
largely, totally *undisturbed*
UNEASY
distinctly, extremely, somewhat *uneasy*
UNEXPECTED
absolutely, comparatively, completely, entirely, relatively *unexpected*
UNFAIR
blatantly, extremely, grossly, notoriously, particularly, totally *unfair*
UNFAMILIAR
completely, relatively, totally *unfamiliar*
UNFORESEEN
completely, totally *unforeseen*
UNHAPPY
deeply, desperately, dreadfully, profoundly, thoroughly *unhappy*
UNLIKELY
comparatively, extremely, highly, incredibly, somewhat *unlikely*
UNNECESSARY
absolutely, completely, totally *unnecessary*
UNPLEASANT
comparatively, decidedly, extremely, notoriously, thoroughly *unpleasant*
UNPREPARED
completely, hopelessly, relatively, totally *unprepared*
UNREALISTIC
completely, hopelessly, somewhat, totally, wildly *unrealistic*
UNRELIABLE
completely, extremely, hopelessly, notoriously *unreliable*
UNSATISFACTORY
altogether, completely, definitely, highly, notoriously, totally, wholly *unsatisfactory*
UNSTABLE
comparatively, dangerously, emotionally, extremely, inherently, intrinsically, notoriously *unstable*

UNTRUE

absolutely, basically, completely, demonstrably, fundamentally, obviously, palpably, patently, totally *untrue*

UPSET

upset sb for no good reason

accidentally, deliberately, unwittingly *upset* sb

UPSET (adj)

dreadfully, extremely, terribly, visibly *upset*

UPSETTING

deeply, dreadfully, extremely, thoroughly *upsetting*

UP-TO-DATE

absolutely, almost, comparatively, completely, reasonably, totally *up-to-date*

URGE

repeatedly, strongly *urge* (you) to ...

URGENT

comparatively, extremely, particularly *urgent*

USE

use sth carefully, cautiously, constantly, constructively, efficiently, effectively, regularly, profitably, sparingly, wisely

generally, hardly ever, occasionally *use* sth

USED

commonly, generally, seldom, widely *used*

USEFUL

always, comparatively, extremely, increasingly, incredibly, particularly, relatively, surprisingly, theoretically, undoubtedly *useful*

USELESS

absolutely, comparatively, completely, relatively, totally, utterly *useless*

V

VALUABLE

enormously, extremely, particularly, tremendously, uniquely *valuable*

VALUE

value sth above all else, tremendously

VALUED

greatly, highly *valued*

VANISH

vanish into thin air, without trace

completely, mysteriously, suddenly, utterly *vanish*

VARY

vary considerably, enormously, greatly, substantially, unpredictably, widely

VIEW

view sth dispassionately, (un)favourably, impartially, positively, realistically, sceptically, seriously, with alarm/caution/dismay/distaste/horror/suspicion

VINDICATED
completely, totally, triumphantly, utterly *vindicated*
VIOLATE
violate (the law, rules) openly
VIOLENT
extremely, gratuitously, increasingly, notoriously, particularly *violent*
VISIBLE
barely, clearly, hardly, plainly, scarcely *visible*
VISIT
visit sb frequently, rarely, regularly
VOTE
vote by a show of hands, by secret ballot, consistently, decisively, (overwhelmingly/unanimously) against/in favour of ...
VULNERABLE
extremely, particularly, somewhat, surprisingly *vulnerable*

WAIT
wait anxiously, apprehensively, expectantly, in vain, nervously, (im)patiently, politely, quietly, respectfully for sb/sth
WALK
walk back and forth, briskly, close behind, on tip-toe, up and down

> **WALK**
> Verbs which describe an action – for example, *act, smile, walk* – can be used with many different adverbs of manner which tell you how the person did the action. You can 'walk' *thoughtfully, carefully, distractedly*. These collocations are correct, but are not strong enough or frequent enough to be listed here. To help you with questions you may have when, for example, writing an essay, we include only the most useful collocations.

WANT
want sth badly, desperately, passionately
WARN
warn sb bluntly, expressly, frequently, repeatedly
WASH
wash carefully, thoroughly
WATCH
watch anxiously, carefully, closely, enviously, helplessly, impassively, intently, uneasily, unobtrusively

> **WATCH**
> *Watch* is similar to other verbs which describe how we look, for example, *observe, notice*. Because they also describe an action, they collocate with many different adverbs of manner.

WEAKEN
greatly, seriously *weaken* sth
WEALTHY
enormously, extremely, fabulously, tremendously *wealthy*
WEEP
weep bitterly, openly, uncontrollably
WELCOME
welcome sb enthusiastically, reluctantly, warmly, with open arms
WHISPER
whisper (in)audibly, gently, hoarsely, huskily, in a low voice, softly
WHISTLE
whistle cheerfully, softly
WIDEN
(the gap) has *widened* considerably, noticeably, perceptibly, rapidly, significantly, steadily
WIN
win against all (the) odds, by a hair's breadth, by a huge/narrow margin, by default, decisively, easily, effortlessly, narrowly, outright
WISH
fervently, just, sincerely *wish* that...
WITHDRAW
withdraw hastily, unconditionally, voluntarily
WORDED
badly, carefully, carelessly, clearly *worded*
WORK
work abroad, alone, amicably, carefully, closely with sb, conscientiously, constructively, continuously, creatively, effectively, (in)efficiently, fast, flat out, full-/part-time, hand-in-hand with sb, hard, harmoniously, locally, methodically, non-stop, steadily, systematically, temporarily, tirelessly, together, untiringly
WORK (function)
work automatically, beautifully, continuously, erratically, faultlessly, fine, now and again, perfectly, properly, round the clock, smoothly, well
WORK OUT
(Things/Everything) *worked out* all right, eventually, fine, in the end, perfectly, satisfactorily, splendidly
WORRIED
constantly, deeply, desperately, dreadfully, extremely, increasingly, not unduly, seriously, terribly *worried*
WORRY
worry constantly, needlessly, unnecessarily
WORSE
definitely, infinitely, noticeably, progressively, substantially, visibly *worse* than ...
WORTHLESS
absolutely, completely, entirely, practically, to all intents and purposes, virtually *worthless*
WOUNDED
badly, deeply, fatally, mortally, seriously, slightly *wounded*
WRITE
write beautifully, clearly, (il)legibly

WRITE (style)

write amusingly, authoritatively, brilliantly, convincingly, elegantly, fluently, frankly, interestingly, knowledgeably, lucidly, movingly, plainly, superbly, vividly, wittily

WRITTEN

badly, carelessly, clearly, superbly *written*

WRONG (mistaken)

badly, completely, definitely, fundamentally, not altogether, seriously, totally, utterly *wrong*

WRONG (morally)

absolutely, clearly, fundamentally, inherently, intrinsically, morally, obviously, totally, utterly *wrong*

Y

YOUNG

young at heart

extremely, terribly *young*

SENTENCE ADVERBS

Some adverbs used at the beginning of a sentence refer to the whole sentence. They show how the sentence which follows relates to the rest of the text. Using these sentence adverbs and adverbials makes your writing easier to read because you show the reader the connections between one part of your text and another. Here are some of the most important expressions which do this:

Accordingly,
Admittedly,
All in all,
All things considered,
Alternatively,
Anyway,
Apparently,
As a (general) rule,
As a result,
As far as we know,
Astonishingly,
At the same time,

Basically,
Briefly,
Broadly,
By and large,
By contrast,

Characteristically,
Clearly,
Coincidentally,
Conveniently,
Conversely,
Curiously,

Disappointingly,

Equally,
Essentially,
Even so,
Eventually,
Explicitly,

Finally,
Firstly,
Fortunately,
Fundamentally,
Funnily enough,
Furthermore,

Generally speaking,

Hopefully,
However,

Incredibly,
Interestingly,
Ironically,
In addition,
In conclusion,
In consequence,
In contrast,
In that case,
In essence,
In fairness,
In general,
In many/some cases,
In other words,
In a nutshell,
In particular,
In practice,
In reality,
In retrospect,
In short,
In spite of this/that,
In theory,
In the same way,
In these circumstances,
In view of this,

Luckily,
Lastly,

Meanwhile,
Moreover,
More interestingly/seriously/specifically,

Naturally,
Nevertheless,
Nonetheless,

Obviously,
Officially,
On average,
On balance,
On reflection,
On the contrary,
On the one hand,
On the other hand,
On the whole,
Overall,

Paradoxically,
Personally,
Potentially,
Predictably,
Presumably,
Primarily,
Probably,
Put simply,

Remarkably,

Sadly,
Secondly,
Seemingly,

Significantly,
Similarly,
Subsequently,
Surprisingly,
Theoretically,
Therefore,
Thus,
To all intents and purposes,
To put it briefly,
To put it bluntly,
To put it crudely,
To put it in a nutshell,
To summarise (the situation),
To sum up,
Typically,

Ultimately,
Unbelievably,
Understandably,
Undoubtedly,
Unfortunately,

With hindsight,

Note

In academic writing, we sometimes indicate the field to which the following text applies by using adverbs such as the following:

commercially
ecologically
financially
logically
numerically
psychologically
socially
technically

culturally
economically
ideologically
morally
politically
scientifically
statistically
traditionally

AN INVITATION

As you will have read in the introduction, this dictionary aims to provide intermediate and advanced learners with collocations which they can use with confidence, particularly when writing. Many more collocations are possible than are listed here. Some have been excluded because they are too common; some because they are too technical; some because they are too colloquial; and some because they could only be used with great difficulty by learners.

If you wish to suggest any collocations which you think should be included in a future edition of this dictionary, please send them to us. All suggestions will be carefully considered, and if any of your suggestions are included, you will be acknowledged in the next edition.

Please address all comments to:

> LTP
> 114a Church Rd
> Hove
> BN3 2EB
> U.K.

We look forward to your involvement.